VERBORGENE RÄUME,
VERSCHWIEGENE BIOGRAFIEN

HIDDEN SPACES,
SILENT BIOGRAPHIES

© 2022 die Autoren und
Wasmuth & Zohlen Verlag
Quedlinburger Straße 11,
10589 Berlin
www.wasmuth-verlag.de

Erste Auflage

Umschlagabbildung / Cover illustration: William Alexander Levy, Hangover House, Laguna Beach, 1938. Fotograf unbekannt / unknown photographer / © University of California, Santa Barbara, Architecture and Design Collection
Übersetzungen ins Englische / Translations into English: Bianca Murphy, Ingrid Nina Bell
Übersetzungen ins Deutsche / Translations into German: Wolfgang Voigt, Uwe Bresan
Grafik & Design: Franziska Langner

Alle Rechte vorbehalten, insbesondere das des öffentlichen Vortrags sowie der Übertragung durch Rundfunk und Fernsehen, auch einzelner Teile. Kein Teil des Werkes darf in irgendeiner Form (durch Fotografie, Mikrofilm oder andere Verfahren) ohne schriftliche Genehmigung der Autoren reproduziert oder unter Verwendung elektronischer Systeme verarbeitet, vervielfältigt oder verbreitet werden.

All rights reserved. No part of this book may be reproduced in any form by any electronic or mechanical means (including photocopying, recording, or information storage and retrieval) without permission in writing from the authors.

ISBN 978 3 8030 2378 0

**VERBORGENE RÄUME,
VERSCHWIEGENE BIOGRAFIEN**
SCHWULE ARCHITEKTEN VOM 18. BIS ZUM 20. JAHRHUNDERT

HIDDEN SPACES,
SILENT BIOGRAPHIES
GAY ARCHITECTS FROM 18TH TO 20TH CENTURY

Wolfgang Voigt, Uwe Bresan, Hg./Ed.

Inhalt

8 **You Can't Be What You Can't See – ein Vorwort**
von Wolfgang Voigt, Uwe Bresan

34 **Hamburg im 18. Jahrhundert: Der Baumeister Ernst Georg Sonnin und sein Liebling**
von Wolfgang Voigt

42 **Die Erfindung der Queer Gothic: Horace Walpole**
von Uwe Bresan

52 **Exzentrisches Eremitentum: William Beckford**
von Uwe Bresan

64 **Wie Castor und Pollux für immer verbunden: Percier und Fontaine, die Architekten Napoleons**
von Wolfgang Voigt

72 **Die Architekten der Wiener Hofoper: Eduard van der Nüll und August Sicard von Sicardsburg**
von Richard Kurdiovsky

82 **Der Architekt und der Kürassier: Franz Heinrich Schwechten**
von Wolfgang Voigt

90 **Zwei Stadtbauräte, zwei Junggesellen: Fritz Schumacher und Gustav Oelsner**
von Wolfgang Voigt

100 **Die erste deutsche Architektin und die bauende Lesbe als Zerrbild im homophoben Roman: Emilie Winkelmann und Blanka Wild**
von Wolfgang Voigt

110 **Mein Zuhause soll nicht sein: Austen St. Barbe Harrison**
von Ron Fuchs

118 **Die Jagd auf schwule Architekturlehrer – drei amerikanische Fälle: Bruce Goff, Charles Moore, Lionel Pries**
von Wolfgang Voigt

126 **Nur die Sonne war Zeuge: Barry Dierks und Eric Sawyer**
von Uwe Bresan

138 **Sissie Architects: John Seely und Paul Paget**
von Uwe Bresan

Contents

9	**You Can't Be What You Can't See – a Preface** by Wolfgang Voigt, Uwe Bresan
35	**Hamburg in the 18th Century: The Architect Ernst Georg Sonnin and his "Liebling"** by Wolfgang Voigt
43	**The Invention of Queer Gothic: Horace Walpole** by Uwe Bresan
53	**Eccentric Hermitism: William Beckford** by Uwe Bresan
65	**Like Castor and Pollux Forever United: Percier and Fontaine, Napoleon's Architects** by Wolfgang Voigt
73	**The Architects of the Vienna Court Opera: Eduard van der Nüll and August Sicard von Sicardsburg** by Richard Kurdiovsky
83	**The Architect and the Cuirassier: Franz Heinrich Schwechten** by Wolfgang Voigt
91	**Two City Planning Officials, Two Bachelors: Fritz Schumacher and Gustav Oelsner** by Wolfgang Voigt
101	**The First German Female Architect and the Lesbian Builder as a Caricature in a Homophobic Novel: Emilie Winkelmann and Blanka Wild** by Wolfgang Voigt
111	**My Home Is Not To Be: Austen St. Barbe Harrison** by Ron Fuchs
119	**The Hunt for Gay Architecture Professors – Three American Cases: Bruce Goff, Charles Moore, Lionel Pries** by Wolfgang Voigt
127	**The Sun Was the Only Witness: Barry Dierks and Eric Sawyer** by Uwe Bresan
139	**Sissy Architects: John Seely and Paul Paget** by Uwe Bresan

146	**Eine Villa für zwei Junggesellen:**
	St. Ann's Court von Raymond McGrath
	von Uwe Bresan
156	**Amüsante und weniger amüsante Erlebnisse: Alfred Roth**
	von Wolfgang Voigt
162	**Dreischeibenhaus und Schloss: Helmut Hentrich**
	von Wolfgang Voigt
172	**Durch die Kollegen gerettet: Friedrich Wilhelm Kraemer**
	von Wolfgang Voigt
180	**Der Abenteurer, sein Ghostwriter und ihr Architekt:**
	William Alexander Levy
	von Uwe Bresan
194	**Ein Gentlemen's Agreement: Patrick Gwynne**
	von Neil Bingham
200	**Der Architekt und sein Engel: Chen Kuen Lee**
	von Uwe Bresan
212	**Das Geheimnis des Architekten: Paul Rudolph**
	von Uwe Bresan
220	**Ich danke für die entsprechende Anrede:**
	Die Trans-Architektin Hildegard Schirmacher
	von Wolfgang Voigt
228	**To be Openly Gay at that Time would not have been Good**
	for Business: Arthur Erickson und Francisco Kripacz
	von Uwe Bresan
242	**Der Architekt im Playboy: Charles Moore**
	von Uwe Bresan
252	**Der Architekt von Fire Island: Horace Gifford**
	von Uwe Bresan
262	**Last, But Not Least: Von Ashbee bis Gropius**
	von Wolfgang Voigt und Uwe Bresan

Anhang

280	Anmerkungen
300	Register
304	Abbildungen

147	**A Mansion For Two Bachelors:**
	St Ann's Court by Raymond McGrath
	by Uwe Bresan
157	**Amusing and Less Amusing Experiences: Alfred Roth**
	by Wolfgang Voigt
163	**Dreischeibenhaus and Castle: Helmut Hentrich**
	by Wolfgang Voigt
173	**Saved by Colleagues: Friedrich Wilhelm Kraemer**
	by Wolfgang Voigt
181	**The Adventurer, His Ghost-writer and Their Architect:**
	William Alexander Levy
	by Uwe Bresan
195	**A Gentlemen's Agreement: Patrick Gwynne**
	by Neil Bingham
201	**The Architect And His Angel: Chen Kuen Lee**
	by Uwe Bresan
213	**The Architect's Secret: Paul Rudolph**
	by Uwe Bresan
221	**Thank You For The Appropriate Form of Address:**
	Trans-Architect Hildegard Schirmacher
	by Wolfgang Voigt
229	**To Be Openly Gay at That Time Would Not Have Been Good**
	For Business: Arthur Erickson and Francisco Kripacz
	by Uwe Bresan
243	**The Architect in Playboy: Charles Moore**
	by Uwe Bresan
253	**The Architect of Fire Island: Horace Gifford**
	by Uwe Bresan
263	**Last, But Not Least: From Ashbee to Gropius**
	by Wolfgang Voigt and Uwe Bresan
	Appendix
281	Annotations
300	Index
304	Figures

Wolfgang Voigt, Uwe Bresan

You Can't Be What You Can't See
– ein Vorwort

Vor fünfzig Jahren, in der Nacht vom 27. auf den 28. Juni 1969, löste eine willkürliche Polizeirazzia in dem vor allem von Schwulen, Lesben und Transsexuellen besuchten Lokal Stonewall Inn in der New Yorker Christopher Street schwere Unruhen aus. Das Publikum widersetzte sich vehement der Verhaftung und es kam über mehrere Tage hinweg zu heftigen Auseinandersetzungen und Straßenschlachten mit der Polizei. Getragen wurde der spontane Widerstand des Stonewall Inn-Publikums von einer breiten Welle der Solidarität, die schon bald zu einer Liberalisierung der US-amerikanischen Gesellschaft im Umgang mit Homo- und Transsexuellen führte. Die Vorkommnisse im Juni 1969 wurden zum Gründungsmoment der internationalen Schwulen- und Lesbenbewegung. In Deutschland kam es im gleichen Jahr durch die Änderung des berüchtigten Paragraphen 175 des Strafgesetzbuches zu einer ersten Liberalisierung. Der 1871 eingeführte, unter den Nationalsozialisten verschärfte und in dieser Form bis 1969 gültige Paragraph stellte jegliche sexuelle Handlungen zwischen Personen männlichen Geschlechts unter Strafe. Die endgültige Abschaffung des Paragraphen 175 und damit die generelle Festlegung eines Schutzalters für sexuelle Handlungen auf 14 Jahre erfolgte erst zum 31. Mai 1994. Schon vor dem Ende der strafrechtlichen Diskriminierung hatte in der deutschen Gesellschaft eine breite Liberalisierung eingesetzt. Offen homosexuelle Prominente und Politiker sorgen heute nicht mehr für Irritationen. Sexuelle Vielfalt ist an vielen Stellen im deutschen Alltag, in den Großstädten mehr als auf dem Land, Wirklichkeit geworden.

In unserem eigenen Feld allerdings – der Architekturgeschichte – ist die Entdiskriminierung der letzten Jahrzehnte noch nicht angekommen. Homosexualität wird hier selbst bei Architekten der Vergangenheit als ein Makel behandelt. Dabei ist die Interpretation eines künstlerischen Werkes im Zusammenhang mit der privaten Biografie seines Schöpfers in Kunst-, Musik-, Film- und Literaturgeschichte längst gängige Praxis. Ganz selbstverständlich darf dabei auch die sexuelle Identität des Künstlers berücksichtigt werden. Ja, sie muss mitunter sogar Eingang in die Deutung finden: Was verstünden wir etwa von der Kunst David Hockneys, der Musik Peter Tschaikowskis, den Filmen Luchino Viscontis oder den Werken von Thomas Mann ohne das Wissen um deren Homosexualität? Was in den anderen Disziplinen längst unumstrittener Standard

You Can't Be What You Can't See
– a Preface

Fifty years ago, on the night of 27-28 June 1969, an arbitrary police raid on the Stonewall Inn on New York's Christopher Street, frequented mainly by gays, lesbians, and transsexuals, triggered major riots. The crowd resisted arrest and there were violent confrontations and street fights with the police lasting days. The spontaneous resistance of the Stonewall Inn patrons was supported by a broad wave of solidarity, which soon led to a liberalization of US society in dealing with homosexuals and transsexuals. The events of June 1969 became the founding moment of the international gay and lesbian movement. In Germany, a first liberalization occurred in the same year with the amendment of the notorious Article 175 of the Criminal Code. The article, introduced in 1871, reinforced under the National Socialists and valid in this form until 1969, made all sexual acts between persons of the male sex a punishable offence. The final abolition of Article 175 and thus the establishment of an age of consent for sexual acts at the age of 14 did not occur until May 31st, 1994. Even before the end of legal discrimination, a broad liberalization had begun in German society. Today, outspoken homosexual celebrities and politicians no longer attract attention. Sexual diversity has become a reality in many parts of everyday life in Germany, more so in the big cities than in rural areas.

In the history of architecture, however, a rollback of discrimination of recent decades has not yet arrived. Stigma is even attached to Homosexuality among architects of the past. At the same time, the interpretation of an artistic work in connection with the private life of its creator has long been common practice in the history of art, music, film and literature. It goes without saying that the sexual identity of the artist may also be considered. Sometimes, it even has to be part of the interpretation: How would we understand the art of David Hockney, the music of Peter Tchaikovsky, the films of Luchino Visconti or the works of Thomas Mann without knowing about their homosexuality? What has long been a common practice in other disciplines is still a taboo, at least within German-language architectural history, that is only slowly beginning to be lifted. In recent portrayals of architects, for example, their homosexuality is often completely ignored, thus running the risk of misinterpretation. While in the US-American discourse it has long been possible and politically correct to name

ist, ist zumindest innerhalb der deutschsprachigen Architekturgeschichte noch ein Tabu, das sich erst langsam auflöst. So wird noch in neueren Darstellungen über Architekten deren Homosexualität gern vollständig ausgeblendet und damit die Gefahr von Fehlinterpretationen in Kauf genommen. Während es im US-amerikanischen Diskursraum schon länger möglich und politisch korrekt ist, homosexuelle Architekten aus Geschichte und Gegenwart beim Namen zu nennen, erzeugt unsere deutsche Initiative noch immer Irritationen.

Ein uns gegenüber nicht selten geäußerter Einwand stellt die Qualität des architektonischen Entwurfs kategorisch über die Frage nach der Person des Entwerfers. Der Entwurf müsse gut sein, alles andere sei zweitrangig. Die Person dahinter sei uninteressant und ihre sexuelle Orientierung noch weniger. Das Werk soll für sich sprechen, sein Autor soll wegen eines Details seiner Person, das mit dem Entwurf nichts zu tun habe, nicht benachteiligt sein. Daher sei die Frage nach der sexuellen Orientierung obsolet, heute ebenso wie für die Vergangenheit. Das ist nobel gedacht und trotzdem unbefriedigend, weil es den sozialen Kontext ignoriert und die Frage eines durch das Anders-Sein gegebenen Handicaps erst gar nicht zulässt. Unverständnis spricht auch aus der scherzhaft gemeinten Frage, ob unser nächstes Buch einem ähnlich unwichtigen Thema, zum Beispiel „Architekten mit roten Haaren", gewidmet sein würde. Da gibt es nur eine Antwort: Dafür kam man nicht ins Gefängnis; der homosexuelle Mann hingegen war mit einem Bein immer schon drin. Die abweichende sexuelle Orientierung bedeutete Zwang zu schizophrener Heimlichkeit und war oft genug Anlass zu Schuldgefühlen und Depression; sie war stets mit Gefahr verbunden; schlimmstenfalls mit Skandal und Verlust der bürgerlichen Existenz. Noch nach 1945 gab es allein in Westdeutschland mehr als 50.000 Verurteilungen wegen homosexueller Handlungen. Dass die Mehrzahl der in diesem Buch vorgestellten schwulen Architekten skandalfrei existierte und von Netzwerken geschützt wurde, ändert nichts an der Tatsache, dass auch sie der Gefahr stets ausgesetzt waren.

Bemerkenswert ist auch, dass uns jener Einwand kaum im Zusammenhang mit der emanzipatorischen Selbstbehauptung von Architektinnen begegnet, die – angefangen mit dem 1986 von Verena Dietrich herausgegebenen Sammelband *Architektinnen: Ideen, Projekte, Bauten*[1] – für sich sehr wohl eine Eigenständigkeit innerhalb der Architektur beanspruchen. Schon die entsprechenden Buchtitel wie *Wege zur nicht-sexistischen Stadt. Architektinnen und Planerinnen in den USA,*[2] *Wie Frauen bauen: Architektinnen von Julia Morgan bis Zaha Hadid*[3] oder *Architektur: eine weibliche Profession*[4], um nur eine kleine Auswahl deutschsprachiger Titel zu nennen, lassen eine klar gesonderte Positionierung von Frauen innerhalb der Profession erkennen.

homosexual architects from the past and present, our German initiative still attracts attention.

An objection that is frequently raised with us categorically places the quality of the architectural design above issues concerning the designer's personality. The design had to be good, everything else was secondary. The person behind it was uninteresting and their sexual orientation even less so. The work should speak for itself; its author should not be disadvantaged because of a personal matter that had nothing to do with the design. Therefore, the question of sexual orientation was as irrelevant misplaced, today as well as for the past. This is a noble concept and yet unsatisfactory, because it ignores social context and does not even allow for the question of a handicap resulting from being different. For instance, we were asked if our next book would be dedicated to a similarly unimportant topic, for example "architects with red hair." There is only one answer to this: you didn't go to prison for having red hair; homosexual men, on the other hand, always had one foot in prison. The deviant sexual orientation meant compulsion to schizophrenic secrecy and was often enough cause for feelings of guilt and depression; it was always associated with danger, at worst with scandal and loss of bourgeois existence. Even after 1945, there were more than 50,000 convictions for homosexual acts in West Germany alone. The fact that the majority of gay architects presented in this book lived without any scandal and were protected by networks does not change the fact that they too were always exposed to danger.

It is also remarkable that we hardly encounter this objection in connection with the emancipatory self-assertion of women architects, who – starting with the anthology published in 1986 by Verena Dietrich entitled *Architektinnen: Ideen, Projekte, Bauten*[1] – claim for themselves autonomy within architecture. Even the corresponding book titles such as *Wege zur nicht-sexistischen Stadt – Architektinnen und Planerinnen in den USA*,[2] *Wie Frauen bauen: Architektinnen von Julia Morgan bis Zaha Hadid*[3] or *Architektur: eine weibliche Profession*,[4] to name just a small selection of German-language titles, reveal a clearly separate positioning of women within the profession.

The fact that homosexual architects also occupy a comparably independent and quite identifiable position in architecture is hardly disputed in the US architectural discourse today. The pioneering role of our colleagues on the other side of the Atlantic is closely related to the outbreak of the AIDS crisis in the mid-1980s, when the "gay disease" also claimed many victims among prominent American architects.

Dass auch homosexuelle Architekten eine vergleichbar eigenständige und durchaus lokalisierbare Stellung in der Architektur einnehmen, wird im US-amerikanischen Architekturdiskurs heute kaum mehr bestritten. Die Vorreiterrolle unserer Kollegen jenseits des Atlantiks steht dabei in engem Zusammenhang mit dem Ausbruch der AIDS-Krise Mitte der 1980er-Jahre, als die „Schwulenkrankheit" auch unter prominenten amerikanischen Architekten viele Opfer fand.

Das Coming-out der Architektur

Einer der ersten Betroffenen, dessen Tod die US-amerikanische Architektenschaft nachhaltig erschütterte, war der gefeierte New Yorker Architekt Alan Buchsbaum (1935-1987),[5] zu dessen Klienten zahlreiche Stars der amerikanischen Unterhaltungsindustrie gehörten. Für die Schauspielerin Diane Keaton etwa entwarf Buchsbaum 1982 in New York ein minimalistisches, weißes Loft, dessen Böden, Decken und Wände mit einer glänzenden Lackschicht überzogen waren und dadurch wie riesige Spiegelflächen wirkten.[6] Für die Sängerin Bette Midler wiederum, die später auf Buchsbaums Beerdigung singen sollte, verwandelte er das Innere eines alten Lagerhauses in eine Art modernen Art-Nouveau-Salon mit metallisch glänzenden Stoffen über den weit ausladenden Fauteuils.[7] Und für den Musiker Billy Joel und seine Model-Freundin Christie Brinkley gestaltete er noch kurz vor seinem Tod ein schrilles Apartment am Central Park mit Wänden aus Glasbausteinen, Möbeln aus polierten Marmorplatten und dickbauchigen Sesseln in leuchtenden Neonfarben.[8] Seine bekannteste Arbeit war jedoch die Gestaltung seines eigenen Apartments im New Yorker Stadtteil Soho aus dem Jahr 1976. Mit geschwungenen Glasbaustein-Wänden, die von einer Reihe Flugfeld-Leuchten in stahlblaues Licht getaucht wurden, wurde das Apartment zu einer Ikone des sogenannten High-Tech-Stils.[9] Dass Buchsbaum hier kaum mit Frau und Kind lebte, sieht man der Wohnung deutlich an. Architekturbüro, Wohnzimmer, Küche und Bett gehen fließend ineinander über. Keine Tür trennt die einzelnen Lebensbereiche voneinander ab. Gleichwohl wurde die Homosexualität des Architekten in keinem der unzähligen Artikel, die in Architektur- und Designzeitschriften über Buchsbaums Apartment erschienen, jemals thematisiert. Erst nach seinem AIDS-Tod 1987 ließ sich das Offensichtliche nicht länger verbergen.

Auf Buchsbaum folgte der New Yorker Architekturvisionär Roger Ferri (1949-1991), dessen Studien zu begrünten Wolkenkratzern wie Blaupausen zu den pflanzenüberwucherten Hochhäusern wirken, die heute vornehmlich in den Metropolen Südostasiens entstehen.[10] Auch der kalifornische Architekt Frank Israel (1945-1996) fiel der Krankheit in den 1990er-Jahren auf dem Höhepunkt

Das Gennaro Andreozzi Office aus dem Jahr 1982 ist ein typisches Werk des New Yorker Architekten Alan Buchsbaum

The Gennaro Andreozzi Office from 1982 is is a typical example for the work of the New York architect Alan Buchsbaum

The coming out of architecture

One of the first people affected, whose death had a lasting impact on the US architectural community, was the celebrated New York architect Alan Buchsbaum (1935-1987)[5], whose clients included numerous stars of the American entertainment industry. For actress Diane Keaton, for example, Buchsbaum designed a minimalist white loft in New York in 1982, the floors, ceilings and walls of which were finished with a shiny layer of varnish, making them look like huge mirrored surfaces.[6] For singer Bette Midler, who was later to sing at Buchsbaum's funeral, he transformed the interior of an old warehouse into a kind of modern art-nouveau salon with shiny metallic fabrics stretched over the expansive fauteuils.[7] And for musician Billy Joel and his girlfriend the model Christie Brinkley, he designed a garish flat near Central Park shortly before his death, with walls made of glass blocks, furniture made of polished marble slabs and bulbous armchairs in bright neon colours.[8] His best-known work, however, was the 1976 design of his own flat in New York's Soho district. With curved glass block walls bathed in steelblue light from a row of airfield lights, the flat became an icon of the so-called high-tech style.[9] You can clearly tell from the flat that Buchsbaum didn't exactly live here with a wife and children. The architectural office, living room, kitchen and bed merge seamlessly into one another. No door separates the individual living areas from each other. Nevertheless, the architect's homosexuality was never discussed in any of the many articles about Buchsbaum's flat that appeared in architecture and design magazines. It was only after he died of AIDS in 1987 that the fact could no longer be concealed.

seiner Karriere zum Opfer. Israel galt damals neben Frank O. Gehry, der sein Mentor war, als hoffnungsvollster Westküsten-Architekt seiner Generation. Zunächst vor allem als Designer für alle großen Film- und Fernseh-Studios in Hollywood tätig, entwickelte sich Israel in den letzten Jahren vor seinem Tod zu einem der gefragtesten Villen-Architekten von Los Angeles. Seine spektakulären Häuser, die er fast mimetisch in die zerklüfteten Berghänge der Stadt einfügte, gehören zum Besten, was die amerikanische Architektur in den 1990er-Jahren hervorgebracht hat.[11] Es war aber nicht nur der überraschende AIDS-Tod vieler etablierter Architekten wie Buchsbaum, Ferri und Israel, der die amerikanische Architektenschaft verunsicherte. Es war vor allem auch der tragische Tod des gerade erst 30-jährigen Chicagoer Architekten Scott Weston (1959-1990),[12] der als außerordentliches Nachwuchstalent galt, der mehr als deutlich machte, welche Auswirkungen die Krankheit auf die gesamte Profession hatte und in Zukunft noch haben konnte. Schweigen war an dieser Stelle nicht länger möglich.

Parallel zur AIDS-Krise der 1980er- und 1990er-Jahre lockerte sich das über homosexuellen Architekten schwebende Tabu. Ihr Anderssein wurde benannt und ihre mitunter erhebliche Bedeutung für die Architekturgeschichte neu entdeckt. Und los ging es gleich mit einem Paukenschlag: „There is a good deal of evidence – some personal, some architectural – to suggest that Louis Sullivan may have been homosexual." Mit diesen Worten beginnt das erste Outing der modernen Architekturgeschichte. Sie stammen von dem Historiker Robert Twombly aus seiner 1986 erschienenen Biografie über den Chicagoer Architekten Louis Sullivan (1856-1924).[13] Sullivan wird bis heute als der Übervater einer von ihren Bindungen an die europäische Architekturgeschichte befreiten, genuin amerikanischen Architektur verehrt. Er schuf den Typus des amerikanischen Hochhauses und gab mit seinem Ausspruch „form follows function" der Moderne beiderseits des Atlantiks ein eingängiges Motto. Was Twombly nun in der Person – aber vor allem in der Architektur – Sullivans erkannte, das für ihn den Schluss zuließ, der Architekt „könnte" homosexuell gewesen sein, beschreibt er auf den letzten Seiten des Kapitels *Frustrated Hopes*.[14] Einerseits verweist Twombly hier auf Sullivans Interesse an der Kunst Michelangelos, zum anderen beschäftigt er sich mit dem auffälligen dekorativen Reichtum von Sullivans Inneneinrichtungen und der überbordenden Ornamentik seiner Bauten. Letzteres ist für Twombly Ausdruck einer „feminin-emotionalen" Seite Sullivans, die oft im Widerspruch zu den „maskulin-rationalen" Grundriss- und Konstruktionslösungen seiner Gebäude stehe.

Tatsächlich galt Sullivan spätestens seit der Inneneinrichtung des 1889 eingeweihten Auditorium Buildings in Chicago als der führende Innenarchitekt

The architectural visionary Roger Ferri (1949-1991) from New York followed Buchsbaum, whose studies of green skyscrapers seem like blueprints for the plant-covered high-rises that are being built today, primarily in Southeast Asian metropolises.[10] California architect Frank Israel (1945-1996) also fell victim to the disease in the 1990s at the height of his career. Alongside Frank O. Gehry, who was his mentor, Israel was considered the most promising West Coast architect of his generation. Initially working primarily as a designer for all the major film and television studios in Hollywood, Israel evolved to become the most sought-after mansion architects in Los Angeles in the last years before his death. His spectacular houses, which he inserted almost mimetically into the city's rugged hillsides, are among the best that American architecture produced in the 1990s.[11] Yet it was not only the surprising death from AIDS of many established architects such as Buchsbaum, Ferri and Israel that unsettled the American architectural community. Above all, it was the tragic death of the 30-year-old Chicago architect Scott Weston (1959-1990)[12], who was considered an extraordinary young talent, that made it abundantly clear what effects the disease was having on the entire profession and might still have in the future. Silence was no longer possible at this point.

Parallel to the AIDS crisis of the 1980s and 1990s, the taboo hovering over homosexual architects was loosening. Their otherness was called by its right name, and their occasionally considerable significance for architectural history was rediscovered. And it all started with a bang: "There is a good deal of evidence – some personal, some architectural – to suggest that Louis Sullivan may have been homosexual." These words mark the beginning of the first outing in modern architectural history. They come from historian Robert Twombly's 1986 biography of the Chicago architect Louis Sullivan (1856-1924).[13] To this day, Sullivan is revered as the father figure of a genuinely American architecture freed from its ties to European architectural history. He created the American type of high-rise buildings and gave modernism on both sides of the Atlantic a catchy motto with his statement "form follows function". On the last pages of the chapter *Frustrated Hopes*, Twombly describes what he recognized in Sullivan's person, but above all in his architecture, that led him to conclude that the architect "could" have been homosexual.[14] On the one hand, Twombly refers to Sullivan's interest in the art of Michelangelo, on the other hand, he deals with the conspicuous decorative richness of Sullivan's interiors and the exuberant ornamentation of his buildings. For Twombly, the latter is an expression of Sullivan's "feminine-emotional" side that often contradicts the "masculine-rational" floor plan and structural solutions of his buildings.

seiner Generation, während die nicht weniger erstaunlichen konstruktiven Lösungen des riesigen Hotel-, Büro- und Opernhaus-Komplexes eher seinem Büropartner Dankmar Adler (1844-1900) zugeschrieben wurden. Weil er die Vorliebe des Architekten für opulent vergoldete und mit floralen Dekorationen angefüllte Räume als Ausdruck einer homosexuellen Neigung deutete, wurde Twombly nicht zu Unrecht vorgeworfen, ein Stereotyp zu bedienen.[15] Gleichwohl fand seine These in späteren biografischen Studien Bestätigung, und so gilt die Homosexualität Sullivans heute als unstrittig.[16]

Einen Höhepunkt erlebte das schrittweise Coming-out der amerikanischen Architektenschaft dann 1996, als sich Philip Johnson (1906-2005) für das Cover des bekannten Schwulenmagazins *Out* porträtieren ließ.[17] Ganz überraschend war die Sache allerdings nicht. Denn dass Johnson homosexuell war, konnte man schon zwei Jahre vorher in der Architekten-Biografie *Philip Johnson. Leben und Werk* nachlesen.[18] Deren Autor, der Kunsthistoriker Franz Schulze, berichtet darin ebenso über die Liebhaber Johnsons wie über die Bauten des Architekten. So erfahren wir von Johnsons „erster regelrecht vollzogenen sexuellen Erfahrung […] mit einem Aufseher in einer dunklen Ecke des Museums von Kairo" im Jahr 1927,[19] von der „sexuellen Erregung", die Johnson bei einer Veranstaltung der Nationalsozialisten 1932 in Berlin „angesichts aller dieser blonden Burschen in schwarzem Leder"[20] spürte, und wie er sich im New York der 1940er- und 1950er-Jahre „einer stattlichen Anzahl von Partnern hingab",[21] bevor er 1960 den späteren Kunstgaleristen David Whitney kennen lernte, mit dem er den Rest seines Lebens verbringen sollte.

Während das Buch in Nordamerika vor allem deshalb überzeugte, weil es eben keine reine Architekten-Biografie war, sondern auch das Private bis hin zu ethisch-moralischen Fragezeichen der Person Johnsons mit einbezog, wurde es hierzulande, als es in einer deutschen Übersetzung erschien, als geschwätzig und kapriziös abgetan. Dass Schulze „die Liebhaber so ausführlich wie die Bauten" behandele, kam 1996 noch nicht gut an.[22] Gleichwohl hat die Veröffentlichung Johnsons Karriere weder in Amerika noch im Ausland geschadet. So darf Schulzes Biografie, in der erstmals ein noch lebender Architekt prominent geoutet wurde, als Meilenstein innerhalb unseres Themas gelten.

In den mehr als 20 Jahren, die seitdem vergangen sind, haben die Werke zu homosexuellen Architekten auf dem nordamerikanischen Kontinent stetig zugenommen. Was alle diese Arbeiten – so unterschiedlich sie im Detail auch sein

Der Chicagoer Architekt Louis Sullivan und sein gemeinsam mit Dankmar Adler errichtetes Auditorium Building

Chicago architect Louis Sullivan and his Auditorium Building, jointly built with Dankmar Adler

In fact, Sullivan was considered the leading interior designer of his generation at least since designing the interiors of the Auditorium Building in Chicago, which was inaugurated in 1889, although the no less astonishing structural solutions of the huge hotel, office and opera house complex were rather attributed to his office partner, Dankmar Adler (1844-1900). Because he interpreted the architect's preference for opulently gilded rooms filled with floral decorations as an expression of a homosexual inclination, Twombly was not unjustly accused of perpetuating a stereotype.[15] Nevertheless, his thesis was confirmed in later biographical studies, and Sullivan's homosexuality is now considered beyond dispute.[16]

The gradual coming out of American architects reached a climax in 1996, when Philip Johnson (1906-2005) had himself portrayed on the cover of the well-known gay magazine *Out*.[17] However, this did not come as a big surprise. The fact that Johnson was homosexual had already been revealed two years earlier in the architect's biography *Philip Johnson. Life and Work*.[18] The author, art historian Franz Schulze, reports as much about Johnson's lovers as about the architect's buildings. For example, we learn of Johnson's "first real sexual experience […] with an attendant in a dark corner of the Cairo Museum" in 1927,[19] of the "sexual arousal" Johnson felt at a Nazi event in Berlin in 1932 "in the face of all those blond fellows in black leather,"[20] and how he "abandoned himself to a number of handsome partners,"[21] in New York in the 1940s and 1950s before meeting the future art gallerist David Whitney in 1960, with whom he was to spend the rest of his life.

Der Architekt Philip Johnson auf dem Cover des Schwulenmagazins Out

Architect Philip Johnson on the cover of gay magazine Out

mögen – aufzeigen, ist, dass homosexuelle Architekten einen wichtigen Beitrag zur Entwicklung der Architektur geleistet haben und bis heute leisten. Sie besitzen also eine lokalisierbare Stellung innerhalb ihrer Profession. Diese Stellung herauszuarbeiten und an Beispielen deutlich zu machen, ist Teil eines umfassenden emanzipatorischen Prozesses der Sichtbarmachung. Wie erfolgreich dieser Prozess in den zurückliegenden Jahrzehnten tatsächlich war, kann man heute an US-amerikanischen Architekten ablesen, die ihre Homosexualität selbstbewusst als Teil auch ihrer professionellen Identität begreifen und in diesem Sinne thematisieren. Dieser Erfolg scheint schlussendlich die zu Beginn mitunter stark umstrittenen Methoden der Biografik vom Ende her zu rechtfertigen.

Im Unterschied zu den USA fehlte es in Deutschland in den 1980er- und 1990er-Jahren an prominenten AIDS-Opfern aus der Unterhaltungsbranche und aus der Kunst, deren Schicksal Identifiktionsmöglichkeiten geboten hätte, wie dies in den angelsächsischen Ländern mit dem Schauspieler Rock Hudson, dem Rockmusiker Freddy Mercury und dem Künstler Keith Haring der Fall war. Bei den deutschen AIDS-Toten wurde auf Diskretion geachtet. Diese bestimmte auch den Umgang mit dem 1988 an AIDS verstorbenen Architekten Antoine Laroche (1950–1988) aus Köln, der in den 1980er-Jahren als eines der hoffnungsvollen Talente im Lande galt und – wie Jeff Wall oder Candida Höfer, mit denen er eng befreundet war – zum Kölner Künstlerzirkel jener Jahre gehörte. In der posthum über ihn publizierten Monographie mit dem Titel *Innenräume* heißt es schlicht, das Leben des Architekten sei nach „einer schweren Krankheit" zu Ende gegangen.[23] Und so will es scheinen, als sei nie ein deutscher Architekt jemals an AIDS gestorben.

While the book was especially compelling in North America because it was not a pure biography of an architect but also covered his private life, including ethical and moral ambiguities about Johnson as a person, here in Germany it was dismissed as gossipy and capricious when the German translation was published. The fact that Schulze covered "the lovers as extensively as the buildings" was not well received in 1996.[22] Yet the publication has not damaged Johnson's career, neither in America nor abroad. Thus, Schulze's biography, which was the first to prominently out a still-living architect, may be considered a milestone within our subject.

In the more than 20 years that have passed since, the number of works on homosexual architects in North America has steadily increased. What all these works – however different in detail – reveal is that homosexual architects have made, and continue to make, an important contribution to the development of architecture. They therefore have a definite position within their profession. Identifying this position and making it clear through examples is part of a comprehensive, emancipatory process of rendering it visible. How successful this process has actually been in the past decades can now be seen by the number of US architects who self-confidently understand their homosexuality as part of their professional identity and address it in this sense. In the end, this success seems to justify the methods of biographical research, which were at times in the beginning highly controversial.

Unlike the USA, Germany in the 1980s and 1990s lacked prominent AIDS victims from the entertainment industry and the arts whose fate would have offered opportunities for identification, as was the case in Anglo-Saxon countries with actor Rock Hudson, rock musician Freddy Mercury and artist Keith Haring. Discretion was observed in the case of German AIDS-related casualties. This also determined the way architect Antoine Laroche (1950-1988) from Cologne, who died of AIDS in 1988, was treated. In the 1980s, he was considered one of the country's most promising talents and, like Jeff Wall or Candida Höfer, with whom he was close friends, belonged to Cologne's artistic circle of those years. The monograph published posthumously about him, entitled *Innenräume* (Interiors), simply states that the architect's life came to an end after "a serious illness."[23] Thus it might seem if no German architect has ever died of AIDS.

Ist Architektur gay-friendly?

Wie weit wir in Bezug auf unser Thema in Deutschland und Europa von den Entwicklungen in Nordamerika entfernt sind, hat in den vergangenen Jahren auch das britische *Architects Journal* untersucht. „Is architecture gay-friendly?", fragte das traditionsreiche Blatt im Jahr 2013 seine Leser.[24] Hinter der einleitenden Frage verbarg sich die Auswertung einer repräsentativen Erhebung unter 300 homosexuellen Architekten aus ganz Großbritannien, die das Architekturmagazin initiiert hatte. Befragt wurden die Teilnehmer zu ihren persönlichen Erfahrungen mit Homophobie innerhalb ihres beruflichen Umfeldes und ihren Umgang damit. Die Studie zeigte, dass fast die Hälfte der Teilnehmer in den vergangenen zwölf Monaten in ihrem Arbeitsumfeld direkt oder indirekt mit homophoben Äußerungen konfrontiert worden war. Dabei gaben zwar drei Viertel der Befragten an, bei einem Coming-out im Architekturbüro keine negativen Reaktionen von Vorgesetzten oder Kollegen befürchten zu müssen, gefragt nach dem Umgang mit dem Thema Homosexualität bei Terminen mit Auftraggebern, Zulieferern oder Baufirmen äußerte allerdings nur noch jeder Dritte, keine Bedenken hinsichtlich eines offenen Verhaltens zu haben. Auf der Baustelle wiederum sah darin nur noch jeder sechste Studienteilnehmer keinerlei Gefahr.

Angeregt wurde die Umfrage des *Architects' Journal* aus dem Jahr 2013 durch den Workplace Equality Index, der jährlich von der einflussreichen britischen Non-Profit-Organisation Stonewall, die sich für die Gleichberechtigung von Homosexuellen in Großbritannien engagiert, erstellt wird. Der sogenannte Stonewall Report untersucht und bewertet die Arbeitsbedingungen von Schwulen und Lesben im Vereinigten Königreich und kürt alljährlich die 100 Unternehmen, die sich besonders engagiert und vorbildlich um die Belange ihrer homosexuellen Arbeitnehmer kümmern. Die Tatsache, dass sich unter den 100 ausgezeichneten Unternehmen des Jahres 2013 weder ein Arbeitgeber aus dem Architekturbereich noch aus dem Immobilien- und Bausektor befand,[25] führte schließlich dazu, dass sich das *Architects' Journal* mit seiner Umfrage dem Thema annahm.

Welche Bedeutung die Zahlen aus der Befragung haben, erläuterte das *Architects' Journal* mit Bezug auf aktuelle wissenschaftliche Untersuchungen. Sie zeigen, dass homosexuelle Arbeitnehmer, die in ihrem Job gezwungen sind, ihre sexuelle Identität zu verbergen, deutlich weniger produktiv sind als ihre Kollegen. So bindet etwa die ständige Vorsicht, sich nicht durch unbedachte Äußerungen oder Handlungen zu verraten, enorme Energien, die bei der Konzentration auf die eigentliche Tätigkeit fehlen. Zudem erschwert das Verheimlichen beziehungsweise

Is architecture gay-friendly?

In recent years, the British *Architects' Journal* has also investigated how far we are from developments in North America with regard to our topic in Germany and Europe. "Is architecture gay-friendly?," the tradition-steeped journal asked its readers in 2013.[24] Behind the introductory question was the evaluation of a representative survey of 300 homosexual architects from all over the UK, initiated by the architecture magazine. The participants were asked about their personal experiences with homophobia within their professional environment and how they dealt with it. The study showed that almost half of the participants had been confronted directly or indirectly with homophobic statements in their working environment in the past twelve months. Although three quarters of the respondents said that they did not have to fear negative reactions from superiors or colleagues if they came out in their architectural profession, when asked about how they dealt with the topic of homosexuality during appointments with clients, suppliers, or construction companies, only one in three said that they had no concerns about being frank about it. On the construction site, only every sixth participant in the study saw no threat at all.

The 2013 *Architects' Journal* survey was inspired by the Workplace Equality Index, which is produced annually by Stonewall, an influential British non-profit organization committed to equal rights for homosexuals in the UK. The so-called Stonewall Report examines and evaluates the working conditions of gays and lesbians in the UK and annually selects the 100 companies that are particularly committed and exemplary in looking after the interests of their homosexual employees. The fact that there was neither an employer from the architecture sector nor from the real estate and construction industry among the 100 winning companies in 2013,[25] prompted the *Architects' Journal* to take up the issue with its survey.

The *Architects' Journal* explained the significance of the survey figures with reference to current scientific research. These studies show that homosexual employees who are forced to hide their sexual identity at work are significantly less productive than their colleagues. For example, the vigilance not to reveal oneself through thoughtless statements or actions ties up enormous energies that are lacking when concentrating on the actual job. In addition, concealing or denying one's sexual identity makes it more difficult to maintain sustainable professional contacts or networks, which may have a negative impact on work and career. It is therefore in the interest of both the employees and the employer

Verleugnen der eigenen sexuellen Identität den Aufbau von nachhaltigen beruflichen Kontakten oder Netzwerken, was einen negativen Einfluss auf die Arbeit wie auch die Karriere der Betroffenen haben kann. Es liegt also sowohl im Interesse der betroffenen Mitarbeiter selbst als auch im Interesse des Arbeitgebers, dass Unternehmen eine gegenüber Homosexuellen offene und tolerante Atmosphäre schaffen. Auch zu diesem Thema erhob das *Architects' Journal* 2013 Zahlen. Sie zeigten, dass lediglich 38 Prozent der Befragten das Gefühl hatten, ihre Vorgesetzten würden bei diskriminierenden Vorfällen gut reagieren. 16 Prozent der Studienteilnehmer hätten sich zum Zeitpunkt der Studie hingegen nicht einmal getraut, entsprechende Vorfälle anzusprechen. Neun von zehn Teilnehmern bemängelten zudem, dass Kollegen bei homophoben Kommentaren und Beleidigungen nicht reagieren würden. Viele der Befragten wünschten sich daher eine stärkere Unterstützung gegen Diskriminierung sowohl von Seiten ihrer Arbeitgeber als auch von Seiten ihrer Berufsverbände sowie von den öffentlichen und privaten Institutionen innerhalb der Architektur – von Hochschulen, Museen und Fachmedien.

In diesem Zusammenhang hoben die Teilnehmer immer wieder die Bedeutung von sogenannten Role Models, von Vorbildern innerhalb der Profession, hervor, das heißt von bekannten und erfolgreichen Architekten, die ihre Homosexualität offen und stolz – „out and proud" – lebten. Darauf verwiesen auch die Interviews der beiden Folgestudien, die das *Architects' Journal* in den Jahren 2015 und 2017 initiierte.[26] Die beiden Umfragen zeigten hinsichtlich der konkreten Zahlen wenig Veränderungen zur Situation der Betroffenen im Vergleich zu 2013. Einen Grund dafür erkannten viele Studienteilnehmer, wie sie in den begleitenden Interviews angaben, nicht zuletzt in der nach wie vor mangelhaften Präsenz offen schwuler und lesbischer Führungspersönlichkeiten innerhalb der Architektur. Gerade für jüngere Betroffene sei das Vorhandensein älterer Role Models in Architekturbüros, Verbänden und Institutionen von großer Wichtigkeit, um Selbstvertrauen zu entwickeln, betonte die Studie von 2015.

Wo sind unsere Role Models?

Für das kontinentale Europa fehlen vergleichbare Aussagen bisher. Man darf aber davon ausgehen, dass entsprechende Studien sowohl hinsichtlich der konkreten Zahlen als auch in Hinsicht auf Erlebnisberichte, Wünsche und Forderungen der Betroffenen zu ähnlichen Ergebnissen führen würden. In diesem Sinne können die biografischen Forschungen zu homosexuellen Architekten, wie sie die vorliegende Textsammlung erstmals für den deutschsprachigen Diskursraum unternimmt, wesentlich zur Emanzipation schwuler und lesbischer Architekten

that companies create an open and tolerant atmosphere towards homosexuals. The *Architects' Journal* also collected figures on this topic in 2013. They revealed that only 38 per cent of the respondents felt that their superiors reacted appropriately to discriminatory behavior. Moreover, 16 per cent of the survey participants did not even dare to bring up such behavior at the time of the study. Nine out of ten participants also complained that colleagues did not censure homophobic comments and insults. Many of the respondents would like to see stronger resistance to discrimination both from their employers and from their professional associations, from public and private institutions within architecture – from universities, museums and trade media.

In this context, the participants repeatedly emphasized the importance of so-called role models within the profession, i.e. well-known and successful architects who lived their homosexuality openly and proudly – "out and proud." This was also pointed out in the interviews of two follow-up studies initiated by *Architects' Journal* in 2015 and 2017.[26] In terms of concrete figures, both surveys showed little change in the situation of those affected compared to 2013. One reason for this, as many study particpants stated in the accompanying interviews, was the continued lack of openly gay and lesbian leadership personalities in the architectural sector. Especially for younger people, older role models in architectural offices, associations and institutions are of great importance in order to develop self-confidence, the 2015 study emphasized.

Where are our role models?

Comparable findings are still lacking for continental Europe. However, it can be assumed that corresponding studies would lead to similar results, both in terms of concrete numbers and with regard to experience reports, wishes and demands of those affected. In this sense, biographical research on homosexual architects, as this collection of texts undertakes for the first time for the German-speaking discourse, can contribute significantly to the emancipation of gay and lesbian architects. After all, every successful homosexual architect from the past and present can serve as a role model for current and future generations. This is where we see the particular benefit of the biographical case studies presented in the following chapters. Here, too, the statement attributed to African American human rights activist Marian Wright Edelman applies: "You can't be what you can't see."

In the USA, it was gay architects who self-organized for the first time. The Organization of Lesbian and Gay Architects and Designers (OLGAD), based

New-York-Führer der Organization of Lesbian and Gay Architects and Designers zu Denkmälern der schwul-lesbischen Stadtgeschichte

Organization of Lesbian and Gay Architects and Designers' New York guide to monuments of gay and lesbian urban history

beitragen. Denn letztlich kann jeder erfolgreiche homosexuelle Architekt aus Geschichte und Gegenwart als Role Model für jetzige und zukünftige Generationen dienen. Besonders darin sehen wir den Nutzen der in den folgenden Kapiteln vorgestellten biografischen Fallbeispiele. Es gilt auch hier der der afroamerikanischen Menschenrechtsaktivistin Marian Wright Edelman zugeschriebene Satz: „You can't be what you can't see". Du kannst nicht sein, was Du nicht siehst.

In den USA waren es schwule Architekten, die sich erstmals selbst organisierten. Dort gibt es seit 1991 die Organization of Lesbian and Gay Architects and Designers (OLGAD) mit Sitz in New York City.[27] Sie wurde als Netzwerk zur Jobsuche, aber auch als Plattform für politischen Aktivismus und gegen Benachteiligungen im Beruf gegründet. Eine wichtige Rolle spielen die Bemühungen um die Anerkennung des Beitrags, den LGBT-Architekten und -Designer im Verlauf der Geschichte in ihren Disziplinen geleistet haben. An die Öffentlichkeit ging man 25 Jahre nach Stonewall, 1994, mit einer Design Pride-Konferenz[28] und einer Ausstellung zur Erinnerung an besonders talentierte Architekten, deren Karrieren durch AIDS abrupt beendet wurden.[29] Auch Erinnerungsarbeit gehört 1994 zu den Aktivitäten. Erstmals wurden Orte in Greenwich, Harlem und Midtown kartiert und publiziert, die als Marksteine lesbischer und schwuler Geschichte angesehen werden.[30] So gelang nicht nur die Eintragung der Stonewall-Bar in die Denkmalliste, sondern 2016 unter Präsident Obama auch die Erhebung des inzwischen angelegten Christopher Parks und der angrenzenden Straßen in den Rang eines Nationaldenkmals der Vereinigten Staaten.[31]

Woran könnte es liegen, dass es eine vergleichbare Organisation in Deutschland nicht gibt und sich bisher kaum ein prominenter Architekt zu seiner

in New York City, has existed since 1991.[27] It was founded as a job search network, but also as a platform for political activism and against disadvantages at work. Efforts made to gain recognition for the contribution LGBT architects and designers have made to their disciplines throughout history play an important role. The organization went public 25 years after Stonewall, in 1994, with a Design Pride Conference[28] and an exhibition to commemorate particularly talented architects whose careers were abruptly ended by AIDS.[29] Remembrance work was part of the activities in 1994. For the first time, places in Greenwich, Harlem and Midtown that are considered landmarks of lesbian and gay history were mapped and published.[30] Thus, not only did the Stonewall Bar succeed in being inscribed on the list of monuments, but in 2016, under President Obama, it was also possible to raise the now established Christopher Park and the adjacent streets to the status of a national monument of the United States.[31]

What could be the reason that there is no comparable organization in Germany and that hardly any prominent architect has admitted his homosexuality so far? Why do those affected, although no one has to fear criminal prosecution anymore, still keep a low profile? One reason is certainly the conservative attitude of many clients and investors in the building industry, which is a sector characterized by normative masculinity, not only in Germany. The same client who admires artists for their bohemianism, who purchases works by Andy Warhol or Keith Haring for his private art collection and would never be bothered by their sexual orientation, looks more strictly on the architect than on the artist. The architect turns his money into buildings and is supposed to produce a value-creating property for him. The fear of being rejected is probably the reason why homosexual architects prefer to be cautious. They cannot assume that they, whom the heterosexual philistine associates first and foremost with unrestrained hedonism, will enjoy the same standards of business conduct and character. There are no official statements or even quotable remarks on this topic, because no one openly professes to practice discrimination or to be afraid of it. Therefore, it also remains open whether the concerns of homosexual architects are as justified today as they were in the past. After all, clients, developers and investors are also part of society that has made big steps towards rolling back discrimination and promoting acceptance.

A precarious existence

The following presentations of homosexual architect biographies are not intended to prove a specifically gay design style. Susan Sontag's thesis of the culture of camp misled people in the 1960s to believe in a connection between the sexual

Homosexualität bekannt hat? Warum halten sich die Betroffenen, obwohl sich niemand mehr vor Strafgesetzen fürchten muss, nach wie vor bedeckt? Eine Ursache dafür ist sicherlich die konservative Haltung vieler Auftraggeber und Investoren im Bauwesen, das nicht nur in Deutschland eine von normativer Maskulinität geprägte Branche darstellt. Derselbe Bauherr, der Künstler für ihre Bohème bewundert, der für seine private Kunstsammlung Werke von Andy Warhol oder Keith Haring anschafft und sich an deren sexueller Orientierung nie stören würde, schaut auf den Architekten strenger als auf den Künstler. Dieser verbaut sein Geld und soll ihm eine Wert schöpfende Immobilie herstellen. Die Angst, hier abgelehnt zu werden, dürfte den Beweggrund dafür abgeben, dass homosexuelle Architekten es vorziehen, vorsichtig zu sein. Dass ihnen, die der heterosexuelle Spießer zuallererst mit hemmungslosem Hedonismus in Verbindung sieht, die notwendige geschäftliche und charakterliche Solidität zugebilligt wird, darauf können sie nicht bauen. Es gibt zu diesem Thema keine offiziellen Stellungnahmen oder auch nur zitierfähige Äußerungen, denn niemand bekennt sich offen dazu, Diskriminierung zu üben beziehungsweise sich davor zu fürchten. So bleibt es auch offen, ob die Befürchtungen homosexueller Architekten heute noch genauso berechtigt sind wie früher. Denn auch die Bauherren, Auftraggeber und Investoren sind ein Teil der Gesellschaft, die große Schritte in Richtung Entdiskriminierung und Akzeptanz gemacht hat.

Konstant gefährdete Existenz

Es geht uns bei den folgenden Darstellungen homosexueller Architektenbiografien nicht darum, einen spezifisch schwulen Entwurfsstil nachzuweisen. Susan Sontags These von der Kultur des Camp hat in den 1960er-Jahren dazu verführt, an einen Zusammenhang von sexueller Abweichung und innovativer Gestaltung zu glauben.[32] In dieselbe Richtung ging Aaron Betsky mit seinem Werk *Queer Space. Architecture and Same-Sex Desire*, in dem er homosexuelle Architekten und Interior Designer und ihre Werke von der Antike bis ins 20. Jahrhundert versammelte.[33]

Selbstverständlich kann es hier einen Zusammenhang geben, der in einigen der von uns präsentierten Porträts auch eine Rolle spielt. Jedoch wäre es naiv anzunehmen, man könne einem Gebäude oder einem Interieur ansehen, welche sexuelle oder bloß geschlechtliche Identität sein Entwerfer besitzt oder besaß. Unser primäres Interesse gilt der Frage, wie sich die sexuelle Orientierung früher und heute auf die Arbeit als Architekt auswirken kann. Vor allem aber fragen wir nach den speziellen Umständen, unter denen homosexuelle Architek-

deviance of architects and innovative design.[32] Aaron Betsky followed the same direction with his work *Queer Space. Architecture and Same-Sex Desire*, in which he compiled homosexual architects and interior designers and their works from antiquity to the 20th century.[33]

Of course, there may be a connection here, which also plays a role in some of the portraits we present. It would, however, be naïve to assume that one can look at a building or an interior and see which sexual or just gender identity its designer has or had. Our primary interest is the question of how sexual orientation in the past and today can affect one's work as an architect. Above all, we ask about the specific circumstances in which homosexual architects have worked throughout history, which have almost always also been times of discrimination and persecution. On the one hand, it is about the reconstruction of precarious existences and thus about the conditions under which well-known homosexual architects in the older and more recent history were able to practice their profession – be it through the total shielding of their privacy or the complete renunciation of their own sexual life. On the other hand, the influence of stable gay networks among professional colleagues or within certain client circles is of interest. Last but not least, individual buildings and designs are also reinterpreted from a biographical perspective that includes sexual identity.

In the past, the social existence of homosexual architects was constantly at risk. Older gay men can still remember the stressful aspects of everyday life – the hardships of discretion, frequently feelings of guilt, depression, fear of scandal. Discreet defensive strategies were needed to protect oneself. These shaped their behavior and did not remain without impact on the relationships between architects, colleagues and clients and thus ultimately had an effect on the genesis of buildings and projects. In many cases, this results in a special tension between biography and œuvre that is worth exploring. It would be a misunderstanding to interpret the perspective we have adopted as a voyeuristic glimpse through the keyhole. Rather, where previously concealed facts are revealed, a look behind doors that were firmly closed for reasons of self-protection in times of persecution is opened up. The reputation of the protagonists is not damaged. On the contrary, we show the architects respect by making them visible as complete personalities.

The fact that our research can often only draw on a narrow basis of source material is understandably due to the subject matter itself. The smoking gun proof is not always to be found in this field. Thus, it also requires the courage to draw conclusions when circumstantial evidence suggests this. The deviant sexual orien-

ten in der Geschichte, die fast immer auch Zeiten der Diskriminierung und Verfolgung gewesen sind, gearbeitet haben. Es geht also einerseits um die Rekonstruktion prekärer Existenzen und damit um die Bedingungen, unter denen namhafte homosexuelle Architekten in der älteren und jüngeren Geschichte ihren Beruf ausüben konnten – sei es durch die totale Abschirmung des Privaten oder den vollkommenen Verzicht auf ein eigenes Sexualleben. Zum anderen interessiert etwa der Einfluss von stabilen schwulen Netzwerken unter Berufskollegen oder innerhalb bestimmter Auftraggeber-Kreise. Nicht zuletzt werden aber auch einzelne Bauten und Entwürfe unter einer biografischen, die sexuelle Identität einschließenden Perspektive neu gelesen und interpretiert.

In der Vergangenheit war die soziale Existenz homosexueller Architekten konstant gefährdet. An die stressbildenden Faktoren des Alltags – die Mühen der Diskretion, nicht selten auch Schuldgefühle, Depression, Angst vor Skandal – können sich ältere Schwule noch gut erinnern. Zur Absicherung bedurfte es diskreter defensiver Strategien. Diese prägten das Verhalten und blieben nicht ohne Einfluss auf die Beziehungen zwischen Architekten, Kollegen und Auftraggebern und wirkten sich damit letztlich auch auf die Genese von Bauten und Projekten aus. Daraus ergibt sich in vielen Fällen ein besonderes Spannungsverhältnis zwischen Biografie und Werk, dem nachzuspüren sich lohnt. Es wäre ein Missverständnis, die dafür von uns eingenommene Perspektive als voyeuristischen Blick durchs Schlüsselloch zu deuten. Wo bisher Verdecktes offenbar wird, öffnet sich vielmehr der Blick hinter Türen, die in Zeiten der Verfolgung zum eigenen Schutz fest verschlossen wurden. Das Ansehen der Protagonisten wird nicht verletzt. Ihnen wird im Gegenteil Respekt bezeugt, indem wir sie als ganze Persönlichkeiten sichtbar machen.

Dass sich unsere Forschungen vielfach nur auf einer schmalen Quellenbasis aufbauen lassen, ist dabei begreiflicherweise dem Gegenstand selbst geschuldet. Der in der Kriminalistik erwünschte Beweis à la smoking gun ist ist auf diesem Feld nicht immer zu finden. So bedarf es auch des Mutes zur Schlussfolgerung, wenn Indizien dies nahelegen. Die abweichende sexuelle Orientierung war zu Lebzeiten meist ein gut gehütetes Geheimnis; Zeitgenossen und Nachkommen taten wiederum in der Regel alles dafür, dass es so blieb. Was trotzdem an Wissen und Zeugnissen überliefert wurde, haben spätere Biografen und Historiker zumeist wohlmeinend ignoriert oder in kryptischen Formeln versteckt. Ein geläufiges Muster ist dabei das Bild des einsamen Genies, das seine ganze Existenz der Architektur verschrieben hat und vor lauter Hingabe an die großen Aufgaben angeblich keine Chance hatte, ein Privatleben zu führen. Besonders

tation was usually a well-kept secret during a person's lifetime; contemporaries and descendants, for their part, usually did everything they could to keep it that way. The knowledge and testimonies that were passed on nonetheless were mostly well meaningly ignored or hidden in cryptic formulas by later biographers and historians. A common pattern here is the image of the lonely genius who dedicated his entire existence to architecture and supposedly had no chance to lead a private life because of his devotion to the great tasks. This image is particularly popular in the Catholic environment, where Antoni Gaudì (1852-1926), Jose Plecnik (1872-1957) and Luis Barragán (1902-1988) were and still are considered celibate geniuses. In the Protestant camp, Fritz Schumacher (1869-1947) until recently belonged to this group of selfless saints of architecture. Those who suspect a hidden homosexuality behind this image are on the right track with Barragán and Schumacher[34]; with the other two, it was very probably no different.

Queer reading of architectural history

It is often sufficient to read the existing sources from a queer perspective that is, to decipher the poetically veiled formulas of the biographies and to recognize what is probable behind the neutralizing shells. Frequently, however, it is also accidental discoveries that advance our work. Nevertheless, the lack of systematic transmission means that both our understanding of individual homosexual architects and the overall picture will always remain fragmentary. Nevertheless, since we have been conducting targeted research, the list of homosexual architects with well-known, sometimes even famous names has become longer and longer. It was by no means only designers with a penchant for style, décor, elegance and surface who correspond to the gay cliché that emerged. Certainly, there were those, but we also find the "structive" architect, the imaginative builder, the representative of regionalism and elaborate detail, as well as the modernist dedicated to objectivity and the socially committed urban planner. The selection made for this book includes primarily biographies of male homosexual architects of the 18th, 19th and 20th centuries from Europe and North America. A more balanced distribution in terms of gender would certainly have been desirable. Although there were individual female pioneers in the field of architecture – a profession dominated by men until well into the 20th century – whom the Deutsches Architekturmuseum (German Architecture Museum) in Frankfurt am Main honored in 2017 with the exhibition *Frau Architekt*[35], finding a lesbian architect in retrospect is difficult due to the discretion exercised to protect oneself. This is why only one lesbian architect and one female trans-architect were included in our book.

beliebt ist dieses Bild im Umfeld des Katholizismus, wo Antoni Gaudì (1852-1926), Jose Plecnik (1872-1957) und Luis Barragán (1902-1988) als zölibatäre Genies geführt worden sind und noch werden. Im protestantischen Lager gehörte bis vor kurzem Fritz Schumacher (1869-1947) in diese Gruppe der selbstlosen Heiligen der Baukunst. Wer hinter diesem Bild eine verborgen gehaltene Homosexualität vermutet, ist bei Barragán und Schumacher[34] auf der richtigen Spur; bei den anderen beiden war es sehr wahrscheinlich nicht anders.

Architekturgeschichte queer lesen

So genügt es oft, die vorhandenen Quellen queer zu lesen; das heißt, die poetisch verbrämten Formeln der Biografik zu entziffern und hinter den neutralisierenden Hüllen das Wahrscheinliche zu erkennen. Nicht selten sind es aber auch zufällige Entdeckungen, die unsere Arbeit voranbringen. Gleichwohl bedingt das Fehlen systematischer Überlieferungen, dass sowohl unser Bild einzelner homosexueller Architekten wie auch die Gesamtschau immer fragmentarisch bleiben werden. Nichtsdestotrotz ist, seitdem von uns gezielt geforscht wird, die Liste homosexueller Architekten mit bekannten, manchmal auch berühmten Namen immer länger geworden. Zum Vorschein kamen dabei keineswegs nur Entwerfer mit Hang zu Stil, Dekor, Eleganz und Oberfläche, die dem schwulen Klischee auf dankbare Weise entsprechen. Gewiss hat es diese gegeben, aber genauso finden wir den „struktiven" Architekten, den fantasiebegabten Konstrukteur, den Vertreter des Regionalismus und des durchdachten Details und ebenso wie den der Sachlichkeit verpflichteten Modernisten und den sozial engagierten Städtebauer. Die für den vorliegenden Band getroffene Auswahl umfasst vorrangig Biografien männlicher homosexueller Architekten des 18., 19. und 20. Jahrhunderts aus Europa und Nordamerika. Eine ausgewogenere Verteilung hinsichtlich der Geschlechter wäre sicher wünschenswert gewesen. Zwar gab es in dem bis weit ins 20. Jahrhundert von Männern dominierten Berufsfeld des Architekten einzelne Pionierinnen, die das Deutsche Architekturmuseum in Frankfurt am Main 2017 mit der Ausstellung *Frau Architekt* würdigte.[35] Rückblickend eine lesbische Architektin zu finden, stößt wegen der zum eigenen Schutz geübten Diskretion allerdings auf Schwierigkeiten. So fanden lediglich eine einzige frauenliebende Architektin sowie eine Trans-Architektin Aufnahme in unseren Band.

Die Idee zu der nun vorliegenden Veröffentlichung entstand vor mehr als zehn Jahren während des von uns im November 2009 initiierten Symposiums *Queer Spaces*, das gemeinsam mit der Architekturfachzeitschrift *AIT* und dem Hamburger *AIT-Architektursalon* veranstaltet wurde.[36] Damals stellten wir die

Jose Plecnik und das Torgebäude seines Zale-Friedhofs in Ljubljana

Slovenian architect Jose Plecnik's gate building of his Zale cemetery in Ljubljana

The idea for this publication developed more than ten years ago during the Queer Spaces symposium we initiated in November 2009, which was organized in cooperation with the architecture journal *AIT* and the Hamburg AIT Architektursalon.[36] At that time we presented the first results of our biographical research on homosexual architects. It was the first step to break the general silence and to trigger the discussion of the topic, which is possible on the other side of the Atlantic, in Germany, as well: for what is certainly not lacking in this country is the successful homosexual architect. What is lacking, however, is the courage to profess his homosexuality. Only an architect who is not afraid of coming out is suited to lead the way as a role model for contemporaries and future generations. With our book we want to support this process.

We would like to thank Barry Bergdoll, Ulf Bollmann, Helge Bofinger (†), Olaf Gisbertz, Franz-Josef Hamm, Hans-Georg Lippert, Gottfried Lorenz, Alan Powers, Mary Pepchinski, Axel Schildt (†), Despina Stratigakos, Lars Strominski and Christoph Waldecker for information on individual architects and help with research; thanks to Koos Bosma (†), Jochen Fischer and Dirk van den Heuvel for their friendly support of our project. Our thanks also go to the external authors Neil Bingham, Ron Fuchs and Richard Kurdiovsky, who supported this anthology with their contributions.

ersten Ergebnisse unserer biografischen Recherchen zu homosexuellen Architekten vor. Es war der erste Schritt, um das allgemeine Schweigen zu brechen und die jenseits des Atlantiks mögliche Auseinandersetzung mit dem Thema auch in Deutschland anzustoßen: Denn woran es hierzulande sicher nicht fehlt, ist der erfolgreiche homosexuelle Architekt. Woran es indessen mangelt, ist der Mut zum Bekenntnis! Nur ein bekennender, das Outing nicht fürchtender Architekt ist geeignet, als Role Model, als Vorbild, für Zeitgenossen und zukünftige Generationen voran zu gehen. Mit unserem Buch wollen wir diesen Prozess unterstützen.

Für Hinweise zu einzelnen Architekten und Architektinnen und Hilfe bei der Recherche bedanken wir uns bei Barry Bergdoll, Ulf Bollmann, Helge Bofinger (†), Olaf Gisbertz, Franz-Josef Hamm, Hans-Georg Lippert, Gottfried Lorenz, Alan Powers, Mary Pepchinski, Axel Schildt (†), Despina Stratigakos, Lars Strominski und Christoph Waldecker; für die freundschaftliche Begleitung unseres Projekts bei Koos Bosma (†), Jochen Fischer und Dirk van den Heuvel. Genauso geht unser Dank an die externen Autoren Neil Bingham, Ron Fuchs und Richard Kurdiovsky, die diesen Sammelband mit ihren Beiträgen unterstützen.

Wolfgang Voigt

Hamburg im 18. Jahrhundert: Der Baumeister Ernst Georg Sonnin und sein Liebling

Der Baumeister Ernst Georg Sonnin (1713-1794) war im 18. Jahrhundert der bekannteste Vertreter der spätbarocken Baukunst in Norddeutschland. Von ihm und Johann Bernhard Prey stammt das traditionelle Wahrzeichen Hamburgs, die „Michel" genannte Hauptkirche Sankt Michaelis mit ihrem charakteristischen Turmhelm, fertiggestellt 1782.[1] Der hochgebildete und im Zeichnen begabte Pastorensohn wollte zunächst Theologe werden, verließ dann aber die Universität und tat sich mit dem etwa gleichaltrigen Freund Cord Michael Möller zusammen, den er 17-jährig kennengelernt hatte, als beide in Hamburg bei einem Töpfer in Kost und Logis wohnten. Schon vor Sonnins Studentenjahren waren sie „ein Herz und eine Seele, keiner konnte den anderen entbehren."[2] In Hamburg reüssierte Möller zunächst als Maler blauer Kacheln, bevor er erst allein und dann mit Sonnin eine Werkstatt für Apparate betrieb. So entwickelte sich dieser zu einem gefragten „Mechanicus" und Ingenieur, dessen Spezialität es war, durch die Wucht der Nordsee-Stürme schief gewordene Turmhelme von Kirchen mit Seilzügen wieder in die Vertikale zu ziehen. Je öfter er mit baukonstruktiven Aufgaben konfrontiert war, desto mehr entwickelte er baumeisterliche Fähigkeiten, bis aus ihm schließlich der führende Architekt der Stadt wurde.

1824 erschien eine detaillierte Lebensbeschreibung Sonnins,[3] verfasst von seinem Schüler Johann Theodor Reinke (1749-1825), der später in das Amt eines hamburgischen Grenzinspektors und Strom- und Kanal-Baudirektors befördert wurde.[4] Sonnins Privatleben, das Reinke selbst über Jahrzehnte mit ihm geteilt hatte, wird darin dem aufmerksamen Leser mit bemerkenswerter Offenheit geschildert. Sonnin blieb zeitlebens unverheiratet und lebte über ein halbes Jahrhundert mit männlichen Hausgenossen zusammen; zuerst mit dem ebenfalls ledigen Freund Cord Michael Möller, mit dem er auch die mechanische Werkstatt betrieb. Sie führten gemeinsame Kasse und wohnten zusammen, bis sie sich nach mehr als drei Jahrzehnten zerstritten. Schon vorher hatten Sonnins Einkünfte aus dem Bau der Michaeliskirche den Bezug eines „niedlichen Wohnhauses von mäßiger Größe" mit Garten in der Nähe des Alstertors erlaubt.[5] Was der Autor wohl nicht ohne Absicht außerdem über das Haus mitteilte, war seine versteckte Lage. Es befand sich hinter einem verschließbaren Gang und war von nirgendwo einsehbar. Die Intimität des „einsamen, fast von der Hamburgischen Welt abgesonderten Locals" in der Nähe des Alstertors entzog den Haushalt den Blicken der Nachbarschaft.

Hamburg in the 18th Century:
The Architect Ernst Georg Sonnin
and his "Liebling"

In the 18th century, the master builder Ernst George Sonnin (1713-1794) was the best-known representative of late-Baroque architecture in northern Germany. Together with Johann Bernhard Prey, he designed the traditional landmark of Hamburg, the Sankt Michaelis main church called Michel with its characteristic spire completed in 1782.[1] The son of a pastor was highly educated and gifted as a draughtsman who initially wanted to become a theologian but then left university and joined his friend Cord Michael Möller of about the same age whom he had met when they were 17 when both were boarding with a potter in Hamburg. Already previous to Sonnin's student years, they had been "hand in glove, neither could do without the other."[2] In Hamburg, Möller first succeeded as a painter of blue tiles before running a workshop for machines, first on his own and then together with Sonnin. The latter thus developed into a sought-after "Mechanicus" and engineer whose specialty was to use pulleys to straighten church spires which had become tilted due to the force of North Sea storms. The more often he was confronted with tasks of building construction, the more he developed master-builder skills until finally he became the leading architect of the city.

In 1824, a detailed life story of Sonnin's life was published,[3] written by his student Johann Theodor Reinke (1749-1825), who was later promoted to the position of a Hamburg border inspector and stream- and canal-construction director.[4] Sonnin's private life, which Reinke himself had shared over decades, is described to the discerning reader in the publication with remarkable openness. Sonnin remained unmarried all his life and for more than half a century lived together with male housemates: first with his likewise unmarried friend Cord Michael Möller, with whom he also ran the mechanical workshop. They pooled their money and lived together until they fell out after more than three decades. Prior to this, income from the building of the Sankt Michaelis church had allowed Sonnin to move into a "charming residence of moderate size" with a garden in the vicinity of the Alstertor.[5] What the author furthermore imparted about the house, probably not unintentionally, was its hidden location. It stood behind a lockable passage and was not observable from any direction. The privacy of the "remote locality, almost separated from the Hamburg world" close to the Alstertor kept the household from the gaze of the neighbours.

Porträt des Baumeisters Ernst Georg Sonnin; im Hintergrund der markante Turmhelm von Sonnins Kirche Sankt Michaelis in Hamburg

Portrait of the architect Georg Sonnin; in the background, the prominent spire of his Sankt Michaelis church in Hamburg

Sonnins Biograf war im Alter von elf Jahren als „Zögling" und Lehrling in den Haushalt von Sonnin und Möller aufgenommen worden.[6] Von Sonnin erhielt er Unterricht in Latein, Mathematik und „anderen Zweigen des Wissens". Als Sonnin und Möller sich trennten, wollte jeder den Jungen bei sich behalten. Wie Reinke berichtet, entschied er selbst sich für Sonnin und blieb bei ihm bis an dessen Lebensende im Jahre 1794. Mit der Lebensbeschreibung erfüllte er noch als alter Mann ein nach Sonnins Tod sich selbst gegebenes Versprechen. Wer war kompetent, seine Lebensbeschreibung zu verfassen, wenn nicht er, „denn ich war Sonnins Zögling von meinem elften Jahre an, und während eines Zeitraumes von 34 Jahren, sein Hausgenosse bis an seinen Tod; wurde bald sein Liebling, und in der Folge sein – fast einziger – Vertrauter und zuletzt – fast möchte ich sagen, sein Alles in allem. Deshalb möchte wohl keiner von Sonnin zu erzählen wissen, was ich davon weiß."[7]

Bei der Schilderung des Privatlebens leistete Reinke einen bemerkenswerten Spagat: Einerseits erklärte er sich offen zu Sonnins „Liebling", andererseits sollte die Nachwelt glauben, dass zuerst Sonnin und Möller und später Sonnin und Reinke nur eine schlichte Freundschaft verbunden habe. Zur Abwehr des Verdachts wurde eine Episode von durchscheinend defensivem Charakter eingefügt. So hätten Möller und Sonnin schon als Jünglinge als Basis ihrer Freundschaft ein gemeinsames Gelübde getan: „Keiner wollte sich je einer unsittlichen oder niederträchtigen Handlung schuldig finden lassen."[8] Sowohl

Titelblatt der 1824 erschienenen Lebensbeschreibung von Sonnin, verfasst von seinem Schüler und „Liebling" Johann Theodor Reinke

Title page of Sonnin's biography published in 1824, written by his student and "darling" Johann Theodor Reinke

Sonnin's biographer had been taken into the household of Sonnin and Möller as a "pupil" and apprentice at the age of eleven.[6] Sonnin gave him lessons in Latin, mathematics and "other fields of knowledge." When Sonnin and Möller separated, each wanted to keep the boy with him. As Reinke tells it, he himself decided in favor of Sonnin and stayed with him until the end of his life in 1794. With the biography, as an old man already he fulfilled a promise he had made to himself after Sonnin's death. Who would be competent to write Sonnin's biography if not he "because I was Sonnin's pupil starting in my eleventh year and for a period of 34 years, his housemate until his death; I soon became his darling and, as a consequence his – almost only – confidant and last, I would almost like to say, his one and all. That is why nobody could be able to tell anything about Sonnin compared to what I know about him."[7]

When describing Sonnin's private life, Reinke managed a remarkable balancing act: On the one hand, he openly declared himself to be Sonnin's "darling" while, on the other hand, posterity was to believe that first Sonnin and Möller and later Sonnin and Reinke were only connected through a simple friendship. To dispel any suspicion, an episode of a transparently defensive nature was added. Möller and Sonnin had thus already as youths taken a shared vow: "Neither wanted ever to be found guilty of an indecent or vile act."[8] In the house at the Alstertor as well as in the later occupied house at Kleiner

im Haus am Alstertor als auch im später bewohnten Haus am Kleinen Michaeliskirchhof lebten auch Frauen, die den Haushalt besorgten, darunter Reinkes nur beiläufig erwähnte Ehefrau, jedoch keine Kinder.[9]

Sonnins Zögling, Hausgenosse und „Liebling" wurde auch sein Erbe. In der mit ihm geteilten Wohnung blieb Reinke auch nach Sonnins Tod bis an sein eigenes Ende. Mit der Selbstdarstellung als „Liebling" des großen Baumeisters nahm Reinke die Mehrdeutigkeit des Wortes in Kauf. Das Wörterbuch der Brüder Grimm nennt eine ganze Reihe von Bedeutungen von „Liebling", die im späten 18. Jahrhundert und später in Gebrauch waren. Auch wenn die Hauptbedeutung des Wortes dem „Favoriten" entsprach, stand „Liebling" im erotischen Zusammenhang eindeutig für Liebhaber.[10] Johann Wolfgang Goethe, vom gleichen Jahrgang wie Reinke, und andere Schriftsteller der Zeit haben das Wort in diesem Sinne benutzt. Zu Sonnins Lebzeiten konnten die so genannten „sodomitischen" Verbrechen, zu denen auch der mann-männliche Sexualakt gehörte, nach Artikel 116 des Strafgesetzes Karls V. mit der Todesstrafe belegt werden. Zu gerichtlichen Verfahren kam es aber nur selten. In Hamburg erging ein solches Urteil zuletzt 1768; es wurde aber nicht mehr vollstreckt. Der Anlass waren Vorfälle im Waisenhaus der Stadt, in dem 18 männliche Jugendliche zwischen zwölf und 18 Jahren miteinander Sex hatten und darüber Geständnisse ablegten. In einem geheimen Prozess wurden alle verurteilt, der Älteste von ihnen zur Höchststrafe.[11]

Das am Rödingsmarkt gelegene alte hamburgische Waisenhaus galt als überbelegt und unhygienisch. Die in den großen Städten Europas im 17. und 18. Jahrhundert eröffneten Waisenhäuser waren, neben ihrer offiziellen Zweckbestimmung, Heterotopien, zu denen sie Foucault gezählt hat: Orte, in denen unter anderem verdrängte sexuelle Praktiken im Verborgenen ausgeübt wurden, die in der sich konstituierenden Ordnung des Bürgertums keinen Platz hatten. Weil dies so war, gab es in der Mitte des 18. Jahrhunderts in Hamburg Überlegungen für einen im Sinne Foucaults „modernen" Neubau an gleicher Stelle, der besser sauber zu halten war, vor allem aber besser kontrollierbar sein sollte und dessen äußere Gestalt das starke Gewicht ausdrücken sollte, das man der moralisch-religiösen Erziehung beimaß.

Kein anderer als Sonnin entwarf ein solches Projekt: eine Hofanlage mit integrierter Kirche auf einem Zentralgrundriss, die der Hansestadt einen im Norden einzigartigen Kuppelbau beschert hätte. Mit 25 Metern Innendurchmesser der Kuppel sollte sie die Maße der Dresdner Frauenkirche und der Karlskirche in Wien erreichen. Die Lage an einem der „Fleete" genannten Wasserläufe garantierte eine respektable städtebauliche Wirkung.[12] Das Projekt wurde jedoch ebenso wenig realisiert wie ein zweites, nicht zufällig im Oktober 1768, also bald nach Aufdeckung der Vorfälle unter den Jugendlichen,

Michaeliskirchhof, women lived who as well took care of the household, among them Reinke's later wife who was only mentioned in passing, but no children.[9]

Sonnin's pupil, housemate and "Liebling" also became his heir. After Sonnin's death as well, Reinke remained in the flat he had shared with him right up to his own death. With the self-portrayal as the darling of the famous master builder, Reinke accepted the ambiguity of the term. The dictionary by the Brothers Grimm lists a whole series of meanings for "Liebling" which were used in the late 18th century and thereafter. Although the main meaning of the word corresponded to the German word for "favourite," in an erotic context "Liebling" clearly stood for lover.[10] Johann Wolfgang Goethe, born the same year as Reinke, and other authors of the time have used the word in this sense.

When Sonnin was alive, the so-called "sodomitic" crimes, among which the man-man sexual act also belonged, could be punished with death according to Article 116 of the penal code of Charles V. Legal proceedings, however, were only rare. In Hamburg, such a sentence was last passed in 1768; it was, however, no longer enforced. The occasions were incidences in the orphanage of the city where 18 male youths aged between twelve and 18 had had sexual relationships with each other and confessed to them. In secret trial, they were all condemned, the oldest of them to the maximum penalty.[11]

The old Hamburg orphanage situated in Rödingsmarkt was considered to be overcrowded and unsanitary. The orphanages opened in the major cities of Europe in the 17th and 18th century were, besides their official purpose, also heterotopies, as Foucault categorized them: places where, among other acts, repressed sexual practices were furtively conducted which were not compatible with the bourgeois order which was in the process of being constituted. Since this was the case, in the middle of the 18th century it was deliberated in Hamburg whether to have a "modern" new building – in the sense of Foucault – constructed in the same place, which was to be easier to keep clean and, above all, to control and with an external appearance that was to express the prime importance one was attributing to moral-religious education.

Sonnin himself developed such a project: a courtyard ensemble with an integrated church on a central layout which would have added to the hanseatic city a domed structure unique in the north. With its inside diameter of 25 metres, the dome was to achieve the dimensions of the Dresden Frauenkirche and the Karlskirche in Vienna. The location at one of the waterways called "Fleet" ensured a respectable effect as to the urban development.[12] The project, however, was just as little implemented as was a second one, not coincidentally originating in October 1768, hence shortly after the exposure of the incidences among the youths, for a narrower site in Gänsemarkt. It was also designed by

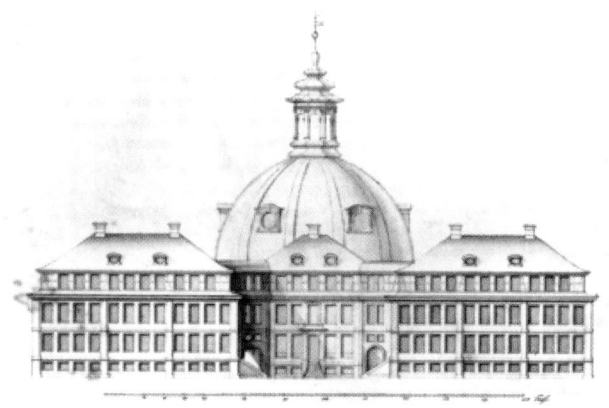

Sonnins erstes Projekt für ein neues Hamburger Waisenhaus: Im Zentrum war ein überkuppelter Kirchenbau mit 25 Metern Durchmesser geplant.

Sonnin's first project for a new Hamburg orphanage: A domed church building with a diameter of 25 metres was planned in the centre.

entstandenes Projekt für ein schmaleres Grundstück am Gänsemarkt. Es war ebenfalls von Sonnin und sah statt des an dieser Stelle nicht realisierbaren Kuppelbaus einen Kirchturm vor. Als Architekt der Obrigkeit, der diese Projekte im Auftrag des Senats entwickelte, befand sich Sonnin in einer delikaten Position. Denn mit dem, was mit Hilfe des Neubaus unter anderem eingedämmt werden sollte, dürfte er sich besser ausgekannt haben, als seine Auftraggeber es wissen durften.

Sonnin und seine Lebensgefährten waren zweifellos in besserer Lage als die proletarischen und mehr oder weniger rechtlosen Insassen des Waisenhauses, doch hatten sie dennoch Grund zur Vorsicht. Kamen in Hamburg während des 18. Jahrhunderts Fälle mann-männlicher „Sodomiterey" zur Verhandlung, wurden die Verurteilten zu Haft im „Spinnhaus" verurteilt – das war die hamburgische Bezeichnung für das gefängnisartige Armenhaus – oder in die Verbannung geschickt. Wurden wohlhabende Bürger verurteilt, konfiszierte man außerdem Teile des Vermögens.

Als Reinke seine Lebensbeschreibung Sonnins 1824 veröffentlichte, war das Strafgesetz Karls V. in Hamburg durch einen milderen Paragrafen ersetzt worden. Doch noch immer drohten bei mann-männlicher Liebe Haftstrafen. Allerdings war Reinke selbst schon 75 Jahre alt und die pikanten Dinge, die er nun andeutete, lagen ein halbes Jahrhundert zurück. Reinkes Text, der in der restaurativen Periode des Vormärz erschien, erlaubt verschiedene Lesarten. Die eher biederen Bürger durften das eingeflochtene Dementi jeglicher unsittlichen Handlung für bare Münze nehmen. Den freieren Geistern bot es einen Subtext mit auffindbaren Chiffren, der es möglich machte, die Schrift als Offenlegung einer Existenz unter Einschluss mann-männlicher Liebe zu entziffern; einer gleichwohl prekären Existenz, abgeschirmt und von Vorsicht bestimmt.

Sonnin and included a church tower instead of the dome construction which could not be implemented in this place. As the architect of the authorities who developed these projects by order of the senate, Sonnin was in a delicate position. This was because he was no doubt more familiar with what was to be curbed with the help of the new building than his clients should ever know.

Sonnin and his companions were no doubt in a better position than the proletarian residents, more or less without any rights of the orphanage, yet they had reason to be careful all the same. Whenever, in Hamburg during the 18th century cases of male-male "sodomy" were prosecuted, the convicted were sentenced to imprisonment in the "Spinnhaus" – this was the Hamburg term for the prison-like poorhouse – or they were sent into exile. Whenever affluent members of the bourgeoisie were convicted, parts of their estates were confiscated as well.

At the time when Reinke published his description of Sonnin's life in 1824, the criminal code of Charles V had been replaced in Hamburg by a milder law. But still man-man love was threatened with imprisonment. Reinke himself, however, was already 75 years old and the spicy matters he now insinuated happened more than half a century ago. Reinke's text, which was published in the restorative pre-March period, allows various interpretations. The rather staid citizens could take the built-in denial of any indecent act take at face value. To freer spirits, it offered a subtext with discernible codes, which made it possible to decipher the writing as the disclosure of an existence including man-man love; yet a precarious existence, shielded by caution.

Uwe Bresan

Die Erfindung der Queer Gothic: Horace Walpole

Weiß strahlt der lang gestreckte Baukörper im Sonnenlicht. Ziselierte Kamine und feingliedrige Ecktürmchen ragen in den Himmel. Ihre Verteilung gibt Aufschluss über die verschiedenen Bau- und Erweiterungsphasen des Hauses. Früher reichte der Blick von hier bis hinunter zur Themse. Doch längst haben sich mehrere Reihen stattlicher Wohnhäuser zwischen den Fluss und Strawberry Hill geschoben. Strawberry Hill, so nannte der englische Politiker, Schriftsteller und emsige Chronist seiner Zeit Horace Walpole (1717-1797) seinen beschaulichen Landsitz in Twickenham vor den Toren Londons. Den Ursprungsbau, ein bescheidenes Cottage, hatte Walpole 1748 von einer Londoner Witwe erworben, dazu zwei Hektar des umgebenden Landes. Bald darauf begannen die ersten Umbauarbeiten. Sie sollten fast 30 Jahre dauern und aus dem unscheinbaren Besitz eines der berühmtesten Anwesen im England des späten 18. Jahrhunderts machen.[1]

Dabei waren es weder seine Größe noch seine Pracht, wie man zunächst vielleicht vermuten könnte, die den Ruf von Strawberry Hill begründeten. Tatsächlich gab es damals eine Vielzahl weit größerer und weitaus prächtigerer Anwesen. Was Walpoles Landhaus über die Grenzen Englands hinaus berühmt machte, war sein so ganz anderer Charakter, sein neuartiger Stil. Denn während überall im Land Villen nach dem Vorbild des venezianischen Renaissance-Baumeisters Andrea Palladio entstanden und sich die Gentry, die englische Oberschicht der Zeit, in eine italienische Villeggiatura, ein sonniges Arkadien, träumte, schuf Walpole mit Strawberry Hill den Ausgangspunkt eines kommenden Gothic Revival. Es sollte der vorherrschende Baustil des 19. Jahrhunderts werden. Walpole vertauschte das klassizistische Ideal seiner Zeitgenossen gegen ein idealisiertes Mittelalter, eine romantische Gotik: Gegen die ruhigen, zentral-symmetrisch geordneten Baukörper des Palladianismus mit ihren strengen dorischen, ionischen oder korinthischen Säulenordnungen, ihren vorspringenden Tempelfronten und ihren pseudo-antiken Dekorationen setzte er sein aus unterschiedlichsten Baukörpern malerisch komponiertes Schlösschen. Mit Zinnen besetzte Mauern, ein runder Festungsturm, ein schmaler Bergfried und unzählige Erker gaben Strawberry Hill das Aussehen einer mittelalterliche Burg – einer Burg allerdings im Diminutiv, das heißt: einer Burg im Puppenstubenformat. Das Gebäude ist eine reine Attrappe: Hinter den Zinnen verbirgt sich kein Wehrgang, der vermeintliche Festungsturm würde keinem feindlichen Ansturm widerstehen und kein Feind ließe sich aus dem Bergfried erspähen. Strawberry Hill ist das Spielhaus eines erwachsenen Mannes, eine spleenige Folly, aber vor allem ist es eine Provokation gegen die Geschmacks- und Stilkon-

The Invention of Queer Gothic: Horace Walpole

The elongated building volume shines white in the sunlight. Chiselled chimneys and slender corner turrets rise into the sky. Their distribution talks about the various construction and expansion phases of the building. In former times, one could look from here all the way down to the Thames. But for a long time now, several rows of stately residential buildings have squeezed between the river and Strawberry Hill. Strawberry Hill, this is how Horace Walpole, the English politician, author, and busy chronicler of his time called his tranquil country estate in Twickenham outside London. In 1749, Walpole had bought the original building, a modest cottage, from a London widow, together with two hectares of the surrounding land. Soon afterwards, the first conversion work started. It was to last for almost 30 years and turn the inconspicuous property into one of the most famous estates in the England of the late 18th century.[1]

Yet it was neither its size nor its magnificence, as one might at first have assumed, which established the reputation of Strawberry Hill. As a matter of fact, there existed at the time a multitude of much larger and much more magnificent properties. What made Walpole's country home famous beyond the borders of England was its so completely different character, its novel style. Whereas, all over the country, mansions modelled on the works by the Venetian Renaissance builder Andrea Palladio were being constructed and the gentry, the English upper class of the time, dreamt itself into an Italian *villegiatura*, a sunny Arcadia, with Strawberry Hill, Walpole established the starting point of the coming Gothic Revival. It was to become the dominating architectural style of the 19th century. Walpole exchanged the classicist ideal of his contemporaries for a kind of idealized Middle Ages, a romantic Gothic period: To the calm, centrally-symmetrically arranged buildings of Palladianism with their strict Doric, Ionic or Corinthian arrangements of columns, their projecting temple fronts and their pseudo-antique decorations, he opposed his picturesque little castle composed of a variety of building structures. Walls equipped with battlements, a round fortress tower, a narrow keep, and countless oriels gave Strawberry Hill the appearance of a medieval fortress – a fortress, however, with diminutive dimensions, meaning: a fortress in the format of a dolls house. The building is a sheer mock-up: There is no wall-walk behind the battlements, the pretended fortress tower would not resist any hostile attack and no enemy could ever be spotted from the keep. Strawberry Hill is the playhouse of a grown-up man, a self-indulgent folly, but it is above all a provocation against the conventions of taste and style of the time. And this not only applies to the

ventionen der Zeit. Und das gilt nicht nur für das Äußere von Strawberry Hill, sondern erst recht für das Innere von Walpoles neogotischer Miniatur: Der Grundriss widersetzt sich jeder formalen Ordnung. Man findet keine Spur einer klassischen Raumhierarchie oder Raumverteilung. Selbst Bodenniveaus und Raumhöhen wechseln mitunter von Zimmer zu Zimmer, so als ob der Bau tatsächlich über Jahrhunderte gewachsen wäre. Dazu kommen Dekorationen, die sich frei und lustvoll, das heißt ohne jeden Anspruch auf stilistische Einheitlichkeit, Genauigkeit oder auch nur Angemessenheit, aus der englischen Gotik des 12. bis 16. Jahrhunderts speisen. Das Vorbild eines gotischen Grabmals aus der Abtei von Westminster etwa wird kurzerhand in einen beschaulichen Kaminsims verwandelt, während sich das Muster des steinernen Rosettenfensters der 1666 zerstörten, nur in Stichen überlieferten Londoner Kathedrale Old Saint Paul's als Stuckdecke des so genannten „Runden Salons" wiederfindet. Seinen Höhepunkt feiert Walpoles Zitatenspiel allerdings im Treppenhaus. Hier verbinden sich so viele Vorlagen zu einer alle Oberflächen beherrschenden gotischen Rocaille, dass es kaum noch möglich ist, exakt übernommene Zitate von phantasievollen Interpretationen und wohl auch manchem frei erfundenen Detail zu unterscheiden.

Als Mitglied der englischen Oberschicht und Parlamentspolitiker wird Walpoles unausgesetzte Bautätigkeit im nahe gelegenen Twickenham natürlich von der Londoner Gesellschaft mit großem Interesse und zunächst auch mit großer Skepsis verfolgt. Diese weicht jedoch spätestens nach 1764 einer allgemeinen Neugier. Es ist das Jahr der Veröffentlichung des Romans *The Castle of Otranto*,[2] mit dem Walpole en passant die Gattung des modernen Schauerromans, der Gothic Novel, begründet. Über Nacht verbreitet sich die im Mittelalter angesiedelte Erzählung um den Erben von Otranto, dessen Ahnen einst durch einen heimtückischen Mord in den Besitz des Schlosses kamen und der nun deshalb

Mit Strawberry Hill schuf Horace Walpole das Abbild einer mittelalterlichen Burg – einer Burg im Puppenstubenformat.

Horace Walpole, 4. Earl of Orford, war Politiker, Schriftsteller und ein bedeutender Chronist seiner Zeit.

With Strawberry Hill Walpole created the image of a medieval castle – a castle of dollhouse size format.

Horace Walpole, 4th Earl of Orford, politician, writer, and an important chronicler of his time.

exterior of Strawberry Hill but even more to the inside of Walpole's neo-Gothic miniature: The layout opposes any formal order. One finds no trace of a classic hierarchy of rooms or space distribution. Even the floor levels and the ceiling heights in some places change from room to room as if the building had indeed grown in the course of centuries. Then there are the decorations which are free and full of relish, meaning without any claim to stylistic consistency, exactness or even derived from the English Gothic of the 12th to the 16th century. The model of a Gothic tomb in Westminster Abbey, for instance, is without further ado turned into a sedate mantelpiece, whereas the pattern of the stone rose windows of the Old Saint Paul's Cathedral in London, destroyed in 1666 and only preserved in etchings, is found again as a stucco ceiling of the so-called round parlour. But Walpole's play with architectural quotations celebrates has its climax in the staircase. So many models here combine into a Gothic rocaille which dominates all the surfaces that it is almost no longer possible to differentiate exactly taken-over quotations from fanciful interpretations and probably also many a freely invented detail.

As a member of the English upper class and a politician in the parliament, it goes without saying that Walpole's continual construction activity in nearby Twickenham is observed by the London society with a strong interest and, at first, also with great scepticism. The latter, however, is replaced by general curiosity after 1764 at the latest. It is the year when the novel *The Castle of Otranto*[2] is published and Walpole, en passant as it were, establishes the genre of the modern horror story, the Gothic novel. Overnight, the story set in the Middle Ages and centred on the heir of Otranto – whose ancestors formerly took possession of the castle after committing an insidious murder and are therefore now haunted by ghosts and demons – spreads over half of Europe. And it does not take long

von Geistern und Dämonen heimgesucht wird, in halb Europa. Und es dauert nicht lange, da stellen die Leser einen Bezug zwischen dem fiktiven mittelalterlichen *Schloss von Otranto* und dem merkwürdigen Zuhause des Autors in Twickenham her. Kurzerhand machen sie Strawberry Hill zur Pilgerstätte. Walpole verlangt ein Eintrittsgeld von einem Pfund, öffnet sein Haus von Mai bis Oktober jeweils für drei Stunden am Nachmittag und bittet seine Besucher im allerhöflichsten Ton darum, auf das Mitbringen von Kindern zu verzichten. Für wen die Anreise – etwa vom Kontinent – zu beschwerlich ist, für den lässt Walpole in der hauseigenen Druckerei, der Strawberry Hill Press, wiederum einen umfassenden Führer drucken: *A Description of the Villa of Horace Walpole, Youngest Son of Sir Robert Walpole Earl of Orford, at Strawberry Hill, near Twickenham. With an inventory of the furniture, pictures, curiosities, etc.*[3] Zunächst als reiner Textband ausgeführt, später auch mit Stichen ausgestattet, erläutert Walpole in den *Descriptions* nicht nur minutiös die einzelnen Räume seines Hauses, ihre Ausstattung und Gestaltung, sondern listet auch pedantisch seine diversen, den unterschiedlichsten Kunst- und Interessensgebieten entstammenden Sammlungen auf – darunter Gemälde, Ritterrüstungen und Porzellangeschirre. Ganz nebenbei erfindet Walpole damit auch noch das moderne Genre der Haus- oder Gebäudemonografie.

Im Angesicht seiner vielfältigen und umfassenden Lebensleistungen darf es nicht verwundern, dass seit Walpoles Tod im März 1797 Historiker, Literaten und Architekten gleichermaßen mit seinem Erbe ringen. Den Historikern hinterließ er tausende Briefe, Notizen und Tagebuchaufzeichnungen, die ein lebendiges Bild der Zeit malen. Sie füllen heute die 48 Bände der *Yale Edition of Horace Walpole's Correspondence*. Den Schriftstellern und Drehbuchautoren wiederum schenkte er mit seinem *Schloss von Otranto* die moderne Horrorfiktion. Eine Serie wie *Games of Thrones* wäre ohne ihn undenkbar! Den Architekten schlussendlich hinterließ er Strawberry Hill als ersten Versuch einer neuen gotischen Baukunst. Sein Einfluss wirkte hier bis weit ins 19. Jahrhundert hinein.

Wie aber lässt sich nun ein solches Lebenswerk in seiner erstaunlichen Vielgestaltigkeit mit der Biografie Walpoles verbinden? Oder besser: Wie lässt sich dieses umfassende und übergroße Werk aus der Lebensgeschichte des Politikers, Dichters und Architekten heraus begründen? Das ist eine der zentralen Fragen, die seit dem Tod Walpoles immer wieder diskutiert wird. Am wirkmächtigsten und langlebigsten hielt sich dabei die Theorie vom übermächtigen Vater Robert Walpole, einem der politisch einflussreichsten Männer seiner Zeit und dem ersten Premierminister Großbritanniens, demgegenüber sich der Sohn in allem, was er tat, beweisen wollte. Seit den achtziger Jahren des vergangenen Jahrhunderts allerdings verschiebt sich der Akzent: In ihrem Buch *Between Men: English Literature and Male Homosocial Desire* von 1985 stellt die US-amerikanische Literaturwissenschaftlerin Eve Kosofsky Sedgwick erstmals einen Zusammenhang zwischen der

Das Treppenhaus von Walpoles neogotischer Miniatur

The staircase of Walpole's neo-gothic miniature

until the readers make the connection between the fictitious medieval "castle of Otranto" and the strange home of the author in Twickenham. Without further ado, they turn Strawberry Hill into a place of pilgrimage. Walpole charges an admission fee of one pound, opens his house from May to October for three hours in the afternoon and, as politely as possible, asks his visitors not to bring their children. For those for whom the journey – from the Continent, for instance – is too cumbersome, Walpole has a comprehensive guidebook printed in his own printing shop, the Strawberry Hill Press: *A Description of the Villa of Horace Walpole, Youngest Son of Sir Robert Walpole Earl of Orford, at Strawberry Hill, near Twickenham. With an inventory of the furniture, pictures, curiosities, etc.*[3] In what initially was just a text volume, later also equipped with etchings, Walpole meticulously explains in the Descriptions not only the individual rooms of his house, their furnishing and their design, put also pedantically lists his various collections from a wide variety of art genres and areas of interest – among them paintings, suits of armour and porcelain tableware. By the way, Walpole thus also invents the modern genre of the house- or building monography.

In view of the manifold and comprehensive achievements in his life, it is not surprising that, since Walpole's death in March 1797 – he lived to be almost 80 years old! – historians, men of letters and architects are equally struggling with his heritage. For the historians, he left behind thousands of letters, notes and diary entries which paint a lively picture of his time. Today, they fill the 49 volumes of the *Yale Edition of Horace Walpole's Correspondence*. The writers and screenplay writers, in turn, he presented with the modern

Der aufwendigste Raum des Hauses ist die so genannte „Galerie" im Obergeschoss. Ein vergoldetes Fächergewölbe überfängt den Saal.

The most elaborate room of the house is the "gallery" on the upper floor. A gold-plated fan vault surmounts the hall.

Entstehung der Gothic Novel, dem Schauerroman im 18. Jahrhundert, und dem Thema Homosexualität her.[4] In der bewussten Wirklichkeitsüberschreitung, im plötzlichen Auftreten von Geistern, Untoten und Gespenstern innerhalb des neuen Genres, sieht sie ein sprechendes Symbol für den Wunsch der Autoren, sich über gesellschaftliche Normen und geschlechtsspezifische Zuordnungen hinweg zu setzen. Den Rückgriff auf eine weit zurückliegende Vergangenheit deutet Sedgwick dabei als notwendigen Schritt: In seiner historischen Wahrheit noch kaum erforscht, kann das Mittelalter den Autoren der Gothic Novel als ideale Projektionsfläche einer von den strengen, bürgerlichen Konventionen der Neuzeit noch unberührten, freien Gesellschaft dienen. Zugleich kann sich mit dem Mittelalter die homoerotische Vorstellung einer idealen Männergesellschaft verbinden, bevölkert von weisen, väterlichen Königen und poetisch gesinnten jugendlichen Prinzen, von agilen Bauernburschen und den gestählten Körpern tapferer Ritter.

Für Sedgwick war der zeitlebens unverheiratet und kinderlos gebliebene und von Freunden wie Feinden als zartgliedrig und effeminiert geschilderte Erfinder des *Schlosses von Otranto* geradezu ein Musterexemplar des von ihr beschriebenen Autorentyps. Nicht zuletzt stützten Briefe Walpoles und seine engen Beziehungen zu anderen Junggesellen Sedgwicks Theorie. In Walpole fand Sedgwick aber letztlich nur die idealste Verkörperung: Ihr Schema ließ sich leicht auch auf andere Autoren des Genres übertragen – von William Beckford bis zu Lord Byron. Der Literaturwissenschaftler George Haggerty wiederum fasste das Phänomen in der Nachfolge Sedgwicks unter dem Begriff der Queer Gothic zusammen,[5] wobei das amerikanische „queer" hier als Synonym für homosexuell verwendet wird.

Das Innere des Hauses wird von einer gotischen Rocaille beherrscht. Sie setzt sich zusammen aus Zitaten, Interpretationen und frei Erfundenem.

The interior of the house features a Gothic rocaille. It is composed of quotes and interpretations, some of them freely invented.

horror fiction by having written *Castle of Otranto*. A series such as *Games of Thrones* would be inconceivable without him! Finally, to the architects he left Strawberry Hill as the first attempt of a new Gothic architecture. In this field, he had an influence until far into the 19th century.

But how can such an œuvre in its astonishing variety be linked with Walpole's biography? Or rather: How can this comprehensive and excessive work be derived from the life story of a politician, poet and architect? This is one of the central questions which continue to be discussed since Walpole's death. Most efficacious and enduring was the theory of the overpowering father Robert Walpole, one of the politically most influential men of his time and the first Prime Minister of Great Britain, arguing that the son wanted to prove himself in his father's eyes in everything he did. Since the eighties of the past century, however, the accent has been shifting: In her book *Between Men: English Literature and Male Homosocial Desire* from 1985, the US-American literary scientist Eve Kosofsky Sedgwick for the first time establishes a link between the origin of the Gothic novel, the horror story in the 18th century, and the topic of homosexuality.[4] In the deliberate transgression of reality, in the sudden appearance of ghosts, undead and spirits in the new genre, she sees an outspoken symbol of the authors' desire to override social norms and gender-specific classifications. Sedgwick interprets the recourse to a long-ago past as a necessary step: hardly investigated for historic truth, the Middle Ages can serve the authors of the Gothic novel as the ideal projection surface of a society still untouched by the strict, bourgeois conventions of the modern era. At the same time, the homoerotic notion of an

Betrachtet man nun Walpoles gotisches Schlösschen in Twickenham, das, wie bereits erwähnt, bewusst mit den ästhetischen Regeln und Konventionen der Zeit bricht und ein neues Mittelalter evoziert, lässt sich Haggertys genuin literaturwissenschaftlicher Begriff der Queer Gothic problemlos auch auf die Architektur von Strawberry Hill übertragen.[6] Das Haus wird so zum Ausdruck eines homoerotischen Eskapismus, einer Flucht in ein utopisches Mittelalter vor einer als bedrohlich und feindselig wahrgenommenen Umwelt. Wir dürfen nicht vergessen, dass homosexuelle Handlungen in England bis weit ins 19. Jahrhundert hinein mit dem Tode bestraft wurden!

Walpole mag nun der Erste gewesen sein, der sich mit Strawberry Hill aus einer ständigen Angst vor gesellschaftlicher Ächtung heraus in eine romantische Gegenwelt – in eine Queer Gothic – flüchtete, er war in den letzten zweihundert Jahren aber sicher nicht der einzige homophile Neogotiker. Man denke nur an den englischen Schriftsteller William Beckford und seine um 1800 entstandene einsame Abtei in den Wäldern von Fonthill;[7] an das Schloss Neuschwanstein des Bayernkönigs Ludwig II.;[8] an den Kunst- und Antiquitätensammler Henry Davis Sleeper und seine nach 1908 errichtete grandiose Mittelalteradaption von Beauport House in Gloucester an der amerikanischen Ostküste;[9] oder auch an den deutschstämmigen Stummfilmregisseur Friedrich Wilhelm Murnau, den Erschaffer des *Nosferatu*, der in den späten 1920er-Jahren in den Hügeln von Hollywood die Kopie eines mittelalterlichen französischen Kastells bezog.[10] Sie alle schufen sich zu ihrer Zeit und vor dem Hintergrund homophober gesellschaftlicher Umstände ihre eigenen mittelalterlichen Phantasieburgen und -Schlösser. Bis heute haben diese Bauten nichts von ihrer Faszination verloren. Manche – Walpoles Strawberry Hill, Sleepers Beauport House oder Ludwigs Neuschwanstein – sind regelrecht zu Touristenmagneten geworden. Über den Hintergrund ihrer Entstehung allerdings wissen nur die wenigsten Besucher Bescheid.

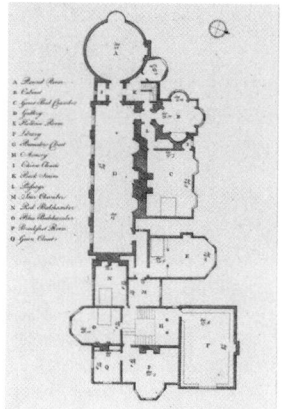

Strawberry Hill, Grundriss des Obergeschosses

Strawberry Hill, floor plan of the upper floor

ideal male society can be connected with the Middle Ages which is populated by wise, fatherly kings and poetic-minded, youthful princes, by agile country lads and the toughened bodies of gallant knights.

For Sedgwick, the inventor of the "castle of Otranto" who had remained unmarried and childless all his life and was described by friends as well as by enemies as fine-boned and effeminate was nothing less but a prime example of the type of author she focuses on. Not least, Walpole's letters and his close relationships with other bachelors are taken to support Sedgwick's theory. In the end, however, Sedgwick only found the most ideal incarnation in Walpole: Her scheme could easily be transferred onto other authors of the genre – from William Beckford all the way to Lord Byron. The literary scientist George Haggerty, in turn, as a follower of Sedgwick summarized the phenomenon by applying to it the term of Queer Gothic,[5] with the American expression "queer" here used as a synonym for homosexual.

If one now looks at Walpole's little Gothic castle in Twickenham which, as already mentioned, deliberately breaks the aesthetic rules and conventions of the time and evokes a new Middle Ages, Haggerty's term of Queer Gothic genuinely used in literary science can also be transferred onto the architecture of Strawberry Hill.[6] The house thus becomes an expression of homoerotic escapism, of a flight into utopian Middle Ages from an environment felt to be threatening and hostile. We must not forget that homosexual acts were punished by death in England until far into the 19th century.

With Strawberry Hill, Walpole may well have been the first who fled fora constant fear of social condemnation into a romantic alternative world – into Queer Gothic – but, during the last two hundred years, he was certainly not the only homophile neo-Goth. If we think of the English author William Beckford and his remote abbey built around 1800 in the forests of Fonthill;[7] of Neuschwanstein, the castle of the Bavarian king Ludwig II;[8] of the collector of art and antiques Henry Davis Sleeper and his medieval adaptation of Beauport House built in Gloucester on the American east coast after 1908;[9] or also of the director of silent films Wilhelm Murnau of German origin, the creator of Nosferatu who, in the late 1920s, moved into the copy of a medieval French fortress in the hills of Hollywood.[10] In their time and against the background of homophobic social conditions, they all created their own medieval fantasy fortresses and castles. To this day, these buildings have lost nothing of their fascination. Some – such as Walpole's Strawberry Hill, Sleeper's Beauport House or Ludwig's Neuschwanstein – have become proper tourist magnets. Only a very small number of the visitors, however, know about the background of their origin.

Uwe Bresan

Exzentrisches Eremitentum: William Beckford

Hier muss es sein! Die flache, kaum hüfthohe Mauer, die uns schon seit einigen Kilometern begleitet, bricht plötzlich ab und von der schmalen Waldstraße zweigt unvermittelt eine lange schnurgerade Allee ab. Es ist die Great Western Avenue. Einen Kilometer führt sie, immer geradeaus, mitten in den Wald hinein. Es ist das letzte Stück unserer Reise, die vor zwei Stunden in London begann. Knapp 100 Meilen, 160 Kilometer, Fahrt durch die sanft gewellte südenglische Landschaft liegen hinter uns. Wir sind in der Grafschaft Wiltshire im Südwesten der Insel. Stonehenge liegt eine halbe Autostunde entfernt, genauso wie die Stadt Salisbury mit ihrer berühmten gotischen Kathedrale, deren Erbauern Ken Follett mit seinem Roman *Die Säulen der Erde* 1989 ein fulminantes Denkmal setzte. Auch wir sind auf einer literarischen Spurensuche, haben Salisbury und Follett jedoch links beziehungsweise südlich liegen gelassen. Stattdessen führte unser Weg in das Dorf Fonthill Gifford – ein paar Häuser, eine Kirche, knapp 100 Einwohner –, in dem 1760 der Schriftsteller William Beckford (1760-1844) das Licht der Welt erblickte. Er war der Erbe eines für die damalige Zeit schier unermesslichen Vermögens, das seine Familie durch die Ausbeutung riesiger Zuckerrohrplantagen in den britischen Überseekolonien und zum Teil wohl auch durch den Handel mit Sklaven erwirtschaftet hatte. Umfassend gebildet, gelang Beckford bereits in jungen Jahren der Durchbruch als Schriftsteller. Als sein Hauptwerk gilt der Roman *Vathek*,[1] geschrieben mit 21 Jahren, der Legende nach in nur drei Tagen, wie im Rausch; halb Schauermärchen, halb faustische Tragödie; angesiedelt im Orient und in seiner ganzen Stimmung verwandt mit den magischen Erzählungen aus Tausendundeiner Nacht, die damals überall in Europa in Mode waren. Lord Byron, Edgar Allen Poe und noch Jorge Luis Borges ließen sich später von Beckfords Erzählung inspirieren. Die Literaturwissenschaften sprechen heute von einem Frühwerk der Schwarzen Romantik, einer klassischen Gothic Novel, dem Vorläufer der modernen Horrorliteratur. Doch zurück auf die Great Western Avenue, den letzten Teil unserer Reise, die nun nach einem Kilometer mitten im Wald abrupt in einer weiten Lichtung endet. Hier muss er gestanden haben: Beckfords legendärer Palast, seine Kathedrale, sein persönlicher Turmbau zu Babel.[2]

Kaum vorstellbar ist es heute, dass hier, in the middle of nowhere, einst ein gigantischer Baukomplex mit seiner höchsten Spitze 90 Meter in den Himmel hochragte. Gäbe es nicht die Gemälde von William Turner, dem großen englischen Landschaftsmaler, die unzähligen Stichwerke und zeitgenössischen Baubeschreibungen, die glaubhaft von

Eccentric Hermitism:
William Beckford

This must be it. The flat, barely waist-high wall, which has accompanied us for several miles, suddenly ends, and a long, dead straight avenue branches off from the narrow forest road called Great Western Avenue. For one mile it leads straight into the forest. It is the last part of our journey, which began two hours ago in London and took us almost 100 miles through the gently undulating landscape in the South of England. We are in Wiltshire County, which is located in Southwest England. Stonehenge is half an hour's drive away, as is the City of Salisbury with its famous Gothic cathedral, for the builders of which Ken Follett erected a brilliant monument 30 years ago with his novel *The Pillars of the Earth*. We, too, are on a literary search for traces, but have left Salisbury and Follett behind. Instead, our route led us to the village of Fonthill Gifford – few houses, a church, about 100 inhabitants –, where writer William Beckford was born in 1760. He was the heir to a fortune almost immeasurable at the time, which his family had earned through the exploitation of huge sugar cane plantations in Britain's overseas colonies and in part probably also from slave trade. Comprehensively educated, Beckford achieved his breakthrough as a writer at a young age. His main work is the novel *Vathek* he wrote at the age of 21 – according to legend, he finished it in only three days, as if in a rush, half a horror story, half a Faustian tragedy, set in the Orient, with its general mood being related to the magical tales of *The Arabian Nights*, which were in vogue all over Europe at the time.[1] Lord Byron, Edgar Allen Poe and Jorge Luis Borges were later inspired by Beckford's narrative. Today, literary studies speak of an early work of Black Romanticism, a classic gothic novel, the predecessor of modern horror literature. But let's return to the Great Western Avenue, the last part of our journey, which now, after running through the middle of the forest for one mile, abruptly ends in a wide clearing. Beckford's legendary palace must have stood here, his cathedral, his personal Tower of Babel.[2]

It is hardly imaginable today that here, in the middle of nowhere, a gigantic building complex rose up 90 metres into the sky. If it weren't for the paintings by William Turner, the great English landscape painter, countless engravings and contemporary architectural descriptions that plausibly testified to its existence, we considered Fonthill Abbey, as Beckford called his grotesque home, to be pure fiction of history. There are hardly any traces of it left on the site: a small, square tower with an adjoining short section of a nave with a hexagonal choir apse and the rest of a cloister next to it. Everything seems as if it was an abandoned, old village church that has stood here since the Middle Ages. However, if one

William Beckford gilt als Paradebeispiel eines englischen Exzentrikers. Er betätigte sich als Schriftsteller und Kunstsammler.

William Beckford is considered a prime example of an English eccentric. He was active as a writer and art collector.

ihrer Existenz zeugten, wir hielten Fonthill Abbey, wie Beckford sein groteskes Zuhause nannte, für eine reine Erfindung der Geschichte. Am Ort selbst jedenfalls finden sich kaum noch Spuren davon: ein kleiner quadratischer Turm, daran angesetzt ein kurzes Stück Langhaus mit einem sechseckigen Chorabschluss, daneben der Rest eines Kreuzgangs. Alles macht den Anschein, als könnte es sich um eine verlassene alte Dorfkirche handeln, die hier seit dem Mittelalter steht. Vergleicht man den Bau jedoch mit den Zeichnungen, die uns von Fonthill Abbey überliefert sind, entpuppt sich das romantische Gemäuer, das einsam am Rande der weiten Lichtung steht,[3] in Wirklichkeit als ein Fragment, als ein letztes erhalten gebliebenes Teilstück von Beckfords bizarrem Landsitz.

Niemand Geringerer als James Wyatt,[4] der Star-Architekt seiner Zeit, war für den ursprünglichen Bau verantwortlich. Im Auftrag von Beckford errichtete er über einem Kreuzgrundriss mit vier annähernd gleichlangen Armen die überspannte Illusion einer einsamen gotischen Abtei im Wald. Wo die vier Kreuzarme aufeinander trafen, ragte ein achteckiger Turm 300 Fuß zum Himmel hinauf. Das untere Drittel seines Schaftes barg mit dem sogenannten Oktagon die wohl eindrucksvollste Raumschöpfung des Architekten. Von mächtigen Pfeilern umstanden, reichte der Raum fast 24 Meter beziehungsweise sechs Geschosse in die Höhe und bildete das Zentrum der gesamten Anlage. Nach Osten lagen die Sammlungsräume. Hier beherbergte Beckford eine der stattlichsten privaten Kunstsammlungen, die das englische Königreich jemals besaß. Dazu kamen kostbare Bücher und zahllose Antiquitäten. Südlich des Oktagons erstreckte sich wiederum eine von einem zarten Fächergewölbe überspannte Galerie, die dem Heiligen Michael gewidmet war, während sich nach Norden die von einer goldenen Kassettendecke überfangene Galerie zu Ehren König Edwards III. öffnete. Sie führte einst in die als Sanctuary und

90 Meter hoch ragte der Turm von Fonthill Abbey in den Himmel. Heute ist nur noch ein kleiner Rest der Anlage erhalten.

The 90 meter high tower of Fonthill Abbey. Only a small remnant of the complex is preserved.

compares the building with the drawings of Fonthill Abbey that have been preserved, the romantic masonry, which stands isolated at the edge of the wide clearing,[3] urns out to be a fragment, the last remaining part of Beckford's bizarre country estate.

None other than James Wyatt,[4] the star architect of his time, was responsible for the original building. Commissioned by Beckford, he constructed the exaggerated illusion of an isolated Gothic abbey in the forest on top of a cruciform ground plan with four arms of almost equal length. Where the four arms of the cross intersected, an octagonal tower rose 90 metres into the sky. The lower third of its well accommodated the so-called octagon, probably the architect's most impressive spatial creation. Surrounded by mighty pillars, the room reached a height of almost 24 metres or six storeys and formed the centre of the entire complex. The rooms holding the art collections were located to the east. Here, Beckford housed one of the most impressive private art collections ever owned in the United Kingdom. In addition, there were precious books and countless antiques. To the south of the octagon was a gallery dedicated to Saint Michael, which was covered by a delicate fan vault, while to the north the gallery, covered by a golden coffered ceiling, opened up in honour of King Edward. It led to the outermost rooms of the north wing, known as the Sanctuary and the Oratory, which, together with the stairwell tower on the side, form the relic of Fonthill Abbey described above. The fourth arm of the cross, oriented to the west, served only to stage arrival. After passing through a portal more than ten metres high, the visitor arrived in a high and wide cathedral room, the Great Western Hall, at the end of which a wide staircase led up into the central octagon. To increase the impression of immense size and height, Beckford employed a dwarf servant whose duties included receiving visitors at the heavy oak door of the west wing.

Die Galerie des Südflügels, von einem zarten Fächergewölbe überspannt, war dem Heiligen Michael, Beckfords Schutzpatron, gewidmet.

The gallery of the south wing, surmounted by a delicate fan vault was dedicated to St. Michael, Beckford's patron saint.

Oratory bezeichneten äußersten Räume des Nordflügels, die zusammen mit dem sich seitlich anschließenden Treppenhausturm das oben beschriebene, noch heute erhaltene Relikt von Fonthill Abbey bilden. Der vierte, nach Westen gerichtete Kreuzarm wiederum diente allein der Inszenierung des Ankommens. Nachdem der Besucher ein mehr als zehn Meter hohes Portal durchschritten hatte, öffnete sich vor ihm ein einziger hoher und weiter Kathedralraum, die Great Western Hall, an deren Ende eine breite Treppe in das zentrale Oktagon hinauf führte. Um den Eindruck gewaltiger Größe und Höhe noch zu steigern, beschäftigte Beckford einen zwergwüchsigen Diener, zu dessen Aufgaben es gehörte, Besucher an der schweren Eichenholztür des Westflügels zu empfangen.

Aber nicht nur das Gebäude selbst ließ Beckford nach seinen Vorstellungen von märchenhafter Größe und Prachtentfaltung gestalten, sondern auch die umgebende Landschaft hatte sich dem ebenso fantastischen wie fanatischen Gestaltungswillen des Literaten unterzuordnen. So ließ er etwa einen künstlichen See anlegen und beschäftigte ein Heer von Gärtnern, die sich um die Ansiedlung und Pflege zahlloser exotischer Gewächse zu kümmern hatten. Zu guter Letzt umgab der Bauherr sein artifizielles Paradies mit einer Mauer – dreieinhalb Meter hoch und insgesamt elf Kilometer lang –, deren Überreste man noch heute entlang der Zufahrtsstraße findet. Früher schirmte sie Beckfords Abtei hermetisch gegen die Außenwelt ab. Nur wenigen Menschen war der Zutritt gestattet. Vor allem Künstlern wie Turner und Constable öffnete Beckford seine Welt; der britische Thronfolger hingegen, der Fonthill Abbey dringend zu sehen wünschte, wurde abgewiesen. Überhaupt hielt Beckford Abstand zu den gesellschaftlichen Eliten seiner Zeit.

Es war ein exzentrisches Eremitentum, das William Beckford in Fonthill Abbey zelebrierte – prunkvoll eingerichtet und umgeben von exquisiten Sammlungen.

Fonthill Abbey was an eccentric hermitage sumptuously furnished by William Beckford and surrounded by exquisite collections.

However, it was not only the building itself that Beckford had designed according to his ideas of fabulous size and splendour, but also the surrounding landscape had to subordinate itself to the writer's fantastic and fanatical design intentions. He had an artificial lake built and employed an army of gardeners who had to take care of the planting and cultivation of countless exotic plants. Last but not least, Beckford surrounded his artificial paradise with a wall – three and a half metres high and a total of eleven kilometres long – the remains of which can still be found along the access road. In the past it hermetically shielded Beckford's abbey from the outside world. Only a few people were allowed in. Beckford opened his world mainly to artists such as Turner and Constable; the British heir to the throne, on the other hand, who desperately wanted to see Fonthill Abbey, was rejected. Beckford generally kept his distance from the social elites of his time.

This was not always the case: young Beckford, due to his origins, his excellent education, and ultimately his immense fortune,[5] entertained justified hopes of a brilliant social, political, and literary career, and was not averse to such a development. In 1784, however, a homoerotic relationship with William Courtenay, who was eight years younger, became his downfall.[6] When this was discovered by chance, an unprecedented smear campaign began. The press reported, friends distanced themselves, and Beckford was rejected by society. He left England and settled for the next ten years near Lake Geneva in Switzerland. When he returned in the mid-1790s, the scandal may have been forgotten, but Beckford had not forgotten how he had been treated. In exile, he had forged a plan. He wanted his father's house demolished and his own secluded world built in the forest. No

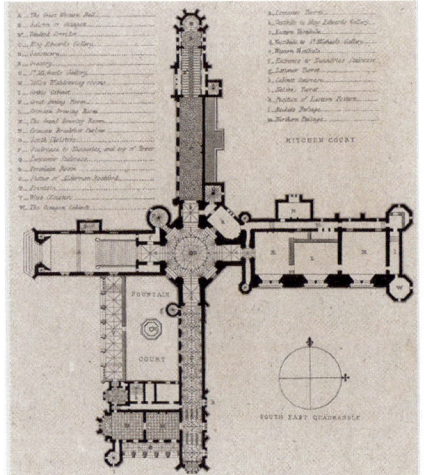 

Das war allerdings nicht immer so: Der junge Beckford konnte sich aufgrund seiner Herkunft, seiner ausgezeichneten Bildung und letztlich seines immensen Vermögens[5] durchaus berechtigte Hoffnungen auf eine glänzende gesellschaftliche, politische und literarische Karriere machen und war einer entsprechenden Entwicklung auch nicht abgeneigt. Im Jahr 1784 wurde ihm jedoch eine homoerotische Beziehung mit dem um acht Jahre jüngeren William Courtenay zum Verhängnis.[6] Als diese durch Zufall entdeckt wird, beginnt eine beispiellose Hetzkampagne. Die Presse berichtet, Freunde nehmen Abstand und Beckford wird von der Gesellschaft verstoßen. Er verlässt England und lässt sich für die nächsten zehn Jahre am Genfer See in der Schweiz nieder. Als er Mitte der 1790er-Jahre auf die Insel zurückkehrt, mag der Skandal vergessen sein, aber Beckford hat nicht vergessen, wie er behandelt wurde. Im Exil hat er einen Plan geschmiedet. Er wird sein Vaterhaus abreißen lassen und sich im Wald seine eigene, abgeschlossene Welt bauen. Niemand wird ihn hier stören. Eine Mauer wird ungebetene Besucher abhalten und sein Tun den missgünstigen Blicken der Welt entziehen. Zuletzt wird ein Turm ihn über seine verhassten Mitmenschen erheben: Der Bau von Fonthill Abbey beginnt!

1812 sind die Arbeiten abgeschlossen. Mehr als 500 Handwerker waren oft gleichzeitig mit dem Bau beschäftigt. Und auch nach der Fertigstellung braucht es Unmengen von Angestellten, um das Gebäude und die umgebenden Gärten zu unterhalten. Zudem hält sich Beckford einen kleinen Hofstaat, der vornehmlich aus jungen attraktiven Männern der Mittelschicht besteht. In Briefen nennt er sie andeutungsvoll seinen Bijou, seinen Ambrose, seinen Poupee oder – ganz unmissverständlich – seine Miss Butterfly. Es ist ein exzentrisches, dekadentes Eremitentum, das Beckford in Fonthill lebt, prunkvoll eingerichtet, umgeben von zahllosen Kunstwerken und exquisiten Sammlungen und begleitet

Grundriss der Gesamtanlage von Fonthill Abbey und Schnitt durch das zentral gelegene Oktagon

Floor plan of the entire Fonthill Abbey complex and section of the centrally located octagon

Die Great Western Hall diente der machtvollen Überwältigung des Ankommenden.

Upon arrival the Great Western Hall overpowered its guests.

one would bother him here. A wall was to keep away unwelcome visitors and hide his activities from the disapproving eyes of the world. Finally, a tower would raise him above his hated fellow men: The construction of Fonthill Abbey began.

Works were completed in 1812. More than 500 craftsmen were often working simultaneously. And even after completion, it took a huge number of staff to maintain the building and the surrounding gardens. In addition, Beckford maintained a small household, consisting primarily of young, attractive middle-class men. In letters he calls them his Bijou, his Ambrose, his Poupee or – unmistakably – his Miss Butterfly. It was an eccentric, decadent hermitage that Beckford lived in Fonthill, splendidly furnished, surrounded by countless works of art and exquisite collections, and accompanied by a spoiled entourage of young, pretty favourites. Beckford lived the life of a modern aesthete and 100 years later still provided a blueprint for the depiction of homophile characters of the Décadence, for example for Oscar Wilde's *Dorian Gray* or the figure of Jean des Esseintes from Joris-Karl Huysman's novel *À rebours*. Another comrade in spirit as in fate was the legendary

von einer verwöhnten Entourage junger hübscher Günstlinge. Beckford lebt das Leben eines modernen Ästheten und liefert damit noch 100 Jahre später eine Blaupause für die homophilen Charakterzeichnungen der Décadence – etwa für Oscar Wildes *Dorian Gray* oder die Figur des Jean des Esseintes aus Joris-Karl Huysmans Roman *Gegen den Strich*. Ein anderer Verwandter im Geiste wie im Schicksal war der legendäre Bayernkönig Ludwig II.[7] Auch er geriet – mehr an den Stallburschen als an den Damen seines Hofes interessiert – im Laufe seiner Regentschaft immer stärker in Konflikt mit den moralischen Vorstellungen seiner Zeit und seiner Gesellschaft. Und auch er flüchtete sich davor in sein eigenes, einsames Exil: Schloss Neuschwanstein, das er auf einem unwegsamen Felsen im bayrischen Voralpenland errichten ließ und das, wie schon Beckfords Abtei, im Grunde zwar einem asketischen mittelalterlichen Modell – dem der Burg – folgte, letztlich aber genauso wie Fonthill Abbey als hoch artifizielle, vollkommen übersteigerte Traumwelt Realität gewann. Und wie schon Beckford ein halbes Jahrhundert vor ihm übernahm sich auch König Ludwig II. mit den Bau- und Unterhaltskosten seines Märchenschlosses. Die horrenden Summen, die er in Neuschwanstein steckte, kosteten den Monarchen am Ende sein Amt.

Auch Beckford scheiterte mit der Finanzierung seines gigantomanen eskapistischen Unterfangens, im Untergang bewies er allerdings weitaus mehr Geschick und Witz als die schwüle Figur des Bayernkönigs. Napoleons Kontinentalsperre, die zwischen 1806 und 1811 britische Erzeugnisse vom europäischen Markt abschnitt, sowie das 1807 von Großbritannien erlassene Gesetz zum Verbot des Sklavenhandels versetzten den Geschäften von Beckfords Familie nach 1800 schwere Schläge. Dazu kam die Erfindung moderner Industrieverfahren zur Zuckergewinnung aus heimischen Rüben, was die jährliche Apanage aus dem Zuckerhandel noch einmal dramatisch sinken ließ. Damit wurde es für Beckford immer schwieriger, den kostspieligen Unterhalt von Fonthill Abbey zu finanzieren. 1822 entschied er sich deshalb für einen Verkauf des Anwesens. Zudem ließ er Teile seiner Kunstsammlungen versteigern. Dass er sich und seinen Besitz jahrelang vor der Öffentlichkeit verborgen hatte, konnte Beckford nun für einen letzten großen Coup nutzen. Denn schon die Ankündigung der Versteigerung verbreitete sich wie ein Lauffeuer im ganzen Land. Immer wieder hatte es Berichte über Beckfords ominöse Bautätigkeit und sein geheimes Leben im Wald von Fonthill Gifford gegeben. Nun wollten Alle – Feinde wie Freunde – sehen, wie der „Foul of Fonthill" lebte.[8] Beckford hatte mit diesem Interesse gerechnet und ließ vorab einen Katalog seiner zu versteigernden Sammlungen produzieren. Mehr als 70.000 Exemplare wurden davon binnen weniger Wochen verkauft. Zudem öffnete er nun erstmals die Tore zu Fonthill Abbey und nahm von jedem Interessierten ein ordentliches Eintrittsgeld. Er selbst allerdings verließ noch vor der Versteigerung seinen Besitz in einer Kutsche in Richtung Bath, seiner neuen Heimat, und überließ alles weitere dem Auktionshaus Christie's. Allein das Gebäude und seine Umge-

Ein Verwandter Beckfords im Geiste wie im Schicksal war der Bayernkönig Ludwig II. Sein Exil war Schloss Neuschwanstein.

A kindred spirit of Beckford was the Bavarian King Ludwig. His hiding place was Neuschwanstein Castle.

Bavarian King Ludwig II.[7] In the course of his reign, he too – more interested in the stable boys than in the ladies of his court – came increasingly into conflict with the moral ideas of his time and society. He also fled into his own lonely exile: Neuschwanstein Castle, which he had built on an impassable rock in the Bavarian foothills of the Alps and which, like Beckford's abbey, basically followed an ascetic medieval model – that of the castle – but which, like Fonthill Abbey, ultimately emerged as a highly artificial, completely exaggerated dream world. And like Beckford half a century before him, King Ludwig II took over the construction and maintenance costs of his fairy-tale castle. The horrendous sums he invested in Neuschwanstein ultimately cost the monarch his throne.

Beckford also failed to finance his gigantomaniac escapist venture, but in the downfall, he proved to have far more skill and wit than the sultry character of the Bavarian king. Napoleon's Continental System, which cut off British products from the European market between 1806 and 1811, and the Act prohibiting slave trade, adopted by Great Britain in 1807, severely affected the businesses of Beckford's family after 1800. In addition, the invention of modern industrial processes for the production of sugar from domestic sugar beet caused the annual turnover from the sugar trade to drop dramatically. This made it increasingly difficult for Beckford to finance the costly maintenance of Fonthill Abbey. In 1822, he therefore decided to sell the property and have part of his art collections auctioned. Beckford could now use the fact that he had hidden himself and his possessions from the public for years for one last big coup. The announcement of the auction alone spread like wildfire throughout the country. Time and again, there had been reports about

bung gingen für die spektakuläre Summe von 330.000 Pfund in den Besitz des Schießpulver-Fabrikanten John Farquhar über. Dieser Erfolg erlaubte Beckford bis zu seinem Tod im Jahr 1844 einen nicht weniger aufwendigen Lebensstil, als er ihn von Fonthill Abbey gewohnt war. Für Farquhar allerdings sollte sich das Geschäft schon bald als große Fehlinvestition erweisen: Denn schon drei Jahre nach dem Kauf stürzte am 21. Dezember 1825 der Turm der Abtei in sich zusammen und begrub weite Teile des Gebäudes unter sich. So rächte sich schließlich die Eile, mit der Beckford den Bau betrieben hatte und mit der er seine Architekten immer wieder zu noch gewagteren Konstruktionen drängte. Als Beckford von dem Einsturz hörte, bedauerte er – ganz englischer Exzentriker, der er war! – weniger die Vernichtung seines Lebenswerks als vielmehr den Umstand, dieses letzte und vielleicht größte Spektakel von Fonthill Abbey verpasst zu haben.

Was von William Beckfords fantastischer Fonthill Abbey übrig geblieben ist, sind die äußersten Räume des Nordflügels.

What remains of William Beckford's fantastic Fonthill Abbey are the outermost rooms of the north wing.

Beckford's ominous building activity and his secret life in the Fonthill Gifford forest. Now everyone – both foes and friends – wanted to see how the "Foul of Fonthill" lived.[8] Beckford had expected this interest and had a catalogue of his collections to be auctioned produced in advance. More than 70,000 copies were sold within a few weeks. In addition, he opened the gates to Fonthill Abbey for the first time and took a substantial entrance fee from everyone interested. Before the auction, however, Beckford left his property in a carriage in the direction of Bath, his new home, and left everything else to Christie's Auction House. The building and its grounds alone became the property of gunpowder manufacturer John Farquhar for the spectacular bid of 330,000 pounds. The successful auction allowed Beckford a no less elaborate lifestyle than he was used to at Fonthill Abbey until he died in 1844. For Farquhar, however, the deal soon proved to be a malinvestment: only three years after the purchase, the tower of the abbey collapsed on 21 December 1825 and buried large parts of the building beneath it. Thus, the haste with which Beckford had the building constructed and with which he urged his architect to ever more daring constructions finally took its toll. When Beckford heard about the collapse, he regretted – all English eccentric he was – less the destruction of his life's work but rather the fact that he had missed this last and perhaps greatest spectacle of Fonthill Abbey.

Wolfgang Voigt

Wie Castor und Pollux für immer verbunden: Percier und Fontaine, die Architekten Napoleons

In Frankreich vereinigten sich um 1800 zwei junge Architekten zu einer der ersten Architektenfirmen der Neuzeit, als Atelier mit zwei gleichberechtigten Partnern, ein bis heute geläufiges Modell. Pierre François Léonard Fontaine (1762-1853) und Charles Percier (1764-1838) waren darüber hinaus „in seltener Ausdauer und in liebevoller Anhänglichkeit miteinander verbunden", wie es nach Fontaines Tod in einem Nachruf hieß.[1] In den letzten Jahren des 18. Jahrhunderts wurden die beiden Architekten das, was man heute eine Marke nennt. In der Schickeria des nachrevolutionären Paris wurde es zur Mode, Möbel von Percier und Fontaine zu besitzen. Ihre Entwürfe wurden prägend für den Stile des Empire, der auf Eleganz abzielte und mit schlanken Gliedern und metallenen Applikationen an den Möbeln arbeitete, weg vom „reinen" und puristischen Klassizismus in den Jahren davor.

Fontaine war der Sohn eines Baumeisters in der Provinz, Percier der Sohn eines Brückenwärters in Paris. Beide lernten sich als Jugendliche im Alter von 15 und 17 Jahren an der Académie royale d'architecture in Paris kennen. Dort studierten sie ab 1779 noch unter dem Ancien Régime vor der Französischen Revolution. Stets traten sie gemeinsam auf. 1783 erhielt Percier das begehrte Stipendium „Prix de Rome"; drei Jahre später begann sein mehrjähriger Aufenthalt in der Ewigen Stadt; Fontaine folgte ihm 1787 auf eigene Kosten nach. Im Zeitalter des frühen Klassizismus übten die antiken Ruinen eine starke Anziehung auf Architekten aus. Beide, vor allem aber Percier, nutzten die Jahre in Rom für intensive Studien an Bauten aller Zeitepochen; dabei entstanden exakte Zeichnungen, die sie später in Büchern publizierten, die weite Verbreitung fanden. Zurück in Paris bezogen Percier und Fontaine eine gemeinsame Wohnung und lebten von Entwürfen für Möbel und Interieurs. 1793 gelang es Percier, als Chef-Bühnenbildner an die königliche Oper berufen zu werden; er nahm die Stelle unter der Bedingung an, dass Fontaine offiziell mitarbeiten konnte.

1799 kam Napoleon Bonaparte als erster Konsul der Republik an die Regierung und wurde auf die beiden aufmerksam. Wieder zog der eine den anderen nach. Als Fontaine engagiert wurde und darauf bestand, dass auch Percier einbezogen werden sollte, erklärt er dem Herrscher sogar mehr oder weniger offen ihr Verhältnis: „Ich habe ihn darauf hingewiesen, dass ich zwar allein die Gnade genieße, in die Nähe seiner Majestät

Like Castor and Pollux Forever United: Percier and Fontaine, Napoleon's Architects

In France around 1800, two young architects joined forces to form one of the first architectural firms of modern times, a studio with two equal partners, a model that is still common today. Moreover, Pierre François Léonard Fontaine (1762-1853) and Charles Percier (1764-1838) were "linked with each other in rare perseverance and in loving attachment," as it was said in an obituary after Fontaine's death.[1] In the last years of the 18th century, the two architects became what is now called a brand. In the haut monde of post-revolutionary Paris, it became fashionable to own furniture by Percier and Fontaine. Their designs became formative for the Empire style, which focused on elegance and worked with slender legs and metal applications on the furniture, away from the "pure" and purist classicism of the previous years.

Fontaine was the son of a master builder working in the province, Percier the son of a bridgemaster in Paris. Both met as young men at the age of 15 and 17 at the Académie royale d'architecture in Paris, where they studied from 1779 under the Ancien Régime before the French Revolution. They always appeared together. In 1783 Percier received the coveted "Prix de Rome" scholarship; three years later he went to the Eternal City for several years; Fontaine followed him in 1787 at his own expense. In the age of early classicism, the ancient ruins had a strong appeal with architects. Both of them, but above all Percier, used the years in Rome for intensive studies of buildings from all eras, resulting in exact drawings that they later published in books that became widely distributed. Back in Paris, Percier and Fontaine moved into a shared apartment and lived off furniture and interior designs. In 1793 Percier managed to be appointed chief stage designer at the Royal Opera House; he accepted the position on condition that Fontaine could officially work with him.

When in 1799 Napoleon Bonaparte came to power as the first Consul of the republic, he became aware of the two architects. One was trailing the other. When Fontaine was engaged and insisted that Percier should also be included, he more or less openly explained their relationship to the ruler: "I pointed out to him that although I alone enjoyed the grace of having been summoned to be close to His Majesty; I was also better known than Percier; but he would share with me the honour of serving him. I have asked his permission for our two names to be mentioned together, as we were together as men."[2]

Nach ihrer gemeinsamen Ausbildung blieben sich Percier (l.) und Fontaine (r.) ein Leben lang verbunden.

After their joint training, Percier (l.) and Fontaine (r.) remained close throughout their lives.

berufen worden zu sein; auch sei ich bekannter als Percier; aber dieser würde die Ehre, ihm zu dienen, mit mir teilen. Ich habe ihn um die Erlaubnis gebeten, dass unsere beiden Namen zusammen genannt würden, so wie wir als Menschen zusammen waren."[2]

Es begann damit, dass sie Paläste für Bonaparte restaurierten und die Ausstattungen neu entwarfen; zuerst das Schloss Malmaison, den Wohnsitz von Joséphine de Beauharnais, der späteren Kaiserin. 1804 erhob sich Bonaparte als Napoleon I. selbst zum Kaiser. Von da an waren es Percier und Fontaine, die die Inszenierung der Kaiserherrschaft in der Hand hatten, indem sie die Bühnen für dessen Auftritte gestalteten – zum Beispiel die Innendekoration der Kathedrale Notre Dame für die Zeremonie der Kaiserkrönung. In dieser Stellung blieben sie auch nach dem Sturz Napoleons, denn auch die nachfolgenden Monarchen der Restaurationszeit bis 1848 bedienten sich gern der Fähigkeiten von Percier und Fontaine. Der Tourist kommt heute in Paris immer wieder mit Percier und Fontaine in Berührung – etwa an der stilprägenden, einen Kilometer langen Arkadenzeile der Rue de Rivoli (1801) oder am Arc de Triomphe du Carrousel (1809), mit dem die siegreichen Feldzüge Napoleons gefeiert wurden. Die Zusammenarbeit der beiden blieb bis zum Tod Perciers 1838 bestehen.

In der 2004 erschienenen *Queer Encyclopedia of the Visual Arts* werden die beiden als schwules Paar aufgeführt.[3] In Werken der Architekturgeschichte ist die gemeinsame Biografie von Percier und Fontaine bis heute Anlass zu gewundenen Bemerkungen. In der 1904 erschienenen, ersten Monografie – und nur dieses eine Mal – wurde vom Autor Maurice Fouché ein zentrales Detail über die private Seite mitgeteilt, das den nachfolgenden Autoren anscheinend zu delikat gewesen ist, um es wieder aufzugreifen. Fouché teilte nämlich mit, dass die beiden als junge Leute schon während ihres Rom-Aufenthalts einen Vertrag geschlossen hatten, in dem sie sich versicherten, dass sie immer zusammen arbeiten und vor allem nie heiraten würden.[4] Diesem Vertrag trat in Rom ein weiterer Architekt bei: Claude-Louis Bernier (1755-1830), „le troisième membre du trio".[5] Dieser

Vereint bis in den Tod: das gemeinsame Grab von Percier und Fontaine (sowie Claude-Louis Bernier) auf dem Pariser Friedhof Père Lachaise

United until death: the common grave of Percier and Fontaine (as well as Claude-Louis Bernier) in the Père Lachaise cemetery in Paris

They began by restoring palaces for Bonaparte and redesigning their furnishings; the first was Malmaison Castle, the residence of Joséphine de Beauharnais, the future empress. In 1804, Bonaparte crowned himself emperor as Napoleon I. From then on, Percier and Fontaine were responsible for staging the imperial reign by designing the stages for his appearances – for example, the interior decoration of Notre Dame Cathedral for the ceremony of the imperial coronation. They remained in this position even after the fall of Napoleon, as the subsequent monarchs of the Restoration period until 1848 were also happy to make use of the expertise of Percier and Fontaine. Today, tourists in Paris repeatedly come into contact with Percier and Fontaine – for example on the style-defining, one-kilometre-long arcade of Rue de Rivoli (1801) or at the Arc de Triomphe du Carrousel (1809), which celebrated Napoleon's victorious campaigns. Their collaboration continued until Percier's death in 1838.

In the *Queer Encyclopedia of the Visual Arts*, published in 2004, the two are listed as a gay couple.[3] In works on architectural history, the joint biography of Percier and Fontaine has been the reason for ambiguous comments to this day. In the first monograph published in 1904 – and only this once – the author Maurice provided a central detail about the private side, which the subsequent authors apparently found too delicate to take up again. Fouché stated that, as young people, the two had already signed a contract during their stay in Rome in which they assured each other that they would always work together and, above all, would never get married.[4] Another architect joined this contract

1812 veröffentlichten Percier und Fontaine eine Auswahl ihrer Interieur-Arbeiten. Das Buch prägte den sogenannten Empirestil.

In 1812, Percier and Fontaine published a selection of their interior works. The book coined the so-called Empire style.

brach jedoch später das Abkommen, indem er eine Ehe einging. Später wurden alle drei in einem gemeinsamen Grab auf dem Friedhof Père Lachaise zusammengeführt.[6] Die lateinische Inschrift „Hic tres in unum" („Hier die drei vereint") verrät nichts, lädt aber zu Spekulationen über eine Dreiecksbeziehung ein.

In den engsten Kreis der beiden Freunde trat um 1800 mit Sophie Dupuis (1777-1846) eine talentierte junge Frau ein, die das Kolorieren der Titelseiten ihres schwarz-weiß gedruckten Werks *Palais, maisons et autres édifices modernes dessinés à Rome* besorgte. Zwischen ihr und Fontaine entwickelte sich bald mehr als eine spezielle Sympathie. 1803 wurde eine Tochter geboren, die vor der Öffentlichkeit mit Sorgfalt verborgen gehalten wurde. Erst nach Perciers Tod kam es zu einer späten Heirat.

Von Fontaine sind Tagebücher überliefert, die in zwei dicken Bänden ediert worden sind, die im Wesentlichen nur die gemeinsame Arbeit dokumentieren.[7] An wenigen

Für Napoleon und seine Frau Joséphine gestalteten Percier und Fontaine das Schloss Malmaison bei Paris als private Residenz.

Fontaine and Percier designed the Malmaison Castle near Paris as a private residence for Napoleon and his wife Joséphine.

in Rome: Claude-Louis Bernier (1755-1830), "le troisième membre du trio."[5] However, he later broke the agreement by entering into marriage. All three were brought together in a common grave in the Père Lachaise cemetery.[6] The Latin inscription "Hic tres in Unum" ("The three united here") discloses nothing but invites speculation about a ménage à trois.

Around 1800, Sophie Dupuis (1777-1846), a talented young woman, joined the inner circle of the two friends. She was responsible for colouring the front pages of their black and white printed work *Palais, maisons et autres édifices modernes dessinés à Rome*. Soon more than a special affection developed between her and Fontaine. In 1803 a daughter was born, carefully hidden from the public. It was only after Percier's death that they married.

Fontaine's diaries have survived, edited in two thick volumes that essentially document only the work they did together.[7] In a few places more shines through, for example when Fontaine writes in 1816: "Joined together by our studies since our youngest days, by our common taste and interests, we have lived off more than thirty years of perfect harmony and enjoyed the gentleness of a friendship that has never been tarnished and will only vanish when we do."[8] When Percier died in 1838, a mourning Fontaine wrote to a friend: "I've lost half of myself."[9] When the diaries were published in 1987 it was apparently not yet possible to call a spade a spade. The editor described the undoubtedly intimate character of the relationship with remarkable garlands of words: "This diary in the first person is also that of a couple. It is much influenced by friendship and fidelity. […]

Der Arc de Triomphe du Carrousel gehört zu den bekanntesten Werken von Percier und Fontaine im Zentrum von Paris.

The Arc de Triomphe du Carrousel is one of the most famous works of Percier and Fontaine in the center of Paris.

Stellen schimmert mehr durch, etwa wenn Fontaine 1816 schreibt: „Miteinander verbunden durch unsere Studien seit der zartesten Jugend, durch unseren gemeinsamen Geschmack und unsere Interessen, haben wir mehr als dreißig Jahre von perfekter Übereinstimmung gezehrt und die Sanftmut einer Freundschaft genossen, die nie getrübt wurde und erst mit uns vergehen wird."[8] Als Percier 1838 gestorben war, schrieb der trauernde Fontaine an einen Freund: „Ich habe die Hälfte meines Selbst verloren."[9] Bei der Herausgabe der Tagebücher war es 1987 offenbar noch nicht möglich, die Sache beim Namen zu nennen. Den zweifellos intimen Charakter der Beziehung umschrieb der Herausgeber mit bemerkenswerten Wortgirlanden: „Dieses Tagebuch in der ersten Person ist auch das eines Paares. Es steht unter dem Zeichen der Freundschaft und der Treue. (...) Percier und Fontaine sind für immer verbunden, wie Achill und Patroklus, Castor und Pollux. (...) Fontaine schreibt, Fontaine spricht, aber er stützte sich auf eine unerschütterliche Brüderlichkeit, die allem Tun und Lassen eine solide Grundlage gab. (...) ‚Ich' bedeutet eben ‚wir', das heißt, Fontaine und Percier."[10]

Als persönliche Architekten von vier Monarchen, die von Napoleon bis zum „Bürgerkönig" Louis-Philippe alle Regimewechsel überstanden, waren Percier und Fontaine keine Freunde der französischen Revolution. Sie profitierten aber von der mit ihr verbundenen Liberalität, die 1791 zur Aufhebung der Gesetze gegen die sogenannte Sodomie geführt hatte. Seitdem wurde Homosexualität, wenn sie einvernehmlich unter Erwachsenen stattfand, in Frankreich strafrechtlich nicht mehr verfolgt.

Auch die Planung der Pariser Rue de Rivoli mit ihren fortlaufenden Arkaden ist ein Werk von Percier und Fontaine.

The planning of the Parisian Rue de Rivoli with its continuous arcades is also a Percier and Fontaine work.

Percier and Fontaine are forever connected, like Achill and Patroclus, Castor and Pollux. […] Fontaine writes, Fontaine speaks, but he relied on an unwavering brotherhood that gave a solid foundation to all his doings. 'I' simply means 'we'. Fontaine and Percier."[10]

As personal architects of four monarchs who survived all regime changes from Napoleon to the Citizen King Louis-Philippe, Percier and Fontaine were no friends of the French Revolution. They did, however, benefit from the liberality associated with it, which had led to the abolition of the laws against so-called sodomy in 1791. Since then, homosexuality, if it took place consensually among adults, has not been prosecuted in France.

Richard Kurdiovsky

Die Architekten der Wiener Hofoper: Eduard van der Nüll und August Sicard von Sicardsburg

Im Frühjahr 1868 erregten zwei aufeinander folgende Todesfälle stadtbekannter Architekten das Wiener Publikum. Eduard van der Nüll (1812-1868) und August Sicard von Sicardsburg (1813-1868), die miteinander enge Freundschaft pflegten und ein gemeinsames Atelier führten, waren die Baumeister des k. k. (kaiserlich-königlichen) Hofopernhauses in Wien, nachdem sie den Wettbewerb von 1860/61 zum Bau des besonders prestigeträchtigen Projekts, nämlich des allerersten Staatsbaus an der neu angelegten Ringstraße, gewonnen hatten. Dessen feierliche Eröffnung am 25. Mai 1869 in Anwesenheit von Kaiser Franz Josef I. erlebten beide nicht mehr. Am 3. April 1868 hatte sich van der Nüll erhängt, Sicardsburg starb nur wenig später.

Seit rund einem Jahr hatte van der Nüll den Bau bereits allein geleitet, weil sein Partner Sicardsburg der Baustelle krankheitshalber hatte fern bleiben müssen. Der heiß umfehdete Opernbau an der Wiener Ringstraße war in den Tageszeitungen seit Jahren scharf kritisiert worden. Den Anfeindungen und Schwierigkeiten dieses ersten öffentlichen Monumentalbaus des neuen Stadtareals entlang der Ringstraße war van der Nüll allein ausgesetzt gewesen. Unter anderem war der Bau als „Königgrätz der Baukunst" geschmäht worden[1] – in Anspielung auf die militärische Niederlage, die Österreich im Krieg von 1866 durch Preußen erlitten hatte. Ein Hauptpunkt der Kritik betraf das Fehlen eines monumentalen Sockels, der die Oper in den Vorstellungen der Zeitgenossen erst zu einem Denkmal gemacht hätte, während das Gebäude jetzt stattdessen in der Erde zu versinken schien. Am Ende sollen es abfällige Bemerkungen aus dem unmittelbaren Umkreis des Kaisers gewesen sein,[2] die van der Nüll in den Freitod getrieben haben. Sicardsburgs Gesundheitszustand sei so schwach gewesen, dass ihm der Tod seines Partners gar nicht habe als Selbstmord mitgeteilt werden können.[3] Er verstarb kurz danach am 11. Juni 1868 an Tuberkulose.[4]

Das tragische Ereignis geschah zu einer Zeit, als erstmals Begriffe für homosexuelles Empfinden in Druckschriften veröffentlicht und für individuelle Identitätsbildungen verfügbar wurden: Ab 1864 erschienen die *Zwölf Schriften über das Rätsel der mannmännlichen Liebe* von Karl Heinrich Ulrichs, in denen gleichgeschlechtlich empfindende Männer mit einem eigenen Wort als „Urning" bezeichnet wurden, und um 1869 dürfte Karl Maria Kertbeny erstmals den Begriff „homosexual" geprägt haben.[5] Die Erbauer des Hofopernhauses gelten heute als eines der frühen Paare homosexueller

The Architects of the Vienna Court Opera: Eduard van der Nüll and August Sicard von Sicardsburg

In the spring of 1868, the consecutive deaths of two well-known architects caught the attention of the Viennese public. Eduard van der Nüll (1812-1868) and August Sicard von Sicardsburg (1813-1868), who cultivated a close friendship and had a joint studio, were the architects of the Imperial and Royal Court Opera House in Vienna after winning the competition held in 1860/61 for the construction of the particularly prestigious project, namely the very first state building on the newly constructed Ringstrasse. Neither of them lived to see its grand opening on 25 May 1869 in the presence of Emperor Franz Josef I. On 3 April 1868, van der Nüll hung himself, Sicardsburg died only a little later.

Van der Nüll had already overseen the construction on his own for about a year, because his partner Sicardsburg had had to stay away from the building site due to illness. The fiercely contested opera building on Vienna's Ringstrasse had been severely criticized in the daily newspapers for years. Van der Nüll alone had had to face the hostility and difficulties of this first public monumental building in the new city area along the Ringstrasse. Among other things, the building had been reviled as the "Königgrätz of architecture"[1]– named after the humiliating military defeat that Austria had suffered in the Austro-Prussian War in 1866. One of the main points of criticism concerned the lack of a monumental plinth, which would have made the opera a monument in the eyes of contemporaries, instead of a building which rather seemed to be sunk into the ground. In the end, it is said that it was derogatory remarks from the immediate circle of the emperor,[2] that caused van der Nüll to commit suicide. Sicardsburg's state of health had been so weak that the death of his partner could not be reported to him as suicide.[3] He died shortly afterwards on 11 June 1868 of tuberculosis.[4]

The tragic event happened at a time when for the first time terms for homosexual feelings were published in printed material and made available for individual identity formation: From 1864 onwards, Karl Heinrich Ulrichs' *Zwölf Schriften über das Rätsel der mannmännlichen Liebe* (Twelve Papers on the Mystery of Man-manly Love) were published, in which men with same-sex feelings were described with a special word as "Urning", and around 1869 Karl Maria Kertbeny probably first coined the term "homosexual".[5] The builders of the Court Opera House are today regarded as one of the early couples of homosexual architects. In connection with the construction of the Court Opera

Porträts der Architekten van der Nüll (l.) und Sicardsburg (r.)

Portraits of the architects van der Nüll (l.) and Sicardsburg (r.)

Architekten. So vermerkt der „schwule" Stadtführer von Wien im Zusammenhang mit dem Bau der Hofoper, dass „deren prominentes schwules Architektenpaar heftig angefeindet war."[6] Tatsächlich beschrieben schon die Zeitgenossen das Verhältnis von Sicardsburg und van der Nüll auf eine Art, die eine ganz besonders enge Bindung zwischen den beiden Architekten vermuten lässt.

Ausgangspunkt dieser Untersuchung sind die Nachrufe auf van der Nüll und Sicardsburg in den Wiener Zeitungen. Sie entstanden mit dem Ziel, das Andenken der Verstorbenen zu würdigen und jenen Kritiken und als ungerecht empfundenen Vorwürfen, die in den vorangegangenen Jahren geäußerten worden waren, etwas entgegen zu setzen.[7] Im Hintergrund freilich enthalten diese Berichte auch Formulierungen, die sich bei bewusstem „queer" Lesen als schwule Topoi entziffern lassen und somit Andeutungen über die persönliche Beziehung der beiden Männer enthalten können.[8] Zwischen den Zeilen galt es – und die Grenzen der im Moment von Trauer und Gedenken gebotenen Pietät wurden dabei durchaus strapaziert –, die Neugier und die Sensationslust des Publikums über zwei Künstler zu befriedigen, die wohl schon länger Anlass zu Gerüchten gegeben hatten.

Ein fester Bestandteil aller Äußerungen zu van der Nüll und Sicardsburg waren Beschreibungen ihrer engen Freundschaft, die einen wesentlichen Teil des zeitgenössischen Narrativs über die beiden Männer ausmachte. „Seit den Studienjahren [war van der Nüll] mit dem Architekten Siccardsburg [sic] durch das Band der Freundschaft innigst verbunden."[9] Unter den 1869 installierten Vorhängen, die in der Hofoper Bühne und Zuschauerraum voneinander trennten, gab es einen – heute nicht mehr vorhandenen – zum Thema der tragischen Oper, auf dem ihre Partnerschaft eine bildliche Darstellung

House, the "gay" Vienna city guidebook states that "[t]he prominent gay architect couple met with fierce hostility."[6] Indeed, contemporaries already described the relationship between Sicardsburg and van der Nüll in a way that suggested a particularly close connection between the two architects.

The starting point for this investigation is the obituaries for van der Nüll and Sicardsburg in the Vienna newspapers. They were written with the intention of honoring the memory of the deceased and to remedy the criticisms and accusations considered unjust that had been voiced in previous years.[7] In the background, of course, these reports also contain formulations which, when read with a "queer eye", can be deciphered as gay topoi and thus contain hints about the personal relationship between the two men.[8] Between the lines it was necessary – and the limits of the piety required at the time of mourning and remembrance were certainly strained – to satisfy the public's curiosity and sensationalism about two artists who had probably given rise to rumours for some time.

An integral part of all comments about van der Nüll and Sicardsburg were descriptions of their close friendship, which formed an essential part of the contemporary narrative about the two men. "Since the academic years [van der Nüll] was closely tied to the architect Siccardsburg [sic] through the bond of friendship."[9] Among the curtains installed in 1869, which separated the stage from the auditorium in the opera house, there was one designed on the theme of the tragic opera. The representation depicts their partnership: in the group of artists shown, who died during the construction period, Sicardsburg places his hand on van der Nüll's shoulder, a gesture modelled on the ancient San Ildefonso Group. This curtain no longer exists today.

Sicardsburg and van der Nüll were repeatedly referred to as the "Dioscuri".[10] They were thus compared to the ancient legendary heroes Castor and Polydeuces, who as twin brothers did all their deeds together. Above all, however, the Dioscuri loved each other so much that the demigod Polydeuces, when the human Castor was mortally wounded, preferred to give up his eternal life in order to be united with Castor in death. In this way the *Gemeinde-Zeitung* mourned "the two 'architect twins' who had grown together and who [...] could not bear to be separated and quickly joined each other in death."[11] On the one hand, the comparison with the Dioscuri provided an obvious metaphor for the jointly created œuvre and the dates of death that were so close together. On the other hand, it was possible to allude to the intimacy of the relationship between the two, the intensity of which seemed to exceed the contemporary norm of relationships between men. The reference to the topoi of classical mythology and even the Bible legitimized this relationship: "The names of both artists [...] had to be pronounced in the same breath as Castor and Pollux, Orestes and Pylades,[12] David and Jonathan,[13] Schiller and Goethe!"[14]

Um 1900 entstandene Aufnahme des von van der Nüll und Sicardsburg entworfenen Hofopernhauses an der Wiener Ringstraße

Photograph taken around 1900 of the Court Opera House on Vienna's Ringstrasse, designed by van der Nüll and Sicardsburg.

fand. In der dort abgebildeten Gruppe jener Künstler, die während der Bauzeit verstorben waren, legt Sicardsburg ganz nach dem Vorbild des antiken San Ildefonso-Doppelstandbildes seine Hand auf die Schulter van der Nülls.

Sicardsburg und van der Nüll wurden wiederholt als „Dioskurenpaar" bezeichnet.[10] Damit verglich man sie mit jenen antiken Sagenhelden Castor und Pollux, die als Zwillingsbrüder alle ihre Taten gemeinsam begingen. Vor allem aber liebten die Dioskuren einander so sehr, dass der Halbgott Pollux, als der Mensch Castor tödlich verwundet worden war, lieber sein ewiges Leben aufgab, um noch im Tod mit Castor vereint zu sein. So betrauerte die Gemeinde-Zeitung „die beiden ineinander verwachsenen ‚Architekten-Zwillinge', welche [...] die Trennung nicht ertrugen und sich im Tode rasch an einander schlossen."[11] Der Vergleich mit den Dioskuren bildete zum einen eine sinnfällige Metapher für das gemeinsam geschaffene Œuvre und die so nahe beieinander liegenden Sterbedaten. Andererseits ließ sich auf die Innigkeit der Beziehung zwischen beiden anspielen, deren Intensität das zeitgenössische Normalmaß der Beziehung zwischen Männern zu übersteigen schien. Der Verweis auf Topoi der klassischen Mythologie und selbst der Bibel legitimierte diese Beziehung: „Die Namen beider Künstler [...] mußte [man] in Einem Athemzuge aussprechen wie Castor und Pollux, Orestes und Pylades,[12] David und Jonathan,[13] Schiller und Goethe!"[14]

Ganz dem romantischen Künstlerideal entsprechend sahen die Zeitungen van der Nüll „bisher einsam und nur seiner Kunst"[15] verpflichtet und umgeben von einem „engvertrauten Kreis von Freunden, mit denen er über wissenschaftliche oder Kunstfragen verkehrte."[16] Räumliche Zurückgezogenheit vom öffentlichen Leben und Konzentration

Der Vorhang des Wiener Hofopernhauses zeigt am linken Rand eine Gruppe von am Bau beteiligten, jedoch während der Bauzeit verstorbenen Künstlern, darunter van der Nüll und Sicardsburg.

The curtain of the Vienna Court Opera House shows on the left edge a group of artists involved in the construction, who died during the construction period, among them van der Nüll and Sicardsburg.

In keeping with the romantic ideal of the artist, the newspapers saw van der Nüll as "hitherto lonely and committed only to his art"[15] aand surrounded by a "close-knit circle of friends with whom he discussed issues of science and art."[16] Spatial seclusion from public life and concentration on a small social group that is familiar with one another, that allows room for personal feelings – this hinted at an ultimately gay topos. The architectural isolation also offered a protected space for the expression of deviant sexual orientation:[17] "It is a quiet, rather remote house,"[18] the *Fremden-Blatt* reported, where van der Nüll spent the last months of his life and committed suicide, which at first became known "only in informed circles."[19] This included "his most intimate friend La Vigne, whom we found deeply moved at the scene of the tragedy, almost speechless with pain,"[20] which is not surprising in view of the tragic death. The person referred to is sculptor August La Vigne, known for his decorative work for the imperial court,[21] and "in whose house, Windmühlgasse no. 28, van der Nüll lived since his marriage."[22] We know little about the lives and activities of other personalities mentioned, such as the architect Käßmann[23] or the decorative painter Holle, who decorated Café Kappelmayer, opened in 1843,[24] in whose house, Coburgbastei no. 12, van der Nüll had lived until 1867.[25]

The move to La Vignes' house in the Vienna suburb is remarkable because the inner city, where van der Nüll had previously lived, was the preferred residential area of the Viennese "refined" society. "La Vigne invited him to move to his house in Mariahilf, a true 'artist's villa'," the *Neues Wiener Tagblatt* reported: "At the beginning of spring, van der Nüll moved out of the city to his Tusculum."[26] The impression is of an escape from the centre of social attention to the remote suburb, where life could take place far from the jealous watch of one's own social group. There van der Nüll "lived on the second floor with

auf eine kleine soziale Gruppe, die untereinander vertraut ist, die einen Freiraum für das persönliche Empfinden gewährt – damit war ein letztlich schwuler Topos angedeutet. Die bauliche Abgeschiedenheit bot auch einen geschützten Raum für die Entfaltung abweichender sexueller Orientierung:[17] „Es ist ein stilles, ziemlich abgelegenes Haus",[18] so konnte man im *Fremden-Blatt* lesen, in dem van der Nüll seine letzten Lebensmonate verbracht habe und sich das Leben nahm, was zunächst „nur in den eingeweihten Kreisen"[19] bekannt wurde. Dazu gehörte „sein intimster Freund La Vigne, den wir an der Unglücksstelle tief ergriffen fanden, vor Schmerz fast sprachlos",[20] was angesichts des tragischen Todes nicht verwunder. Es handelt sich um den Bildhauer August La Vigne, der wegen seiner Dekorationsarbeiten für den kaiserlichen Hof bekannt ist[21] und „in dessen Haus, Windmühlgasse Nr. 28, van der Nüll seit seiner Vermählung wohnte."[22] Vom Leben und der Tätigkeit weiterer erwähnter Persönlichkeiten wissen wir kaum etwas: etwa vom Architekten Käßmann[23] oder dem Dekorationsmaler Holle, der das 1843 eröffnete Café Kappelmayer dekorierte[24] und in dessen Haus Coburgbastei Nr. 12 van der Nüll bis 1867 gewohnt hatte.[25]

Der Umzug in das Haus La Vignes in der Wiener Vorstadt ist bemerkenswert, weil die Innenstadt, wo van der Nüll bisher gewohnt hatte, das bevorzugte Wohngebiet der Wiener „besseren" Gesellschaft war. „La Vigne lud ihn ein, in sein in Mariahilf befindliches Haus, eine wahre ‚Künstler-Villa', zu ziehen", wusste das *Neue Wiener Tagblatt* zu berichten: „mit Beginn des Frühlings zog van der Nüll aus der Stadt in sein Tusculum."[26] Der Eindruck einer Flucht aus dem Zentrum gesellschaftlicher Aufmerksamkeit in die abgeschiedene Vorstadt, in der das Leben fernab der Argusaugen der eigenen Sozialgruppe stattfinden konnte, stellt sich durchaus ein. Dort bezog van der Nüll „mit seiner jungen Gattin das zweite Stockwerk".[27] Auffallend ist, dass van der Nüll erst 1867 die Ehe mit der 30 Jahre jüngeren Maria Killer einging; ob es sich dabei um eine Scheinehe gehandelt haben könnte, lässt sich nicht sagen, stand die rund 26-Jährige zum Zeitpunkt des Selbstmordes doch kurz vor ihrer Entbindung.[28] Jedenfalls geben die Umstände der Eheschließung zu denken: Angeblich habe van der Nüll gehofft, dass Maria Killer, „die früher in seinen Diensten stand", ihm „über die Beschwerden des Alters hinweghelfen werde. Als er das Mädchen seine kranke Tante pflegen sah, war der Gedanke es zu heiraten in ihm entstanden und er führte ihn aus, trotz dem Abrathen von Freunden und Verwandten."[29]

Bei Sicardsburg kann ein in den Tageszeitungen mitgeteiltes Detail als Andeutung einer Neigung zum männlichen Geschlecht gelesen werden. Die Wortwahl lässt uns aufhorchen: „Als die Künstler in Salzburg waren, befand sich eben […] ein Zigeunerlager in der Nähe. Siccardsburg [sic], ein geborener Ungar, in dem das Blut seiner Heimat mitunter aufwallte, machte sich eines Abends nach diesem Lager auf und verbrachte mitten unter den Zigeunern, mit denen er anstieß und Bruderschaft trank, ein paar

Um 1840 von Sicardsburg gezeichnete Darstellung eines antiken Dreifußes mit Satyrn (l.), das Original stammt aus dem Gabinetto Segreto in Neapel (r.).

A drawing by Sicardsburg of an ancient tripod with satyrs from around 1840 (l.) The original comes from the Gabinetto Segreto in Naples (r.).

his young wife."[27] It is striking that van der Nüll did not enter into marriage with Maria Killer, 30 years his junior, until 1867; whether this could have been a fictitious marriage cannot be said, since the 26-year-old woman was about to give birth at the time of his suicide.[28] In any case, the circumstances of the marriage provide food for thought: van der Nüll allegedly hoped that Maria Killer, "who used to be in his service," would "help him get over the discomfort of old age. When he saw the girl nursing his sick aunt, the thought of marrying her arose in him and he pursued it, despite the advice of friends and relatives."[29]

In Sicardsburg's case, a detail reported in the daily newspapers can be read as an indication of an inclination towards the male sex. The incident is described in a socially acceptable way, but punctuation marks suggestively insert a pause for thought: "When the artists were in Salzburg, there was […] a gypsy camp nearby. Siccardsburg, a native Hungarian, with the blood of his homeland sometimes surging within him, set off one evening for this camp and spent a few … romantic hours among the gypsies with whom he toasted and befriended."[30] That this was a group of men is illustrated by another obituary, which described them as a "band of voluntary hussars."[31] In contrast, another incident had a clear sexual connotation: Because of the difficulties involved in building the opera house, van der Nüll, suffering from insomnia, had retired to his apartment, while Sicardsburg "went for walks at night, visited inns and cafes. Since after midnight only those cafes are usually open, which conduct a so-called 'night-time business' and are visited almost exclusively by female guests of ambiguous character and their following, one could often see Siccardsburg sitting in such places, where he was distracted by the colourful hustle and bustle around him."[32] Viennese night cafés,[33] however, were also considered secret meeting places for man-manly love.[34] It is remarkable that such a report, which deals with an environment that is considered sexually indecent, can be found in a

tollromantische Stunden."[30] Dass es sich um eine Runde von Männern handelte, verdeutlicht ein weiterer Nachruf, der sie als „Schaar freiwilliger Husaren"[31] bezeichnete. Eindeutig sexuell konnotiert war dagegen eine andere Begebenheit: Wegen der Schwierigkeiten beim Opernbau an Schlaflosigkeit leidend, habe sich van der Nüll in seine Wohnung zurückgezogen, Sicardsburg dagegen machte „nächtlicher Weise Spaziergänge, besuchte Gast- und Kaffeehäuser und da nach Mitternacht nur jene Kaffeehäuser offen zu bleiben pflegen, welche ein sogenanntes ‚Nachtgeschäft' haben, in dem sie fast ausschließlich von weiblichen Gästen zweideutigen Charakters und ihrem Anhang aufgesucht werden, so konnte man gar oft Siccardsburg [sic] in solchen Lokalen sitzen sehen, wo er sich an dem bunten Treiben um ihn her zerstreute."[32] Die Wiener Nachtcafés[33] galten indessen auch als geheime Treffpunkte für die mann-männliche Liebe.[34] Es ist auffällig, dass ein derartiger Bericht, der ein als sexuell-anrüchig geltendes Umfeld thematisiert, in einem öffentlichen Medium des 19. Jahrhunderts zu finden ist; wurde hier doch ein respektables Mitglied der Gesellschaft, noch dazu ein Akademieprofessor, seit 1844 mit Luise Janschky verheiratet und Vater dreier Kinder, dabei präsentiert, wie er die Grenzen gesellschaftlich-normierten Verhaltens überschritt.

Ein Indiz für eine homosexuelle Neigung bietet auch eine Zeichnung des Satyr-Dreifuß aus dem legendären Gabinetto Segreto in Neapel.[36] Sicardsburg dürfte ihn aus Jean-Claude Richards *Voyage Pittoresque* kopiert haben[37] – mit allen Unstimmigkeiten gegenüber dem Original (Feigenblätter anstelle der erigierten Penisse der Satyrn). Eigentlich zeichnete Sicardsburg hier eines der großartigsten Werke homoerotischer Kunst der römischen Antike. War er sich dessen bewusst? Ob er das Original während seines Neapel-Besuchs um 1840 sehen konnte oder ob er nur die zensierte Nachzeichnung kannte (oder nur sie ertragen konnte), bleibt uns verborgen.

Dass van der Nüll und Sicardsburg eine enge Beziehung verband, steht außer Frage. Wie intim die Beziehung tatsächlich war, ob sie mehr als eine Freundschaft unter Männern darstellte und in heutigen Augen als schwul bezeichnet werden kann, offenbaren die zwischen gezielter Andeutung und Diskretion lavierenden Quellen freilich nicht. Andererseits tangieren manche Charakterisierungen Sicardsburgs die Grenzen der zeitgenössischen Moral auf so direkte Weise, dass wir es nicht von der Hand weisen sollten, in den beiden Architekten tatsächlich ein Paar von „Urningen" zu sehen, wie die Anhänger der mann-männlichen Liebe in ihrer Zeit genannt wurden.

19th century publication; after all, a respectable member of society, and an academy professor to boot, married to Luise Janschky since 1844 and father of three children, was presented here as a man crossing the boundaries of socially standardized behavior.

That Sicardsburg had an unbiased eye for male sexuality is suggested by a drawing attributed to him[35] of the bronze tripod with Satyrs from the legendary Gabinetto Segreto in Naples,[36] which he possibly created during his stay in Italy around 1840. The aforementioned tripod was known since the 18th century through pictorial representations.[37] Sicardsburg's drawing is revealing in one detail, however: he drew the three young Satyrs with erect penises and thus completely in accordance with the original model – a detail that most representations had meticulously avoided until then.

There is no question that van der Nüll and Sicardsburg were very close. How intimate the relationship actually was, whether it was more than a friendship between men and whether it could be called gay from today's viewpoint is not revealed by the sources, which waver between deliberate insinuation and discretion. On the other hand, some of Sicardsburg's characterizations touch on the boundaries of contemporary morality in such a direct way that we should not deny that the two architects are actually a couple of "Urninge", as the followers of man-male love were called in their time.

Eine Gedenktafel am Haus Schadekgasse 4 in Wien benennt das Gebäude als gemeinsames „Wohn- und Sterbehaus" von van der Nüll und Sicardsburg. Die Angabe muss allerdings bezweifelt werden. Die offiziellen Adressbücher der Stadt Wien verzeichnen lediglich für die frühen 1840er-Jahre eine gemeinsame Wohnung der beiden Architekten in der heutigen Praterstraße.[22]

A memorial plaque on the house at Schadekgasse 4 in Vienna names the building as the joint "residence and death house" of van der Nüll and Sicardsburg. This statement must be doubted. The official address books of the city of Vienna record a joint apartment of the two architects only for the early 1840s in today's Praterstrasse.[22]

Wolfgang Voigt

Der Architekt und der Kürassier: Franz Heinrich Schwechten

Berlin war zu Beginn des 20. Jahrhunderts eine stürmisch gewachsene, vibrierende Metropole. Mit 3,5 Millionen Einwohnern war es nach London und Paris 1914 die drittgrößte Stadt der damaligen Welt. Für die Schwulen ein besonderer Ort: Hier lag der Sitz des 1897 gegründeten Wissenschaftlich-Humanitären Komitees (WHK), das die erste organisierte Befreiungsbewegung für die Homosexuellen darstellte. Unter der Leitung des Arztes Magnus Hirschfeld leistete es Pionierarbeit für die junge Disziplin der Sexualwissenschaft, besonders aber für die Entdiskriminierung der Homosexualität.[1] Den Schwulen und Lesben der Stadt widmete Hirschfeld 1904 mit *Berlins Drittes Geschlecht* ein warmherziges Porträt. Es sei kein Zufall, dass sie „dorthin strebten, wo sie in der Fülle und dem Wechsel der Gestalten unauffälliger und daher unbehelligter leben können."[2] Zwar gab es das gefürchtete Strafgesetz mit dem Paragraphen 175 und sammelte die Berliner Polizei „rosa" Listen über tausende schwule Männer, doch könnten die Homosexuellen trotzdem „im Großen ruhig in Berlin ihren Trieben und Wünschen nachgehen [...], wenn sie nicht zu auffällig ihr Wesen treiben", stellte 1906 ein anderer Autor fest. Nur ab und zu greife die Polizei „irgendeinen heraus aus den Tausenden", um dem Gesetz Respekt zu verschaffen und die Homosexuellen in Furcht zu halten.[3] Die Strafandrohung bot einen günstigen Nährboden für Erpressungen. Die Polizei verfolgte die Erpresser, wenn sie den sexuellen Verkehr ihrer Opfer bezeugen konnten, wanderten aber auch diese ins Gefängnis. In der für Homosexualität zuständigen Inspektion B im Berliner Polizeipräsidium teilte man bereits die Auffassung des WHK über die fällige Abschaffung des Paragraphen 175. Sie gelang allerdings erst 1994. Der Leiter der Inspektion war von 1896 bis 1919 Hans von Tresckow (1866-1934), ein Kriminalkommissar aus preußischer adliger Familie, der mit Hirschfeld freundlich verbunden war.[4]

Nach dem Ende des Kaiserreichs veröffentlichte von Tresckow unter dem Titel *Von Fürsten und anderen Sterblichen* seine Erinnerungen aus drei Jahrzehnten des kriminalistischen Alltags. Das 1922 erschienene Buch stieß auf großes Interesse des Publikums und wurde mehrmals nachgedruckt.[5] Zu von Tresckows informellen Aufgaben gehörte es auch, Sexualaffären mit Beteiligung von Angehörigen des Adels und anderer hochgestellter Persönlichkeiten diskret zu bereinigen, bevor die Presse etwas erfuhr und ehe die Justiz offiziell tätig wurde. Das Ansehen von Monarchie und Hofgesellschaft sollte nicht beschädigt werden! Im Kapitel „Die Homosexuellen" berichtete von Tresckow über einen Berliner Architekten mit ausgeprägtem Fetisch. In der Hauptstadt, so von Tresckow,

The Architect and the Cuirassier: Franz Heinrich Schwechten

At the beginning of the 20th century, Berlin was a rapidly growing, vibrant metropolis. With 3.5 million inhabitants, it was the third-largest city in the world after London and Paris around 1914. For gays, it was a special place: This was the location of the Wissenschaftlich-Humanitäres Komitee (WHK) founded in 1897, which was the first organized liberation movement for homosexuals. Under the direction of the physician Magnus Hirschfeld, the committee achieved pioneering work for the fledgling discipline of sexology, but particularly for the non-discrimination of homosexuality.[1] With the publication *Berlins Drittes Geschlecht*, Hirschfeld in 1904 dedicated a warm-hearted portrait to the gays and lesbians of the city. He thought that it was no coincidence that "they flock to where they can live more inconspicuous and thus more undisturbed among the masses and the constantly changing people."[2] Although the feared penal code with the article 175 existed and the Berlin police was collecting "pink" lists of thousands of gay men, it was all the same possible for "the homosexuals to by and large quietly satisfy their drives and desires […] if they do not act too conspicuously," a different author stated in 1906. The police would only now and then "seize anyone out of the thousands" in order to earn the law respect and to keep the homosexuals in fear.[3] The threat of punishment was a favourable breeding ground for extortions. The police prosecuted the extortionists but if these were able to testify to the sexual intercourse of their victims, these as well went to jail. In the Inspektion B responsible for homosexuality in the Berlin police headquarters, one already shared the opinion of the WHK regarding the due abolition of article 175. However, it only succeeded in 1994. From 1896 until 1919, Hans von Tresckow (1896-1934) was the head of the department, a detective superintendent from a Prussian, aristocratic family who had friendly ties with Hirschfeld.[4]

After the end of the Empire, von Tresckow published his memoirs from three decades of forensic career with the title *Von Fürsten und anderen Sterblichen*. The book came out in 1922, met with strong interest of the public and was reprinted several times.[5] Among von Tresckow's informal tasks was also to discretely cover up sexual affairs with the participation of members of the nobility and other distinguished personages before the press found out about them and before the judicial system officially took action. The prestige of the monarchy and the court society was not to be damaged. In the chapter "Die Homosexuellen", von Tresckow wrote about a Berlin architect with a pronounced fetish. According to von Tresckow, many homosexuals in the capital had a "liking for soldiers

Der Architekt Franz Schwechten, ein Freund Kaiser Wilhelms II.

The architect Franz Schwechten, a friend of Kaiser Wilhelm II.

fänden viele Homosexuelle „Gefallen an Soldaten oder Matrosen" wegen ihrer virilen Uniformierungen.⁶ Als größte Garnison des Reiches war Berlin vor 1914 von mehr Militärpersonen bevölkert als jede andere deutsche Stadt. Nicht wenige der karg besoldeten Soldaten verdienten sich mit sexuellen Diensten ein Taschengeld, was zu wiederholten Beschwerden und Lokalverboten durch die Kommandeure der Berliner Regimenter Anlass gab, jedoch ohne durchschlagenden Erfolg. Auch Hirschfeld berichtete über die Uniformliebhaber, „welche vielfach ihre Spitznamen nach den Truppenteilen bekommen, für die sie sich besonders interessieren"; so gab es eine „Dragonerbraut", eine „Kürassieranna", eine „Kanoniersche" und andere mehr.⁷

Jener Architekt, so von Tresckow, interessierte sich nicht für einfache Infanteristen, sondern ausschließlich „für Kürassiere, aber sie mussten Trompeter sein und auf ihren Schultern die Schwalbennester tragen."⁸ Das in Potsdam stationierte und von Wilhelm II. persönlich kommandierte Kürassierregiment Garde du Corps war die berittene Leibgarde des Kaisers, auffällig durch weiße Uniformen, über das Knie aufsteigende Husarenstiefel, weiß-metallene Brustpanzer und besonders dekorierte Paradehelme. Berühmte Kürassiere, die in Potsdam ihren Dienst geleistet hatten, waren so gegensätzliche Persönlichkeiten wie Otto von Bismarck und der AEG-Direktor und spätere Außenminister Walter Rathenau. Den Namen des Architekten behielt von Tresckow für sich, aber er legte eine Spur: Es handele sich um einen „bekannten Baumeister, dem Berlin einige seiner schönsten Monumentalbauten verdankt."⁹ Der im ausgehenden Kaiserreich in Berlin tätige Personenkreis, der das Format mitbrachte, um diesem hohen Rang zu entsprechen, war klein. Nicht aus der Sicht der Moderne, sondern mit den Augen eines preußischen Konservativen gesehen, kommen nur fünf Architekten jener Zeit ernsthaft in Frage.

Kürassier-Offizier des Garde du Corps-Regiments, um 1880

Cuirassier officer of the Garde du Corps regiment, around 1880

and sailors" because of their virile uniforms.[6] As the largest garrison of the Empire, prior to 1914 Berlin had had more military persons living there than any other German city. Not a few of the meagrely salaried soldiers also earned some pocket money with sexual services which repeatedly led to complaints and bans from pubs by the commanders of the Berlin regiments, without resounding success, however. Hirschfeld as well wrote about the lovers of uniforms "who are often given nicknames according to the military units in which they take a special interest"; there was thus a "dragoon's bride," a "cuirassier's Anna," a "gunner's darling," and others.[7]

The respective architect, according to von Tresckow wrote, was not interested in simple infantry soldiers but exclusively in "cuirassiers, but they had to be trumpeters and, on their shoulders, they had to wear what were called swallow's nests [epaulettes]."[8] The Garde du Corp regiment of cuirassiers, stationed in Potsdam and commanded by William II personally, was the mounted lifeguard of the Emperor, standing out with white uniforms, hussar boots to above the knees, white-metallic cuirasses and especially decorated parade helmets. Famous cuirassiers, who had performed their military service in Potsdam, were such contrasting personalities as Otto von Bismarck and the director of AEG and later foreign minister Walter Rathenau. Von Tresckow kept the name of the architect to himself but he left a trail: It was said to be a "well-known master builder to whom Berlin owes some of its most beautiful monumental buildings."[9] The group of persons active in Berlin at the end of the Empire who had the quality necessary for this high rank was small. Not from the point of view of the modern age but seen with the eyes of a Prussian conservative, only five architects of the time are seriously worth considering.

Anhalter Bahnhof in Berlin, 1880

Anhalt Train station in Berlin, 1880

Zu den fünf gehören, neben dem Berliner Stadtbaurat Ludwig Hoffmann (1852-1932) und Alfred Messel (1853-1909), dem Entwerfer luxuriöser Warenhäuser und des Pergamon-Museums, drei Architekten, die Wilhelm II. und dem kaiserlichen Hof besonders nahe standen: Ernst von Ihne (1848-1917) war seit 1888 der offizielle Hofarchitekt. Von ihm kennt man das Bode-Museum auf der Berliner Museumsinsel und in Kronberg am Taunus das Schloss Friedrichshof für die Kaiserin-Witwe Victoria, die Mutter Wilhelms II. Julius Carl Raschdorff (1823-1914) baute in Potsdam das Mausoleum für Friedrich III., Wilhelms Vater, und in Berlin den monumentalen Dom. Außerdem kommt Franz Heinrich Schwechten (1841-1924), Architekt der Kaiser-Wilhelm-Gedächtniskirche, in Frage. Von allen fünf sind die Lebensläufe bekannt, fast alle waren Familienväter mit zahlreichen Kindern.

Einer fällt, wie wir gleich sehen werden, hinsichtlich des Privatlebens jedoch auf auffällige Weise aus der Reihe: Franz Heinrich Schwechten.[10] Sein Meisterwerk in Berlin war der Anhalter Bahnhof (1872-1880), einer der herausragenden Großbauten des 19. Jahrhunderts. Das Bauwerk mit dem mächtigen Bogengiebel war nach dem Zweiten Weltkrieg nur mäßig beschädigt und wurde trotzdem in den 1960er-Jahren abgebrochen, nachdem die entsprechende Bahnlinie durch die Grenzziehungen nach 1945 nicht mehr vorhanden war. Nur noch ein Fassadenfragment ist heute übrig. Als der junge Wilhelm II. 1889 den Kaiserthron bestieg, gelang es Schwechten, das Vertrauen des jungen Monarchen zu gewinnen und über Jahrzehnte für sich zu erhalten. Mit positiven Folgen für ihn, denn auf Veranlassung Wilhelms und oft durch Direktauftrag entstanden neben zahlreichen anderen Kirchen und weltlichen Bauten in Berlin auch die bereits erwähnte Kaiser-Wilhelm-Gedächtniskirche (1890-1895) und der Grunewaldturm (1899), außerdem die Erlöserkirche in Bad Homburg (1908) und das einer mittelalterlichen Kaiserpfalz nachgebildete Residenzschloss in Poznan/Posen (1903-1910). Die Bauten für den Kaiser waren in dem von diesem bevorzugten neuromanischen Stil gehalten. Oft hatte Wilhelm II. hierfür stilistische Wünsche geäußert, die dann von Schwechten nach dessen Vorstellungen materialisiert wurden. Die Nähe Schwechtens zum Kaiser war den Architektenkollegen ein Dorn im Auge. Von Paul Wallot, dem Architekten des von Wilhelm wenig geschätzten Reichstags-

Kaiser-Wilhelm-Gedächt-
niskirche in Berlin, 1895

*Kaiser Wilhelm Memorial
Church in Berlin, 1895*

Besides the Berlin director of urban development Ludwig Hoffmann (1852-1932) and Alfred Messel (1853-1909), the designer of luxurious department stores and of the Pergamon Museum, three architects belonged to those five who were particularly close to William II and the imperial court: Ernst von Ihne (1848-1917) had been the official court architect since 1888. He designed the Bode Museum on the Berlin Museum Island and, in Kronberg am Taunus, Schloss Friedrichshof for the Emperor's widow Victoria, the mother of William II. Julius Carl Raschdorff (1823-1914), who had the mausoleum in Potsdam built for Frederick III, William's father, and in Berlin the monumental cathedral. In addition, Franz Heinrich Schwechten (1841-1924), the architect of the Kaiser-Wilhelm-Gedächtniskirche, is worth considering. The biographies of all five are known, almost all of them were family men with numerous children.

One of them, however, conspicuously stands out regarding his private life, as we shall soon see: Franz Heinrich Schwechten.[10] His masterwork in Berlin was Anhalter Bahnhof (1872-1880), one of the eminent large-scale constructions of the 19th century. After the Second World War, the building with the enormous arched gable was only moderately damaged and was nevertheless demolished in the 1960s because the corresponding railway line no longer existed following the border demarcation after 1945. Only a fragment of the façade remains today. When young William II became Emperor in 1889, Schwechten succeeded in winning the young monarch's confidence and maintaining it for several decades. With positive consequences for him since, at the instigation of William and frequently with a direct commission, besides numerous other churches and

Königliches Residenzschloss in Posen/Poznan, 1913

Royal Residence Castle in Poznan, 1913

gebäudes in Berlin, ist die folgende Klage überliefert: „Warum häuft Majestät all seine Liebenswürdigkeit auf Männer, wie jene Schwechten oder Raschdorff, und warum ergiesst er allen Schwall seines rohen Unverstandes über mein Haupt?"[11]

Im Gegensatz zu den anderen genannten Architekten war Schwechten unverheiratet und hinterließ keine Angehörigen. Bis zu seinem 50. Lebensjahr lebte er mit seiner Mutter zusammen. In Köln, wo er seine Jugend verbrachte, war seit 1850 auch das preussische Kürassierregiment Nr. 8 stationiert, das ähnlich auffällig uniformiert war wie das Garde du Corps-Regiment des Kaisers in Potsdam und Berlin. Wenn es sich also um Schwechten handelt, konnte dieser schon als junger Mann bei Paraden auf dem Kölner Neumarkt die Augen schweifen lassen. Sein Werk ist gut dokumentiert. Schwechten selbst oder die mit dem Nachlass befassten Personen sorgten dafür, dass mehr als 5.000 Blatt Pläne und Zeichnungen an die Stiftung Kaiser-Wilhelm-Gedächtniskirche übergeben wurden. Dagegen drang über sein Privatleben nichts nach außen. In der 1999 erschienenen Monographie über ihn spricht der Autor Peer Zietz von einer „merkwürdigen Anonymität" der Person Schwechtens, über den er trotz Bemühungen nichts herausfinden konnte: „Es existieren von ihm zwei Photos, einige Briefe, sonst nichts, kein schriftlicher Nachlass."[12] Ich vermute, dass dies nicht zufällig so war. Während für den Nachruhm des Baukünstlers Schwechten alles geregelt war, blieb das Private im Dunkeln. Dass unter den Architektenkollegen schon damals über von Tresckows Andeutung gerätselt wurde, davon darf man ausgehen. Wenn der Junggeselle Schwechten der Liebhaber von Kürassieren gewesen ist, dann hatte er in seinen letzten Lebensjahren noch Gelegenheit, zu reagieren und dafür zu sorgen, dass die Details seines schon vorher abgeschirmten Privatlebens auch nach seinem Tod verschleiert blieben. Wenn – wie vermutet – er es war, dann ist ihm dies vollkommen gelungen.

Flirt mit Blicken: Skulpturen an der Ostfassade des Residenzschlosses in Posen/Poznan

Flirting with fleeting glances: Sculptures on the East Façade of the Residence Castle in Poznan

secular buildings in Berlin, the Kaiser-Wilhelm-Gedächtniskirche (1890-1895) and the Grunewaldturm (1899) were built, furthermore the Erlöserkirche in Bad Homburg (1908) and the residential palace in Poznan (1903-1910) emulating a medieval imperial palace. The buildings for the Emperor were designed in the neo-Romanesque style he preferred. Often, William II had expressed stylistic wishes regarding them which Schwechten then fulfilled according to his ideas. Schwechten's closeness to the Emperor was a nuisance to his fellow architects. By Paul Wallot, the architect of the Berlin Reichstag building, which Wilhelm little appreciated, the following complaint is passed on: "Why does His Majesty pile all his kindness onto men such as Schwechten or Raschdorff, and why does he pour a flood of his rough ignorance on my head?"[11]

In contrast to the other architects mentioned, Schwechten was unmarried and did not leave any relatives. His work is well documented. Schwechten himself or those administrating his estate made sure that more than 5,000 pages of plans and drawings were handed over to the Kaiser-Wilhelm-Gedächtniskirche foundation. About his private life, however, nothing was publicly known. In the monograph on him published in 1999, the author Peer Zietz writes about a "strange anonymity" regarding Schwechten as a person about whom he could not find out anything despite his efforts: "There exist two photographs of him, some letters, nothing else, no written legacy."[12] I assume that this was not by chance. Whereas everything was seen to for Schwechten's posthumous fame as an architect, what was private remained in the dark. That, already at the time, his fellow architects puzzled over von Tresckow's insinuation is very likely. If the bachelor Schwechten had been the lover of cuirassiers, he would still have had the chance in his final years to react and to ensure that the details of his private life – already shielded previously – also remained concealed after his death. If – as presumed – it had been him, he completely succeeded with this.

Wolfgang Voigt

Zwei Stadtbauräte, zwei Junggesellen: Fritz Schumacher und Gustav Oelsner

Fritz Schumacher (1869-1947)[1] und Gustav Oelsner (1878-1956)[2] waren in der Zwischenkriegszeit die Stadtbauräte in den damals noch nicht vereinigten Städten Altona und in Hamburg, Schumacher mit dem Titel eines Oberbaudirektors, der andere als Bausenator. Beide wurden 1933 von den Nationalsozialisten aus ihrem Amt entlassen. Sie waren als Reformer angetreten und nutzten die Chance des Umbruchs, um der jeweils eigenen Stadt ein charakteristisches Profil zu geben. Fritz Schumacher ist als derjenige in die Geschichte eingegangen, der dem Stadtbild Hamburgs in besonderer Weise Farbe verlieh; alles was der hamburgische Staat damals baute, einschließlich der damals neuen Siedlungen des sozialen Wohnungsbaus, wurde in rotem bis dunkelbraunem Backstein gemauert. Mit der schieren Menge und Dominanz der von ihm selbst entworfenen neuen Schulen, Krankenhausbauten, Gerichte, Polizei- und Feuerwachen stellte Schumacher jeden seiner Kollegen in den Schatten.[3] Für die kleinere Nachbarstadt Altona war die so auffällig umgefärbte Hansestadt eine Herausforderung, die von seinem Kollegen Oelsner bravourös gemeistert wurde. Seine Antwort auf die homogenen dunkelroten Klinkerfassaden in Hamburg war nicht die Zurückweisung des Mauerziegels, sondern der Aufbruch in andere Farbakzente, von denen Oelsners Gelb zur Erkennungsmarke des „Neuen Altona" wurde. So erhielt die von traditionalistischen Hanseaten nicht immer für voll genommene Schwesterstadt ein lebendiges Profil, und dies war das Verdienst Gustav Oelsners.

In ihrem jeweiligen Amt waren Schumacher und Oelsner nur ihrer eigenen Stadt verpflichtet und somit offiziell Konkurrenten. Tatsächlich nahmen sie früh Kontakt auf, besuchten sich zum Tee am Nachmittag – das geht aus Briefen zwischen den beiden hervor – und sie trafen Absprachen, wenn dies zum Nutzen der beiden Städte war, die längst zusammengewachsen waren. Beide waren Junggesellen, Oelsner war aus jüdischer Familie und homosexuell.[4] Bei Schumacher gibt es keinen eindeutigen Beleg, aber doch Hinweise auf seine Orientierung. Ein Paar waren sie nicht. Beide lebten in einer Zeit, in der „widernatürliche Unzucht" unter Männern, wie das im Gesetz hieß, mit Gefängnis bestraft wurde. Wer kein Risiko eingehen wollte, bemühte sich um strikte Unauffälligkeit, wie Oelsner sie praktizierte, oder um Enthaltsamkeit, wie sie bei Schumacher für weite Strecken seines Lebens angenommen werden darf.

Two City Planning Officials, Two Bachelors: Fritz Schumacher and Gustav Oelsner

In the period between the World Wars, Gustav Oelsner (1878-1956)[1] and Fritz Schumacher (1869-1947)[2] were both head of the municipal planning and building control office in the then not yet united cities of Altona and Hamburg, Schumacher with the title of Oberbaudirektor (chief planning officer), the other as Bausenator (senator for the built environment). Both were dismissed from office by the National Socialists in 1933. They had started out as reformers and used the opportunity of the upheaval to give their respective city a characteristic profile. Fritz Schumacher has gone down in history as the man who gave Hamburg's cityscape a special identity; everything the Hamburg state built at that time, including the then new social housing estates, was built in red to dark brown brick. With the sheer quantity and dominance of the new schools, hospital buildings, courthouse, police and fire stations that he himself designed, Schumacher outshone all his colleagues.[3] For the smaller neighbouring city of Altona, the hanseatic city with its distinctive new brick-coloured identity was a challenge that was brilliantly met by his colleague, Oelsner. His answer to the homogenous dark red brick façades in Hamburg was not to reject brick but to move on to other colour emphases, of which Oelsner's yellow became the identifying feature of the "New Altona". Thus, the sister city, which was not always taken seriously by traditionalist Hanseatic citizens, was given a vibrant profile, and this was thanks to Gustav Oelsner.

In their respective positions, Schumacher and Oelsner were bound only to their respective cities and were thus officially competitors. Actually, they made contact with each other at an early stage, visited each other for afternoon tea – this is evident from letters between the two – and they made arrangements if this was to the benefit of the two cities, which had long since grown together. Both were bachelors, Oelsner was from a Jewish family and homosexual.[4] In Schumacher's case there is no clear evidence, but there are indications of his sexual orientation. They were not a couple. Both lived in a time when "unnatural fornication" among men was punishable by imprisonment. Those who did not want to take a risk made every effort to be strictly inconspicuous, as Oelsner practiced it, or to abstain – as may be assumed of Schumacher for long periods of his life.

Both had heard of the conviction of Oscar Wilde and the scandal surrounding Friedrich Alfred Krupp when his sexual escapades with young men on the island of Capri came to light;[5] they also knew about the Eulenburg affair concerning the Emperor's circle

Porträt des Hamburger Oberbaudirektors Fritz Schumacher, Holzschnitt um 1925

Portrait of the Hamburg chief planning officer Fritz Schumacher, woodcut around 1925

Beide hatten die Verurteilung Oscar Wildes und den Skandal um Friedrich Alfried Krupp mitbekommen, als dessen sexuelle Eskapaden mit jungen Männern auf der Insel Capri ans Licht kamen;[5] auch wussten sie von der Eulenburg-Affäre um den von Schwulen durchsetzten Freundeskreis des Kaisers.[6] Krupp hatte danach 1902 Selbstmord begangen und der Skandal um Eulenburg endete mit einer Serie von Prozessen und Verurteilungen. All das musste auf die Generation Oelsners und Schumachers alarmierend wirken. Beide waren hochgestellte, aus dem Bürgertum stammende Beamte. Sexuelle Abweichung als solche mochte unter der Hand toleriert sein, solange sie im Verborgenen blieb. Wurde sie öffentlich und versagten die schützenden Netzwerke, drohte gesellschaftliche Ächtung, waren Position und Amt in Gefahr und damit die eigene bürgerliche Existenz.

Von 1909, dem Jahr seiner Berufung nach Hamburg, bis zu seinem Tod lebte Schumacher 37 Jahre lang mit seinen beiden Schwestern zusammen, die ihm den Haushalt führten. Die Mitwelt kannte ihn als extremen workoholic, dessen schriftstellerische Produktion alle Grenzen sprengte. Dass allein der Umfang – 40 Bücher, etwa 500 Zeitschriftenaufsätze – ein Privatleben kaum zuließ, leuchtet ein.[7] Die Tragik des Diplomatensohns Schumacher bestand darin, dass er durch seine viktorianische Erziehung und angesichts der hohen Risiken doppelt gehemmt war. Die in sein Werk geflossene beispiellose Energie verdanken wir letztendlich Schumachers notgedrungener Askese. Auffällige Zuwendung von Schumachers Seite erhielt ein junger Architekt in Hamburg. Gerhard Langmaack (1898-1986)[8] war gebildet und frisch verheiratet, als er auf Empfehlung Schumachers die eigentlich diesem anvertraute Kulturwissenschaftliche Bibliothek Aby Warburgs (1925/26) bauen durfte.[9] Aus der Verbindung entwickelte sich eine lebenslange Freundschaft, die Züge einer Vater-Sohn-Beziehung annahm. Nach Schumachers Tod gehörten Langmaack und seine Familie zu den Erben.

Gustav Oelsner, Bausenator in Altona bis 1933. Porträtaufnahme aus den 1950er-Jahren

Gustav Oelsner, in charge of construction in Altona until 1933. Portrait photograph from the 1950s

of friends which included many gay men.⁶ Krupp committed suicide in 1902 and the Eulenburg scandal ended with a series of trials and convictions. All this must have been alarming for the generation of Oelsner and Schumacher. Both were high-ranking civil servants from bourgeois family backgrounds. Sexual deviance as such might be tolerated on the quiet as long as it remained hidden. If it became public and the protective networks failed, one was threatened with social ostracism, position and function were in danger and with it one's own bourgeois existence.

From 1909, the year of his appointment to Hamburg, until his death, Schumacher lived with his two sisters, who ran his household, for 37 years. His contemporary world knew him as an extreme workaholic, whose literary production pushed all boundaries. It is obvious that the amount alone – 40 books, about 500 articles in magazines – hardly left any room for a private life.⁷ The tragedy of Schumacher, the son of a diplomat, was that he was doubly inhibited by his Victorian upbringing and in the face of the high risks involved. The unprecedented energy he invested in his work was ultimately due to Schumacher's forced asceticism. A young architect in Hamburg got a conspicuous amount of attention from Schumacher. Gerhard Langmaack (1898-1986)⁸ was well-educated and newly married when, on Schumacher's recommendation, he was allowed to build Aby Warburg's cultural studies library, which had been entrusted to him (1925-26).⁹ A lifelong friendship developed from this connection, which took on the characteristics of a father-son relationship. After Schumacher's death, Langmaack and his family were among the heirs.

Gustav Oelsner staged himself as a celibate, middle-class intellectual whose private life remained shielded. As he later revealed to his students, he found distraction, far

Schule im Stadtteil Berne in Hamburg, 1930, entworfen von Fritz Schumacher

School in the Berne district of Hamburg, 1930, designed by Fritz Schumacher

Gustav Oelsner inszenierte sich als zölibatärer Bildungsbürger, dessen Privatleben abgeschottet blieb. Wo er Zerstreuung fand, weit weg von Altona und Hamburg, offenbarte er später vor seinen Studenten im Exil in der Türkei. Als Beispiel, wie man in einer Halle durch Licht von oben besondere Wirkung erzielen könne, nannte er die türkischen Bäder in Budapest, und er ließ sie wissen, dass ihn dort das Spiel des Lichts auf den athletischen Körpern der männlichen Besucher fasziniert habe.[10] Die Bäder dort waren als diskrete Treffpunkte bekannt. Nach 1949 wirkte Oelsner einige Jahre als Senior des Hamburger Städtebaus. Nach seinem Tod 1956 erinnerte sich der Architekt Werner Kallmorgen – er war in den 1920er-Jahren einer der jungen Mitarbeiter in Oelsners Bauverwaltung – an die scheinheilige Frage unter Oelsners Mitarbeitern im Amt, ob einer wie er „wohl jemals sündigen könnte?" Nach Oelsners Tod gab Erich Lüth, der Pressesprecher des hamburgischen Senats, 1960 ein Gedenkbuch für Oelsner heraus;[11] dort gab es einen Beitrag von Kallmorgen, in dem wir das lesen können.[12] Die extreme Verschlossenheit des Verstorbenen in privaten Dingen wurde im Gedenkbuch als Tugendhaltung eines selbstlosen Staatsdieners erklärt; „als Beamter" habe Oelsner jede Publizität gescheut.[13] Die Formulierung „als homosexueller Beamter" hätte die Sache präzise getroffen. Dies zu offenbaren hätte jedoch den Ruf des Bausenators jedoch auch posthum noch schwer beschädigt.

Die erste Reform des Paragraphen 175 des Strafgesetzbuchs in Westdeutschland erfolgte erst neun Jahre später. Dabei wussten die Beteiligten durchaus, was verborgen bleiben sollte, denn Erich Lüth war Teil eines diskreten Dreierzirkels aus Sozialdemokraten und früheren Nazigegnern, dem außer ihm Gustav Oelsner und der ebenfalls homosexuelle Altonaer Architekt Rudolf Lodders angehörten,[14] der wie Kallmorgen als junger Architekt in den 1920er-Jahren im Hochbauamt unter Oelsner gearbeitet hatte. Lodders' wichtigstes, zusammen mit anderen Architekten realisiertes Werk in Hamburgs Wiederaufbau waren

Schule Angerstraße in Hamburg, 1927, entworfen von Fritz Schumacher

Angerstrasse School in Hamburg, 1927, designed by Fritz Schumacher

away from Altona and Hamburg, in his exile in Turkey. As an example of how special effects can be achieved in a hall by light from above, he mentioned the Turkish baths in Budapest, and he told the students that he was fascinated by the play of light on the athletic bodies of the male visitors.[10] The baths there were known as discreet meeting places. After 1949, Oelsner worked for a few years as senior official of the Hamburg city development authority. After his death in 1956, the architect Werner Kallmorgen – one of the young employees in Oelsner's planning department in the 1920s – remembered the hypocritical question among Oelsner's employees in the department whether someone like him "could probably ever sin." After Oelsner's death, Erich Lüth, the press spokesman of the Hamburg Senate, published a commemorative book for Oelsner in 1960;[11] it includes an article by Kallmorgen which mentions this anecdote.[12] The extreme secrecy of the deceased in private matters was explained in the memorial book as the virtue of a selfless public servant; "as a civil servant" Oelsner had shunned any publicity.[13] The wording "as a homosexual civil servant" would have accurately described the matter. To reveal this, however,

Wohnblock am Lunapark in Altona, 1928, entworfen von Gustav Oelsner

Apartment block at Lunapark in Altona, 1928, designed by Gustav Oelsner

die bis zu 14 Stockwerke hohen Grindelhochhäuser in Eimsbüttel (1946-56), in Deutschland die erste Anlage dieser Art.[15] Nach dem Krieg waren die drei führende Mitglieder der neu gegründeten Freien Akademie der Künste in Hamburg, die das Kulturleben entscheidend prägte; dort wirkten diese drei als einflussreiche „Strippenzieher".

Gustav Oelsners Bürgermeister in Altona vor 1933 war Max Brauer, der während des Dritten Reiches nach den USA emigrierte, danach zurückkehrte und 1946 Nachkriegsbürgermeister Hamburgs wurde.[16] Für das Gedenkbuch lieferte Brauer eine Würdigung seines früheren Bausenators und benutzte dabei so ziemlich alle Klischees, die für die Eingeweihten genau den Typus des diskreten Gentleman-Homosexuellen beschrieben, wie er der Gesellschaft vor 1968 genehm war: Junggeselle, unverheiratet, zierlicher Wuchs, Wärme des Auges, empfindlich, leicht verletzbar, kultivierte Häuslichkeit, leidenschaftlicher Koch.[17]

Nach der Machtübernahme der Nationalsozialisten war Oelsner ebenso wie Brauer und Schumacher aus seinem Amt entlassen worden. Als Jude war er nach Jahren des Abwartens zunehmend in Gefahr und suchte nach Möglichkeiten der Emigration. Es war Schumacher, der 1939 seine Verbindungen ins Ausland spielen ließ, so dass Oelsner im buchstäblichen letzten Augenblick eine Einladung in die Türkei erhielt. Er wurde Professor an der TH in Istanbul und blieb dort zehn Jahre lang.

Während des Zweiten Weltkrieges und danach war der Kontakt zwischen Oelsner und Schumacher jahrelang unterbrochen. Schumacher hatte sein eigenes Haus an die Familie Langmaack übergeben und war in eine Wohnung im Stadtteil Uhlenhorst gezogen, die wenig später im Luftkrieg zerstört wurde. Krank und unterernährt lebte er nach 1945

Wohnblock Schützenstraße in Altona, 1927, entworfen von Gustav Oelsner

Residential block Schützenstrasse in Altona, 1927, designed by Gustav Oelsner

would have severely damaged the reputation of the building senator at the time even posthumously.

The first reform of Paragraph 175 of the German Penal Code in West Germany only took effect nine years later. Those involved knew exactly what was to remain hidden, for Erich Lüth was part of a discreet trio of Social Democrats and former Nazi opponents, which included Gustav Oelsner and the likewise homosexual architect from Altona, Rudolf Lodders,[14] who, like Kallmorgen, had worked as a young architect in the Building Department under Oelsner in the 1920s. Lodders' most important work in Hamburg's reconstruction, implemented together with other architects, were the up to 14-storey Grindel high-rise buildings in Eimsbüttel (1946-56), the first of their kind in Germany.[15] After the war, the three of them were leading members of the newly founded Freie Akademie der Künste in Hamburg, which had a decisive influence on cultural life; there, they acted as influential "string-pullers."

im nahe gelegenen Lüneburg. Als man 1946 wieder Briefe von und nach Deutschland schreiben konnte, meldete sich Oelsner bei Schumacher.[18] Was folgte, waren ein intensiver Briefwechsel, der sich erhalten hat, und eine Kaskade von Paketen mit Medikamenten und Lebensmitteln, die Schumacher und seine Schwestern geschickt bekamen. Die Briefe sind Dokumente einer Freundschaft, bei der sich die stets gewahrte respektvolle Distanz zweier Herren, die sehr viktorianisch erzogen worden waren und die sich noch immer sehr förmlich mit ihren Titeln anredeten, am Ende auflockerte. Als Oelsner einen Brief mit „Lieber, lieber Herr Oberbaudirektor" begann, verstand Schumacher die Bitte um einen herzlicheren Ton und antwortete ihm mit „Du" und „Lieber Freund". Nach Schumachers Tod im November 1947 schrieb Oelsner, tief erschüttert, einen Kondolenzbrief an dessen Schwester, in dem er die gefühlte Nähe zum verstorbenen Freund zum Ausdruck brachte: „Ich habe niemanden außer meinem Bruder so lieb gehabt in diesen Jahren wie ihn, ich habe niemanden in meinem Innern so hoch geehrt wie diesen gütigen, vornehmen Menschen. Seit 24 Jahren sehe ich ihn so. Und sehe ihn hinter mir stehen und helfen und dann nach 33 mich schützen, wie er konnte. Am Ende die Hilfe, vor dem Naziterror ins Ausland zu kommen, im letzten Augenblick zu fliehen. Und jetzt? Ich bitte Sie sehr, senden Sie mir, wenn Sie können, ein Bild von ihm, daß ich ihm bei mir einen kleinen Altar der Freundschaft aufbaue."[19] Ein bewegendes Dokument von zwei schwulen Architekten, die Junggesellen und Kollegen waren und natürlich voneinander wussten.

„Edolino", Bronze-Kopie nach antiker Skulptur, im Vestibül von Fritz Schumachers Wohnhaus in Hamburg

"Edolino", bronze copy of an ancient sculpture, in the vestibule of Fritz Schumacher's residence in Hamburg

Gustav Oelsner's mayor in Altona before 1933 was Max Brauer, who emigrated to the USA during the Third Reich, then returned and became the post-war mayor of Hamburg in 1946.[16] For the commemorative book, Brauer provided a tribute to his former building senator, using pretty much all the clichés that for insiders described exactly the type of discreet gentleman-homosexual that was acceptable to pre-1968 society: bachelor, unmarried, petite build, a warm eye, sensitive, vulnerable, prefers cultivated domesticity and is a passionate cook.[17]

After the National Socialists came to power, Oelsner was dismissed from his office, as were Brauer and Schumacher. As a Jew, after years of waiting, he was increasingly in danger and was looking for ways to emigrate. It was Schumacher who in 1939 let his connections play abroad, so that Oelsner received an invitation to Turkey at the literal last moment. He became a professor at the Technical University in Istanbul and stayed there for ten years.

During the Second World War and afterwards the contact between Oelsner and Schumacher was interrupted for years. Schumacher had handed over his own house to the Langmaack family and had moved into an apartment in the Uhlenhorst district, which was destroyed shortly afterwards in the aerial war. Sick and malnourished he lived in nearby Lüneburg after 1945. In 1946, when letters to and from Germany could be exchanged again, Oelsner contacted Schumacher.[18] There was an intensive correspondence that followed, which has been preserved, and a cascade of parcels of medicine and food sent to Schumacher and his sisters. The letters are documents of a friendship in which the always maintained respectful distance between two gentlemen, who had been brought up in a very Victorian tradition and who still addressed each other very formally with their titles, loosened up at the end. When Oelsner began a letter with "Lieber, lieber Herr Oberbaudirektor" ("Dear, dear Mr. Chief Planning Officer"), Schumacher understood the request for a more cordial tone and answered him with the informal "du" and "Dear Friend." After Schumacher's death in November 1947, Oelsner, deeply shocked, wrote a letter of condolence to his sister, in which he expressed the closeness he had felt to his deceased friend: "In these years, I have loved no one but my brother like him, I have honored no one in my heart as highly as this kind, noble man. For 24 years I have seen him like this. I see him standing behind me helping and then after 1933 protecting me as he could. In the end, the help to get abroad to escape from the Nazi terror, to flee at the last moment. And now? I beg you, if you can, send me a picture of him, that I may build him a small altar of friendship in my home."[19] A moving document of two gay architects who were bachelors and colleagues and of course knew of one another.

Wolfgang Voigt

Die erste deutsche Architektin und die bauende Lesbe als Zerrbild im homophoben Roman: Emilie Winkelmann und Blanka Wild

Noch Ende des 19. Jahrhunderts gab es in Deutschland keine einzige Architektin. Ein Anfang wurde um 1900 gemacht, als man dem Drängen engagierter Frauen nachgab und ihnen gestattete, mit Sondererlaubnis an Architekturfakultäten zu hospitieren.[1] Eine von diesen war Emilie Winkelmann (1875-1951): eine junge Frau, die bewusst anderes im Sinn hatte als das obligate bürgerliche Leben einer von ihrem Mann unterhaltenen Gattin.[2] Im Zimmereibetrieb ihrer Großeltern hatte sie sich bereits mit dem praktischen Bauen vertraut gemacht. Als sie nach fünf Jahren Studium an der Technischen Hochschule Hannover 1907 die Diplomprüfung ablegen wollte, wurde ihr dies noch verwehrt; erst 1909 wurden Frauen für das volle Studium an den deutschen TH's zugelassen.[3] Emilie Winkelmann gab nicht auf, wobei ihr der Umstand zugute kam, dass die Berufsbezeichnung Architekt noch nicht geschützt war. Sie zog nach Berlin und eröffnete in der Reichshauptstadt ihr eigenes Büro, das schon bald genügend Aufträge hatte und bis zu 15 weiblichen und männlichen Angestellten Arbeit gab.

Mit ihrem 1907 etablierten eigenen Büro war Emilie Winkelmann die erste Architektin in Deutschland. Sie war rasch erfolgreich, wobei früh geknüpfte Verbindungen in die Frauenbewegung eine nicht unwichtige Rolle spielten. Emilie Winkelmann blieb zeitlebens unverheiratet. Irgendwelche Allianzen mit Männern scheint es nicht gegeben zu haben; mit großer Wahrscheinlichkeit war sie eine Lesbe. In ihrer Familie, mit der sie offenbar so wenig Kontakt wie möglich pflegte, erinnert man sich an „Tante Emilie" als „eine etwas herrische Dame mit kurzen Haaren und Hosen." Ein um 1930 entstandenes Porträtfoto zeigt sie im Profil mit konzentrierter, ernster Miene. Vielleicht, um den Gedanken an eine lesbische Verwandte gar nicht erst aufkommen zu lassen, gab man sich mit der Annahme zufrieden, die Tante sei wohl frigide.

Neben Villen und Miethäusern für ein bürgerliches Publikum entwarf sie Heime für Frauen, die sich wie sie selbst für einen Beruf entschieden hatten oder nach einem mit Arbeit verbrachten Leben nicht allein wohnen wollten. In Potsdam baute sie 1913/14 für die Genossenschaft für Frauenheimstätten ein mit modernen Service-Einrichtungen versehenes Haus für berufstätige Frauen im Ruhestand.[4] 1914 bis 1916 folgte unter der

The First German Female Architect and the Lesbian Builder as a Caricature in a Homophobic Novel: Emilie Winkelmann and Blanka Wild

At the end of the 19th century, there was still not a single female architect in Germany. A beginning was made around 1900 when the urgings of committed women were yielded to and they were allowed to sit in on lectures in the architectural faculties with a special permission.[1] One of these women was Emilie Winkelmann (1875-1951): a young woman who deliberately had something other in mind than the obligatory bourgeois life of a wife financially supported by her husband.[2] She had already familiarized herself with the practice of building in the carpentry business of her grandparents. When, after five years of studying at the Technische Hochschule in Hanover, she wanted to pass her diploma examination in 1907, however, she was still denied to do so; it was not until in 1909 that women were admitted for the full course of studies at German technical universities.[3] Emilie Winkelmann did not give up whereby she benefited from the fact that the professional title "architect" was not yet protected. She moved to Berlin and opened her own office in the German capital which soon had sufficient contracts and provided work for up to 15 female and male employees.

With her office established in 1907, Emilie Winkelmann was the first female architect in Germany. She quickly became successful and early on established connections to the women's movement played an important role in this. Emilie Winkelmann remained unmarried all her life. There appear not to have been any relationships with men; in all probability, she was a lesbian. In her family with which she apparently maintained as little contact as possible, one remembers "Aunt Emilie" as a "somewhat domineering lady with short hair and trousers." A portrait photograph taken around 1930 shows her in profile with a concentrated, serious expression. Perhaps to not even let the notion of a lesbian relative come up, one was content with the assumption that the aunt was possibly frigid.

Besides mansions and blocks of flat for a bourgeois clientele, she designed homes for women who, like her, had decided in favour of a profession or did not want to live on their own after a life spent working. In Potsdam, she designed in 1913/14 for the Genossenschaft für Frauenheimstätten a building equipped with modern service facilities for professional women in retirement.[4] From 1914 to 1916 and under the patronage of

Emilie Winkelmann, Porträtaufnahme um 1930

Emilie Winkelmann, portrait photograph around 1930

Schirmherrschaft der Kaiserin das Viktoria-Studienhaus in Charlottenburg als Wohnheim und Bildungseinrichtung für weibliche Studierende.[5]

1914 schafft sie es auf eine der prominenten Ausstellungen, die seit 1900 die Fortschritte auf den Gebieten der Gestaltung dokumentierten. Für die Internationale Buchgewerbe-Ausstellung (Bugra) in Leipzig entwarf sie das „Haus der Frau", in dem ausschließlich Entwürfe von Frauen präsentiert wurden.[6] Während sie mit Räumen für Frauen und als Pionierin im Architektenberuf aus dem Rahmen fiel, legte sie es nicht darauf an, sich der modernen Avantgarde anzuschließen. Einen Vergleich mit den Werken der männlichen Kollegen halten ihre im Reformstil der Zeit gestalteten Bauten dennoch locker aus. Winkelmann vermied eine vorgefasste Ordnungs- oder Gestaltidee, die Bauten zeigten Funktionalität und Materialität ebenso wie einen ausgeprägten Sinn für Proportionen. In die Öffentlichkeit drängte es sie nicht. Hans-Georg Lippert sieht sie unter denen, „die nicht die Lufthoheit in den Medien haben, durch ihr Tun aber trotzdem die Dinge voranbringen – vielleicht sogar wirksamer und nachhaltiger als die lauten Stimmen im Konzert."[7] Es dauerte bis 1928, bis die Kollegen sie für würdig genug hielten, in den Bund Deutscher Architekten aufgenommen zu werden.

Obwohl bis zum Ersten Weltkrieg nur sehr wenige Frauen in der Kunst auftraten oder Architektur studierten, provozierte ihr Vordringen in die kreativen Disziplinen gereizte Reaktionen bei verunsicherten Männern. Überraschend hysterisch reagierte der Kunst- und Architekturkritiker Karl Scheffler, der ansonsten als scharfsinniger Beobachter der frühen modernen Architektur und des Städtebaus bekannt war. In seinem 1908 erschienenen Buch *Die Frau und die Kunst* nannte er die Gleichberechtigung eine ansteckende Krankheit und prophezeite den Künsten den Niedergang, würden sich die Frauen gegen ihre Natur und bei schleichendem Verlust ihrer Weiblichkeit in ihnen etablieren.[8] Den Frauen, die hier den Männern eine Domäne streitig machten, sagte er

„Haus der Frau" auf der Internationalen Ausstellung für Buchgewerbe und Graphik, Leipzig 1915

"House of the Woman" at the International Exhibition of Book and Graphic Arts, Leipzig 1915

the Empress, there followed the Viktoria-Studienhaus in Charlottenburg as a hostel and educational facility for female students.[5]

In 1914, she made it into one of the prominent exhibitions which had been documenting the advances in the field of design since 1900. For the Internationale Buchgewerbe-Ausstellung (Bugra) in Leipzig, she designed the "Haus der Frau" where exclusively designs by women were shown.[6] While she fell outside the norm with rooms for women and as a pioneer in the profession of an architect, she had no interest in associating herself with the modern avant-garde. The buildings she designed in the reform style of the time do, however, easily stand a comparison with the works by her male colleagues. Winkelmann avoided preconceived ideas of order or design, the buildings showed functionality and materiality just as much as a keen sense of proportions. She did not feel the urge to be a public figure. Hans-Georg Lippert sees her among those "who do not have the sovereignty in the media but, despite this, further matters by their activities – perhaps even more efficiently and sustainably than all the loud voices in concert."[7] It took until 1928 for the colleagues to deem her worthy enough to be accepted into the Bund Deutscher Architekten.

Although, until the First World War, only a very few women appeared in the arts or studied architecture, their advance into the creative disciplines provoked irritated reactions among insecure men. The art and architecture critic Karl Scheffler, otherwise known as an astute observer of early modernist architecture and urban development, reacted in a surprisingly hysterical way. In his book *Die Frau und die Kunst* published in 1908, he called gender equality a contagious disease and predicted a decline of the arts in case women were to establish themselves in them against their nature and with the gradual loss of their femininity.[8] He predicted for the women who were here challenging a male domain a hermaphroditic change of their personalities; in the end, they would not only be threatened

eine hermaphroditische Persönlichkeitsveränderung voraus; am Ende drohe ihnen nicht nur Vermännlichung, sondern Prostitution und Lesbianismus. Eins war Scheffler besonders wichtig: Vor allem von der Architektur habe sich die Frau fernzuhalten.

Es kann kein Zufall sein, dass auf diesem Gebiet die unverhüllt frauenfeindliche Argumentation zur der Zeit entwickelt wurde, als Winkelmann und andere den Männern einen Fuß in die Tür setzten. Die Disziplin gegen die Frauen abgrenzend, forderte Scheffler für die Architektur 1909 ganz allgemein mehr Maskulinität. Die Arbeit erfülle dem Architekten die höchsten Sehnsüchte eines Mannes; ihn wünschte sich Scheffler robust, energisch, autokratisch, als einen „Mann der Tat".[9] Selbstredend würden nur echte Männer, nicht aber vermännlichte Frauen diese Rolle ausfüllen können. Gerüchte um eine eventuell nie eingestandene Homosexualität bei Scheffler lassen es auch als möglich erscheinen, dass seine Hymnen an die Maskulinität dazu dienten, Zweifel an der eigenen Männlichkeit zu zerstreuen.

Ähnlich wie er äußerte sich auch der ansonsten so besonnene Otto Bartning, als er 1911 auf die Frage „Sollen Damen bauen?" die Antwort gab, das was zur Gesundung der Baukunst nötig sei, in der Tat keine Architektinnen, sondern in höchstem Maße männliche Männer seien.[10] Im Deutschen Werkbund war die Abwehrfront nicht einheitlich. Einerseits durften die Frauenverbände in der Kölner Werkbundausstellung, die 1914 zehn Tage nach der Leipziger Bugra eröffnet wurde, ebenfalls ein „Haus der Frau" errichten. Andererseits wurde den Frauen im Jahrbuch des Bundes wiederum nahegelegt, die Architektur zu meiden und stattdessen ihrem Geschlecht angeblich gemäße, traditionelle Sparten wie die kunstgewerblichen Handarbeit zu pflegen.[11]

Als nach den Jahrzehnten des Aufbruchs in die Moderne, der unorthodoxe Lebensstile begünstigt hatte, in den 1930er-Jahren mit dem aufkommenden Faschismus eine gegenteilige Stimmung an Boden gewann, äußerte sich Scheffler erneut zu Wort. In seiner Schrift *Der neue Mensch* (1932) übte er Kritik an den Nationalsozialisten und ihrem Rassismus, aber seine Abneigung gegen kreative Frauen war so lebendig wie vorher.[12] Mit Rousseau, Goethe und Edouard Manet als Zeugen wies er sie, nun aus dem Blickwinkel einer fortgeschrittenen Moderne, erneut in die Schranken. So hätten sich in den vergangenen Jahrzehnten im Kunstgewerbe den Frauen Aufgaben aufgetan, denn dort könnten sie „mit fertigen, leicht nachzuahmenden oder zu variierenden Formen spielen." Allerdings gebe es dafür keine Basis mehr, seit die Architekten den Hausbau wieder ganzheitlich auffassen würden; folgerichtig würde dekorativer Überfluss aus den Bauten verbannt, um funktional-sachlichem Gerät Platz zu machen.[13]

Leistikowhaus in Berlin-Charlottenburg, 1907, entworfen von Emilie Winkelmann

Leistikowhaus in Berlin-Charlottenburg, 1907, designed by Emilie Winkelmann

by masculinization, but even by prostitution and lesbianism. One issue was particularly important to Scheffler: A woman had above all to keep away from architecture.

It can be no coincidence that in this field the unveiled misogynous argumentation was developed at the same time when Winkelmann and others got a foot in men's doors. Demarcating the discipline against women, in 1909 Scheffler demanded more masculinity in general for architecture. He stated that this line of work fulfilled the strongest longings of a man; Scheffler wanted the latter to be robust, vigorous, autocratic, a "man of action".[9] It went without saying that only true men but not masculinized women were able to fulfil this role. Rumours about Scheffler's perhaps never admitted homosexuality also make it appear possible that his hymns to masculinity served to resolve any doubt about his own masculinity.

The otherwise so prudent Otto Barning, when answering the question "Sollen Damen bauen?" [Should ladies build?] expressed himself in a similar way in 1911 by stating that what was needed to heal architecture was indeed not female architects but men who were masculine in the highest degree.[10] In the Deutscher Werkbund, the line of defence was not united. On the one hand, women's associations were allowed to likewise construct a "Haus der Frau" in the Cologne Werkbund exhibition which was opened ten days after the Leipzig Bugra. However, in the yearbook of the Werkbund women were recommended to avoid architecture and to, instead, cultivate fields more suited to their sex such as artisanal handicrafts.[11]

Der Roman von Johanna Böhm: *Das Haus der alleinstehenden Frauen*, 1932

The House of Single Women. *The novel by Johanna Böhm, 1932*

Despina Stratigakos verdanken wir die Wiederentdeckung des im Verlauf des gleichen kulturellen Roll-Backs entstandenen Romans *Das Haus der alleinstehenden Frauen*, erschienen 1932, verfasst von der Schweizer Autorin Johanna Böhm.[14] Als Hauptfigur sehen wir eine zur Karikatur verzerrte und mit lesbischen Attributen versehene Architektin namens Blanka Wild. Die nur ihrem Beruf ergebene kaltherzige Blanka, die selbst weder an Männern noch an Kinder interessiert ist, errichtet – nicht anders als Emilie Winkelmann zwei Jahrzehnte früher – ein Wohnheim für selbstständig lebende Frauen, das aus drei schneeweißen, mit flachen Dächern bedeckten Zeilenbauten besteht und damit leicht als Erzeugnis der klassischen Architekturmoderne zu erkennen ist. Als Vorbild dürfte die Autorin die Siedlung Neubühl vor Augen gehabt haben, die kurz zuvor in Zürich fertig geworden war; ein Pionierprojekt des Neuen Bauens in der Schweiz. Der Schutzumschlag des Buches lässt bereits das Unheil ahnen, das die Bewohnerinnen ereilen wird: Man sieht eine modern frisierte Frau mit melancholischem Gesichtsausdruck, überblendet von einer schematischen Ansicht kubistischer Flachdach-Architektur. Das Motiv ist nach links gekippt, so dass der Eindruck entsteht, dass im nächsten Moment die Frau mitsamt dem Haus kopfüber in einen Abgrund gleitet ...

Die Bewohnerschaft setzt sich aus älter gewordenen Frauen zusammen, die das richtige Leben verpasst haben und durch das unbewusste Böse dieses als „Haus des Horrors"

Siedlung Neubühl bei Zürich, fertiggestellt 1932

Neubühl housing estate near Zurich, completed in 1932

When, after decades of the awakening of modernism which had favoured unorthodox lifestyles, with the nascent fascism in the 1930s, a contrary opinion gained ground, Scheffler again had his say. In his publication *Der neue Mensch* (1932), he criticized the national socialists and their racism, but his aversion to creative women was as strong as before.[12] With Rousseau, Goethe and Édouard Manet as witnesses, he again put them into their place, now from the point of view of an advanced modernism. Thus, in the past decades, tasks had opened up for women in arts and crafts because there "they could play with ready-made, easy to imitate or varying forms." There would, however, no longer be a basis for this since architects would once again holistically view the building of houses; consequently, decorative surplus would be banned from the buildings to make room for functional-objective elements.[13]

We say here Despina Stratigakos thanks for the rediscovery of the novel *Das Haus der alleinstehenden Frauen* [The house of single women], originated in the course of the same cultural roll-back, published in 1932 and written by the Swiss Author Johanna Böhm.[14] As the protagonist, we see a female architect called Blanka Wild, twisted into a caricature and with lesbian attributes. The cold-hearted Blanka, only dedicated to her profession, who herself is interested neither in men nor in children, designed – no different from Emilie Winkelmann two decades previously – a hostel for independently living women which consists of three snow-white row houses covered with flat roofs and thus easily recognizable as the result of classic modernist architecture.

The residents are elderly women who have missed the correct life and are drawn into the abyss by the subconscious evil of this building described as a "house of horror."

gezeichneten Bauwerks in den Abgrund gezogen werden. Alle haben hier nach einem feministischen Surrogat für Familie gesucht, aber was sie finden, sind aber Alkoholismus, Wahnsinn, Suizid und Frauen, die mangels erotischer Alternativen einander in die Arme sinken. Der Tiefpunkt der Degeneration ist erreicht, als die einzige glückliche Bewohnerin während ihrer Verlobungsfeier mit einem Mann von einer eifersüchtigen Nachbarin ermordet wird. Als es schlimmer nicht mehr kommen kann, gerät die für alles verantwortliche Blanka in die Krise. Auf dem Behandlungsstuhl einer Zahnärztin, die ihr einen schmerzend verfaulten Zahn aus dem Mund entfernt, verliert sie zugleich symbolisch ihre feministische Bissigkeit. Das erlaubt ihre Läuterung, die Architektin entwickelt mütterliche Gefühle, distanziert sich von ihrem gescheiterten Haus und büßt für ihre Fehler durch den Bau eines Waisenkindern gewidmeten Heimes. Für ein erlöstes Leben ist die Zeit jedoch abgelaufen; Blankas spät erwachte Sehnsucht nach Mann und Familie bleibt unerwidert. Soweit diese reaktionäre Fiktion feministischen Unglücks, als Warnung verfasst von einer bigotten Autorin, die ansonsten Kinderbücher verfasste. Die um eine Architektin gesponnene Gruselgeschichte ist ein allerdings extremes Beispiel für homophobe Projektionen, wie sie in Zeiten der Gender-Verunsicherung zur Abwehr devianter Lebensmodelle in Umlauf kommen.

Zurück in die Wirklichkeit des 20. Jahrhunderts: Emilie Winkelmann war im Alter davon überzeugt, weltweit die erste Architektin gewesen zu sein. Dass ihr dieser Titel nicht zustand, konnte sie vermutlich nicht wissen. Kurz vor ihr hatte es die Amerikanerin Julia Morgan (1872-1957) nicht nur geschafft, als erste Frau einen Abschluss der École des Beaux-Arts in Paris zu bekommen; drei Jahre vor Winkelmann gelang es ihr, sich 1904 in San Francisco als Architektin selbstständig zu machen.[15] Ihr bekanntester Bau ist das phantasievolle Hearst Castle (1919-47) in San Simeon für einen superreichen Zeitungsverleger. Mit Julia Morgan hatte Winkelmann einiges gemeinsam; beide waren selbstbewusste Frauen, denen der zielstrebig eroberte Beruf es erlaubte, aus den bürgerlichen Konventionen auszubrechen und sich in einem männlich dominierten Umfeld zu behaupten. Beide verfügten über ein Netzwerk von Frauen, das ihnen manchen Auftrag zuführte. Auch Morgan blieb unverheiratet; über ihr Privatleben ist zu lesen: „Little is known for certain about her emotional and affectional attachments, but she is believed to have been a lesbian."[16]

All have been looking here for a feminist surrogate for a family but what they find are alcoholism, madness, suicide and women who, for lack of erotic alternatives, fall into each other's arms. Rock bottom of the degeneration is reached when the only happy resident is killed by a jealous neighbour at her engagement party to a man. When it cannot get any worse, Blanka, who is responsible for it all, enters a state of crisis. On the treatment chair of a female dentist who removes a rotten tooth, she symbolically loses her feminist mordant humour at the same time. This allows her to reform herself, the architect develops maternal feelings, distances herself from the failed hostel and makes amends for her mistakes by designing a home dedicated to orphans. Yet the time for a redeemed life has run out; Blanka's late awakened longing for a man and a family remains unrequited. That much about this reactionary fiction about feminist misery, penned as a warning by a female bigot who was otherwise writing children's books. The horror story woven around a female architect is indeed an extreme example of homophobic projections as they were circulating at a time of gender-insecurity for keeping deviant ways of life at bay.

Back to the reality of the 20th century: In old age, Emilie Winkelmann was convinced of having been the first female architect worldwide. She probably could not know that she had no claim to this title. Shortly before her, the American Julia Morgan (1872-1957) had not only succeeded in being the first woman to graduate from the École des Beaux-Arts in Paris; three years previous to Winkelmann, she managed to become self-employed as a female architect in San Francisco in 1904.[15] Her best-known building is the fanciful Hearst Castle (1919-47) in San Simeon for a super-rich newspaper publisher. Winkelmann had quite some things in common with Julia Morgan; both were self-confident women whose purposefully conquered profession allowed them to break out of the bourgeois conventions and to assert themselves in a male-dominated environment. Both had a network of women which awarded them many a contract. Morgan as well remained unmarried; one can read about her private life: "Little is known for certain about her emotional and affectional attachments, but she is believed to have been a lesbian."[16]

Ron Fuchs
Mein Zuhause soll nicht sein: Austen St. Barbe Harrison

Er „war eine edle Persönlichkeit mit seinem fein ausgeprägten, byzantinischen Kaiserkopf und der athletischen Ruhe seiner hohen Gestalt. Seine funkelnden Augen und sein lebhafter Humor überspielten jedoch die Strenge seiner Erscheinung."[1] So beschreibt der Schriftsteller Lawrence Durrell 1957 den britischen Architekten Austen St. Barbe Harrison (1891-1976), nachdem er ihn in seinem Haus in Lapithos auf Zypern besucht hatte. Harrisons Werdegang als typische Karriere der Kolonialzeit zusammenzufassen wäre zutreffend; zugleich wäre eine solche Beschreibung zu trocken, um ihm damit wirklich gerecht zu werden.[2] Gleichwohl sind damit die Schauplätze – zumeist britische Besatzungen im Nahen Osten und rund um das Mittelmeer – wie auch der Zeitraum seiner Karriere – vom Zenit des britischen Empire nach dem Ersten Weltkrieg bis zu seinem Untergang nach dem Zweiten Weltkrieg – benannt.

Das bedeutendste Kapitel von Harrisons Karriere ist dabei zweifellos seine Tätigkeit als Architekt im Public Works Department des Mandatsgebiets Palästina (1922-1937). Die in dieser Zeit entstandene High Commissioner's Residence (1931) und das Palestine Archaeological Museum (1937, heute Rockefeller Museum), beide in Jerusalem, gehören zu den besten Arbeiten britischer Architekten in der Zwischenkriegszeit. Seine Karriere nach der Station Palästina umfasst wiederum eine Reihe von Großprojekten, die mit einer Ausnahme alle außerhalb Großbritanniens entstanden.[3] Dazu gehören das Nuffield College in Oxford (1938-58), ein Plan für den Wiederaufbau von Valletta auf Malta (1943) und – sein größtes Projekt – die Gold Coast University in Legon an der Goldküste, dem heutigen Ghana (begonnen 1949).[4]

Während seines Studiums in Montreal sowie an der Londoner Universität unter Stanley Davenport Adshead scheint Harrison ein von der Beaux-Arts-Tradition inspiriertes, rationalistisches Denken verinnerlicht zu haben, an dem er während seiner gesamten Karriere festhielt. Auch die progressive britische Architektur der 1920er-Jahre wie die späten Arbeiten von Edwin Lutyens oder das Werk von Charles Holden dürften ihm als Vorbild gedient haben. Doch bei Harrison verband sich der britische Rationalismus und dessen elementares Formenvokabular mit einer regionalistischen Sensibilität für lokale Landschaft und einheimische Architekturen, die er mit intensiver Hingabe und Engagement studierte. Dies fügte sich gut in die allgemeine Vorliebe der britischen Kolonialherren für auf den Ort bezogene Gesten in der Architektur ein.[5] Es war Harrisons

My Home Is Not To Be:
Austen St. Barbe Harrison

He was a noble personage, with his finely featured Byzantine emperor's head and the spare athletic repose of his tall figure. But the austerity was belied by a twinkling eye and brisk lively humours."[1] This is how the British architect Austen St. Barbe Harrison (1891-1976) is described by the writer Lawrence Durrell in 1957, after visiting him in his house in Lapithos, Cyprus. "A colonial career" would rightly sum up Harrison's career, but this would be too dry an observation to do it justice.[2] One should mention the scene – mostly British possessions in the Middle East and around the Mediterranean – and the period – from the zenith of the Empire after World War I to its demise after World War II.

Harrison's greatest achievements belong to his work as architect in the Public Works Department of Mandate Palestine (1922-1937), and his High Commissioner's Residence (1931), and the Palestine Archaeological Museum (1937, now Rockefeller Museum) both in Jerusalem, should rank with the best work of British architects of the interwar era. His post Palestinian career includes a number of large projects, all but one outside Britain.[3] Among these are Nuffield College, Oxford (1938–58), a post-war reconstruction town plan for Valletta, Malta (1943), and – his greatest undertaking – the Gold Coast University, in Legon, the Gold Coast (now Ghana, begun 1949). Most of these projects were designed in partnership with Pearce Hubbard and Thomas S. Barnes, with Harrison as the dominant figure.[4]

In his studies in Montreal and in London University, under Stanley Davenport Adshead, Harrison seems to have absorbed Beaux Arts inspired rationalistic thinking, which he kept adhered throughout his career. British progressive architecture of the 1920s, such as Edwin Lutyens' later work, or Charles Holden, must have served as a model as well. However, with Harrison, rationalism and "elemental manner" were combined with a regionalist sensitivity to local landscapes and indigenous architectural idioms, which he studied with intense dedication and involvement. This meshed well with general British preference for localizing gestures in architecture.[5] It was Harrison's engagement with foreign, sun-drenched landscapes that produced his uniqueness as an architect. Harrison's aesthetic strategy was most successful in Palestine, perhaps because the simple domed volumes of the Palestinian vernacular readily lent themselves to his abstracting treatment. The Archaeological Museum in Jerusalem, with its domed and vaulted turrets, serenely looks over the intramural city, offering a refined and perfected paraphrase of the historic townscape, an image of heavenly Jerusalem, as it were.

Auseinandersetzung mit fremden, sonnenverwöhnten Landschaften, die seine einzigartige Architektsprache hervorbrachte. Harrisons ästhetische Strategie war dabei in Palästina am erfolgreichsten, vielleicht weil die einfachen gewölbten Volumina der einheimischen, anonymen Architektur sich besonders für seine abstrahierende Behandlung eigneten. Das Archäologische Museum in Jerusalem mit seinen Kuppeln und gewölbten Türmen blickt gelassen über die Stadt und bietet eine raffinierte und perfektionierte Paraphrase des historischen Stadtbildes, sozusagen ein Abbild des Himmlischen Jerusalem.

Es scheint, dass Harrison schon früh eine Karriere im Ausland plante. So suchte er nach dem Ende seines Universitätsstudiums nach Arbeitserfahrungen in fernen Ländern. Unter anderem arbeitete er einige Monate in Lutyens' Indien-Büro in London und schloss sich 1919 einer britischen Delegation von Fachleuten für den Wiederaufbau nach dem Krieg in Griechenland an. 1922 meldete er sich auf eine Suchanzeige des Office of the Crown Agents, wurde in den Kolonialdienst aufgenommen und als Architekt für das Public Works Department der britischen Mandatsregierung nach Palästina entsandt. Nachdem er England für diese neue Aufgabe verlassen hatte, kehrte er zeitlebens nur noch für kurze Aufenthalte in seine Heimat zurück. Die meiste Zeit verbrachte er fortan im Mittelmeerraum, in orientalischen Ländern, und lebte unter anderem in Jerusalem, Kairo, Zypern, Malta und Athen. Er war sicher nicht der erste Europäer, der der Anziehungskraft des Orients folgte, aber er band sein Leben enger daran als andere.

Harrisons Karriere brachte ihn in Kontakt mit zahlreichen Persönlichkeiten von Rang – Kolonialbeamten, Architekten, Künstlern und Planern, Archäologen und anderen Briten im Nahen Osten –, von denen viele zu persönlichen Freunden wurden. Der Chef der Mandatsregierung, High Commissioner Lord Plummer, betraute ihn mit dem Bau seiner Residenz und des Archäologischen Museums. Die Liste von Bekanntschaften umfasste darüber hinaus Ronald Storrs, den Gouverneur von Jerusalem, sowie die Architekten Charles Robert Ashbee[6], Erich Mendelsohn und in Ägypten Hasan Fathy, der ein enger Freund wurde. Auch mit dem Grafiker und Bildhauer Eric Gill, den Harrison nach Jerusalem einlud, um von ihm Flachreliefs für das Archäologische Museum zu bekommen, entstand eine lebenslange Freundschaft. Gill, der keine Scheu vor erotischen Themen hatte, entwarf für Harrison auch ein Exlibris mit durchaus homoerotischem Unterton.

Sein Privatleben hütete Harrison eifersüchtig, so dass heute kaum etwas über die Umstände und Hintergründe seines privaten Daseins bekannt ist.[7] „Er ist ein extremer Einsiedler – aber kann man ihm das verübeln?", schrieb Durrell nach dem Besuch bei Harrison auf Zypern. „Ein geselliger Typ oder ein Vereinsmensch würde sich wohl nicht so weit von den Mitmenschen entfernen, wie es er tat."[8] Harrison unternahm gern lange einsame Spaziergänge in der Wildnis, eine Angewohnheit, die er fast sein ganzes Leben

Austen St. Barbe Harrison, fotografiert von Dimitri Papadimos, 1970er-Jahre

Austen St. Barbe Harrison, photographed by Dimitri Papadimos, 1970s

It seems that Harrison planned for an overseas career at an early stage. Once he finished his university studies, he proceeded to seek experience in far-off lands. He worked for several months in Lutyens' India office in London, and in 1919 joined an English Technical Mission for post-war reconstruction in Greece (under T. H. Mawson). In 1922 he responded to a Crown Agents' "wanted" notice, was accepted to the Colonial Service and dispatched to Palestine as architect to the Public Works Department of the newly established civil government of the British Mandate there. Having left England for this new job, he would not return home but for short visits. He spent most of his life in Mediterranean, Oriental, lands, living variously in Jerusalem, Cairo, Cyprus, Malta and Athens. He would not be the first European to have followed the allure of the Orient, but his life was centred in its territories.

Harrison's life brought him in contact with a wide gallery of figures of distinction – British colonial officials, architects, artists and planners, archaeologists, and other British Expatriates in the Middle East – many of whom became personal friends. High Commissioner Lord Plummer entrusted him with the major projects of the Residence and the Archaeological Museum. The list includes Ronald Storrs, the Governor of Jerusalem, the architects Charles Robert Ashbee,[6] Erich Mendelsohn, and in Egypt, Hasan Fathy, who became a friend. Eric Gill, the graphic designer, and sculptor, whom Harrison invited to Jerusalem to create the bas-reliefs for the Museum, kept his friendship. Gill, never shying eroticism, designed for Harrison an exlibris with a whimsical homoerotic touch.

Harrison was always jealous of his privacy, so his personal life and motivations would never be fully accessible.[7] "He's an awful recluse – can one blame him?" wrote Durrell, describing Harrison in his Cyprus days. "One wouldn't come so far from the haunts of

lang beibehielt. „Wie ich die Wüsten, die leeren Räume und die Sonne liebe!", ließ er in einem Brief, in dem er von einem Spaziergang in der ägyptischen Wüste berichtete, den Maler David Bomberg wissen.[9] Die gleiche Sehnsucht nach dem Erhabenen, die in diesem Brief anklingt, liegt vielleicht auch seinen besten architektonischen Arbeiten zugrunde. „Ich bin wirklich ein geselliger Mensch, trotz des gegenteiligen Anscheins", kommentierte Harrison in einem seiner Briefe, „nur muss ich in der Lage sein, von der Gesellschaft wegzukommen, wenn sie mich zu ersticken droht."[10] In Jerusalem mied er notorisch gesellschaftliche Termine, sogar höchst offizielle Einladungen ins Government House schlug er aus. Als er zu einer Cocktailparty bei Erich Mendelsohn in Jerusalem eingeladen war, antwortete er: „Ich gehe nie zu Hahn-[Cock]-und-Henne-Partys." „Er mochte keine Frauen", bemerkte dazu Luise, die Gattin Mendelsohns.[11] Einen seltenen Einblick in privatere Verbindungen bieten gelegentlich nur Harrisons Briefe, etwa seine Beschreibung des berühmten Kairoer Hauses des britischen Sanitätsoffiziers John Gayer-Andersons, das dieser mit traditionellen ägyptischen Möbeln, Teppichen und Kunstwerken ausgestattet hatte, und seines bunten Hofstaats von jungen, Djellaba tragenden Dienern.[12]

Um 1935 lernte Harrison in Kairo einen griechisch-stämmigen jungen Mann kennen: Dimitri Papadimos (1918-1994), den er fortan förderte und unterstützte. So half er ihm 1939, nach Paris zu gehen, um dort Kinematografie zu studieren.[13] Später machte sich Papadimos einen Namen als Fotograf.[14] Die Verbindung zwischen den beiden hielt für den Rest ihres Lebens.

Als Harrison 1937 (verärgert) seinen Posten beim Palestine Public Works Department verließ, glaubte er, dass seine berufliche Laufbahn beendet sei. Tatsächlich genoss er aber noch weitere zwanzig Jahre als angesehener Architekt mit einer erfolgreichen Baupraxis. Doch als sich nach dem Zweiten Weltkrieg eine neue Weltordnung abzeichnete, zerbröckelte das koloniale System allmählich unter seinen Füßen. Die Orte, an denen er gelebt hatte – Palästina, Zypern, Ägypten und sogar Malta –, wurden zunehmend unwirtlich oder von politischen Unruhen und Gewalt überrollt. Man kann nur darüber spekulieren, ob Harrison wahrnahm, dass mit dem sich stetig dekolonisierenden Empire auch die Möglichkeit, einen schwulen Lebensstil zu verfolgen, immer mehr unter Druck geriet. Selbst im Mutterland des Empires sah es damals nicht besser aus.[15]

Der Gedanke, dass er gezwungen sein könnte, wieder in England leben zu müssen, ließ Harrison einen „kalten Schauer" über den Rücken laufen. „Wie kann ich an einem Ort glücklich sein, an dem die Sonne nicht immer scheint?", schrieb er an seine Mutter.[16] An einen Freund, den Physiker Markus Reiner in Palästina, schrieb er wiederum: „Ich versuche, mir einzureden, dass ich wie ein Jude dazu bestimmt bin, ein Wanderer auf dieser Erde zu sein. Meine Zuhause soll nicht sein", und fügte hinzu: „Mir fehlt – hat immer

Palestine Archaeological Museum (heute Rockefeller Archaeological Museum) in Jerusalem, 1938, entworfen von Austen St. Barbe Harrison

Palestine Archaeological Museum (now Rockefeller Archaeological Museum) in Jerusalem, 1938, designed by Austen St. Barbe Harrison

man if one were a gregarious or clubby type."[8] Taking long solitary walks in the wilderness was a habit that he kept for many years. "How I love the deserts, the empty spaces & the sun," he exclaimed in a letter to the painter David Bomberg reporting a walk in the Egyptian desert.[9] This yearning for the sublime perhaps underlies his best architectural work. "I am really a sociable person despite appearances," Harrison commented in one of his letters, "Only I must be able to get away from society which suffocates me."[10] In Jerusalem he notoriously avoided social events, even at Government House. When invited to a cocktail party at Erich Mendelsohn's in Jerusalem he responded: "I never go to Cock or Hen Parties." "He did not like women," remarked Luise, Mendelsohn's wife.[11] A rare glimpse into more private associations is offered occasionally in his letters, e.g. his description of John Gayer-Anderson's old Arab house in Cairo and its colorful household of galabiya wearing boy servants.[12] Around 1935 Harrison met in Cairo an Egyptian born Greek youth, Dimitri Papadimos (1918-1994), whom he cultivated and supported. In 1939 he helped Papadimos go to Paris to study cinematography.[13] Papadimos would eventually make a name for himself as a photographer.[14] The bond between the two lasted for the rest of Harrison's life.

In 1937, when Harrison left his post at the Palestine Public Works Department (in a huff), he believed that his professional career had ended, but in fact he enjoyed another twenty years of prestigious architectural practice. However, as a new world order was emerging after World War II, the colonial system gradually crumbled under his feet. The places where he had lived – Palestine, Cyprus, Egypt, even Malta – each became unwel-

gefehlt – Ihre geistige Elastizität und Anpassungsfähigkeit an jede Umgebung; und ich habe nicht Ihre Art der Flucht aus den Verstrickungen dieser Welt in die seltene Luft der höheren Mathematik. Sie werden lachen, wenn ich von Verstrickungen spreche – Sie, der Sie zwei Frauen hatten und ich weiß nicht, wie viele Kinder ins Meer des Lebens geworfen haben. Aber ich nehme an, dass diese familiären Verpflichtungen für Sie den Rhythmus und die Disziplin geschaffen haben, ohne die der Mensch wie ein Korken im rauen Meer ist. Die Praxis der Architektur – fast ihre Anbetung – gab mir diese Disziplin."[17]

Während Harrison den architektonischen Prinzipien, die er sich in den 1910er-Jahren zu eigen gemacht hatte, treu blieb, geriet er gleichzeitig und zunehmend in Widerspruch mit dem Zeitgeist. Das umfangreiche Projekt für die Universität von Ghana, das er in Legon, einem Stadtteil von Accra, realisierte, wurde in den Architekturpublikationen der Zeit konsequent ignoriert. „Ich schließe die Tür zur Architektur", schrieb er Ende der 1960er-Jahre verbittert an einen Freund.[18] In seinen letzten Jahren beschäftigte er sich in Zusammenarbeit mit der British School of Archaeology in Athen damit, eine Geschichte des Johanniterordens auf Rhodos zu schreiben, die nie veröffentlicht wurde. Er starb 1976, gepflegt von Dimitri Papadimos und seiner Frau in deren Haus in Athen.

Exlibris von Austen St. Barbe Harrison, gestaltet von Eric Gill

Austen St. Barbe Harrison bookplate, designed by Eric Gill

Griechenland-Relief am Palestine Archaeological Museum, von Eric Gill

Greece relief at the Palestine Archaeological Museum, by Eric Gill

coming or was overtaken by violence. One may speculate that he also discovered that the freedom to pursue a gay lifestyle in the steadily decolonizing Empire become ever more restricted. Nor did it improve in England.[15]

The thought that he may be obliged to live in England sent a "cold shiver" down Harrison's back. "How can I be happy in a place where the sun does not always shine?" he wrote to his mother.[16] To a friend, the Physicist Markus Reiner in Palestine, he wrote: "I am trying to persuade myself that like a Jew, I am destined to be a wanderer on this earth. My 'home' is not to be," adding: "I lack – have always lacked – your mental elasticity and adaptability to any environment and I have not your way of escape from this world's entanglement into the rare air of higher mathematics. You will laugh to hear me talk of entanglements – you who have had two wives and launched I don't know how many children into the sea of life. But I suppose these family responsibilities have created for you the rhythm and discipline without which man is like a cork in a rough sea. The practice of architecture – almost worship of it – gave me this discipline."[17]

At the same time, as Harrison remained loyal to the architectural principles, he had adopted in the 1910s, he found himself increasingly out of pace with the spirit of the times. The extensive project for a University of Ghana that he realized in Legon, Accra, was consistently ignored in architectural publications of the time. "I close the door on architecture," he wrote bitterly to a friend in the late 1960s.[18] In his last years he occupied himself, in association with the British School of Archaeology in Athens, in writing a history of the Order of St. John in Rhodes (never published). He died in 1976, tended by Dimitri Papadimos and his wife in their house in Athens.

Wolfgang Voigt

Die Jagd auf schwule Architekturlehrer - drei amerikanische Fälle: Bruce Goff, Charles Moore, Lionel Pries

Norman, eine Kleinstadt im US-Bundesstaat Oklahoma, im Jahre 1950: So ein Haus hatte noch niemand gesehen. Die Beschreibung fällt schwer, weil das Auge nichts findet, was es als Bestandteil eines Einfamilienhauses zu kennen glaubt. Man sieht zylindrische Glaskörper, die aus einer zyklopischen Mauer herauswachsen. Im weiten Bogen beginnt sie niedrig, um sich als Spirale in einem immer enger werdenden Radius emporzuwinden, bis sie im Kern einen stählernen Mast erreicht. Im Inneren dieses Schneckenhauses gibt es keine Zimmer. Stattdessen gibt es fünf Plattformen, die an Seilen und in aufsteigender Ordnung am Mast hängen. Die Bauherren Gene und Nancy Bavinger waren ein auf absolute Individualität erpichtes Künstlerpaar, das in Bruce Goff (1904-1982) einen gleichgesinnten Architekten fand.[1]

Goffs gebautes Werk, das unter dem Einfluss von Frank Lloyd Wright entstand, lässt sich als Serie flamboyanter Unikate beschreiben. Mit oft exotischen Materialien und stets singulären Formen erfüllte Goff seinen zum Wagnis entschlossenen Bauherren den amerikanischen Traum der unbedingten Freiheit. Die Fantasie eines Antonio Gaudí fand bei ihm eine exzentrische, aber stets organisch grundierte Fortsetzung. Goff ist ein Fall, bei dem sexuelle Abweichung mit kreativem Außenseitertum in der Architektur überzeugend zusammengehen. In der prüden, von Präsident Eisenhower geprägten Nachkriegszeit und noch mehr im konservativen mittleren Westen der USA konnte dies aufs Glatteis führen. Das von den Denunziationen des McCarthyismus vergiftete soziale Klima bedrohte nicht nur die politische Abweichung von der Norm.

Seine Homosexualität behandelte Goff mit Diskretion. 1942 hatte man ihn als Lehrer an die School of Architecture der Universität von Oklahoma berufen; später wurde er deren Chairman. 1955 trat er von diesem Amt zurück und verließ die Schule, offiziell aus gesundheitlichen Gründen. Niemand verstand es, denn die Schule florierte; willige Bauherren hatte er genug und krank wirkte er überhaupt nicht. Den wahren Grund enthüllte wenige Tage später die lokale Presse in genüsslich ausgebreiteten Details. Um ihn als Homosexuellen bloßzustellen, hatte ihm die Polizei eine Falle gestellt. Die Kontaktaufnahme zu einem nicht volljährigen, jungen Mann brachte ihn für kurze Zeit in Haft. Goff plädierte auf „nicht schuldig". Studenten, Kollegen aus der Fakultät und sogar der Präsident der Universität

The Hunt for Gay Architecture Professors - Three American Cases: Bruce Goff, Charles Moore, Lionel Pries

Norman, a small town in the US state of Oklahoma, in the year 1950: Nobody had ever seen such a house. Describing it is difficult since the eye does not find anything which it can take to be a component of a single-family house. One sees cylindrical glass volumes which grow out of a cyclopean wall. In a wide curve, the latter starts low to spiral up in an increasingly tighter radius until its core reaches a steel mast. There are no rooms inside this snail shell. Instead, there are five platforms hanging on ropes and in increasing size from the mast. The building clients Gene and Nancy Bavinger were an artist couple keen on absolute individuality who found in Bruce Goff (1904-1982) a like-minded architect.[1]

Goff's built work, which originated under the influence of Frank Lloyd Wright, can be described as a series of flamboyant unique designs. With often exotic materials and always singular forms, Goff fulfilled the American dream of absolute freedom of his daring building clients. The imagination of someone like Antonio Gaudí found in him an eccentric but always organically based continuation. Goff is a case where sexual deviation is convincingly combined with a creative kind of misfitness in architecture. In the prudish postwar period influenced by President Eisenhower and even more so in the conservative middle west of the USA, this could easily lead onto thin ice. The social climate poisoned by the denunciations of McCarthyism threatened not only the political deviation from the norm.

Goff treated his homosexuality with discretion. In 1942, he had been appointed as a professor to the School of Architecture of the university of Oklahoma; subsequently, he became its chairman. In 1955, he resigned from this office and left the school, officially for reasons of health. Nobody could understand it since the school flourished; he had enough building clients and did not at all give the impression of being ill. A few days later, the local press revealed the real reason with gleefully described details. The police had set a trap to expose him as a homosexual. Seeking contact with an underaged young man caused his imprisonment for a short time. Goff pleaded "not guilty". Students, colleagues from the faculty and even the president of the university stood up for him. Expecting of a long tug of war before court, he preferred to pay a fine.[2] In addition, he was banned for one month from the state of Oklahoma: "in true Wild West fashion –

Bruce Goff, 1947

setzten sich für ihn ein. In Erwartung eines langen Tauziehens vor Gericht zog er es vor, eine Strafe zu bezahlen.² Außerdem wurde er für einen Monat aus dem Staat Oklahoma verbannt: „in true Wild West fashion – asked to leave the town."³ Die Stadt verließ er für immer. Bruce Goffs akademische Karriere war ruiniert, aber viele seiner Bauherren hielten ihm die Treue, so dass in der Folge noch zahlreiche extravagante Goff-Häuser entstanden.

Mit homophoben Hochschulkollegen hatte auch Charles Moore (1925-1993), einer der intellektuellen Väter der Postmoderne, zu kämpfen. Als das Magazin *Progressive Architecture* 1979 die US-amerikanische Architektenschaft nach dem damals einflussreichsten unter ihren Kollegen befragte, bekam Moore die meisten Stimmen.⁴ Moore studierte in den 1950er-Jahren an der Architekturschule von Princeton, einer der traditionsreichen Schulen der Ivy League an der Ostküste. 1957 zum Assistant Professor befördert, machte er aus seiner Abneigung gegen eine inzwischen zur Orthodoxie erstarrte Moderne keinen Hehl. Architekturgeschichte wollte er nicht als faktengestützte Disziplin des Wissens verstanden wissen, sondern als Quelle poetischer Bilder existierender Bauten, die man benutzen konnte, um mit Phantasie und Ironie einprägsame Orte neu zu erschaffen.⁵

Der Moderne-treuen Leitung der Schule war nicht nur seine provokative Lehre nach zwei Jahren zu viel, auch Moores Homosexualität wurde 1959 „behind closed doors" zum Problem erklärt. Im feinen Princeton waren die Mittel, um einen schwulen Professor in die Wüste zu schicken, subtiler als im Mittleren Westen von Oklahoma. Gegenüber der Administration wurde er als unberechenbar und deviant denunziert und es wurde empfohlen, seinen Vertrag nicht zu verlängern. In einem vertraulichen Schreiben an den Präsidenten der Universität wurde die Entscheidung mit vielsagenden Umschreibungen

Bavinger House in Norman/Oklahoma, 1950, entworfen von Bruce Goff

Bavinger House in Norman/Oklahoma, 1950, designed by Bruce Goff

asked to leave the town."[3] He left the town forever. Bruce Goff's academic career was ruined but many of his clients remained loyal to him so that, subsequently, numerous extravagant Goff houses were still built.

Charles Moore (1925-1993), one of the intellectual fathers of postmodernism, also had to fight against homophobic university colleagues. When the *Progressive Architecture* magazine asked among American architects in 1979 who, at the time, was the most influential among their colleagues, Moore received the most votes.[4] Moore studied in the 1950s at the school of architecture of Princeton, one of the most traditional Ivy League universities on the East Coast. Promoted to assistant professor in 1957, he made no secret of his aversion against the kind of modernism which had meanwhile been frozen into orthodoxy. He did not want architectural history to be understood as an evidence-based discipline of knowledge but as a source of poetic images of existing buildings which one could use to newly create memorable places with imagination and irony.[5]

After two years, the directors of the school, who adhered to modernism, found not only his provocative teaching too much but they also declared Moore's homosexuality "behind closed doors" to be a problem in 1959. In the refined town of Princeton, the means of sending a gay professor packing where more subtle than in the middle west of Oklahoma. In front of the administration, Moore was denounced as erratic and deviant and it was recommended not to extend his contract. In a confidential letter to the president of the university, the decision was justified with telling paraphrases: "Single at 35, Moore did not seem stable or mature in respect to his relationships with students, and while brilliant, was an uncertain quantity personally for the long pull."[6] One expressively wanted

Eine Architekturphantasie
von Charles Moore,
1970er-Jahre

*An architectural fantasy
by Charles Moore, 1970s*

begründet: „Mit 35 Jahren noch Junggeselle schien uns Moore nicht stabil und reif genug im Verhältnis zu den Studenten; obwohl brillant, war er uns als Person auf die Dauer eine zu unsichere Größe."[6] Ausdrücklich wollte man kein „Klima wie an Kunstschulen" einreißen lassen, weil diese offenbar im Ruf allzu lockerer Sitten standen.[7]

Den Hinauswurf hat Moore gut überstanden. Seine Lehre konnte er schon wenig später im liberalen Berkeley in Kalifornien fortsetzen. Dort entstanden unter anderem gemeinsam mit seinen Kollegen Donlyn Lyndon, William Turnbull und Richard Whitaker (MLTW) die legendären Bauten der Sea Ranch, die ihm internationale Aufmerksamkeit bescherten. Die Hintergründe des erzwungenen Abschieds aus Princeton wurden erst lange nach seinem Tod publik.

Weit schlimmer traf es den in San Francisco und Seattle tätigen Lionel H. Pries (1897-1968). Während Goff und Moore ihren festen Platz in der Architekturgeschichte bekamen, ist dieser talentierte Entwerfer und leidenschaftliche Architekturlehrer bis heute eine nur an der US-amerikanischen Westküste bekannte Figur. Seit 1928 lehrte er an der Architekturabteilung der Universität des Staates Washington in Seatte. Sein berühmtester Schüler war ohne Zweifel Minoru Yamasaki, dessen Hauptwerk, das World Trade Center in New York, auf doppelte Weise Geschichte machte: als zeitweise höchstes Gebäude der Welt und als Zielscheibe der Angriffe vom 11. September 2001.[8]

Seine Homosexualität hatte Pries auf so perfekte Weise versteckt, dass an der Schule nur wenige davon wussten. Diese schützten ihn zugleich durch diskretes Schweigen. Zum Verhängnis wurde ihm 1958 allerdings ein Ausflug nach Los Angeles, wo er an einem

Charles Moore, 1977

"to avoid a climate too often associated with art centers" from spreading since these apparently had the reputation of all too lax morals.[7]

Moore weathered the dismissal well. Already a little later, he was able to continue his teaching at the liberal Berkeley University in California. This is where, among other things, together with his colleagues Donlyn Lyndon, William Turnbull and Richard Whitaker (MLTW), the legendary buildings of the Sea Ranch were designed which earned him international recognition. The backgrounds of the forced leave from Princeton only became public knowledge long after his death.

Lionel H. Pries (1897-1968), working in San Francisco and Seattle, had a far worse fate. While Goff and Moore were assigned a permanent place in architectural history, the talented designer and passionate architecture professor remains to this day a figure only known at the US American West Coast. Since 1928, he had been teaching at the architecture department of the university of the State of Washington in Seattle. Without any doubt, his most famous student was Minoru Yamasaki whose main work, the World Trade Center in New York, made history in two ways: as the, for a time, highest building in the world and as the target of the 11th September 2001 attacks.[8]

Pries had hidden his homosexuality in such a perfect way that only a few people knew about it at the university. They simultaneously protected him by discrete silence. An excursion to Los Angeles in 1958, however, became his downfall where he was caught by the police at a gay meeting point. The university was sent the police report. Based on the rules of the institution and a clause regarding "moral turpitude", he was faced with

Lionel H. Pries, ca. 1960

schwulen Treffpunkt einem Lockvogel der Polizei ins Netz ging. Die Schule erhielt den Polizeibericht zugesandt. Gestützt auf das Regelwerk der Institution und einen Paragraphen über „moralische Verworfenheit" („moral turpitude") verlangte man von ihm, seinen Rücktritt zu erklären und die Schule zu verlassen, sonst würde der Bericht an die Presse weitergegeben.[9] Nach 30 Jahren als angesehener und von den Schülern vielfach verehrter Lehrer verschwand Pries so von einem Tag auf den anderen von der Bildfläche.

Wie schon bei Bruce Goff lautete die offizielle Version: „Erkrankung". Nur wenige Jahre vor seinem regulären Ausscheiden verlor Pries damit alle Ansprüche auf eine Altersversorgung, die ihm von der Universität zugestanden hätte. Er verkaufte sein Haus und verdingte sich als Zeichner in einer Werbefirma. Er verstarb 1968 einsam und verbittert. Aus dem Gedächtnis der Schule war er gestrichen, bis sich die Überzeugung durchsetzte, dass einem der besten Lehrer der Schule Unrecht widerfahren war. So gibt es seit 1981 zu seinen Ehren eine Annual Lecture. 1984 wurde außerdem ein Lionel Pries Teaching Award ins Leben gerufen und 1988 sein Name auf der Ehrentafel im Auditorium der Schule angebracht.[10]

Als Lehrer waren schwule Architekten erhöhten Risiken ausgesetzt. Getroffen hat es sicher nicht nur die hier genannten. Jedoch dürfte sich die Mehrzahl der Fälle im Verborgenen abgespielt haben. Und sicher nicht nur in den Vereinigten Staaten von Amerika! Auch in Europa wurden nach den Erschütterungen des Zweiten Weltkrieges Sittsamkeit und Kleinfamilie als neue gesellschaftliche Leitbilder besonders groß geschrieben, so dass Homosexuelle noch mehr als vorher zur Zielscheibe wurden. Die Geschichte des Braunschweiger Architekturprofessors Friedrich Wilhelm Kraemer mag einen vergleichbaren deutschen Fall aufzeigen.[11]

James W. O'Brien: Raum für Michelangelos David in einem Kunstmuseum, 1948, Studentenentwurf bei Lionel H. Pries

James W. O'Brien: Space for Michelangelo's David in an Art Museum, 1948, student design of Lionel H. Pries

the alternative of handing in his resignation and leave the university or having the report passed on to the press.⁹ After 30 years as a respected teacher frequently worshipped by the students, Pries disappeared from one day to the next.

As already in the case of Bruce Goff, the official version was: "illness". Just a few years before his regular retirement, Pries thus lost all entitlements to a pension which the university would have owed him. He sold his house and took a job as a draughtsman in an advertising firm. He died in 1968, lonesome and embittered. He was erased from the memory of the university until the conviction prevailed that one of the best teachers of the school had been the victim of an injustice. Since 1981, there has thus been an Annual Lecture in his honour. In 1984, a Lionel Pries Teaching Award was furthermore initiated, and his name was inscribed on a commemorative plaque in the university auditorium in 1988.¹⁰

As teachers, gay architects have been exposed to heightened risks. Certainly not only the ones mentioned here have been affected. The majority of the cases, however, probably took place in secrecy. And definitely not only in the United States of America! In Europe as well, after the turmoil of the Second World War morality and the nuclear family were particularly writ large as the new social leitmotifs so that homosexuals became targets even more than before. The story of the Braunschweig architecture professor Friedrich Wilhelm Kraemer may well describe a comparable German case.¹¹

Uwe Bresan

Nur die Sonne war Zeuge: Barry Dierks und Eric Sawyer

Miramar – Meeresblick – heißt der kleine Küstenort westlich von Cannes an der Côte d'Azur. Von der Croisette über die Corniche d'Or dauert die Fahrt hierher weniger als eine halbe Stunde. Rechts der legendären Küstenstraße ragen die bizarren, roten Felsformationen des Esterel-Massivs, dem die kurvenreiche Passage um 1900 mühevoll abgerungen wurde, in die Höhe, während links das steinige Terrain steil zum Mittelmeer hin abfällt. In Miramar führt die Corniche in einer lang gestreckten Kurve um den Gipfel des Col de l'Esquillon herum, dessen zerklüftete Ausläufer unterhalb der Straße als Pointe de l'Esquillon aus dem Meer heraus ragen. Es ist vielleicht der spektakulärste Abschnitt der Straße, denn das Gelände stürzt hier so schroff zum Meer hin ab, dass es aus dem Auto heraus so scheint, als könnte man schon beim kleinsten Fahrfehler über die niedrige Seitenmauer hinweg direkt ins Meer hinab stürzen. Und genau hier versteckt sich – auf einem schmalen Streifen steinigen Landes unterhalb der Straße – eines der bemerkenswertesten Häuser der Côte d'Azur. Gebaut hat es der amerikanische Architekt Barry Dierks (1899-1960) im Jahr 1926 für sich selbst. Es war sein erstes Haus und der Beginn einer glänzenden Karriere als Architekt der Schönen und Reichen. Mehr als 100 zum Teil äußerst imposanter Villen und Landhäuser entlang der französischen Rieviera können wir heute dem Amerikaner zuordnen.[1] Das vergleichsweise kleine Haus in Miramar, das er mit Mitte zwanzig baute, gilt jedoch – auch aufgrund seiner spektakulären Lage – seit jeher als Dierks' geniales Hauptwerk.

Aus dem Städtchen Miramar, das sich westlich des Col de l'Esquillon erstreckt, führt ein schmaler Schotterweg, der parallel zur Corniche d'Or verläuft, zum Haus. Ein unauffälliges Eisentor markiert am Ende des Weges den Zugang. Von hier winden sich fast drei Dutzend Stufen den steilen Abhang hinunter. Sie führen auf einen kleinen Vorplatz, von dem aus das Haus betreten wird. Die schwere, hölzerne Tür ist von einem fein profilierten Sandsteinportal gerahmt. In den mittig über der Tür vortretenden Schlussstein ist die filigrane Zeichnung eines Dreizacks eingemeißelt, der dem Haus seinen Namen gibt: Le Trident. Die drei scharfkantigen Felseninseln des Pointe de l'Esquillon, die unterhalb des Hauses ins Meer ragen, sollen Dierks zu der Namenswahl inspiriert haben. Betreten wird das Haus im ersten Obergeschoss. Wie zur Entstehungszeit werden von einem schmalen Gang aus mehrere Schlafzimmer und Bäder erschlossen, während die offene Treppenhalle, die von einem filigranen Sterngewölbe überspannt wird, in die Hauptwohnräume im Erdgeschoss führt. Linkerhand lagen früher die Bibliothek, das

The Sun Was the Only Witness:
Barry Dierks and Eric Sawyer

Miramar – sea view – is the name of the small coastal town west of Cannes on the Côte d'Azur. The drive from the Croisette via the Corniche d'Or takes less than half an hour. To the right of the legendary coastal road, the bizarre red rock formations of the Esterel mountain, from which the winding road was painstakingly wrested around 1900, rise up, while on the left the stony terrain plunges towards the Mediterranean. In Miramar, the Corniche runs in a long curve around the summit of Col de l'Esquillon, whose rugged foothills rise from the sea as Pointe de l'Esquillon beneath the road. It is perhaps the most spectacular section of the road as the terrain slopes steeply towards the sea; viewed from inside a car it seems as if even the slightest driving mistake could cause the car to crash through the low side wall and into the ocean. Exactly here, one of the most remarkable houses at the Côte d'Azur is hidden – on a narrow strip of stony land below the road. American architect Barry Dierks built the residence for himself in 1926. It was his first house and the start of a brilliant career as architect of the beautiful people. Today, we can ascribe more than 100, partly highly impressive mansions and country homes located along the French Riviera to the American architect.[1] However, the relatively small house in Miramar, which he built at the age of 26, has always been considered Dierks' ingenious masterpiece – also because of its spectacular location.

From the small town of Miramar, which extends to the west of the Col de l'Esquillon, a narrow gravel road parallel to the Corniche d'Or leads to the house. An inconspicuous iron gate marks the entrance at the end of the path. From here, almost three dozen steps wind down the steep slope. They lead to a small forecourt fleading to the house. The heavy wooden door is framed by a finely profiled sandstone portal. The filigree drawing of a trident, which is eponymous for the house, is carved into the keystone protruding centrally above the door: Le Trident. The three sharp-edged rock islands of Pointe de l'Esquillon, which protrude into the sea below the house, are said to have inspired Dierks to choose the name. The entrance to the house is on the first floor. As at the time of its construction, several bedrooms and bathrooms are accessed from a narrow hallway, while the open stairwell, which is spanned by a filigree stellar vault, leads to the main living areas on the ground floor. The library, dining room and Dierks' study used to be on the left, while the salon was on the right of the staircase. Even today, the room is dominated by a large fireplace made of grey sandstone. Between the salon and

1938 ist Barry Dierks auf dem Höhepunkt seiner Karriere als Architekt der Schönen und Reichen an der Côte d'Azur angelangt.

In 1938, Barry Dierks was at the height of his career as an architect to the rich and famous on the Côte d'Azur.

Speisezimmer sowie Dierks' Arbeitszimmer, während sich rechterhand des Treppenabgangs der Salon befand. Noch heute wird der Raum von einem großen Kamin aus grauem Sandstein beherrscht. Zwischen den Salon und die übrigen Wohnräume des Erdgeschosses legte Dierks eine tiefe und von einem einfachen Kreuzgewölbe überspannte Loggia an, die über drei schmale Fenstertüren aus der Treppenvorhalle heraus betreten wird. Zur sich anschließenden großen Terrasse trennte der Architekt den Freisitz durch zwei dünne Säulen ab, die den offenen Außenraum noch heute in ein intimes Separee verwandeln. Einen Pool gab es früher nicht, nur ein kleines, flaches Wasserbecken saß am Rand der großen Terrasse. Zum Baden musste man über einen schmalen steinigen und nur notdürftig mit einigen Stufen befestigten Weg zum Meer hinabsteigen, wo zwei natürliche Felsbecken zwischen den scharfkantigen Klippen als leidlich komfortable Badeorte dienten. Ein zweiter, nicht weniger beschwerlicher Abstieg führt auch heute noch an einen kleinen Sandstrand in einer benachbarten Bucht.

1921 lernten sich Barry Dierks (l.) und Eric Sawyer (r.) in Paris kennen und wurden ein Paar.

In 1921, Barry Dierks (l.) and Eric Sawyer (r.) met in Paris and became a couple.

the other living rooms on the ground floor, Dierks laid out a deep loggia, which is spanned by a simple cross vault and accessed via three narrow French doors from the front hall. Towards the adjoining large terrace, the architect separated the outdoor sitting area with two slender columns, which still transform the open exterior space into an intimate private space. There used to be no pool, only a small, shallow water basin at the edge of the large terrace. For a swim, one had to go down to the sea via a narrow, stony and only makeshift path with several steps, where two natural rock basins between the sharp-edged cliffs served as moderately comfortable bathing spots. A second, no less arduous descent still leads down to a small sandy beach in a neighbouring bay.

There is primarily one reason why Dierks chose this rocky and difficult to access terrain at Pointe de l'Esquillon of all sites, which locals regarded as unsuited for any development, for the construction of his house – and the reason was Eric Sawyer.[2] He was ten years older than Dierks and an Englishman. Both had come to know and love each other in the early 1920s in Paris. Even though the French society dealt with homosexuality extremely liberally in the period between the two World Wars, Dierks and Sawyer were always aware of their endangered role as outsiders and the strict necessity to protect themselves against hostilities and denunciation. Consequently, the secluded site beneath the Corniche d'Or, which is only visible from the sea, was ideal. Here, Dierks and Sawyer were able to unobtrusively live the life they wished for, without being hampered – open, carefree and with numerous friends and like-minded people. The guestbook of their house,

Warum sich Dierks ausgerechnet jenes felsige und nur schwer zugängliche Terrain am Pointe de l'Esquillon, das bei den Einheimischen als unbebaubar galt, für den Bau seines Hauses aussuchte, dafür gab es vor allem einen Grund – und der hieß Eric Sawyer (1889-1985).[2] Er war zehn Jahre älter als Dierks und kam aus England. Beide hatten sich zu Beginn der 1920er-Jahre in Paris kennen und lieben gelernt. Und auch wenn der Umgang der französischen Gesellschaft mit dem Thema Homosexualität während der Zeit zwischen den Weltkriegen äußerst liberal war, so wussten Dierks und Sawyer doch stets um ihre bedrohte Außenseiterrolle und die strikte Notwendigkeit, sich vor Anfeindungen und Denunziationen zu schützen. Das einsame, nur von der Meerseite aus einsehbare Grundstück unterhalb der Corniche d'Or war deshalb ideal. Hier konnten Dierks und Sawyer unauffällig und ungestört das Leben leben, dass sie sich gemeinsam wünschten – offen, unbeschwert und mit zahlreichen Freunden und Gleichgesinnten. Das Gästebuch ihres Hauses, das sich bis heute erhalten hat, erlaubt einen kleinen Einblick in das sorgenfreie Leben in Le Trident.[3] Dierks und Sawyer liebten es, die Besucher ihres Hauses zu fotografieren und diese Bilder den Einträgen im Gästebuch zuzuordnen. Neben Familienmitgliedern – vor allem Sawyers Mutter – und einer Reihe von Dierks' Auftraggebern zeigen viele der Fotografien einzelne Männer oder kleinere Männergruppen, die oft nur mit Badehosen bekleidet auf der Terrasse oder auf den Felsen unterhalb des Hauses posieren. Die karge Umgebung, das Meer als Hintergrund und die bewusst gewählten Posen erinnern mitunter entfernt an die antikisierenden homoerotischen Akte, die den deutschen Fotografen Wilhelm von Gloeden Ende des 19. Jahrhunderts berühmt machten.[4] Zugleich sind die Bilder aus dem Gästebuch ein klarer Hinweis darauf, dass das Paar an der Côte d'Azur engen freundschaftlichen Kontakt auch zu anderen Homosexuellen pflegte und das abgelegene Küstenhaus gern für diesen Freundeskreis öffnete.

Zuhause fühlten sich Dierks und Sawyer in den 1920er- und 1930er-Jahren aber nicht nur in ihrem privaten Refugium am Pointe de l'Esquillon, sondern auch in den feinen Bars, Restaurants und Hotels an der Croisette in Cannes. Es waren hauptsächlich Amerikaner und Briten, die damals die Côte d'Azur bevölkerten. Viele der Männer hatten nur wenige Jahre vorher im Ersten Weltkrieg in Frankreich gekämpft, sich in das Land verliebt und kamen nun mit ihren Familien und Freunden zurück – manche nur für ein paar Wochen im Jahr, manche – wie Dierks und Sawyer – blieben für immer. Sie hauchten der französischen Riviera nach dem Krieg neues Leben ein. Sie brachten den Jazz mit, die schnellen Sportwagen und die kurzen Sommerkleider – kurz: sie brachten ein neues, modernes Lebensgefühl an das Mittelmeer. Wo früher der europäische Hochadel in den Sommermonaten unter sich war, feierte nun die Jeunesse dorée des amerikanischen Wirtschaftsbooms der 1920er-Jahre ihr Stelldichein – junge Künstler und Intellektuelle, mondäne Abenteurer und Jetsetter. Die Côte d'Azur war dankbar für diese neue Klientel – zumal seit der Oktoberrevolution von 1918 auch die zahlungskräftige russische Oberschicht, die vor dem Ersten Weltkrieg noch wesentlich das Gesicht der Riviera geprägt hatte, nun ausblieb.

Le Trident liegt am Fuße des Col de l'Esquillon, dessen zerklüftete Ausläufer unterhalb des Hauses aus dem Meer ragen.

Le Trident is located at the foot of the Col de l'Esquillon, whose rugged foothills rise from the sea below the house.

which has been preserved, provides a small insight into the blithe life at Le Trident.[3] Dierks and Sawyer loved to take photographs of their visitors and add these photographs to the entries in the guestbook. Besides family members – especially Sawyer's mother – and a number of Dierks' clients, many of the photos show individual men or small groups of men, frequently only dressed in swimming trunks, posing on the terrace or on the rocks underneath the house. The bleak surrounding landscape, the sea as backdrop and the deliberately chosen poses remotely recall antique-like, homoerotic nudes, which brought fame to German photographer Wilhelm von Gloeden at the end of the 19th century. At the same time, the photographs in the guestbook are a clear indication that the couple cultivated close friendly contacts with other homosexuals at the Côte d'Azur and liked to open their remote house on the coast for this circle of friends.

However, in the 1920s and 1930s, Dierks and Sawyer not only felt at home in their private refuge at Pointe de l'Esquillon but also in exquisite bars, restaurants and hotels on the Croisette in Cannes. It was mainly Americans and Englishmen, who populated the Côte d'Azur in those days. Many of these men had fought in France during the First World War only a few years ago, had fallen in love with this country and now returned with their families and friends – some came for a few weeks per year, others like Dierks and Sawyer stayed forever. They breathed new life into the French Riviera after the war. They brought along jazz, fast sports cars and short summer dresses, in short: they introduced a new, modern sense of life to the Mediterranean. Where members of the European aristocracy once spent the summer months among their peers, the jeunesse dorée of the American 1920s

Dierks als Amerikaner und Sawyer als Brite, obendrein aus gutem Hause, erwiesen sich in diesem sozialen Umfeld schnell als charmante Gesellschafter und gern gesehene Gäste auf Partys und privaten Abendgesellschaften. Und natürlich nutzte Dierks diese Möglichkeiten auch zur Akquise neuer Aufträge. Dabei kam dem Architekten zu gute, dass er keine festen architektonischen Überzeugungen besaß, sondern sich jederzeit den Wünschen und Vorstellungen seiner Bauherren anpassen konnte. Der halbmoderne Stil von Le Trident, den Dierks geschickt mit historischen Anleihen und Versatzstücken aus der provenzalisch-mediterranen Architektur zu bereichern wusste, wurde sein Markenzeichen. Dabei beherrschte der Architekt ein erstaunlich breites Repertoire, je nachdem wie weit seine Bauherren bereit waren, sich der Moderne zu öffnen – oder eben auch nicht. In dieser Unentschlossenheit liegt vielleicht auch ein Grund dafür, dass Dierks' Bauten nie die Aufmerksamkeit erfahren haben, wie sie etwa Robert Mallet-Stevens' Villa Noailles in Hyères[5] oder Eileen Grays Maison en Bord de Mer in Roquebrune-Cap-Martin,[6] die zeitlich parallel zu Le Trident an der Côte d'Azur entstanden, noch heute genießen. Aber auch wenn Dierks' Bauten die kompromisslose, avantgardistische Strahlkraft der Häuser von Mallet-Stevens und Gray fehlt, so darf doch nicht übersehen werden, dass Dierks mit seinem moderaten und komfortbetonten Modernismus die Architektur der Rieviera mehr als jeder andere Architekt seiner Zeit prägte und schnell eine Reihe von Schülern und Nachahmern fand.

Das Eklektische seines Stils und sein Talent für freie Kompositionen lässt sich nicht zuletzt auf Dierks' Zeit an der Pariser École des Beaux Arts zurückführen, wohin er 1921 ging, nachdem er bereits sein Architektur-Diplom am Carnegie Institute of Technology in Pittsburgh, seiner Heimatstadt, erworben hatte. Angelegt war das Pariser Studium auf zwei Jahre. Danach, so war es ursprünglich geplant, wollte Dierks zurück nach Amerika gehen. Der Plan ändert sich allerdings, als Sawyer in sein Leben trat. Der 1889 geborene Spross einer wohlhabenden und einflussreichen englischen Familie hatte während des Ersten Weltkriegs als Offizier in Frankreich gedient und blieb nach 1918 im Land, dessen tolerantes und weltoffenes Klima er gerade im Gegensatz zu der engstirnigen Atmosphäre seiner britischen Oberschicht-Herkunft er zu schätzen wusste. In Paris lebte er in einem vornehmen Apartment am Boulevard des Italiens und arbeitete als Filialleiter eines englischen Bankhauses, in das es 1921 auch Dierks verschlug, der sich in der Bank um eine Anstellung als Kassierer bewarb, um seine finanzielle Situation als Student an der École des Beaux Arts aufzubessern. So lernten sich Dierks und Sawyer kennen. Bald zogen sie zusammen und verbrachten ihre Abende vornehmlich in den legendären Bars des Hotel Ritz, wo sich zur Cocktail Hour allabendlich ein amüsierfreudiges, kosmopolitisches Publikum einfand – darunter vor allem Amerikaner, die in Paris für ihre Regierung oder amerikanische Konzerne arbeiteten. Hier pflegten Dierks und Sawyer – wie später in den Salons an der Croisette – ihre gesellschaftlichen Kontakte und hier erhielten sie

Das nur vom Meer aus einsehbare Haus unterhalb der Corniche d'Or war das ideale Zuhause für Dierks und Sawyer.

The house below the Corniche d'Or, visible only from the sea, was the ideal home for Dierks and Sawyer.

economic boom enjoyed life to the full – young artists and intellectuals, sophisticated adventurers and jetsetters. The Côte d'Azur was grateful for this new clientele – especially since the wealthy Russian upper class, which had mainly characterized the appearance of the Riviera before the First World War, failed to appear since the October Revolution in 1918.

Dierks as an American and Sawyer as an Englishman and of a good family quickly proved to be charming companions and welcome guests at parties and private soirées in this social environment. Naturally, Dierks also used these opportunities to acquire new commissions. The architect thereby benefitted from the fact that he was not committed to a fixed architectural conviction but was always able to adapt to the wishes and ideas of his clients. The semi-modern style of Le Trident, which Dierks skilfully enriched with historic borrowings and set pieces from Provencal-Mediterranean architecture, became his trademark. The architect mastered an amazingly broad repertoire, depending on the extent to which his clients were willing to open themselves to modernism – or not. This indecision is one reason why Dierks' buildings never attracted the same attention as, for example, Robert Mallet-Stevens' Villa Noailles in Hyères[5] or Eileen Gray's Maison en Bord de Mer in Roquebrune-Cap-Martin,[6] which were constructed on the Côte d'Azur at the same time as Le Trident, still enjoy today. But even though Dierks' buildings lack the uncompromising, avant-garde radiance of the houses built by Mallet-Stevens and Gray, it should not be overlooked that Dierks, with his moderate and comfort-oriented modernism, shaped the architecture of the Riviera more than any other architect of his time and quickly found a number of students and imitators.

Die Fotos aus dem Gästebuch von Le Trident erinnern vielfach an die antikisierenden homoerotischen Akte, die den deutschen Fotografen Wilhelm von Gloeden um 1900 berühmt machten.

The photos from Le Trident's guestbook are often reminiscent of the antique homoerotic nudes that made German photographer Wilhelm von Gloeden famous around 1900.

unter der Hand eine Reihe lukrativer Anlage-Tipps, die ihnen schon bald ein von ihren jeweiligen Familien finanziell unabhängiges Leben und damit den Umzug an die Côte d'Azur und damit letztlich auch den Bau von Le Trident ermöglichen sollten. Dierks wurde der gefeierte Architekt, Sawyer sein Manager.

Ihr unbeschwertes Leben an der Riviera endete jedoch abrupt mit dem Ausbruch des Zweiten Weltkriegs. Während Sawyer in der Résistance aktiv war, musste Dierks das Land verlassen. Erst 1946 konnten beide nach Le Trident zurückkehren. Dierks fand schnell in die Arbeit zurück und eröffnete nun gemeinsam mit zwei Kollegen, Marc-Pierre Renaut und Claude Magne, ein neues Büro in der Rue d'Antibes in Cannes. Eine schwere Gefäß-Erkrankung machte dem Architekten jedoch zunehmend zu schaffen. 1956 musste ihm ein Bein amputiert werden, was Le Trident, das er so spektakulär auf die Felsen des Pointe de

Das Gästebuch zeigt, dass Le Trident ein beliebter Treffpunkt des homosexuellen Freundeskreises von Dierks und Sawyer war.

The guestbook shows that Le Trident was a popular meeting place for Dierks' and Sawyer's homosexual circle of friends.

The eclectic nature of his style and his talent for free compositions can be traced back to Dierks' time at the École des Beaux Arts in Paris, were he studied in 1921, having already obtained his architecture diploma at the Carnegie Institute of Technology in Pittsburgh, his hometown. His studies in Paris were planned to last two years. After that, as originally planned, Dierks wanted to go back to America. But the plan changed when Sawyer entered his life. Born in 1889 to a wealthy and influential English family, he had served as an officer in France during the First World War and stayed in the country after 1918, where he appreciated the tolerant and cosmopolitan climate, particularly in contrast to the narrow-minded atmosphere of his British upper-class background. In Paris, he lived in a distinguished apartment on Boulevard des Italiens and worked as the branch manager of an English bank, which also employed Dierks in 1921, who had applied for a cashier's position in the bank to improve his financial situation as a student at the École des Beaux Arts. That is where Dierks and Sawyer got to know each other. Soon they moved in together and spent their evenings mainly in the legendary bars of the Ritz Hotel, where a pleasure-loving, cosmopolitan clientele gathered every evening for the cocktail hour – especially Americans who worked in Paris for their government or American corporations. Here, Dierks and Sawyer cultivated their social contacts – as later in the salons on the Croisette – and here they were secretly given a number of profitable investment tips, which were soon to enable them to live a life financially independent of their respective families and thus to move to the Côte d'Azur and ultimately also to build Le Trident. Dierks became the celebrated architect, Sawyer his manager.

Die filigrane Zeichnung eines Dreizacks über der Tür gibt dem Haus seinen Namen: Le Trident.

The filigree drawing of a trident above the door gives the house its name: Le Trident.

l'Esquillon gesetzt hatte, um neugierige Blicke und unliebsame Besucher abzuhalten, letztlich zu einem Gefängnis für ihn selbst machte. Vier Jahre später, am 20. Februar 1960, im Alter von 60 Jahren, erlöste ihn der Tod. Sawyer hingegen überlebte seinen jüngeren Lebensgefährten um ein Vierteljahrhundert. Als er 1985 verstarb, ging Le Trident, ihr gemeinsames Zuhause, in den Besitz eines Neffen über. Heute gehört das Haus einem reichen russischen Geschäftsmann, was einer gewissen Ironie nicht entbehrt, kamen doch Dierks und Sawyer genau in dem Moment an die Côte d'Azur, als die Russen verschwanden. Der neue Besitzer ließ die Villa in den vergangenen Jahren von den deutschen Architekten Matthias Burkart und Ernst Ulrich Tillmanns vom Stuttgarter Architekturbüro 4a Architekten aufwendig sanieren und umbauen.[7] Im Inneren ist nur noch wenig vom Charme der Entstehungszeit übrig geblieben, nach außen jedoch strahlt Le Trident wieder im gleißenden Sonnenlicht des Mittelmeeres – genau wie in den 1920er-Jahren, als sich Barry Dierks und Eric Sawyer hier den Traum eines gemeinsamen Lebens erfüllten.

Nach der Sanierung strahlt Dierks' und Sawyers Le Trident heute wieder wie zu seiner Entstehungszeit.

After refurbishment, Dierks' and Sawyer's Le Trident now shines as it did when it was built.

Their carefree life on the Riviera ended abruptly with the outbreak of the Second World War. While Sawyer was active in the French Resistance, Dierks had to leave the country. Only in 1946, the two men could return to Le Trident. Dierks was able to quickly resume his work, and he opened a new office on Rue d'Antibes in Cannes together with two colleagues, Marc-Pierre Renaut and Claude Magne. A serious vascular disease increasingly discomforted the architect. In 1956, one of his legs had to be amputated, and Le Trident, which he had so spectacularly positioned on the rocks of Pointe de l'Esquillon to keep away curious views and unwelcome visitors, turned into a prison for him. Four years later, on 20 February 1960, Dierks died at the age of 60. Sawyer, on the contrary, survived his younger partner by a quarter of a century. When he died in 1985, Le Trident, their shared home, passed into the ownership of a nephew. Today, a rich Russian businessman owns the house, which is not without a certain irony, because Dierks and Sawyer arrived at the Côte d'Azur exactly at the time when the Russians disappeared. In recent years, the new owner had the mansion elaborately restored and converted by Matthias Burkart und Ernst Ulrich Tillmanns from the Stuttgart-based architectural firm 4a Architekten.[7] Inside, only little is left of the charm of the time of its origin, but towards the outside Le Trident shines again in the glistening sunlight of the Mediterranean – just like in the 1920s, when Barry Dierks and Eric Sawyer fulfilled their dream of living together here.

Uwe Bresan

Sissie Architects:
John Seely und Paul Paget

Henry John Alexander Seely (1899-1963) und Paul Edward Paget (1901-1985) waren über vier Jahrzehnte lang ein Paar. Gemeinsam führten sie eines der prominentesten Londoner Architekturbüros ihrer Zeit.[1] Sie hatten sich um 1920 beim Studium in Cambridge kennen gelernt und gründeten ihr gemeinsames Architekturbüro 1922. Es wurde schon bald sehr erfolgreich! Seely wie auch Paget stammten aus vermögenden Elternhäusern und nutzten ihre guten Kontakte zur britischen Oberschicht auch zur Auftragsakquise. Als ihr bedeutendstes Werk der Zwischenkriegszeit gilt Eltham Palace, eine verfallene Wasserburg im Südosten Londons, die sie im Auftrag des vermögenden Philanthropen Stephen Courtauld und seiner Frau Virginia in den 1930er-Jahren zu einem modernen Landsitz mit 14 Schlafzimmern ausbauten. Einen mittelalterlichen Saalbau von bedeutender Größe und offen liegendem Dachstuhl integrierten Seely und Paget geschickt in das neue Ensemble, das ansonsten einem schlichten französischen Château-Stil verpflichtet war und im Inneren deutliche Art-Deco-Züge trug.[2]

Nach dem Zweiten Weltkrieg beschäftigten sich Seely und Paget vorrangig mit Restaurierungsarbeiten prominenter historischer Gebäude sowie mit Sakralbauaufgaben. Von 1956 bis 1969 hatten sie in der Nachfolge Christopher Wrens die Position eines Surveyor of the Fabric of St. Paul's Cathedral inne und waren damit für alle architekturbezogenen Arbeiten am bedeutendsten Londoner Kirchenbau zuständig. Als Diözesanarchitekten der Diözese London konnten sie darüber hinaus zahlreiche Kirchenneubauten im Umland realisieren. Das vielleicht fortschrittlichste Werk ihrer Karriere war die 1960 fertiggestellte Kirche St. Andrew and St. George in der knapp 40 Kilometer nördlich von London gelegenen New Town Stevenage. Das Mittelschiff der Kirche wird von zwei parallel verlaufenden Reihen hoher, parabelförmiger Betonbögen überspannt. Durch ihre Überlappung entsteht jeweils links und rechts ein Seitenschiff. St. Andrew and St. George ist bis heute der größte Pfarrkirchen-Neubau in Großbritannien seit dem Zweiten Weltkrieg.[3]

Bis zu Seelys Tod 1963 lebten die beiden Männer gemeinsam unter der Adresse 41/42 Cloth Fair im Zentrum von London, nur wenige hundert Meter von der St. Paul's Cathedral entfernt. Ihr Wohnhaus, das sie 1927 erwarben und für ihre Zwecke herrichten ließen, gilt als das älteste der City of London und stammt aus der Zeit um 1600.[4] Eine bekannte Fotografie aus dem Nachlass von Paget zeigt ihren Haushälter Peter Foxwell bei der Reinigung des Badezimmers von 41/42 Cloth Fair. Bemerkenswert ist die Auf-

Sissy Architects:
John Seely and Paul Paget

Henry John Alexander Seely (1899-1963) and Paul Edward Paget (1901-1985) were a couple for over four decades. Together they ran one of the most prominent London architectural offices of their time.[1] They had gotten to know each other around 1920 while studying in Cambridge and founded their joint architectural practice in 1922, which soon became successful. Both Seely and Paget came from wealthy family backgrounds and used their good contacts to the British upper class to acquire commissions. Eltham Palace, a dilapidated moated castle in south-east London, is regarded as their most important work of the interwar period. In the 1930s, they were commissioned by wealthy philanthropist Stephen Courtauld and his wife Virginia to convert the palace into a modern country residence with 14 bedrooms. Seely and Paget skilfully integrated a medieval hall of considerable size with an open roof truss into the new ensemble, which was otherwise designed in a simple French château style with distinct Art Deco features inside.[2]

After the Second World War, Seely and Paget were primarily engaged in the restoration of prominent historical and sacred buildings. From 1956 to 1969, they held the position of Surveyor of the Fabric of St. Paul's Cathedral, succeeding Sir Christopher Wren, and were thus responsible for all architecture-related work on London's most important church building. As diocesan architects of the diocese of London, they were also in a position to realize numerous new church buildings in the surrounding area. Their probably most progressive work was the Church of St. Andrew and St. George that was completed in 1960 in the New Town of Stevenage, located less than 25 miles north of London. The central nave of the church is spanned by two parallel rows of high, parabolic concrete arches. The interlacing arches create a side nave on the left and right. St. Andrew and St. George is until today the largest new parish church in Great Britain since the Second World War.[3]

Until Seely's death in 1963, the two men lived together at 41/42 Cloth Fair in central London, just a few hundred yards from St. Paul's Cathedral. Their house, which they purchased in 1927 and had refurbished for their purposes, is considered to be the oldest in the City of London and dates from around 1600.[4] A well-known photograph from Paget's estate shows their housekeeper Peter Foxwell cleaning the bathroom of 41/42 Cloth Fair. The photograph is particularly noteworthy because it shows two bathtubs standing only about half a meter apart. We can therefore justifiably assume that the two ar-

nahme vor allem, weil sie zwei, nur etwa einen halben Meter voneinander entfernt stehende Badewannen zeigt. Wir können also mit gutem Recht vermuten, dass die beiden Architekten gern bei einem gemeinsamen Bad entspannten. Touristengruppen, denen das Haus heute gezeigt wird, werden bei diesem Anlass auch gern auf das benachbarte, durch einen schmalen Durchgang von 41/42 Cloth Fair getrennte Haus mit der Nummer 43/44 hingewiesen. Im ersten Obergeschoss des Hauses befindet sich auf der Seite des Durchgangs ein Scheinfenster, hinter dessen Glasscheibe sich ein Bild versteckt. Es zeigt einen Seemann bei der Rückkehr zu seiner Familie, wie er gerade die heimische Stube betritt.[5] Die Geschichte des Bildes erläuterte Paget in einem Interview, das er noch kurz vor seinem Tod 1985 gab:[6] Der Durchgang zwischen den beiden Häusern sei so schmal gewesen, dass man aus dem Küchenfenster heraus den gegenüber wohnenden Nachbarn den Sonntagsbraten hätte reichen können. Deshalb hätten sie zusammen mit 41/42 Cloth Fair auch das Nachbarhaus gekauft, das Fenster im ersten Obergeschoss zumauern und stattdessen das Seemannsbild anbringen lassen.[7] Zweifelsohne legten Seely und Paget größten Wert auf ihre Privatsphäre und dies sicher auch im Hinblick auf ihr gemeinsames Lebensmodell. In dem bereits erwähnten Interview beschreibt Paget dieses Modell als „marriage of two minds"; Seely und er seien praktisch eine Person gewesen.[8]

Neben ihrem Londoner Stadthaus hat sich auf der Isle of Wight auch noch das private Ferienhaus der beiden Architekten erhalten.[9] The Shack ist, wie der Name schon verrät, nicht mehr als eine kleine, mit Holzschindeln verkleidete Schäferhütte. Sie ist mobil und lagert auf hochkant stehenden Feldsteinen, um Mäuse und Ungeziefer fernzuhalten. Im Inneren entwarfen Seely und Paget allerdings ein hochmodernes Interieur mit zahlreichen platzsparenden Einbauten sowie einem kleinen Bad. Die Wände sind mit Holzwerkstoffplatten verkleidet; Stahlrohrelemente dienen als Trittleitern und Handläufe; und vor dem Kamin stehen zwei bequeme Bugholzsessel. In die beiden hohen Giebelwände ist jeweils überkopf ein schmales Hochbett eingefügt. Die getrennte Anordnung der Betten sollte bei Besuchern jeglichen Verdacht zerstreuen, dass es sich bei den beiden Bewohnern um mehr als gute Freunde und Geschäftspartner handeln könnte. Denn immerhin galt noch bis 1967 in Großbritannien das so genannte „Labouchere Amendment",[10] das jede sexuelle Handlung zwischen zwei Männern unter Gefängnisstrafe stellte, auch wenn deren Vollzug ausschließlich in den privaten Räumen der Beteiligten stattgefunden hatte.

Der britische Architekturhistoriker Timothy Brittain-Catlin beschreibt die Beziehung von Seely und Paget – sicher auch im Hinblick auf die Ferienlager-Romantik von The Shack – als „eine starke Partnerschaft zwischen zwei Teenagern, die zusammen aufwachsen und möglichst viele Dinge gemeinsam tun wollten."[11] In seinem fulminanten Buch *Bleak Houses. Disappointment and Failure in Architecture* (Trostlose Häuser. Enttäuschung und Misserfolg in der Architektur) geht Brittain-Catlin der Frage nach, warum

Seely (l.) und Paget (r.) bei der gemeinsamen Arbeit

Seely (l.) and Paget (r.) working together

chitects liked to relax in a shared bathroom. Tourist groups, who are shown around the house today, are often made aware of the neighbouring house with the number 43/44, which is separated from 41/42 Cloth Fair by a narrow alleyway. On the first floor of the house, on the side facing the alleyway, there is a fake window with a picture hidden behind a glass pane. It shows a sailor returning to his family as he is just entering his home.[5] Paget explained the story behind the picture in an interview he gave shortly before his death in 1985:[6] The alleyway between the two houses was so narrow that one could have handed over a plate of Sunday roast to the neighbours living opposite. Therefore, they bought the neighbouring house, bricked up the window on the first floor and had the sailor's picture placed there instead.[7] There is no doubt that Seely and Paget attached utmost importance to their privacy and this certainly also with regard to their shared life model. In the aforementioned interview, Paget describes this model as a "marriage of two minds"; Seely and he were virtually one person.[8]

In addition to their townhouse in London, their private holiday home has also been preserved on the Isle of Wight.[9] The Shack, as the name suggests, is nothing more than a small shepherd's hut clad in wooden shingles. It is mobile and sits on upright field stones to keep mice and vermin away. Inside, however, Seely and Paget designed an ultra-modern interior with numerous space-saving fixtures and a small bathroom. The walls are clad with composite wood panels; tubular steel elements serve as stepladders and handrails; and two comfortable bentwood armchairs are placed in front of the fireplace. A narrow bunk bed is fitted overhead in each of the two high gable walls. The separate placement arrangement of the beds allay visitors' suspicions that the two residents might be more than good friends and business partners. After all, the so-called Labouchere Amendment was still in force in Great Britain until 1967,[10] which made any sexual act between two men punishable by imprisonment, even if it had taken place exclusively in the private rooms of the persons involved.

Eltham Palace gilt als das bedeutendste Werk von Seely & Paget in der Zwischenkriegszeit. Der Bau ist typisch für den eklektischen Stil der Architekten – außen französisches Château, innen Art Deco.

Eltham Palace is considered the most important work of Seely & Paget in the interwar period; it is typical for the eclectic style of the architects – French château exterior, Art Deco interior.

manche Architekten, obwohl sie zu ihrer Zeit durchaus erfolgreich waren und ihre Gebäude von Bauherren und Nutzern geschätzt wurden, später fast spurlos aus der Architekturgeschichte verschwinden. Er widmet Seely und Paget dabei einen eigenen Abschnitt seines Buches.[12] Einen gewichtigen Grund für den Erfolg der Architekten und zugleich für das Desinteresse der späteren Architekturgeschichte an ihrem Werk sieht er in der Tatsache, dass sich Seely und Paget in ihrer Arbeit auf keinen „definierbaren Stil" festlegen wollten.[13] Sie nutzten für ihre Gebäude die vielfältigsten historischen Versatzstücke ebenso wie zeitgenössische Elemente. Vor allem in der Zeit nach dem Zweiten Weltkrieg und vor dem Hintergrund eines immer dominierender werdenden Architekturdiskurses der Moderne, der seine zentralen Begriffe wie Materialgerechtigkeit und konstruktive Ehrlichkeit gern noch durch geschlechtsspezifische Attributierungen wie männlich und viril zu überhöhen suchte, konnten die „Sissie Architects", wie Brittain-Catlin seine Protagonisten nennt,[14] keine Anerkennung mehr finden!

St Andrew and St George in Stevenage, errichtet zwischen 1956 und 1960, ist der größte Kirchenbau der Nachkriegszeit in England; zugleich stellt er das modernste Werk von Seely & Paget dar.

St Andrew and St George in Stevenage, built between 1956 and 1960, is the largest post-war church in England and the most modern work by Seely & Paget.

British architectural historian Timothy Brittain-Catlin describes the relationship between Seely and Paget – certainly with regard to The Shack's summer camp romance – as a "strong partnership between two teenagers who wanted to grow up together and do things together."[11] In his brilliant book *Bleak Houses. Disappointment and Failure in Architecture*, Brittain-Catlin explores the question of why some architects, although they were quite successful in their time and their buildings were appreciated by clients and users, later disappeared almost without trace from architectural history. He dedicates a separate section of his book to Seely and Paget.[12] In his view, one important reason for the success of the architects and, at the same time, for the disinterest of later architectural history in their work is the fact that Seely and Paget did not want to commit themselves to a "definable style" in their projects.[13] They used the most varied historical set pieces as well as contemporary elements for their buildings. Particularly in the period after the Second World War and against the background of the increasingly dominant architectural discourse of modernism,

The Shack diente den Architekten als Feriendomizil; moderne Einbauten verleihen der kleinen Hütte ungeahnten Komfort.

The Shack served as the architects' vacation home; modern fixtures add unexpected comfort to the small cabin.

In Seely und Paget sieht Brittain-Catlin auch deshalb zwei exemplarische Vertreter homosexueller Architekten des 20. Jahrhunderts. Als gesellschaftliche Außenseiter hätten sie versucht, mit ihrer Architektur sich selbst eine schönere, vielleicht auch eine sentimentalere Welt zu erschaffen.[15] Zumindest für Paget mag dies schlussendlich zutreffen. Nach Seelys Tod zog sich Paget Ende der 1960er-Jahre aus der Architektur zurück und siedelte nach Northrepps in der Grafschaft Norfolk im Osten Englands über. Hier hatten er und Seely in den späten 1930er-Jahren für einen Onkel von Paget ein kleines palladianisches Landhaus – Templewood – realisiert.[16] Paget nahm das Haus nach dem Tod des Onkels in Besitz und verbrachte hier seinen Lebensabend. Den Kirchenkünstler Brian Thomas, der bereits an zahlreichen Sakralbauten von Seely und Paget mitgewirkt und auch das Seemannsbild am Haus 43/44 Cloth Fair gemalt hatte, beauftragte Paget nun mit einer letzten, großen, romantischen Arbeit: Im Auftrag des Architekten bemalte der Künstler die Decke des großen Hauptraums von Templewood mit Darstellungen aus dem Leben Pagets. Ein Bildausschnitt zeigt ihn unter anderem im Teenageralter als kraftstrotzenden Athleten. Dass Paget als Schüler im Sport in Wirklichkeit eine hoffnungslose Niete war: geschenkt![17]

Errichtet wurde The Shack in den 1930er-Jahren auf dem Anwesen von Seelys Familie in Mottistone auf der Isle of Wight.

The Shack was built in the 1930s on the estate of Seely's family in Mottistone on the Isle of Wight.

which willingly sought to exaggerate its central concepts such as material justice and constructive honesty by gender-specific attributes such as masculine and virile, the "sissy architects", as Brittain-Catlin calls his protagonists,[14] could no longer gain recognition!

For this reason, Brittain-Catlin regards Seely and Paget as two exemplary representatives of homosexual architects in the 20th century. As social outsiders, they had tried to create a more beautiful, perhaps even a more sentimental world for themselves with their architecture.[15] At least for Paget this may ultimately be true. After Seely's death, Paget retired from architecture in the late 1960s and moved to Northrepps in the county of Norfolk in the east of England. Here, he and Seely had built a small Palladian country house – Templewood – for one of Paget's uncles in the late 1930s.[16] Paget took possession of the house after his uncle's death and spent the rest of his life there. He then commissioned the church artist Brian Thomas, who had already contributed to numerous sacred buildings by Seely and Paget and had also painted the sailor's home coming window at 43/44 Cloth Fair, with a last, large, romantic work: on the architect's request, the artist painted the ceiling of the large main room of Templewood with depictions of Paget's life. One section of the painting depicts him in his youth posing as a vigorous athlete. The fact that Paget was in reality hopeless at sports as a schoolboy – so what![17]

Uwe Bresan

Eine Villa für zwei Junggesellen:
St. Ann's Court von Raymond McGrath

Die Straße ist so schmal, dass kaum zwei Autos aneinander vorbei passen – schon gar nicht die großen Land Rover, die in diesem Teil Englands gefühlt noch etwas häufiger vorkommen als in anderen Teilen; was auch damit zusammenhängen könnte, dass es in diesem Teil Englands gefühlt noch immer etwas englandhafter zugeht als in anderen Teilen. Wir sind in der Grafschaft Surrey, im Süden der Insel, keine Autostunde westlich der Londoner City. Das Pro-Kopf-Einkommen ist überdurchschnittlich hoch und auch das Grün der Wiesen, Hecken und Wälder scheint mitunter überdurchschnittlich grün. Die schmale, von Zäunen und alten Mauern gesäumte Straße führt in nordwestlicher Richtung aus der Ortschaft Chertsey hinaus und eine kleine Anhöhe, den St. Ann's Hill, hinauf. Links und rechts begleitet dichtes Unterholz den Fahrtweg und an manchen Stellen wuchern die Büsche, Sträucher und Bäume so stark über die Zäune und Mauern hinweg, dass sich die Straße in einen grünen Tunnel verwandelt. Nur hin und wieder werden die haushohen Laubwände von schmalen Toreinfahrten unterbrochen. Sie sind die einzigen Hinweise auf die prächtigen Herrenhäuser und Anwesen, die sich hinter den grünen Seitenstreifen verbergen. Unser Ziel ist das Haus St. Ann's Court. Es liegt da, wo die Straße den höchsten Punkt der Anhöhe erreicht und ein schlichtes, weißes, zweiflügeliges Holztor die Vorfahrt markiert. Nur auf Zehenspitzen kann man einen Blick in den dahinter liegenden kreisrunden Hof und das weiß-strahlende Herrenhaus an dessen gegenüberliegender Seite erhaschen. Es stammt aus den späten 1930er-Jahren und ist ein Werk des Architekten Raymond McGrath (1903-1977), der heute – wenn überhaupt – nur noch wenigen vor allem als Interior Designer und Textilgestalter bekannt sein dürfte.[1]

Er kam 1926 durch ein Cambridge-Stipendium von Australien nach Großbritannien, beendete hier seine Ausbildung als Architekt und eröffnete 1930 in London sein eigenes Büro, mit dem er schnell für Aufsehen sorgte,[2] als ihn die britische BBC mit der Ausgestaltung des damals gerade fertiggestellten Broadcasting House,[3] der Senderzentrale am Portland Place in London, beauftragte. Für die Umsetzung arbeitete McGrath eng mit Serge Chermayeff (1900-1996) und Wells Coates (1895-1958) zusammen, die sich in der Folge zu führenden Vertretern der Moderne in Großbritannien entwickelten. Zu der Gruppe um McGrath, Chermayeff und Coates stieß bald auch der Landschaftsarchitekt Christopher Tunnard (1910-1979) hinzu. Auch er war von den Ideen der Moderne und ihrer Ästhetik überzeugt und brachte mit dem vermögenden Börsenhändler Gerald L. Schlesinger (1889-1966) auch einen potenten Bauherrn mit in den Freundeskreis. Schlesinger war nicht nur von Tunnards Talent als Garten- und Land-

A Mansion For Two Bachelors: St Ann's Court by Raymond McGrath

The road is that narrow that two cars can hardly pass each other – and definitely not the large Land Rovers which, in this part of England, are seen more frequently than in other parts; this could also be because, in this part of England, everything is still a bit more "englandish" than in other parts. We are in the county of Surrey, in the south of the island, not even an hour by car west of the City of London. The per-capita income is above-average and the green of the meadows, hedges and forests appears to be above-average green in some parts. The narrow road bordered by fences and old walls leads in a north-western direction out of the town of Chertsey and up a small hill, St Ann's Hill. On the left and the right, dense undergrowth accompanies the road, and, in some places, the bushes, shrubs and trees encroach on the fences and the walls in such a way that the road turns into a green tunnel. Only now and then are the walls as high as houses replaced by narrow entrance gates. They are the only indications of the magnificent mansions and properties concealed behind the green verges. Our destination is the building with the name of St Ann's Court. It is located where the road reaches the highest point of the hill and where a plain, white, two-leaf wooden gate marks the entrance. Only on tiptoe can one catch a glimpse of the circular courtyard behind it and the radiant white mansion on the opposite side of it. The latter is from the late 1930s and was built according to plans by the architect Raymond McGrath (1903-1977), who today – if at all – is probably only known to a small number of people mainly as an interior and fabric designer.[1]

On a Cambridge scholarship, McGrath came to Great Britain in 1926, finished his training as an architect here and, in 1930, opened his own office with which he quickly attracted attention[2] when the BBC commissioned him with the interior design of the just completed Broadcasting House,[3] the broadcasting centre in London's Portland Place. For the implementation, McGrath closely worked with Serge Chermayeff (1900-1996) and Wells Coates (1895-1958), who subsequently became the leading representatives of modernism in Great Britain. Shortly afterwards, the landscape architect Christopher Tunnard (1910-1979) also joined the group consisting of McGrath, Chermayeff and Coates. Tunnard was also convinced of the ideas of modernism and its aesthetics and, with the wealthy stockbroker Gerald L. Schlesinger, also added a potent building client to the circle of friends. Schlesinger was not only convinced of Tunnard's talent as a garden- and landscape architect but also felt physically attracted to the young man. Tunnard reciprocated Schle-

St. Ann's Court war das gemeinsame Zuhauses des Landschaftsarchitekten Christopher Tunnard (Bild) und des Börsenmaklers Gerald Schlesinger.

St. Ann's Court was the shared home of landscape architect Christopher Tunnard (pictured) and stockbroker Gerald Schlesinger.

schaftsarchitekt überzeugt, sondern fühlte sich von dem jungen Mann auch körperlich angezogen. Tunnard erwiderte Schlesingers Gefühle und beide waren für einige Jahre ein Paar. Das elegante Herrenhaus hinter dem schlichten weißen Holztor an der von Bäumen und Sträuchern überwucherten St. Ann's Road in Chertsey war ihr gemeinsames Zuhause.[4]

Tunnard hatte Schlesinger dazu überredet, seinen Freund McGrath mit dem Entwurf des Hauses zu beauftragen. Tunnard selbst übernahm die Gestaltung des Gartens – so wie er auch den Garten von Hill House im Londoner Stadtteil Camden gestaltete, dem Haus, das Schlesinger nach der Trennung für seine Frau bauen ließ. Auch das langgestreckte zweigeschossige Hill House mit seinen halbrunden Schmalseiten, der asymmetrischen Fassadengliederung und dem flachen Dach war – wie Schlesingers und Tunnards Haus in Chertsey – ganz der Moderne verpflichtet. Wahrscheinlich abermals auf Tunnards Fürsprache hin hatte Schlesinger mit dem Bau den Architekten Oliver Hill (1887-1968) und damit einen weiteren führenden Vertreter der Avantgarde beauftragt.[5]

Doch zurück zu Schlesingers und Tunnards eigenem Haus in Chertsey, das Raymond McGrath über einem äußerst bemerkenswerten, durch drei konzentrische Kreise gebildeten Grundriss konzipierte.[6] Zur Straße und zum Vorhof hin türmt es sich drei volle Geschosse hoch auf: Eine wuchtige Geste, die jedoch geschickt von der asymmetrischen Gliederung der Fassade unterlaufen wird. So bildet das große, über zwei Geschosse reichende Treppenhausfenster ein klares Gegengewicht zu der in der zentralen, von Tor und Vorfahrt definierten Achse gelegenen Eingangstür. Den größten Reiz des runden Hauses entfaltet jedoch nicht die nach Nordosten gerichtete Eingangspartie, sondern dessen Südseite, die sich fulminant zum Garten und dem abfallenden, parkähnlich gestalteten Gelände hin öffnet. Hier hat McGrath den Rundbau wie einen Laib Käse aufgeschnitten und damit den inneren Aufbau

singer's feelings and, for some years, they became a couple. The elegant mansion behind the plain, white wooden gate at the overgrown by trees and bushes St Ann's Road in Chertsey was the home they shared.[4]

Tunnard had persuaded Schlesinger to commission his friend McGrath with designing the house. Tunnard himself took responsibility for the design of the garden – just as he also designed the garden of Hill House in the London Borough of Camden, the house Schlesinger had built for his wife after their separation. The elongated, two-storey Hill House with its semi-circular narrow sides, the asymmetrical façade structure and the flat roof were completely in line with modernism – as was Schlesinger's and Tunnard's house in Chertsey. Probably also due to Tunnard's recommendation, Schlesinger had commissioned the architect Oliver Hill (1887-1968) – another leading representative of the avant-garde.[5]

But back to Schlesinger's and Tunnard's own house in Chertsey which Raymond McGrath designed based on a remarkable floor plan composed of three concentric circles.[6] Towards the road and the forecourt, it rises three full storeys: a powerful construction which, however, is cleverly offset by the asymmetrical structure of the façade. Thus the large staircase window extending over two levels is a clear counterbalance to the entrance door located in the central axis defined by the gate and the forecourt. The strongest appeal of the circular house, however, is not the entrance towards the northeast but its south side which brilliantly opens onto the garden and the sloping site designed to look like a park. Here McGrath sliced open the circular building like a wheel of cheese and thus made the inner structure of the house visible to the outside – on the ground floor, the large, circular living room whose walls follow the middle ring of the layout; on the floor above it, the bedroom of Tunnard and Schlesinger, whose form in turn corresponds to the smallest of the three concentric circles of the layout. The latter is finally also present on the top floor as a negative shape in the form of a cut-out roof terrace. With this arrangement, McGrath no doubt successfully achieved one of the most fascinating and most idiosyncratic creations of modernism in Great Britain. In every respect, the bedroom Tunnard and Schlesinger shared takes the central position. It represents the focus of the house and occupies its centre in the layout as well as in the cross-section. The whole house appears to be designed solely with this room in mind.

And there was actually a good reason for this. This shared bedroom was for Tunnard and Schlesinger not only the strongest possible expression of their mutual affection but also its most threatened liability. This was because of the fact that a law passed by the British Parliament in 1888, the so-called Laboucher Amendment,[7] took place in the private premises of the participants. The relevant accusation "gross indecency" – major immoral behaviour – could be punished with up to two years of prison "with or without hard labour."

McGrath konzipierte das Haus über einem äußerst bemerkenswerten, durch drei konzentrische Kreise gebildeten Grundriss.

McGrath designed the house on a remarkable floor plan formed by three concentric circles.

des Hauses nach außen sichtbar gemacht – im Erdgeschoss das große runde Wohnzimmer, dessen Wände dem mittleren Grundriss-Ring folgen; im darüber liegenden Geschoss das Schlafzimmer von Tunnard und Schlesinger, dessen Form wiederum dem kleinsten der drei konzentrischen Grundriss-Kreise entspricht. Dieser ist schlussendlich auch im obersten Geschoss als Negativform in Gestalt einer ausgeschnittenen Dachterrasse präsent. Ohne Zweifel ist McGrath mit dieser Anordnung eine der faszinierendsten und eigenwilligsten Schöpfungen der Moderne in Großbritannien gelungen. In jeder Hinsicht nimmt darin das gemeinsame Schlafzimmer von Tunnard und Schlesinger die zentrale Position ein. Es bildet den Fokus des Hauses und besetzt dessen Mittelpunkt sowohl im Grundriss wie auch im Schnitt. Das ganze Haus scheint allein auf diesen Raum hin konzipiert zu sein.

Und dafür gab es durchaus einen guten Grund. Denn dieses gemeinsame Schlafzimmer war für Tunnard und Schlesinger nicht nur der größtmögliche Ausdruck ihrer gegenseitigen Zuneigung, sondern auch deren größte Gefahr. Denn ein 1888 vom britischen Parlament verabschiedetes Gesetz, das so genannte „Labouchere Amendment",[7] stellte bis zu seiner Abschaffung 1967 jede sexuelle Handlung zwischen zwei Männern unter Strafe – auch wenn der Vollzug ausschließlich in den privaten Räumen der Beteiligten stattfand. Die entsprechende Anklage lautete auf „gross indecency" – grob unsittliches Verhalten – und konnte mit bis zu zwei Jahren Gefängnis – „with or without hard labour" – bestraft werden. Der vielleicht berühmteste Angeklagte, der unter dem Labouchere Amendment verurteilt wurde, war der Schriftsteller Oscar Wilde, der 1895 in einem Aufsehen erregenden Prozess das größtmögliche Strafmaß – zwei Jahre bei harter Arbeit – erhielt. Tunnard und Schlesinger hatten also allen Grund, die wahre Natur ihrer Beziehung vor der Öffentlichkeit

Auf der Südseite ist der Rundbau wie ein Laib Käse aufgeschnitten und damit der innere Aufbau nach außen sichtbar.

On the south side, the round building is cut open like a loaf of cheese, revealing the internal structure.

The most famous defendant who was sentenced under the Laboucher Amendment was probably the writer Oscar Wilde who, in 1895 in a sensational trial, was sentenced to the maximum penalty – two years of hard labour. Tunnard and Schlesinger thus had every reason to keep the true nature of their relationship a secret from the public. But even though in Chertsey, far from London, they were hardly in danger of being recognized by business partners or colleagues, and although the remote property on the edges of the small town offered them protection against all too prying eyes, the shared house with the prominent bedroom had to raise suspicion. McGrath, however, had a brilliant architectural idea: On two opposite sides, he designed deep alcoves which connected the inner with the middle layout ring and had their side walls directed to the central point of the house which gave them the shape of circle segments. Officially, these two room components were considered to be the actual bedrooms of the two "bachelors" Tunnard and Schlesinger and the circular room in between was to be the common antechamber. But, in actual fact, the two men had narrow beds resting on concealed castors which, at night, were pushed together and only during the day stood in the two alcoves desultorily separated with some curtains. In case of an unannounced visit by the local police patrol, this kind of charade would certainly not have been convincing but, in the event of a court case, might probably have avoided a conviction as court records of similar cases occurring during that time show.[8]

But it never came to that! Schlesinger and Tunnard were anyway only able to enjoy their shared existence in Chertsey for a short time since soon the outbreak of the Second

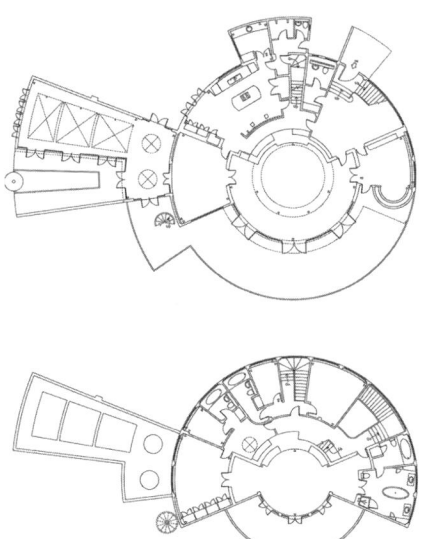

Grundriss Erdgeschoss
Ground floor plan

Grundriss Obergeschoss
Upper floor plan

geheim zu halten. Aber auch wenn sie in Chertsey, weit abseits von London, kaum Gefahr liefen, von Geschäftspartnern oder Kollegen erkannt zu werden, und das einsame Grundstück am Rande der Kleinstadt Schutz vor allzu neugierigen Blicken bot, musste das gemeinsame Haus mit dem prominenten Schlafzimmer doch Argwohn erregen. McGrath hatte jedoch einen genialen architektonischen Einfall: Er versah den Raum an zwei gegenüberliegenden Seiten mit tiefen Nischen, die jeweils den inneren mit dem mittleren Grundriss-Ring verbanden und deren Seitenwände auf den zentralen Punkt des Hauses ausgerichtet waren, wodurch sie die Form von Kreis-Segmenten erhielten. Offiziell galten diese beiden Raumteile als die eigentlichen Schlafzimmer der beiden „Junggesellen" Tunnard und Schlesinger; das dazwischen liegende runde Zimmer als gemeinsames Antichambre. In Wirklichkeit verfügten beide Männer jedoch über auf versteckten Rollen gelagerte schmale Betten, die nachts im Schlafzimmer zusammengestellt wurden und lediglich tagsüber in den beiden nur durch einige Vorhänge halbherzig abgetrennten Nischen standen. Diese Art der Scharade wäre im Falle eines unangekündigten Besuches der örtlichen Polizeistreife sicher nicht überzeugend gewesen, hätte bei einem Prozess jedoch wahrscheinlich eine Verurteilung verhindert, wie Gerichtsakten aus ähnlichen Fällen der Zeit zeigen.[8]

Doch so weit kam es nie! Ohnehin konnten Schlesinger und Tunnard ihr gemeinsames Dasein in Chertsey nur für kurze Zeit genießen, denn schon bald sollte der Ausbruch des Zweiten Weltkriegs ihr Leben und das ihres Architekten vollständig verändern. Tunnard, der ursprünglich aus Kanada kam, musste 1939 England verlassen. Während des Krieges war er für die Royal Canadian Air Force tätig. Noch in England hatte er eine Reihe von

Der Hauptraum des Erdgeschosses ist das Wohnzimmer; ein Ring aus schmalen Metallstützen umsteht das Zentrum des Raumes und verweist auf den Grundriss des darüber liegenden Schlafzimmers.

The main room of the first floor is the living room; a ring of narrow metal supports surrounds the center of the room and refers to the floor plan of the bedroom above it.

World War was to completely change their lives and that of their architect. Tunnard, who originally came from Canada, had to leave England in 1939. During the War, he was part of the Royal Canadian Air Force. While still in England, he had published a series of essays on designing modern landscaped gardens. The resulting book, *Gardens in the Modern Landscape*,[9] made him, who meanwhile was back in his home country, instantly famous. He first taught at Harvard, after the War at Yale, and became one of the most renowned theorists of landscaping and urban development on the North-American continent.[10] When he married Lydia Evans in 1945, it seemed like there had never been a shared time with Schlesinger in Europe. Schlesinger, on the other hand, kept St Ann's Court even after Tunnard's departure. It was not until after his death that the musician Phil Manzanera, guitarist of the legendary New Wave band Roxy Music, purchased the house. He lived there for almost 20 years. When he resold St Ann's Court in 1997, the new owners had the house, whose visible concrete structure had suffered considerably damage in the course of the years, elaborately refurbished.[11] Thus, it is thanks to them that the house today still sits en-

Aufsätzen über die Gestaltung moderner Landschaftsgärten publiziert. Das daraus entstandene Buch, *Gardens in the Modern Landscape*,[9] machte ihn, zurück in seiner Heimat, schlagartig berühmt. Er lehrte zunächst in Harvard, nach dem Krieg in Yale und entwickelte sich zu einem der renommiertesten Landschafts- und Städtebautheoretiker des nordamerikanischen Kontinents.[10] Als er 1945 Lydia Evans heiratete, schien es, als habe es die gemeinsame Zeit mit Schlesinger in Europa nie gegeben. Schlesinger wiederum behielt St. Ann's Court auch nach Tunnards Weggang. Erst nach seinem Tod erwarb es 1977 der Musiker Phil Manzanera, Gitarrist der legendären New-Wave-Band Roxy Music. Er wohnte fast 20 Jahre hier. Als er St. Ann's Court 1997 weiterverkaufte, ließen die neuen Eigentümer das Haus, dessen sichtbare Betonkonstruktion im Laufe der Jahre starke Schäden bekommen hatte, aufwendig sanieren.[11] So ist es ihnen zu verdanken, dass das Haus noch heute auf der kleinen Anhöhe bei Chertsey thront und von dem großen Können seines Architekten Raymond McGrath kündet. Auch dessen Lebensweg änderte sich mit dem Ausbruch des Krieges und seiner Flucht aus London. Er ging nach Dublin und fand eine Anstellung in der staatlichen Bauverwaltung, wo er vor allem für die Ausgestaltung und Möblierung von Staatsbauten im In- und Ausland zuständig war. Dazu gehörten auch Botschaften weltweit, für die McGrath eine Art staatliche Corporate Identity schuf, wobei er ein besonderes Augenmerk auf textile Elemente legte und selbst zahlreiche Teppichentwürfe fertigte. Selber bauen konnte McGrath in dieser Position jedoch nicht mehr und so blieb das runde weiße Haus auf dem St. Ann's Hill in Chertsey, das er Ende der 1930er-Jahre für Tunnard und Schlesinger bauen durfte, nicht nur sein brillantestes, sondern auch sein letztes realisiertes Bauwerk.

Heute steht das Haus unter Denkmalschutz – auch wegen seiner eigenwilligen Form und seiner modernen Beton-Bauweise, doch nicht nur deswegen, sondern auch wegen Tunnard und Schlesinger und der Geschichte ihres gemeinsamen Schlafzimmers. Denn es ist eines der ersten Häuser, die in das von der staatlichen Denkmalpflegebehörde und der Leeds Beckett University initiierte Programm Pride of Place aufgenommen wurden. Es handelt sich dabei um ein in dieser Form weltweit einzigartiges Projekt der staatlichen Denkmalpflege mit dem Ziel, das in der gebauten Umwelt aufgehobene kulturelle Erbe von Schwulen und Lesben gezielt zu erforschen, zu dokumentieren und für die Nachwelt zu erhalten.[12] Nachdem die Initiative im Sommer 2015 erstmals vorgestellt worden war, dauerte es ein knappes Jahr, bis im September 2016 die ersten sechs Gebäude den Status einer LGBTQ Heritage Site erhielten. Neben Tunnards und Schlesingers St. Ann's Court wurden unter anderem auch die Wohnhäuser von Oscar Wilde und Benjamin Britten, aber auch die Royal Vauxhall Tavern, eines der bekanntesten schwulen Lokale Londons, in das Programm aufgenommen. Sie und die Geschichten, die sie von ihren Bewohnern und von deren Kampf um Anerkennung und Gleichbehandlung erzählen, sind damit ein Teil der offiziellen nationalen Kultur Großbritanniens, der Geschichte des Landes und seiner Identität geworden.

throned on a little hill near Chertsey and tells about the great skill of its architect Raymond McGrath. His life as well changed with the outbreak of the War and his flight from London. He went to Dublin and found employment in the Office of Public Works where he was above all responsible for the design and the furnishing of government buildings in Ireland and abroad. Also among his works were embassies for which McGrath established a kind of government corporate identity while paying particular attention to textile elements and coming up with numerous carpet designs. In this position, however, McGrath could no longer design buildings and thus the circular white house on St Ann's Hill in Chertsey, which he was commissioned to build at the end of the 1930s for Tunnard and Schlesinger, remained not only his most brilliant but also the last building he completed.

Today, the house is under a preservation order – because of its idiosyncratic shape and its modern concrete construction method but also because of Tunnard and Schlesinger and the story of their shared bedroom. This is because it is one of the first houses which became part of the Pride of Place programme initiated by the government monument-protection authorities and Leeds Beckett University. This is a worldwide unique project of the government monument protection authorities with the aim to specifically research the cultural heritage of gays and lesbians preserved in the built environment, to document it and to keep it safe for posterity.[12] After the initiative was first presented in summer 2015, it took almost a year until, in September 2016, the first six buildings were assigned the status of an LGBTQ Heritage Site. Besides Tunnard's and Schlesinger's St Ann's Court, among others the residences of Oscar Wilde and Benjamin Britten, but also the Royal Vauxhall Tavern, one of the best-known gay pubs in London, became part of the programme. They and the stories they tell about their residents and their fight for recognition and equal treatment, have thus become part of the official, national culture of Great Britain, the history of the country and its identity.

Wolfgang Voigt

Amüsante und weniger amüsante Erlebnisse: Alfred Roth

Die einen waren begeistert, andere schockiert: flache Dächer, schmucklose kubische Würfel, Scheiben und Terrassen, einzeln und in der Reihe – sollten das die Wohnungen der Zukunft sein? Die 21 Häuser auf einem Hügel über Stuttgart waren von 17 Architekten entworfen worden, unter ihnen mit Le Corbusier, Walter Gropius, Mies van der Rohe, Bruno Taut und Peter Behrens einigen der bekannten Pioniere der neuen Architektur. Die im Rahmen der Ausstellung „Die Wohnung" errichtete Weißenhofsiedlung wurde im Sommer 1927 zum Mekka der Architekturmoderne. Um sie zu sehen, kamen eine halbe Million Menschen.[1] Zu den Höhepunkten der Siedlung gehörten die beiden Häuser von Le Corbusier, die ein gebautes Manifest darstellten.[2] Am langgestreckten Doppelhaus demonstrierte der Architekt sein in fünf Punkten fixiertes Glaubensbekenntnis. Statt massiver Wände gab es ein die Geschossdecken tragendes Stützenskelett aus Stahlbeton. Dadurch war nicht nur ein von Rücksichten auf tragende Wände befreiter Grundriss („plan libre") möglich, sondern auch eine zwanglose Fassadengestaltung. Das traditionelle Lochfenster ersetzte Le Corbusier durch horizontale Fensterbänder. Auf den flachen Dächern legte er Gärten an.

Die Ausarbeitung der Pläne hatte Le Corbusier einem jungen Mitarbeiter anvertraut, den er in einem Brief als „exzellenten Zeichner, sehr korrekt und intelligent" charakterisierte.[3] Der aus der Schweiz stammende Alfred Roth (1903-1998) hatte sein Architekturstudium an der ETH Zürich abgeschlossen, als ihn sein Lehrer Karl Moser ermunterte, im Atelier Le Corbusiers auszuhelfen.[4] Roth folgte dem Rat. Im Januar 1927 zog er nach Paris und unterstützte den aufstrebenden Star der Architekturmoderne zunächst bei der Fertigstellung seines Projekts für den Völkerbundpalast in Genf. Danach, von April bis Juli 1927, überwachte Roth als Bauleiter Le Corbusiers dessen Baustelle am Weißenhof. Eine Besonderheit bildeten multifunktionale Wohnräume, die sich durch variables Interieur für Tages- und Nachtnutzungen herrichten ließen. Als kurz vor der Eröffnung vom Atelier angekündigte Pläne für einzelne Stücke nicht eintrafen, füllte Roth die Lücke mit einem eigenen Entwurf für mobile Betten aus vernickeltem Stahlrohr, die tagsüber in die Wandschränke geschoben wurden. Le Corbusier blieb für Roth fortan der verehrte Mentor, mit dem er sich lebenslang verbunden fühlte. Mit Sorgfalt restauriert und in Teilen rekonstruiert, wurde das Doppelhaus 2006 als Weißenhofmuseum eingerichtet; zehn Jahre später wurde es in den Rang einer Welterbestätte der Unesco erhoben.[5]

Amusing and Less Amusing Experiences: Alfred Roth

Some were enthusiastic, others were shocked: flat roofs, plain, cubic constructions, slabs and terraces, individually and standing in a row – these should be the residences of the future? The 21 houses on a hill above Stuttgart had been designed by 17 architects, among them Le Corbusier, Walter Gropius, Mies van der Rohe, Bruno Taut and Peter Behrens, some of the well-known pioneers of the new architecture. The Weissenhof settlement constructed as part of the "The Dwelling" exhibition became a mecca of modern architecture in summer 1927. Half a million people came to see it.[1] Among the highlights of the settlement were the two houses designed by Le Corbusier which were a built manifesto.[2] massive walls, there was a supporting skeleton consisting of reinforced concrete on which the storey ceilings rested. This not only made a layout ("*plan libre*") possible regardless of load-bearing walls but also a free façade design. Le Corbusier replaced the traditional punched with horizontal bands of windows. On the flat roofs, he had gardens laid out.

Le Corbusier put a young employee in charge of developing the plans whom he characterized in a letter as "an excellent draughtsman, very correct and intelligent."[3] Alfred Roth (1903-1998), born in Switzerland, had completed his studies of architecture at ETH Zurich when his teacher Karl Moser encouraged him to help out in the studio of Le Corbusier.[4] Roth followed the advice. In January 1927, he moved to Paris and initially supported the coming star of architectural modernism in completing his project for the League of Nations Building in Geneva. Subsequently, from April to July 1927, Roth supervised as a site manager of Le Corbusier the latter's construction site at Weissenhof. Special features were multifunction living rooms which could be arranged for being used by day and by night with the help of variable interior furnishings. When, shortly before the opening, plans for individual pieces announced by the studio did not arrive. Roth filled the gap with his own design for mobile beds made of nickel-plated tubular steel which were pushed into the closets during the day. Carefully restored and in part reconstructed, the duplex was set up as the Weissenhofmuseum in 2006; ten years later, it was raised to the rank of a UNESCO World Heritage Site.[5] From then on, Le Corbusier remained for Roth the mentor with whom he felt connected for life.

Alfred Roth und „Pierino"
am Strand von Ischia

*Alfred Roth and "Pierino"
on the beach of Ischia*

Die Weißenhof-Sage ist viele Male erzählt worden; eine Episode blieb jedoch stets ausgespart. Während des Sommers 1927 musste Roth die Stadt Hals über Kopf verlassen, weil ihm die Polizei nachstellte. Roth war homosexuell und anscheinend war er abenteuerlustig genug, um sich in Stuttgart nach Männern umzusehen. Was im Deutschen Reich noch strafbar war, stellte damals in vielen Kantonen der Schweiz nur noch ein minderes Problem dar. Die sogenannte Sodomie war dort kein Offizialdelikt mehr und wurde nur noch auf Antrag verfolgt, weshalb es immer weniger Verurteilungen gab.

Nach einem Zwischenspiel in Schweden in die Heimat zurückgekehrt, wurde Roth mit Bauten, Publikationen und seit den 1950er-Jahren mit seiner Lehre an der ETH Zürich einer der Beweger der Schweizer Moderne und blieb dies bis ins hohe Alter. 1932 gehörte Roth zu den Architekten der gemeinschaftlich entworfenen Siedlung Neubühl bei Zürich, die als bedeutendste Manifestation der neuen Architektur zwischen den Weltkriegen in der Schweiz angesehen wird. Außerdem baute er zusammen mit seinem Cousin Emil Roth und mit Marcel Breuer die Mehrfamilienhäuser im Doldertal in Zürich (1935/36), mit denen die am Weißenhof exerzierten Prinzipien des Meisters in der Schweiz heimisch gemacht wurden.[6]

Von 1942 an war Sex zwischen erwachsenen Männern in der Schweiz straffrei. So kam es, dass Zürich in den 1950er-Jahren für schwule Männer aus Ländern, in denen die barbarischen Strafbestimmungen noch aufrechterhalten wurden, zum beliebten Reiseziel avancierte. Natürlich war in der Schweiz auch danach noch die gesellschaftliche Stellung der Homosexuellen daran geknüpft, dass sie sich angepasst und unauffällig verhielten. Als Roth dann im hohen Alter seinen Lebensbericht *Amüsante Erlebnisse eines Architekten* (1988) veröffentlichte, hatte sich die Lage längst gelockert, und so ließ er auf dezente Weise durchblicken, was ihm die größte Freude bereitete, wenn er die Ferien auf seiner Lieblingsinsel Ischia verbrachte: am Strand und in den Bars das „ungezwungene, fröhliche"

Le Corbusiers Doppelwohnhaus in der Weißenhof-Siedlung in Stuttgart: Den Entwurf zum Bettgestell lieferte Alfred Roth.

Le Corbusier's semi-detached house in the Weißenhof estate in Stuttgart: The design for the bedstead was provided by Alfred Roth.

The Weissenhof saga has been told many times; one episode, however, was always left out. During summer 1927, Roth once had to leave the city in a mad rush because he was wanted by the police. Roth was homosexual and apparently adventurous enough to look for men in Stuttgart. What was still punishable in the German Reich was no more than a minor problem in many cantons of Switzerland. So-called sodomy was no longer a criminal offence there and was only prosecuted on request so that there were increasingly fewer convictions.

Having returned to his home country after an interlude in Sweden, Roth became one of the movers of Swiss modernism with buildings, publications and, since the 1950s, with his teachings at ETH Zurich and remained as such into old age. In 1932, Roth was one of the architects of the jointly designed Neubühl settlement near Zurich which is considered to be the most significant manifestation of the new architecture in Switzerland between the world wars. Together with his cousin Emil Roth and with Marcel Breuer, he also designed the multi-family houses in the Doldertal in Zurich (1935/36), which introduced and anchored in Switzerland the master's principles practiced at Weissenhof in Switzerland.[6]

Starting in 1942, sex between adult men was unpunished in Switzerland. So it happened, that, in the 1950s, Zurich became a favourite travel destination for gay men from countries where the barbaric penal provisions were still maintained. Of course, even afterwards the social standing of the homosexuals in Switzerland obliged them to behave in a conformist and inconspicuous way. When, at an advanced age, Roth published his memoirs *Amüsante Erlebnisse eines Architekten* (1988), the situation had long been relaxed and thus he he subtly implied what had been his greatest joy when spending his holidays on his favourite island of Ischia: on the beach and in the bars, the "casual, merry" meeting with the Italian village youth – the males, of course – with Marco, Pierino, Franco, Michele, Enzo and Paolo, whom he remembered with pleasure.[7]

Alfred Roth, Dolder-Häuser in Zürich, 1930er-Jahre

The Alfred Roth Dolder houses in Zurich, 1930s

Zusammentreffen mit der italienischen Dorfjugend – der männlichen natürlich – mit Marco, Pierino, Franco, Michele, Enzo und Paolo, an die er sich mit Vergnügen erinnerte.[7]

Im Alter hatte Roth das, was mit „schlechter Umgang" umschrieben worden ist. Es kamen männliche Prostituierte ins Haus, darunter auch zwielichtige Gestalten. Mit schlimmen Folgen: wertvolle Bilder kamen abhanden; eines soll plötzlich in London im Kunsthandel aufgetaucht sein; ein wertvolles Mondrian-Gemälde wurde aus der Limmat gefischt. Nach Roths Tod druckte die *Neue Zürcher Zeitung* ein ehrendes Porträt, das Gelegenheit zu befreiender Wahrheit geboten hätte. Sie wurde nicht genutzt; stattdessen kann man hier sehen, wohin das Verschweigen des noch nicht Sagbaren führen kann. An Roths Begegnung mit Kriminellen zu erinnern, erschien kurz vor dem Jahr 2000 offenbar noch als weniger schädlich für das Ansehen des Verstorbenen zu sein als ein ungeschminkter Umgang mit seiner Homosexualität. So enthielt der Nachruf eine ominöse Bemerkung über das „Rumoren des Unplanbaren" und über „Häusliche Unbilden und Pech mit Schlaumeiern und Ganoven", die Roth zu erdulden gehabt habe. Der Verfasser meinte es zweifellos gut mit Alfred Roth, doch war damit die Neugier erst recht geweckt.[8]

Roth hatte sich 1960/61 ein Domizil in schönster Hanglage gebaut. Sein „Fellowship Home" in Zürich war vieles: großzügige Wohnung und Privatatelier des Architekten, Ausstellungsraum für seine Sammlung moderner Kunst und gleichzeitig ein privates Studentenheim mit sechs Zimmern in der unterer Etage. Wegen der wachsenden Wohnungsnot der Architekturstudenten hatte er sich entschlossen, ein Haus nicht nur für sich und seine Gäste zu bauen. Die Studenten, die von ihm auch Betreuung in ihren Entwürfen erhielten, sollten in ihrem Stockwerk ansonsten so frei und unabhängig leben wie er selbst auf der Ebene darüber. So wohnte der Junggeselle seine ganz eigene Version eines Mehrgenerationen-Hauses bis an sein Ende ungestört und allein, aber schaffte es so doch, männliche Jugend in enger Nachbarschaft bei sich zu wissen.

Alfred Roths Fellowship Home: Unten lagen die Studentenzimmer, oben Roths eigene Wohnung.

Alfred Roth's Fellowship Home: The student rooms were downstairs, Roth's own apartment was upstairs.

In his old age, Roth kept what has been described as "bad company". Male prostitutes came to the house, among them shady characters. With dire consequences: valuable paintings disappeared; one was said to have suddenly showed up in the London art trade; a valuable Mondrian painting was fished out of the river flowing through Zurich. After Roth's death, the *Neue Zürcher Zeitung* printed a redeeming portrait which would have offered the opportunity of telling the truth. Instead, one can see where the non-disclosure may lead. A reference to Roth's encounters with criminals seemed, shortly before the year 2000, to be apparently less detrimental to the image of the deceased than openly dealing with his homosexuality. The obituary thus contained an ominous remark about the "rumbling of the unpredictable" and about "domestic tribulations and bad luck with rogues and crooks" which Roth had to endure. The author no doubt meant well with Alfred Roth, but this stimulated the curiosity even more.[8]

In 1960/61, Roth had built for himself a residence in a prime hillside location. His "Fellowship Home" in Zurich was many things: the spacious residence and the private studio of the architect; an exhibition room for his collection of modern art and, at the same time, a private student hostel with six rooms on the lower level. Due to the growing housing shortage affecting the students of architecture, he had decided to build a home not only for himself and his guests. The students, who were also given advice on their designs, were to live on their floor as freely and independently as he himself did on the floor above. The bachelor thus lived alone and undisturbed in his own version of a multi-generation house until the end of life while ensuring that male youth was living in close vicinity.

Wolfgang Voigt

Dreischeibenhaus und Schloss: Helmut Hentrich

Über der Düsseldorfer City erheben sich drei parallel gegeneinander versetzte Scheiben mit Vorhangfassaden aus Glas, Aluminium und poliertem Edelstahl; die mittlere Scheibe 24 Geschosse hoch; ein scharfkantiges gewaltiges Volumen, dessen Gewicht auf wundersame Weise unsichtbar gemacht wurde. Damals wie heute verführt der 1956 bis 1960 für den Phoenix-Rheinrohr-Konzern errichtete Bau zu Metaphern der Schwerelosigkeit; das „Dreischeibenhaus" erscheint schwebend, spielerisch leicht, „im Sonnenlicht von gleißender Anmut." Henry-Russell Hitchcock nannte es eines der schönsten Hochhäuser der Welt und stellte es ausdrücklich auf eine Stufe mit dem zur gleichen Zeit in New York entstandenen Seagram Building von Mies van der Rohe.[1] Ein anderer Kritiker aus den USA sah es auf dem gleichen Rang wie Gio Pontis Pirelli-Hochhaus in Mailand und dem Seagram Building, wegen der noch besser gelungenen Einfügung in das städtische Umfeld, sogar überlegen.[2] Sechzig Kilometer westlich steht wiederum ein nur wenig später entstandenes Werk desselben Architekten: Casteel Groot Buggenum in der niederländischen Provinz Zuid-Limburg, eine kleine Wasserburg wie aus dem 17. Jahrhundert. Wirklich alt sind hier nur die Grundmauern und der Burggraben. Aus einer verlassenen Ruine entstand ein für den eigenen Gebrauch geschaffenes Schloss, das man für einen niederländischen Adelssitz der Vergangenheit halten möchte. Tatsächlich ist es eine mit großem Geschick komponierte Collage aus hunderten Teilen verschiedenster Provenienz. Wer hier naserümpfend ein schräges Pastiche erwartet, kommt nicht auf seine Kosten. Der Architekt war zwar ein obsessiver Sammler, jedoch auch ein begnadeter Arrangeur mit großem Gespür für Harmonie.[3]

Hier das perfekte Dreischeibenhaus, bewunderte Ikone der westdeutschen Moderne, dort das komplett fiktionale Schloss: Der Kontrast könnte kaum größer sein! Der Architekt, dessen Name für beide Werke steht, war Helmut Hentrich (1905-2001). Groot Buggenum war nicht nur sein Ferienhaus, es schützte auch sein Privatleben zu einer Zeit, als die Strafbestimmungen gegen Homosexualität in Teilen aufgehoben, aber nicht beseitigt waren.

Den aus dem Rheinland stammenden Sohn eines vermögenden Bauingenieurs zog es 1925 zum Studium nach Berlin, als die Architekturmoderne im Begriff war, vom Expressionismus zur Neuen Sachlichkeit überzugehen.[4] Sein wichtigster Lehrer wurde Hans Poelzig, der bei aller Sachlichkeit den Hang zu monumentaler, großer Form nie abgelegt hatte.[5] Geldprämien aus Architekturwettbewerben nutzte der junge Hentrich für

Dreischeibenhaus and Castle: Helmut Hentrich

High above the Düsseldorf city centre, three parallel staggered blocks rise up with curtain-wall façades consisting of glass, aluminium and polished stainless steel: the centre block is 24 storeys high; a sharp-edged, enormous volume whose weight has been made indiscernible in a miraculous way. Then as now, the building constructed from 1956 to 1960 for the Phoenix-Rheinrohr Group inspires metaphors of weightlessness: the "Dreischeibenhaus" (roughly translated: three-panel house) appears to be floating, playfully light, as "a thing of gleaming beauty in sunlight." Henry-Russell Hitchcock called it one of the most attractive high-rise buildings of the world and expressly put it on a par with the Seagram Building by Mies van der Rohe[1] constructed in New York around the same time. Another critic from the USA ranked it the same as Gio Ponti's Pirelli high-rise building in Milan and the Seagram Building, actually superior to them due to the even more successful integration into the urban environment.[2] Sixty kilometres further west stands a work by the same architect constructed only little later: Casteel Groot Buggenum in the Netherlands province of Zuid-Limburg, a small, moated castle as if from the 17th century. Only the foundation walls and the castle moat are truly old, however. Based on an abandoned ruin, a castle was designed here for personal use which one might think to be a Netherlands seat of nobility from the past. It is, in fact, a collage assembled with much skill from hundreds of parts from a wide variety of origins. Those who might expect a quirky pastiche will be disappointed. Even though the architect was an obsessive collector, he was also a gifted arranger with a great feeling for harmony.[3]

Here the perfect Dreischeibenhaus, an admired icon of West-German modernism, there the completely fictional castle: the contrast could hardly be stronger! The architect whose name stands for both works was Helmut Hentrich (1905-2001). Groot Buggenum was not only his holiday home but also protected his private life at a time when the penal provisions for homosexuality had in part been lifted but not completely eliminated.

The son of a wealthy civil engineer born in the Rhineland went to Berlin in 1925 for his studies at a time when modernist architecture was about to pass from expressionism to the New Objectivity.[4] Hans Poelzig was to become his most important teacher who, despite all the objectivity, had never relinquished the tendency to monumental, large form.[5] Young Hentrich used financial rewards from architectural competitions for a more than one-year study tour around the globe, which allowed him to gain a kind of world experience

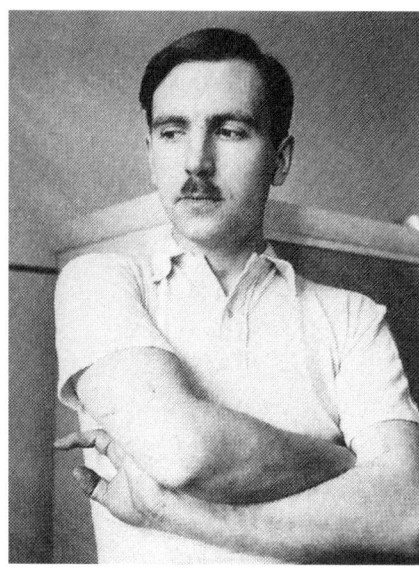

Helmut Hentrich, Architekturstudent in Berlin

Helmut Hentrich, architecture student in Berlin

eine mehr als einjährige Studienreise um den Globus, die ihm eine in seiner Generation ungewöhnliche Welterfahrung einbrachte, bevor er 1933 in Düsseldorf sein eigenes Büro eröffnete. Wenn man seinen Memoiren Glauben schenkt, erlebte er das nationalsozialistische Regime in kritischer Distanz. Zugleich bestand er darauf, an den NS-typischen Bauaufgaben teilzunehmen, und baute mit seinem ersten Büropartner Hans Heuser unter anderem Heime der Hitlerjugend. Die Jahre des Wiederaufbaus brachten dem inzwischen als Hentrich & Petschnigg firmierenden Büro den rasanten Aufstieg, der sich bald in Höhenmetern ablesen ließ. Mit dem Büroturm für die BASF in Ludwigshafen (1953-57) gelang ihnen das erste deutsche Hochhaus mit voller Klimatisierung und einer Höhe von mehr als 100 Metern. Der Rekord wurde gehalten, bis ihm 1963 das auf denselben Reißbrettern entworfene Bayer-Hochhaus in Leverkusen mit 122 Metern den Rang ablief. Anerkennung aus dem In- und Ausland gab es für das bereits erwähnte Phoenix-Rheinrohr-Hochhaus in Düsseldorf, bei dem Hentrichs Mitarbeiter das in Ludwigshafen angewendete Konzept von zwei einen Versorgungskern umschließenden Scheiben intelligent optimierten. Das Dreischeibenhaus markierte Westdeutschlands Anschluss an die internationale Architekturmoderne, von der sich das Dritte Reich einst verabschiedet hatte.

Mit Erfolgen reich gesegnet, gehörte das inzwischen mit wechselnden Partnern geführte Büro unter dem Namen HPP (Hentrich-Petschnigg & Partner) in den 1960er-Jahren zu den größten Architekturfirmen des Landes und blieb es bis heute. Helmut Hentrich war seit den 1950er-Jahren immer weniger selbst der Entwerfer und immer mehr Anreger und operativer Lenker eines Unternehmens, dessen Teams im Übergang in die

unusual in his generation, before he opened his own office in Düsseldorf in 1933. If one is to believe his memoirs, he witnessed the national-socialist regime from a critical distance. At the same time, he insisted on participating in the building tasks typical of National Socialism and, together with his first office partner Hans Heuser, designed homes of the Hitler Youth among other projects. The years of reconstruction meant the rapid ascent for the firm meanwhile operating under the name of Hentrich & Petschnigg – a development which could soon be measured in metres of height. With the BASF office tower in Ludwigshafen (1953-57), the office succeeded in designing the first German high-rise building with full air-conditioning and a height of more than 100 metres. The record was held until 1963, when the Bayer high-rise building in Leverkusen designed on the same drawing boards achieved the first position with its height of 122 metres. The above mentioned Phoenix-Rheinrohr high-rise building in Düsseldorf achieved recognition from Germany and abroad. In it Hentrich's employees intelligently optimized the concept of two blocks enclosing a supply core as it was applied in Ludwigshafen. The Dreischeibenhaus marked West-Germany's connection to the international modernist architecture which the Third Reich had suppressed.

In the wake of success, the firm operated with changing partners under the name HPP (Hentrich-Petschnigg & Partner), ranked among the largest architectural companies of the country and remained as such until today. Since the 1950s, Helmut Hentrich himself had been less and less the designer but more and more the stimulator and operative director of a company whose teams were proficient in diverse design vocabularies during the transition to postmodernism. It had never been Hentrich's "thing" to follow classic modernism like a creed. Only like that had it been possible for him to include without shame a castle born from imagination in his list of works and to proudly publish it.

Hentrich's self-discipline and his always remote refuges allowed him to keep his private life hidden from the Düsseldorf public. The homosexuality of the vivacious bachelor was, however, no secret anywhere, neither among his own employees nor in the Düsseldorf "society". Linchpins of his network of contacts were the Malkasten artists association for which, after the Second World War, he built a new domicile, today called Hentrichhaus, as well as influential male and female building clients with whom he maintained lifelong friendships. Through the Poensgen and the van Meeteren families, connections to the upper echelons of the industry and the financial sector were established which had their administrative headquarters in Düsseldorf. The banker's widow Olga van Meeteren (1896-1976) may be considered a key figure who, in 1952, had commissioned him to design the elegant "aluminium house" which went down in history as an iconic construction of the local post-war modernism. For Hentrich, she took on the role of best friend and accompanied him on his travels for more than two decades.

Helmut Hentrich und Alfred Drexler, um 1930

Helmut Hentrich and Alfred Drexler, around 1930

Postmoderne vielgestaltige Formensprachen beherrschten. Der Klassischen Moderne wie einem Glaubensbekenntnis zu folgen, war Hentrichs Sache nie gewesen. Nur so war es ihm möglich, ohne Scham ein aus der Phantasie geborenes Schloss in seine Werkliste aufzunehmen und stolz zu publizieren.

Hentrichs Selbstdisziplin und seine stets abgelegenen Refugien erlaubten es ihm, sein Privatleben vor der Düsseldorfer Öffentlichkeit verborgen zu halten. Die Homosexualität des lebensfrohen Junggesellen war indessen nirgends ein Geheimnis, weder unter den eigenen Mitarbeitern noch in der Düsseldorfer „Gesellschaft". Angelpunkte seines Beziehungsnetzes waren der Künstlerverein Malkasten, dem er nach dem Zweiten Weltkrieg ein neues, heute Hentrichhaus genanntes Domizil baute, ebenso wie einflussreiche Bauherren und Bauherrinnen, mit denen er lebenslange Freundschaften pflegte. Über die Familien Poensgen und van Meeteren ergaben sich Verbindungen in die oberen Etagen von Industrie und Finanzbranche, die in Düsseldorf ihre Verwaltungssitze unterhielten. Als Schlüsselfigur darf man die Bankierswitwe Olga van Meeteren (1896-1976) ansehen, die ihn 1952 das elegante „Aluminiumhaus" entwerfen ließ, das als ikonischer Bau der lokalen Nachkriegsmoderne in die Geschichte einging. Sie übernahm bei Hentrich die Rolle der besten Freundin und war über zwei Jahrzehnte auf Reisen seine Begleiterin.

In Hentrichs Memoiren *Bauzeit. Aufzeichnungen aus dem Leben eines Architekten*, die er im hohen Alter 1995 erscheinen ließ, bleibt die Diskretion im Prinzip gewahrt.[6] Obwohl im engeren Sinne Persönliches nicht mitgeteilt wird, erlauben gezielt eingestreute Sätze blitzlichthafte Einblicke. So hielt sich Hentrich während seiner Kindheit von den

Helmut Hentrich vor dem Modell des BASF-Hochhauses in Ludwigshafen, 1954

Helmut Hentrich in front of the model of the BASF high-rise building in Ludwigshafen, 1954

In Hentrich's memoirs, *Bauzeit. Aufzeichnungen aus dem Leben eines Architekten*, which he had published in a very old age in 1995, discretion is in principle maintained.[6] Although, strictly speaking, nothing personal is communicated, deliberately interspersed sentences allow brief insights like flashes. Thus, during his childhood, Hentrich kept away from the village boys who were "too rough and coarse when they played."[7] Already early on, he had an eye for well-dressed men; he was a fan of sailor suits. "The young girls were also often wearing such nautical clothes," but: "they suited us better."[8] Already in his youth, he also started focusing on literature and art which he continued all his life, and which was to prevent him from growing lonely when living a solitary life in his old age. The mill he purchased in a remote valley of the Eifel Mountains in the 1950s has the special benefit that it is "barely observable".[9] His friend Olga did not mind the "eccentricities" of her companion,[10] who assesses tables above all as to whether they allow "attractive decorations into the bargain."[11] After Olga's death, he travels alone which "had disadvantages but also major advantages. […] Contrary to the usual routine, I was able to move around freely everywhere."[12] He was now no longer prevented from discovery tours of a special kind.

Among the men who were particularly close to Helmut Hentrich, Fritz Eilers has to be mentioned; in the 1930s, a "cordial friendship" with the young journalist grew which resulted in several joint journeys.[13] When Eilers committed suicide during the war, he was mourned by Hentrich like a family member. Hentrich does not disclose the nature of the "hopeless situation" which had driven Eilers to suicide.[14] Also worth mentioning is the architect Adolf Drexler (1905-1955),[15] like Hentrich a student of Poelzig, from a Jewish family and homosexual; Hentrich visited him in Paris in 1931 and in his Bohemian

Dorfjungen fern, die „in ihren Spielen zu grob und roh" waren.[7] Der Blick auf gut angezogene Männer war ihm früh gegeben; er war ein Fan von Matrosenanzügen. „Auch die jungen Mädchen trugen oft solche seemännischen Kleider", aber: „uns standen sie besser."[8] Schon in der Jugend beginnt auch seine zeitlebens gepflegte Beschäftigung mit Literatur und Kunst, die verhindern soll, dass er im Alter als Einzelgänger vereinsamt. Für die Mühle, die er in den 1950er-Jahren in einem abgelegenen Tal des Eifelgebirges erwirbt, spricht besonders, dass sie „kaum einsehbar" ist.[9] Freundin Olga stört sich nicht an den „Exzentritäten" ihres Gefährten,[10] der Tische vor allem danach beurteilt, ob sie „auch noch schöne Dekorationen" zulassen.[11] Nach Olgas Tod reist er allein, es „hatte Nachteile, aber auch große Vorteile. (...) Ich konnte mich, entgegen den üblichen Gewohnheiten, überall frei bewegen."[12] An Entdeckungstouren der besonderen Art war er nun nicht mehr gehindert.

Unter den Männern, die Helmut Hentrich besonders nahe standen, ist Fritz Eilers zu nennen; mit dem jungen Journalisten ergab sich in den 1930er-Jahren eine „herzliche Freundschaft", was einige gemeinsame Reisen zur Folge hatte.[13] Als Eilers während des Krieges Selbstmord beging, wurde er bei Hentrichs wie ein Familienmitglied betrauert. Welcher Art die „ausweglose Situation" gewesen ist, die Eilers in den Suizid getrieben hatte, lässt Hentrich ungesagt.[14] Erwähnung verdient auch der Architekt Adolf Drexler (1905-1955),[15] wie Hentrich ein Poelzig-Schüler, aus jüdischer Familie und homosexuell; Hentrich besuchte ihn 1931 in Paris und 1932 in seiner böhmischen Heimat. Drexler emigrierte 1939 nach England, um bald nach Kriegsende den Kontakt zu Hentrich wieder aufzunehmen. Zu Hentrichs engstem Kreis gehörte auch der ebenso Männern zugeneigte Gartenarchitekt Roland Weber (1909-1997), der sich nach dem Krieg in Düsseldorf etablierte und seitdem zu vielen Bauten Hentrichs die passenden Naturräume entwarf. 1953 bezogen beide zwei einander benachbarte, von Hentrich entworfene Häuser in der idyllischen Randlage des Vorortes Kalkum.

Ein Architektenfreund, ebenfalls schon im Seminar von Hans Poelzig, war auch Friedrich Tamms (1904-1980), nicht homosexuell, aber als junger Mann blond, blauäugig und von auffallender Attraktivität. Ein von Tamms an Hentrich gerichteter Brief, den dieser für die Nachwelt ins Archiv gelangen ließ, beklagt eine bemerkenswerte Szene: Im April 1933 kam Tamms zu Besuch, um Hentrich seine Verlobte und spätere Ehefrau vorzustellen. Die Begegnung misslang; Hentrich ließ die beiden seine Enttäuschung auf brüskierende Weise spüren.[16] Die männerbündisch fundierte Freundschaft ging darüber allerdings nicht zu Bruch. Nach sieben Jahren Mitarbeit in Albert Speers GBI-Behörde (Generalbauinspektor für die Reichshauptstadt) in Berlin war Tamms 1945 gezwungen, sich neu zu orientieren. Drei Jahre später berief man ihn als Leiter des Stadtplanungsamts nach Düsseldorf. Dass im Hintergrund dieser Personalie der in der Stadt bestens etablierte Hentrich seine Verbindungen spielen ließ, darf man annehmen. Ohne Tamms sähe die Stadt heute

Das Dreischeibenhaus in Düsseldorf: Henry-Russell Hitchcock nannte es eines der schönsten Hochhäuser der Welt.

The Dreischeibenhaus in Düsseldorf: Henry-Russell Hitchcock called it one of the most beautiful skyscrapers in the world.

home in 1932. In 1939, Drexler emigrated to England and got in touch with Hentrich again soon after the end of the war. Also part of Hentrich's inner circle was the garden architect Roland Weber (1909-1997), who likewise leaned towards to men, established himself in Düsseldorf after the war and, since then, designed the suitable natural environments for many of Hentrich's buildings. In 1953, they both moved into neighbouring homes designed by Hentrich in an idyllic peripheral location of the suburb of Kalkum.

An architect friend, also a member of the Poelzig seminar held by Hans Poelzig, was also Friedrich Tamms (1904-1980), not homosexual but, as a young man, blond, blue-eyed and strikingly handsome. A letter written by Tamms to Hentrich, which the latter put into the archive for posterity, bemoans a remarkable scene: In April 1933, Tamms visited to introduce to Hentrich his fiancée and later wife. The encounter failed. Hentrich made the couple feel his disappointment in an affronting way.[16] The friendship based on male bonding, however, did not break up because of it. After seven years of working in the Berlin office of Albert Speer, the general building inspector for the capital of the Reich, Tamms was forced to reorient himself in 1945. Three years later, he was appointed to Düsseldorf as head of the urban planning office. It may be assumed that Hentrich, optimally established in the city, pulled a few strings behind the scenes for this designation. Without Tamms, the city would today look completely different; his master plan for the reconstruction and his bridges of slender steel across the Rhine were decisive for the modern urban image of Düsseldorf.[17]

komplett anders aus; seine Leitplanung für den Wiederaufbau und seine Rheinbrücken aus schlankem Stahl waren entscheidend für das moderne Stadtgesicht Düsseldorfs.[17]

In einem Leben, das fast das gesamte zwanzigste Jahrhundert umfasste, hatte Hentrich verschiedene Intensitäten der antihomosexuellen Repression beobachten können. In seiner Berliner Studentenzeit die relativ liberale Praxis der Weimarer Republik, dann die forcierte Verfolgung im Nationalsozialismus, schließlich die andauernde Strafverfolgung in der frühen Bundesrepublik, in der der 1935 verschärfte Paragraph 175 weiter gültig blieb, so dass erst 1969 eine erste Stufe der Liberalisierung beschlossen wurde. Vor diesem Hintergrund war es 1971 kein Zufall, dass bei der Suche nach einem neuen Refugium ein Angebot aus den Niederlanden für Hentrich doppelt attraktiv war. Die in der Provinz Zuid-Limburg gelegene Ruine von Casteel Groot Buggenum war für den Ritter- und Burgen-Spleen, der Hentrich schon in seiner Jugend eigen gewesen war, der geeignete Platz. Sie lag außerdem in einem Staat, in dem der mannmännlichen Liebe seit den Zeiten Napoleons kein Gesetz mehr entgegenstand. Auch war der Ort von Düsseldorf mit dem Auto schneller zu erreichen als etwa die Mühle im stillen Tal des Eifelgebirges. Mit dem ihm eigenen Geschmack und unterstützt von Roland Weber machte Hentrich Groot-Buggenum zu seinem persönlichen Refugium. In dem Bewusstsein, keine Erben zu hinterlassen, und unter der Bedingung, dass er das Anwesen bis zu seinem Tod allein nutzen würde, schenkte Hentrich den Besitz 1980 der Regierung von Zuid-Limburg.

Die Architekturgeschichte kennt das Künstlerhaus und das Architektenhaus seit längerem als eigene Themen. Zu diesen gehören auch die Rückzugsorte, mit denen Patrick Gwynne, Louis Barragán, Geoffrey Bawa,[18] Helmut Hentrich und andere homosexuelle Architekten die gebotene Abschirmung ihres gefährdeten Privatlebens absicherten. Sie stellen eine eigene Gattung dar, die eine eigene Forschung verdient.

Casteel Groot Buggenum:
Helmut Hentrichs
Refugium hinter der
niederländischen Grenze

*Casteel Groot Buggenum:
Helmut Hentrich's refuge
behind the Dutch border*

During his life, which spanned almost the entire 20th century, Hentrich has been able to observe various intensities of anti-homosexual repression. At the time of his studies in Berlin, the relatively liberal attitude of the Weimar Republic; then, the accelerated persecution during the National Socialism and, finally, the continuous prosecution during the early years of the Federal Republic in which the more stringent "Paragraph 175" remained valid so that not until 1969 a first state of liberalization was decided. Against this background, it was no coincidence in 1971 that, in the search for a new refuge, an offer from the Netherlands was doubly attractive for Hentrich. The ruin of Casteel Groot Buggenum located in the province of Zuid-Limburg was the suitable place for Hentrich due to the fondness for knights and castles which he had already shown in his youth. The ruin was furthermore in a country where there had not been a law against sexual relationships between men since Napoleonic times. The place was also quicker to get to by car from Düsseldorf than, for instance, the mill in the quiet valley of the Eifel Mountains. With his very own taste and supported by Roland Weber, Hentrich turned Groot Buggenum into his personal refuge. Conscious of the fact that he was not going to leave any heirs and on condition that he alone would be using the estate until his death, Hentrich donated the property to the government of Zuid-Limburg in 1980

For some time already, the history of architecture has known artists houses and architects houses as autonomous topics. These also include the refuges which Patrick Gwynne, Louis Barragán, Geoffrey Bawa,[18] Helmut Hentrich and other homosexual architects used to ensure the necessary shielding of their endangered private lives. They represent an independent genre which merits specific research.

Wolfgang Voigt

Durch die Kollegen gerettet: Friedrich Wilhelm Kraemer

Ein Architekt, der als schwuler Mann unter die Räder von Justiz und Verwaltung geriet, aber im richtigen Moment gerettet wurde, war Friedrich Wilhelm Kraemer (1907-1990).[1] Geboren noch im wilhelminischen Kaiserreich, erhielt er in den 1920er-Jahren an der Technischen Hochschule in Braunschweig seine Ausbildung als Architekt. Ab den 1930er-Jahren war er mit einem eigenen Büro in Braunschweig erfolgreich, das mit geschmackvollen Wohnhäusern und Villen im gemäßigten norddeutschen Backstein-Traditionalismus schnell Renommee gewann. Nach dem Zweiten Weltkrieg, aus dem Kraemer schwer verwundet zurück kam, war er 1946 nur acht Monate nach Kriegsende einer der ersten in Braunschweig neu berufenen Architekturlehrer, denen die Aufgabe zufiel, Entwerfer für den Wiederaufbau auszubilden, und – ebenso wichtig – die während der NS-Zeit unfreie Architektur neu auszurichten. Kraemer war überzeugt, dass eine völlige Umkehr hin zu einer klaren Moderne notwendig war, mit der er selbst jedoch keine Berührung gehabt hatte. So begann er mit der Beschaffung von Büchern und Zeitschriften aus Ländern, in denen die Moderne sich freier als in Deutschland hatte entwickeln können. Gestützt auf den Neubeginn nur durch Lektüre schaffte er es, in den Nachkriegsjahrzehnten nicht nur einer der führenden Architekten in Norddeutschland, sondern auch der am meisten respektierte Lehrer an seiner Schule zu sein. In den 1950er-Jahren war Kraemer ein regionaler Star, dessen elegante Bauten in ganz Westdeutschland Anerkennung fanden, auf Augenhöhe mit den Werken von Sep Ruf und Egon Eiermann. Mit Dieter Oesterlen und Walter Henn hatte die „Braunschweiger Schule" der Architektur auch andere im Land bekannte Lehrer. Kraemer überstrahlte sie alle, er war die Galionsfigur der hoch angesehenen Fakultät.[2]

Kraemer hatte eine Familie, aber unter Studenten und Kollegen wusste man von der hinter der bürgerlichen Fassade versteckten Homosexualität. Bald nach seiner Berufung zum Professor ordnete er seine Verhältnisse und heiratete 1947 die deutlich jüngere Inge Roedenbeck, mit der er vier Kinder hatte.[3] Es geschah 1950 in einem Hotel in Hamburg, dass er sich mit einem Mann traf und verraten wurde; die Polizei kam und er wurde offenbar in flagranti ertappt.[4] Dass es ein Strafverfahren gab, ist anzunehmen; wie es eventuell ausging, ist aus den Hamburger Archiven nicht mehr zu ermitteln. Gefahr drohte Kraemer auch von anderer Seite, denn offensichtlich hielt ihn das Kultusministerium in Hannover als Hochschullehrer nicht mehr für tragbar und betrieb ein disziplinarisches Ermittlungsverfahren, das auf seine Entfernung aus der TH hinauslief.[5] In dieser Situation, mitten in

Saved by Colleagues: Friedrich Wilhelm Kraemer

Friedrich Wilhelm Kraemer (1907-1990) was an architect who, as a gay man, was threatened by the judicial system and the administration but was saved at the right moment.[1] Born during the Wilhelmine Empire, in the 1920s he was trained as an architect at the Technische Universität in Braunschweig. As of the 1930s, he was successful with his own office in Braunschweig which quickly gained a reputation for tasteful residential buildings and mansions in the style of moderate North-German brick traditionalism. After the Second World War, from which Kraemer returned seriously injured, in 1946 he became one of the first newly appointed teachers of architecture in Braunschweig just eight months after the war ended. Their task was to train designers for the reconstruction and – just as important – reposition the architecture which had not been independent during the Nazi period. Kraemer was convinced that a complete return to a kind of clear modernity was necessary with which he himself, however, had never been familiar. He thus started by purchasing books and journals from countries where modernism had been able to develop more freely than in Germany. Based on the new start exclusively through reading, in the post-war decades he not only succeeded in becoming one of the leading architects in North Germany but also in being one of the most respected teachers at his university. In the 1950s, Kraemer was a regional star whose elegant buildings found recognition in all of West Germany, on a par with Sep Ruf and Egon Eiermann. With Dieter Oesterlen and Walter Henn, the "Braunschweiger Schule" of architecture also had other teachers known in the whole country. Kraemer outshone them all; he was the figurehead of the highly regarded faculty.[2]

Kraemer had a family, but the students and colleagues knew about his homosexuality hidden behind the bourgeois façade. Soon after his appointment as a professor, he ordered his affairs and, in 1947, married the considerably younger Inge Roedenbeck with whom he had four children.[3] It happened in a Hamburg hotel in 1950 that he met a man and was reported: the police came and he was caught in flagrante.[4] It may be assumed that there was a criminal proceeding; how it eventually ended can no longer be determined based on the Hamburg archives. There was also a serious danger for Kraemer from a different direction, since apparently the ministry of education and the arts in Hanover thought him to be no longer tolerable as a university teacher and started disciplinary preliminary proceedings which resulted in him being dismissed from the Technische Hochschule.[5] In this situation, during the post-war era, which was so bitter for gays, in which the "Para-

Friedrich Wilhelm
Kraemer, 1950er-Jahre

*Friedrich Wilhelm
Kraemer, 1950s*

der für die Schwulen so bitteren Nachkriegszeit, in denen der von den Nationalsozialisten verschärfte Paragraph 175 weiterhin angewendet wurde und Tausende in Haft kamen, fanden sich Kraemers Professorenkollegen zu einer mutigen Aktion zusammen. Sie taten das Richtige und unterschrieben gemeinsam einen Brief, in dem sie Kraemers herausragenden Ruf als Architekt, die außerordentliche Qualität seiner Lehre und den großen Schaden für die TH benannten, wenn er der Hochschule verloren ginge.[6] Auch die Studentenschaft schickte im November 1950 einen Brief. Beides rettete ihm den Kopf.[7]

Den Brief der Professoren hatte Justus Herrenberger formuliert,[8] der am Beginn von Kraemers Hochschullaufbahn zu dessen begabtesten Schülern gehörte und ihm nach dem Diplom über viele Jahre als Assistent diente. In der prüden Adenauerzeit war es für einen wie Herrenberger riskant, mit diesem Thema in der Fakultät zu agieren. Er war nicht schwul, wie auch keiner der übrigen Assistenten Kraemers. Für diesen besonderen Dienst versprach ihm Kraemer, dass er sich auf angemessene Weise revanchieren würde. 1959 war es soweit, Herrenberger rückte zum Professor auf und wurde mit einem Lehrstuhl für Baukonstruktion Kraemers Kollege. Als Assistent an Kraemers Lehrstuhl für Gebäudelehre und Entwerfen war es unter anderem Herrenbergers Aufgabe, dessen Freitagsvorlesungen über die Architektur der Moderne vorzubereiten, die in den gebildeten Kreisen Braunschweigs Kultstatus besaßen und auch ein Publikum von außerhalb der Hochschule anzogen. Die eigene Bekehrung zur Moderne hatte den protestantisch erzogenen Kraemer wie ein Erweckungserlebnis tief berührt. Nicht zufällig wurden die Vorlesungen auch „Abendandachten" genannt.[9] Kraemers neues Idol und sein von ihm selbst so genannter „heimlicher

Geschäfts- und Bürohaus Flebbe in Braunschweig, 1954

Flebbe commercial and office building in Braunschweig, 1954

graph 175" tightened by the national socialists continued in and thousands were put under arrest, Kraemer's colleagues joined together in a courageous initiative. They signed a letter in which they pointed out Kraemer's outstanding reputation as an architect, the extraordinary quality of his teaching and the great damage to the Technische Hochschule in case he were lost to the university.[6] The student body as well mailed a letter in November 1950. Both contributed to saving him.[7]

The letter from the professors had been formulated by Justus Herrenberger[8] who, at the beginning of Kraemer's university career, had been amongst his most talented students and, having graduated, had worked many years as his assistant. During the prudish period of Federal Chancellor Adenauer, it was risky for someone like Herrenberger to act upon this subject in the faculty. He was not gay, and neither were any of the other Kraemer's assistants. For this special service, Kraemer promised him to reciprocate in an appropriate way. In 1959, the time for this had come, Herrenberger was appointed professor and became Kraemer's colleague with a chair for building construction. As an assistant at Kraemer's chair for building theory and design, it was Herrenberger's task, among others, to prepare the former's Friday lectures on modernist architecture which enjoyed cult status in the educated circles of Braunschweig and attracted an audience from outside the university as well. His own conversion to modernism was profoundly touching not unlike an epiphany for Kraemer who had been raised a protestant. The lectures were not by chance also called "evening service".[9] Kraemer's new idol and, as he called him himself, his "secret teacher" became Ludwig Mies van der Rohe who, at Kraemer's instiga-

Jahrhunderthalle in Frankfurt-Höchst, 1962

Century Hall in Frankfurt-Höchst, 1962

Lehrer" wurde Ludwig Mies van der Rohe, dem die TH Braunschweig auf Kraemers Betreiben hin die Ehrendoktorwürde verlieh. Die Überreichung der Urkunde an Mies durch Kraemer war der hauptsächliche Anlass seiner ersten Amerika-Exkursion, die Kraemer 1955 mit einigen engen Mitarbeitern und seiner Ehefrau unternahm. Auf derselben Reise wurde auch der Mies-Schüler Philip Johnson in dessen Glashaus in New Canaan besucht. In den folgenden Jahren wurde der in Westdeutschland um sich greifende „Miesianism" von den perfekt detaillierten Rasterfassaden mit gläsernen Curtain Walls begleitet, die auch Kraemers Verwaltungsbauten ab den späten 1950er-Jahren kennzeichneten.

Nach der Affäre von 1950, die seine Karriere um ein Haar zerstört hatte, war Kraemer ein gebranntes Kind und begann, sein Privatleben wirksamer abzuschirmen. An einem Ort, den man sich einsamer und abgelegener kaum denken kann, erwarb er ein Haus. Der auf den Dünen der Nordspitze der Insel Sylt gelegene Walmdachbau in Backstein und mit Reetdach ist das nördlichste Wohnhaus Deutschlands. In der Zwischenkriegszeit hatte die Tänzerin Gret Palucca hier Ferien gemacht. Unter den in den 1960er-Jahren an der Braunschweiger Schule Studierenden wusste man Bescheid. So auch über Kraemers Freundschaft mit dem jungen Schauspieler Matthias Fuchs, der auffällige Förderung durch den Architekten erfuhr. Ab 1955 war Fuchs als Nachwuchsdarsteller in der Serie der Immenhof-Filme aus der Sparte Heimatfilm aufgetreten. Später wurde er ein seriöser Charakterdarsteller an deutschen Bühnen. Gäste in Kraemers Haus in Braunschweig waren der amerikanische Dirigent und Komponist Leonard Bernstein und dessen deutscher Musiker-Kollege Justus Frantz, der als jugendlicher Pianist im Klassikfach Furore machte. Die Freunde Justus Frantz und Christoph Eschenbach wurden auch zu Bauherren von Kraemer. Für beide entwarf er 1971 die Casa de los Musicos im Süden der Insel Gran

Amerikareise 1955: Kraemer blickt auf das Chrysler Building in New York.

Trip to America 1955: Kraemer looks at the Chrysler Building in New York.

tion, was awarded an honorary doctorate by the TH Braunschweig. The presentation of the certificate to Mies by Kraemer was the main reason for his first excursion to America which Kraemer undertook with some of his close colleagues and his wife in 1955. On the same journey, he also visited the Mies student Philip Johnson in his Glass House in New Canaan. In the following years, the "Miesianism" spreading in Western Germany was accompanied by the perfectly detailed grid façades with glass curtain walls which also characterized Kraemer's administration buildings starting in the late 1950s.

After the affair in 1950, which by a fraction of an inch had destroyed his career, Kraemer had learned his lesson and began to shield his private life more efficiently. He purchased a house in a location that can hardly be imagined any lonelier and more remote. The hipped-roof building consisting of bricks and with a thatched roof located on the dunes at the northern tip of the island of Sylt is the northernmost residential building of Germany. During the interwar period, the dancer Gret Palucca spent her holidays here. The students at the "Braunschweiger Schule" in the 1960s also knew about Kraemer's friendship with the young actor Matthias Fuchs, who received conspicuous support from the architect. Since 1955, Fuchs had played a role as an up-and-coming actor in the series of Immenhof films in the "Heimatfilm". He subsequently became a serious character actor on German stages. Guests in Kraemer's house in Braunschweig were the American conductor and composer Leonard Bernstein and his German fellow musician Justus Frantz, who made headlines as a young pianist in the field of classical music in the 1960s. The friends Justus Frantz and Christoph Eschenbach also became Kraemer's building clients. In 1971, he designed for them the Casa de los Musicos in the south of the island of Gran Canaria where he convincingly succeeded with the modern interpretation of the Mediter-

Umbau Herzog August Bibliothek in Wolfenbüttel, 1962-1981

Reconstruction of the Herzog August Library in Wolfenbüttel, 1962-1981

Canaria, in der er das mediterrane Ambiente einer kanarischen Finca auf überzeugende Weise modern interpretierte. Als Standort hatte man einen Hügel gewählt, der in Sichtweite, jedoch in dezentem Abstand, zu den Dünen von Maspalomas lag, das sich damals in ein schwules Ferienparadies verwandelte.

Im Jahre 2007 veranstaltete die Technische Universität Braunschweig zu Kraemers 100. Geburtstag eine ehrende Ausstellung. Dazu erschien ein Katalog unter dem Titel *Gesetz und Freiheit*, mit dem die virtuose Handhabung von Regel und Variation in Kraemers Moderne gemeint war und nicht der unbarmherzige Paragraph 175 des Strafgesetzbuches, der ihn beinahe seine Freiheit gekostet hätte. Ob die Herausgeber den Doppelsinn bemerkt haben? Im Katalog ist das Thema tabu, auch wenn etwas durchschimmert, wenn geheimnisvoll von „Gerüchten und Andeutungen" die Rede ist und damit erst recht Fragen aufgeworfen werden, ohne dass Antworten folgen.[10] Über die Krise des Jahres 1950 kein Wort, als wäre sie nie passiert! Das ist schade, denn die damals gegenüber Kraemer bewiesene Solidarität der Kollegen und Studenten war nicht nur ein dramatisches Ereignis in Kraemers Biografie; sie verdient es auch, als Glanzpunkt in der Hochschulgeschichte erinnert zu werden.

ranean ambience of a Canary finca. As the location, a hill had been chosen in sight but at a discreet distance from the dunes of Maspaloma which, at the time, was turning into a gay holiday paradise.

In 2007, the Technische Universität Braunschweig organized an exhibition honoring Kraemer on his 100th birthday. Accompanying it, a catalogue was published with the title *Gesetz und Freiheit*, which referred to the virtuoso dealing with rules and variations in Kraemer's modernism and not the merciless "Paragraph 175" of the criminal code which had almost cost him his freedom. Had the editors noticed the double entendre? In the catalogue, the topic is taboo, although something shows through when "rumours and innuendos" are mentioned which only raise more questions.[10] Not a single word about the crisis of 1950, as if it had never happened! This is a pity since the solidarity shown at the time for Kraemer by his colleagues and students was not only a dramatic event in his biography; it is also a highlight in the history of the university.

Uwe Bresan

Der Abenteurer, sein Ghostwriter und ihr Architekt: William Alexander Levy

Drei einfache Schlafräume reihen sich aneinander. Sie sind nahezu gleich groß und bis auf wenige Details identisch gestaltet. Die Einrichtung ist simpel; gleichwohl aber von hoher Qualität. Bett und Stuhl stehen frei im Raum; unterhalb des Fensterbandes ziehen sich hölzerne Regale, Ablagen und Arbeitsflächen von Wand zu Wand; eine Tür führt ins Bad; daneben versteckt sich ein breiter Wandschrank. Böden, Wände und Decken der drei Zimmer bestehen – wie der Rest des Hauses – aus sichtbar belassenem massiven Stahlbeton. Ein breiter Flur verbindet sie mit den anderen Wohnräumen. Über hohe Schiebefenster lässt sich der Gang auf einer Seite fast vollständig nach außen öffnen und gleicht damit mehr einer Loggia oder einem Laubengang. Vier Stufen führen an seinem Ende in das offene Esszimmer hinunter, an das sich über Eck eine schmale Küche anschließt. Eine Glasfaltwand führt vom Essbereich hinaus auf die Terrasse, an deren Ende das Gelände schroff nach unten abfällt. Hinter den dünnen Stützen des Eisengeländers geht es fast senkrecht 100 Meter in die Tiefe! Eine schmale Wendeltreppe aus Stahl führt hingegen hinauf zum Sonnendeck. Der Terrasse gegenüber und um weitere drei Stufen nach unten versetzt liegt wiederum die hohe lichtdurchflutete Wohnhalle. Auch sie wird von der rohen Ästhetik ihrer schalungsrauen Betonoberflächen beherrscht und ist nur spärlich möbliert. Nichts stört den Blick, der durch die raumhohe Fensterfront hinaus wandert, den felsigen Abhang hinunter, über die Dächer der Stadt hinweg und bis zum Meer, das hinter den letzten Häusern beginnt und bald den ganzen Horizont einnimmt.

Nichts an diesem Haus ist gewöhnlich: nicht seine prekäre Lage auf einem schmalen Berggrat, gefangen zwischen einer tiefen Schlucht im Rücken und dem zum Meer hin steil abfallenden Gelände auf der Vorderseite; nicht die scharfkantige Materialität des innen wie außen brutal zur Schau gestellten Stahlbetons; und auch nicht die kühne Präzision seines Planes, der nicht nur jeder Funktion die ihr angemessene Geometrie zuweist, sondern darüber hinaus alle Funktionen in einer bestechend klaren räumlichen Ordnung diszipliniert. Es strahlt eine virile Kompromisslosigkeit aus, die jede Form von Heimeligkeit vermissen lässt. Es besitzt nichts Feminines, nichts Bergendes, nichts Behütendes. So unkonventionell sich das Haus damit darstellt, so unkonventionell war letztlich auch sein Bauherr: der Abenteurer Richard Halliburton (1900-1939).[1] Nach einem Journalismus-Studium an der renommierten Princeton University zog es ihn in den frühen 1920er-Jahren hinaus in die Welt. Anstatt sich einen lukrativen Job zu suchen, zu heiraten und eine Familie zu gründen, wie es seine Kommilitonen taten und wie es seine konser-

The Adventurer, His Ghost-writer and Their Architect: William Alexander Levy

Three simple bedrooms of almost the same size are lined up next to each other. Except for a few details, their design is almost identical. The furnishings are simple, but of high quality. Bed and chair are placed freely in the room; wooden shelves, storage and work areas extend from wall to wall below the window strip; a door leads to the bathroom; a wide wall cabinet is concealed next to it. The floors, walls and ceilings of the three rooms are – like the rest of the house – made of exposed reinforced concrete. A wide hallway connects them with the other living spaces. High sliding windows allow the hallway to be opened almost completely outwards on one side, thus giving it the appearance of a loggia or pergola. At its end, four steps lead down to the open dining room, to which a narrow kitchen adjoins around a corner. A folding glass wall connects the dining area with the terrace, at the end of which the terrain plunges 100 metres behind the thin supports of the iron railing! A narrow spiral staircase made of steel leads up to the sun deck. Opposite the terrace and offset downwards by a further three steps, is the high, light-flooded living hall. It is also dominated by the raw aesthetics of rough concrete surfaces with formwork marks and is sparsely furnished. Nothing disturbs the view that wanders out through the floor-to-ceiling window front, down the rocky slope, over the roofs of the city and to the sea that begins behind the last houses and fills the entire horizon.

Nothing about this house is ordinary: not its precarious location on a narrow ridge, trapped between a deep gorge at the back and the steep slope towards the sea on the front side; not the sharp-edged materiality of reinforced concrete brutally showcased both inside and outside the house, nor the bold precision of its plan, which assigns the appropriate geometry to each function and disciplines them in an impressively clear spatial order. The building exudes a virile uncompromising attitude that lacks any form of homeliness. It has nothing feminine, nothing comforting, nothing protective. The house was as unconventional as its owner, the adventurer Richard Halliburton (1900-1939).[1] After studying journalism at Princeton University, he travelled around the world in the early 1920s. Instead of looking for a job, getting married and starting a family, as his fellow students did and as his conservative parents had planned, he went to Europe, North Africa and Asia. In Egypt, he slept one night on top of the Pyramid of Cheops. In Japan he climbed Fujiyama in the middle of winter. Back in America, he turned his adventures into the book *The Royal Road to Romance*,[2] which became a bestseller overnight and made Halliburton internationally famous. Just one year after its publication, a German translation entitled *Die Jagd*

Der Abenteurer und sein Ghostwriter: Richard Halliburton bei der Überquerung der Alpen mit einem Elefanten und Paul Mooney auf der Baustelle des Hangover Hauses

The adventurer and his ghostwriter: Richard Halliburton crossing the Alps with an elephant and Paul Mooney on the construction site of the Hangover House

vativen Eltern für ihn vorgesehen hatten, ging er nach Europa, nach Nordafrika und Asien. In Ägypten schlief er eine Nacht auf der Spitze der Cheops-Pyramide. In Japan bestieg er mitten im Winter den Fujiyama. Zurück in Amerika verarbeitete er die Erlebnisse seiner Reise in dem Buch *The Royal Road to Romance*,[2] das über Nacht zu einem Bestseller wurde und Halliburton international berühmt machte. Nur ein Jahr nach Erscheinen kam bereits eine deutsche Übersetzung mit dem Titel *Die Jagd nach dem Wunder* auf den Markt.[3] Da war Halliburton allerdings schon wieder unterwegs! Diesmal folgte er den legendären Irrfahrten des Odysseus durch die Ägäis und durchschwamm nebenbei die 65 Kilometer lange Meerenge der Dardanellen, den sogenannten Hellespont. Mit dem darauf folgenden Buch *The Glorious Adventure*[4] – in Deutschland erschien es unter dem Titel *Auf den Spuren des Odysseus*,[5] – wurde Halliburton endgültig zur Legende und für hunderttausende kleine und große Jungen auf der ganzen Welt zum Idol. Weitere Bücher, aber vor allem weitere Abenteuer folgten: die Besteigung des Popocatépetls in Mexiko, die Überquerung der Alpen mit einem Elefanten, die Umrundung der Welt in einem offenen Flugzeug und nicht zuletzt die Durchschwimmung des Panamakanals, seine wohl publikumswirksamste Aktion. Offiziell als Schiff deklariert, zahlte Halliburton am Ende der Passage eine seinem Körpergewicht entsprechende Durchfahrtsgebühr von 36 Cent.

Je halsbrecherischer und aufsehenerregender seine Aktionen wurden, um so mehr stand Halliburton im Licht der Öffentlichkeit. Innerhalb weniger Jahre entwickelte er sich zu einem der gefragtesten und bestbezahltesten Vortragsredner seiner Generation. Mitte der 1930er-Jahre hatten ihn fast sechs Millionen Menschen sprechen gehört. Seine Bücher verkauften sich glänzend. Ein Problem war nur, dass die vielen öffentlichen Auftritte, die Halliburton zu absolvieren hatte, ihm immer weniger Zeit und Muße ließen, um an neuen

Der Architekt: William Alexander Levy an seinem Zeichentisch bei der Arbeit am Hangover Haus

The architect: William Alexander Levy at his drawing table planning the Hangover House

nach dem Wunder was released. By then, Halliburton was already travelling again! This time he traced the legendary odyssey of Ulysses through the Aegean Sea and swam through the 65-kilometre-long Strait of the Dardanelles, the so-called Hellespont. With the next book *The Glorious Adventure*,[4] published in Germany under the title of *Auf den Spuren des Odysseus*,[5] Halliburton finally became a legend and an idol for hundreds of thousands of young and old boys around the world. Further books, but above all further adventures followed: the ascent of Popocatépetl in Mexico, the crossing of the Alps with an elephant, the circumnavigation of the world in an open airplane and last but not least a swim through the Panama Canal, probably his most popular adventure. Officially declared a ship, Halliburton had to pay a passage fee of 36 cents corresponding to his body weight.

The more breakneck and sensational his undertakings became the more Halliburton was in the public eye. Within a few years he became one of the most sought-after and well-paid speakers of his generation. By the mid-1930s, almost six million people had heard him speak. His books were brilliant bestsellers. However, one problem was that the many public appearances Halliburton had to make left him little time to work on new books. The problem was solved when Paul Mooney (1904-1939) appeared in Halliburton's life around 1930 – as a congenial ghost writer and life partner.[6] In both respects, Mooney was a perfect match. The fact that he had to remain hidden from the outside world in both functions did not bother him. Like Halliburton, Mooney came from a middle-class background and initially studied journalism. After only a few semesters, he quit his studies and went to Paris for some time. After his return, he worked in New York as a copywriter, but at the same time tried to establish himself as a freelance author and photographer. When the Great De-

Büchern zu arbeiten. Das Problem löste sich allerdings, als Paul Mooney (1904-1939) um 1930 in Halliburtons Leben trat – als Ghostwriter und als Lebensgefährte.[6] In beiden Funktionen war Mooney ein kongenialer Partner. Dass er in beiden Funktionen der Außenwelt verborgen bleiben musste, störte ihn nicht. Wie Halliburton kam auch Mooney aus mittleren Verhältnissen und studierte zunächst Journalismus. Allerdings brach er das Studium nach nur wenigen Semestern ab, um für einige Zeit nach Paris zu gehen. Nach seiner Rückkehr arbeitete er in New York als Werbetexter, versuchte aber zugleich, sich als freier Autor und Fotograf zu etablieren. Mit der Weltwirtschaftskrise 1929 zog es Mooney – wie viele andere auch – auf der Suche nach Arbeit an die Westküste. Ob sich Mooney und Halliburton zu dieser Zeit bereits kannten, wissen wir nicht. Wo und wie sie sich das erste Mal trafen, ist bis heute ungeklärt. Fest steht allerdings, dass sich Mooneys neue Heimat Los Angeles schon bald auch zu einem Fixpunkt im Leben von Halliburton entwickelte. In Laguna Beach, knapp 80 Kilometer südlich von Los Angeles, erwarb der Abenteurer 1931 das spektakuläre Felsengrundstück, auf dem sein Haus noch heute steht. Der wildromantische Küstenort mit seiner zum Landesinneren hin schnell ansteigenden Topografie zog schon damals viele Hollywood-Berühmtheiten an, die an den steilen Hängen der Stadt elegante Wochenend- und Sommerhäuser errichteten, die oft einen atemberaubenden Meerblick boten. Und noch heute gilt die Stadt mit ihren traumhaften Stränden als bevorzugter Wohnsitz der Schönen und Reichen.

Nachdem die Stadt die notwendigen Erschließungsarbeiten des Grundstücks abgeschlossen hatte, begann Halliburton 1936 den Bau seines Hauses in Laguna Beach zu forcieren. Auf Betreiben von Mooney holte er dafür den noch jungen und unerfahrenen New Yorker Architekten William Alexander Levy (1909-1997) an die Westküste. Mooney und Levy kannten sich seit den späten 1920er-Jahren. Sie waren sich in New York begegnet und bildeten ein Liebespaar. Halliburton tolerierte das andauernde intime Verhältnis der beiden und sah in Levy die ideale Gesellschaft für Mooney während seiner vielen Abwesenheiten. Im Gegenzug nahm sich auch Halliburton die Freiheit, immer wieder intime Beziehungen mit anderen Männern einzugehen. Als Levy 1936 in Laguna Beach eintraf, war er knapp 27 Jahre alt, neun Jahre jünger als Halliburton und fünf Jahre jünger als Mooney. Er hatte an der New York University studiert – unter anderem bei den beiden Hochhaus-Pionieren Ely Jacques Kahn und Raymond Hood, dem Chefarchitekten des Rockefeller Centers. Wahrscheinlich hatte er 1932 im New Yorker Museum of Modern Art auch die legendäre Ausstellung *Modern Architecture* gesehen, die das amerikanische Publikum erstmals mit der europäischen Architekturmoderne der 1920er-Jahre vertraut machte. Den größten Einfluss auf den jungen Architekten besaß allerdings Frank Lloyd Wright, dessen Arbeiten Levy mit tiefer Bewunderung studierte. Er hatte sich sogar um die Aufnahme in Wrights private Schule, den Talesien Fellwoship, bemüht, konnte aber letztlich die notwendigen Studiengebühren nicht aufbringen. Trotzdem verbrachte er

Das Hangover Haus ist ein kaum bekanntes Meisterwerk der kalifornischen Mid-Century-Moderne.

The Hangover House is a little-known masterpiece of California mid-century modernism.

pression of 1929 hit – like many others – he went to the West Coast in search of work. Whether Mooney and Halliburton already knew each other at that time, we do not know. It is still unclear where and how they first met. What is certain, however, is that Mooney's new home in Los Angeles soon became a focal point in Halliburton's life. In Laguna Beach, about 80 kilometres south of Los Angeles, the adventurer bought the spectacular rocky property in 1931 where his house still stands today. The wild and romantic coastal town with its topography ascending steeply towards the hinterland attracted many Hollywood celebrities who built elegant weekend and summer houses on the steep slopes of the city, which often afforded breath-taking sea views. Even today, the city with its beautiful beaches is still the preferred residence of the rich and famous.

After the municipality had completed the necessary land development work, Halliburton accelerated the construction of his house in Laguna Beach in 1936. At the instigation of Mooney, he commissioned the young and inexperienced New York architect William Alexander Levy (1909-1997) and brought him to the West Coast. Mooney and Levy had known each other since the late 1920s. They had met in New York and were lovers. Halliburton tolerated the continuing intimate relationship of the two and saw Levy as an ideal companion for Mooney during his many absences. In return, Halliburton also took the liberty of repeatedly establishing intimate relationships with other men. When Levy arrived in Laguna Beach in 1936, he was almost 27 years old, nine years younger than Halliburton and five years younger than Mooney. He had studied at New York University – among others with the two high-rise pioneers Ely Jacque Kahn and Raymond Hood, chief architect of the Rockefeller Center. He probably had visited the legendary exhibition *Modern Architecture* at the Museum of Modern Art in New York in 1932, which

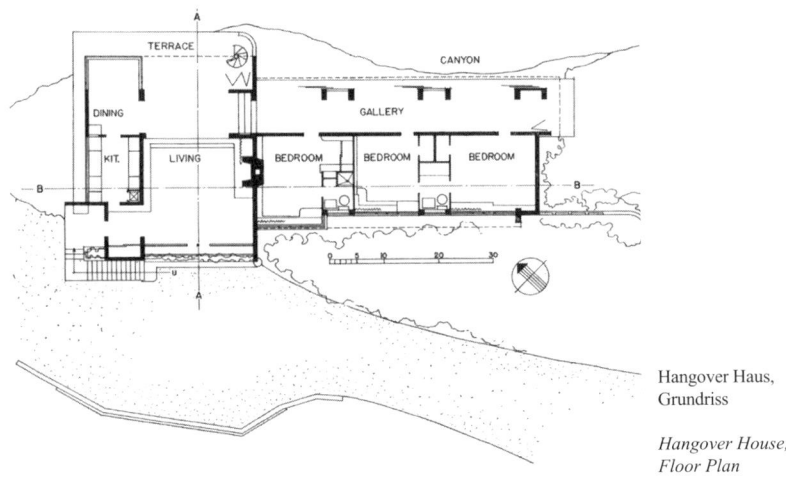

Hangover Haus, Grundriss

Hangover House, Floor Plan

mehrere Wochen in Spring Green, wo Wright seine Schule in den Sommermonaten betrieb. Nach seinem Abschluss 1934 arbeitete Levy dann zunächst für die Stadt New York an verschiedenen Sanierungsprojekten, bevor ihn Halliburton nach Laguna Beach holte. Hier mieteten sich Mooney und Levy ein gemeinsames Haus in Strandnähe, um mit den ersten Planungen zu beginnen, während Halliburton nur selten zwischen seinen vielen öffentlichen Auftritten die Zeit fand, um für ein paar Tage vorbeizuschauen. Der Plan, das Haus nicht für zwei, sondern für drei Bewohner – Halliburton, Mooney und Levy – zu konzipieren, muss bei einem dieser Besuche entstanden sein.

Die Bauarbeiten selbst zogen sich über fast zwei Jahre hin und verschlangen ein Vielfaches des zu Beginn veranschlagten Budgets.[7] Dafür gab es vor allem zwei Gründe: die schwierige Lage des Grundstück, das für schwere Baumaschinen ungeeignet war, und die von Levy gewünschte Ausführung in Stahlbeton, für dessen Einsatz beim Bau von Wohnhäusern es damals noch kaum Vorbilder gab. Beides führte dazu, dass sich kein Bauunternehmer bereit fand, die Realisierung zu übernehmen. So war Levy gezwungen, selbst als Bauunternehmer aufzutreten. Mit dem Material unerfahrene Arbeiter und das Fehlen schweren Geräts machten den Bau zu einem Abenteuer. Allein schon der Transport des Baumaterials auf die unwegsame Baustelle stellte eine gewaltige Kraftanstrengung dar. 100 Tonnen Beton und fast 50 Tonnen Stahl mussten das steile Gelände hinauf gebracht werden. Unterhalb des schmalen Berggrats, auf dem das Haus entstehen sollte, wurde dafür zunächst eine Stützmauer in den Hang getrieben und eine Zufahrt angelegt. Erst danach konnten die Arbeiten am Haus mit dem Errichten der Betonschalungen beginnen. Jede Steckdose, jeder Lichtschalter, jede Strom- und Wasserleitung machte detailgenaue Vorplanungen und eine präzise Umsetzung notwendig. Um Trocknungshorizonte zu ver-

Das Bild zeigt die Schriftstellerin Ayn Rand gemeinsam mit Paul Mooney und William Alexander Levy bei einem Besuch des Hauses; Levy soll Rand zum Roman *The Fountainhead* inspiriert haben.

The picture shows the writer Ayn Rand together with Paul Mooney and William Alexander Levy during a visit to the house; Levy is said to have inspired Rand to write the novel The Fountainhead.

introduced the American public to 1920s European modernism. Frank Lloyd Wright, whose works Levy studied with deep admiration, had the greatest influence on the young architect. He had even sought admission to Wright's private school, the Talesia Fellowship, but was unable to afford the tuition fees. Nevertheless, he spent several weeks in Spring Green, where Wright used to run his school during the summer months. After graduating in 1934, Levy first worked on various refurbishment projects for the City of New York, before Halliburton brought him to Laguna Beach. Here, Mooney and Levy rented a house near the beach to start planning, while Halliburton rarely found time to drop by for a few days between his many public appearances. The plan to design the house not for two but for three residents – Halliburton, Mooney and Levy – must have emerged during one of these rare visits.

  Construction work itself took almost two years and consumed many times the budget originally expected.[7] There were two main reasons for this: the difficult location of the property, which was inappropriate for heavy construction machinery, and the reinforced concrete construction requested by Levy, for which there were hardly any models for use in housing construction at the time. As a result, no building contractor was prepared to take over the project. Consequently, Levy was forced to act as a contractor himself. Workers with no experience with the material and the lack of heavy equipment made the construction an adventure. Transporting the building material to the impassable construction site alone was an enormous effort. 100 tons of concrete and almost 50 tons of steel had to be moved up the steep terrain. Below the narrow mountain ridge on which the house was to be built, a retaining wall was first driven into the slope and an access road was built. Only then was it possible to commence work on the house with the instal-

Eine Glasfaltwand führt vom Essbereich hinaus auf die Terrasse, an deren Ende das Gelände schroff abfällt; seinen Namen verdankt das Hangover Haus seiner spektakulären Lage.

A folding glass wall leads from the dining area onto the terrace, at the end of which the terrain drops away precipitously; the Hangover House owes its name to its spectacular location.

meiden, mussten die Wände des Hauses zudem in einem Stück betoniert werden. 48 Stunden brachten die Arbeiter damit zu, den Beton anzumischen und in die fertigen Wandschalungen einzufüllen. Es waren zwei Tage und zwei Nächte, die alle Beteiligten an den Rand ihrer Kräfte brachten. Nicht weniger aufwendig gestaltete sich der Ausbau und die Einrichtung. Alle Türen- und Fensterelemente wurden nach Levys Plänen aus Stahl gefertigt. Jedes Möbelstück entstand nach den genauen Vorstellungen und Wünschen des Architekten. 1938 war es schließlich fertig: das Hangover Haus. Die weit über den Aliso Canyon hinausragende Terrasse vor dem offenen Essbereich gab dem Haus seinen Namen. Er ist in den Beton der Hangmauer, die die Zufahrt vor dem Haus abstützt, eingegossen. Ob der Schriftzug bewusst spiegelverkehrt gesetzt wurde oder ob es sich um einen Irrtum der Arbeiter gehandelt hat, ist heute nicht mehr nachzuvollziehen. Wir kennen nur das berühmte Foto, auf dem Mooney die Schaltafel mit dem Hangover-Schriftzug lächelnd in die Kamera hält.[8]

Andere Fotos, die nach dem Einzug von Halliburton, Mooney und Levy entstanden, vermitteln wiederum einen Eindruck vom Zusammenleben der drei 'Junggesellen'.[9] Im Schlafzimmer, das der Wohnhalle am nächsten liegt, hängt eine Weltkarte an der Wand. Auf ihr sind die Stationen von Halliburtons Reisen markiert. Es ist sein Zimmer, während Mooney und Levy das mittlere sowie das äußere Zimmer bewohnten. Ein anderes Bild zeigt die russischstämmige New Yorker Schriftstellerin Ayn Rand bei einem Besuch des Hangover Hauses. Levy soll sie zu ihrem berühmten Roman *The Fountainhead* (*Der Ursprung*) von 1943 inspiriert haben,[10] der später mit Gary Cooper in der Rolle des Architekten Howard Roark verfilmt wurde. Wieder auf einer anderen Fotografie sieht man das von Levy entworfene Bücherregal in der großen Wohnhalle. Auf dem obersten Regalboden stehen zwei hohe Porzellanfiguren. Sie stellen zwei stattliche, sich zugewandte

Auf einem Foto der Wohnhalle des Hangover Hauses sieht man auf dem Regal zwei Porzellanfiguren; sie stellen zwei stattliche Matrosen dar, ein beliebtes homoerotisches Sujet.

In a photo of the Hangover House's living room, two porcelain figurines can be seen on the shelf; they represent two handsome sailors, a popular homoerotic theme.

lation of the concrete formwork. Every socket outlet, every power and water supply line required detailed preliminary planning and precise implementation. In order to avoid drying marks, the walls of the house had to be cast in one piece. The workers spent 48 hours mixing the concrete and pouring it into the finished wall formwork. It was two days and two nights that pushed everyone involved to their physical limits. The fittings and furnishing was no less complex. All door and window elements and every piece of furniture was produced from steel according to Levy's precise designs. The Hangover House was finally completed in 1938. The cantilevered terrace in front of the open dining area overlooking Aliso Canyon gave the house its name. It is cast into the concrete retaining wall that supports the access road in front of the house. Today, it is no longer possible to determine whether the lettering was deliberately set in reverse (overhang) or whether it was an error on the part of the workers. We only know the famous photo in which Mooney presents the formwork panel with the Hangover lettering to the camera, smiling.[8]

Other photographs taken after Halliburton, Mooney and Levy had moved in give an impression of how the three bachelors lived together.[9] In the bedroom closest to the

Ein breiter Flur verbindet die Schlaf- mit den Wohnräumen des Hangover Hauses; über hohe Schiebefenster lässt sich der Gang fast vollständig öffnen.

A wide hallway connects the bedrooms with the living rooms of the Hangover House; the hallway can be opened almost completely via high sliding windows.

Matrosen dar, ein beliebtes Sujet homoerotischer Kunst- und Kitschproduktion, und dürften von den Bewohnern als augenzwinkernder Verweis auf den eigenen Lebensstil gedacht gewesen sein. Sie sind das, was Susan Sontag später Camp nannte![11] In der Rückschau bilden die beiden Seemänner auf dem Bücherregal allerdings auch ein unheilvolles Menetekel. Denn die ungewöhnliche ménage-à-trois des Hangover Hauses währte nur wenige Monate. Bereits Ende 1938 brach Halliburton zu einem neuen Abenteuer auf. Mit einer Dschunke, einem traditionellen chinesischen Segelschiff, wollte er von Hongkong aus den Pazifik bezwingen. Geplant war, mit dem Schiff und unter den Augen der Weltöffentlichkeit zur Eröffnung der Golden Gate International Exposition 1939 in San Francisco einzulaufen. Mooney sollte Halliburton dabei begleiten und die Reise von Beginn an dokumentieren. Es wurde allerdings eine Reise ohne Wiederkehr. Weder Halliburton noch Mooney hatten Erfahrungen auf See. In einem schweren Sturm kenterte ihr Schiff in der Nacht vom 23. auf den 24. März 1939 in der Nähe der Midwayinseln, auf halber Strecke zwischen Hongkong und San Francisco. Der letzte Funkspruch lautete bitter: „having wonderful time / wish you were here / instead of me."[12] Ihre Leichen wurden nie gefunden.

Das Hangover Haus besitzt drei fast identische Schlafzimmer; das Zimmer mit der großen Weltkarte gehörte dem Abenteurer Richard Halliburton.

The Hangover House has three almost identical bed rooms; the room with the large world map belonged to the adventurer Richard Halliburton.

living room, a world map is hung on the wall with the places Halliburton visited during his journeys marked on it. It is his room, while Mooney and Levy occupied the middle and the last room. Another picture shows Russian-born New York writer Ayn Rand visiting the Hangover House. Levy is said to have inspired her to write her famous novel *The Fountainhead* from 1943,[10] which was later made into a film with Gary Cooper starring architect Howard Roark. Yet another photograph shows the bookcase in the large living room designed by Levy. On the top shelf there are two tall porcelain figures representing two handsome sailors turned towards each other, a popular subject of homoerotic art and kitsch production, that was probably meant by the inhabitants as a tongue-in-cheek reference to their own lifestyle. They are what Susan Sontag later called camp![11] In retrospect, the two sailors on the bookshelf are also a warning sign: the unusual ménage à trois of the Hangover House lasted only a few months. At the end of 1938, Halliburton embarked on a new adventure. Putting out to sea from Hongkong, he wanted to conquer the Pacific aboard a junk, a traditional Chinese sailing ship. The plan was to arrive with the ship before the eyes of the world at the opening of the Golden Gate International Exposition in San Francisco in 1939. Mooney should accompany Halliburton and document the journey from the beginning. However, it became a journey of no return. Neither Halliburton nor Mooney had experience at sea. In a severe storm, their ship capsized near the Midway Islands, halfway between Hong Kong and San Francisco, during the night of March 23 to 24, 1939. The last radio message was "having wonderful time / wish you were here / instead of me."[12] Their bodies were never found.

Levy was in New York when he heard about Halliburton's and Mooney's disappearance. He never returned to the house in Laguna Beach. Instead, he moved to Los Angeles, where he built himself another spectacular dream house in the Hollywood Hills.

Levy war gerade in New York, als er vom Verschwinden Halliburtons und Mooneys hörte. Er kehrte nicht mehr in das gemeinsame Haus nach Laguna Beach zurück. Er zog stattdessen nach Los Angeles, wo er sich später in den Hollywood Hills noch einmal ein spektakuläres Traumhaus errichtete. Das House in Space, wie er den Bau selbst nannte, entstand an einem steilen Waldhang. Levy ließ schwere Stahlträger horizontal in den Berg treiben und errichtete auf ihnen ein künstliches Plateau, das in der Luft zu schweben schien. In dem Haus, das er darauf baute, lebte der Architekt bis zu seinem Tod 1997. Bis zuletzt hing an der Wand im Arbeitszimmer ein Porträt Mooneys von William Eugene McCown. Das Hangover Haus, Levys geniales Frühwerk, wurde hingegen in den 1940er-Jahren an Wallace Thompson Scott, einen General, und seine Frau, die Tänzerin Zolite Elizabeth Scott, verkauft. Sie liebten das Gebäude und erhielten es in seinem ursprünglichen Zustand. Selbst als ihre Tochter, die das Haus nach dem Tod ihrer Eltern alleine bewohnte, 2009 verstarb, hatte sich noch immer kaum etwas verändert. Halliburtons Landkarte hing nach 70 Jahren noch an der gleichen Stelle im vordersten Schlafzimmer. Alle Einbauten waren noch vorhanden. Maklerfotos[13] sowie Modeaufnahmen,[14] die damals im Haus entstanden, zeigen den nahezu perfekten Erhaltungszustand. Dass es die zuständigen Behörden versäumten, das Haus, als es 2010 zum Verkauf stand, zu erwerben oder zumindest die neuen Eigentümer zum Erhalt wesentlicher Elemente der Inneneinrichtung zu verpflichten,[15] darf als tragischer Fehler gelten. Die neuen Bewohner gingen wenig zimperlich mit dem Haus um. Im Inneren ist es heute kaum mehr wiederzuerkennen. Verloren gegangen ist damit nicht nur ein herausragendes und authentisch erhalten gebliebenes Werk der frühen kalifornischen Architekturmoderne, sondern auch ein faszinierendes Beispiel für eine Mid-Century-Architektur, die nach neuen und angemessenen Formen für ein Zusammenleben jenseits familiär strukturierter, normativer Beziehungen suchte.

The House in Space, as he himself called the building, was built on a steep wooded slope. Levy had heavy steel beams driven horizontally into the mountain and constructed an artificial platform that seemed to float in the air. The architect lived in the house he built on this platform until he died in 1997. A portrait of Mooney by William Eugene McCown hung on the wall of his study throughout his life. The Hangover House, Levy's ingenious early work, was sold to Wallace Thompson Scott, a general, and his wife, the dancer Zolite Elizabeth Scott, in the 1940s. They loved the building and kept it in its original condition. Even when their daughter, who lived in the house alone after her parents' death, died in 2009, hardly anything had changed. After 70 years, Halliburton's map was still in the same place in the front bedroom. All fixtures and built-in units were still in place. Photographs then taken by estate agents[13] as well as fashion shots[14] show the almost perfect state of preservation. The fact that the responsible authorities failed to purchase the house when it was for sale in 2010, or at least to oblige the new owners to maintain essential elements of the interior design,[15] may be regarded as a tragic mistake. The new residents were not very squeamish with the house. The interior is hardly recognizable today. Thus, an outstanding and authentically preserved work of early Californian modern architecture has been lost, as has a fascinating example of mid-century architecture that sought new and appropriate forms of coexistence beyond family-based, normative relationships.

Neil Bingham

Ein Gentlemen's Agreement: Patrick Gwynne

Er war erst 24 Jahre alt, als sich dieser Architekt der britischen modernen Bewegung mit einem großen und luxuriösen Landhaus in einer wunderschönen, vier Hektar großen Landschaft einen Namen machte: 1938 errichtete Patrick Gwynne (1913-2003) das Anwesen The Homewood in Esher im Südwesten von London. Hier sollte er sechzig Jahre lang leben und Architektur praktizieren. Das Haus ist heute im Besitz des National Trust und steht Besuchern offen, die dieses Meisterwerk aus perfektem Stil und modernem Komfort bewundern können.[1]

Patrick Gwynne war so gesellig und zurückhaltend wie die Architektur, die er schuf. Maßgeschneiderte Häuser und Interieurs, Meisterwerke der Moderne aus der Mitte des Jahrhunderts, wurden wie Savile Row-Anzüge für zeitgenössisch gesinnte Kunden maßgeschneidert.[2] Dieser epikureische Architekt nahm alle Aspekte des Essens – den Anbau, das Kochen und die Unterhaltung – als Grundlage für seine Restaurantprojekte, die er als Orte des hingebungsvollen Genusses gestaltete; wie sein wunderschönes Dell Restaurant, das wie eine Seerose über dem Serpentine-Ufer im Hyde Park schwebt. Als „eingefleischter Junggeselle", um den höflichen Euphemismus seiner Generation zu gebrauchen, lebte er das Leben eines englischen Gentleman, das von Diskretion und Zurückhaltung geprägt war. Als Architekt der oberen Mittelschicht, der von The Homewood aus selbstständig praktizierte, stammte er aufgrund seiner Klasse und seines Status aus einer Welt voller Privilegien, die allerdings nicht frei von Verwerfungen war. Während Gwynnes Lebenszeit, die sich fast über das gesamte zwanzigste Jahrhundert erstreckte, ging Großbritannien und insbesondere London durch eine soziale Revolution: architektonisch, politisch und sexuell.

Gwynne entschied sich jedoch, selbst Freunden und Familie gegenüber nie über seine Homosexualität zu sprechen. Das war verständlich. Die Generation seiner Eltern und Lehrer hatte die sehr öffentliche Demütigung Oscar Wildes nach seiner Haft miterlebt. Gwynne musste sich in einer homophoben Männerwelt zurechtfinden; zuerst in dem exklusiven Internat in Harrow, das nur Jungen vorbehalten war, dann als Offizier der Royal Air Force während des Zweiten Weltkriegs – Situationen, in denen homosexuelle Aktivitäten zwar weit verbreitet, aber verurteilt und illegal waren. Auch der Beruf des Architekten war fast ausschließlich männlich, und damit verband sich die maskuline Ethik der Moderne, wie Le Corbusier sagte, eine „gesunde und männliche".[3] The Homewood

A Gentlemen's Agreement:
Patrick Gwynne

In 1938, when just twenty-four years old, the British modern movement architect Patrick Gwynne (1913-2003) came to prominence for creating The Homewood in Esher, on the fringes of southwest London, a large and luxurious country house set in a beautiful 10-acre (4-hectare) landscape. Here Gwynne would live and practice architecture for sixty years. The house is now owned by The National Trust, open to visitors who come to admire his masterpiece of high style and modern comfort.[1]

Patrick Gwynne was as convivial and quietly reserved as the architecture he created. Houses and interiors, many masterworks of mid-century modern, were tailored like Savile Row suits for contemporary-minded clients.[2] For this epicurean architect, food – growing, cooking and as entertainment – informed his restaurant designs as venues of dedicated delight like his beautiful Dell Restaurant which floats like a waterlily over the Serpentine shore in Hyde Park. A "confirmed bachelor" to use the polite euphemism of his generation, he lived an English gentleman's life of discernment and discretion. As an upper middle-class architect practicing on his own from The Homewood he was, by his class and status, from a world of privilege, although it was not without its upheavals. During Gwynne's lifetime, spanning almost the whole 20th century, Britain, and London especially, underwent a social revolution: architectural, political and sexual.

Gwynne, however, chose never to speak of his homosexuality to friends and family. It was understandable. The generation of his parents and teachers had witnessed the very public humiliation and imprisonment of Oscar Wilde. Gwynne had to navigate a homophobic male world, at the exclusive boys-only public school of Harrow and as an officer in the Royal Air Force during the Second World War – enabling situations where homosexual activity was widespread but condemned and illegal. The profession of architecture too was almost exclusively male, and with that came Modernism's masculine ethic, as Le Corbusier said, one of "the healthy and virile."[3] The Homewood may have been Gwynne's greatest homage to Corbusier, but as his career progressed, his domestic work came to be characterized by a total aesthetic approach to beauty: from designing the building, the interior fittings and furnishings, to the landscape. His affluent modern interiors, including The Homewood which he continually enriched, his sensitive colour palette and a tendency to always stylize photo shoots of his work with carefully arranged objects, came in for criticism behind his back by the Macho Modernists as being effeminate, the work of a mere interior decorator.

Patrick Gwynne, The Homewood in Esher, Grafschaft Surrey, errichtet 1938

Patrick Gwynne, The Homewood at Esher in Surrey, built in 1938

mag Gwynnes größte Hommage an Le Corbusier gewesen sein. Im Laufe seiner Karriere wurden seine Wohnhäuser jedoch mehr von einem ganzheitlich ästhetischen Ansatz zur Schönheit geprägt: vom Entwurf des Gebäudes, der Innenausstattung und Einrichtung bis hin zur Landschaft. Die üppigen modernen Interieurs – auch in The Homewood –, die er ständig bereicherte, seine sensible Farbpalette und die Tendenz, Fotoshootings seiner Arbeit stets mit sorgfältig arrangierten Objekten zu stilisieren, wurden hinter seinem Rücken von den Macho-Modernisten als verweichlicht kritisiert, als das Werk eines bloßen Innenarchitekten.

Patrick Gwynnes Unterdrückung des homosexuellen Ausdrucks lag mehr in seiner Zurückhaltung und seinem Schweigen als in seinen Handlungen. Seine erste Serie von Aufträgen in den 1930er-Jahren waren allesamt Innenräume für schwule Architektenfreunde. Wie in einer Szene aus Christopher Isherwoods Roman *Leb wohl Berlin* wurde der 21-jährige Gwynne mit seinem Reisegefährten aus Harrow beim Sonnenbaden am Ufer des Genfer Sees fotografiert, während sie unbeschwert durch Europa fuhren, nur einmal gestört durch eine Begegnung mit einer Bande von Nazis. In Stuttgart sahen sie die geschmeidige Moderne des Schocken-Kaufhauses (1926-28, abgebrochen 1960) des Architekten Erich Mendelsohn. Gwynne erinnerte sich, dass sie beim Fotografieren des Gebäudes von einer Gruppe aufdringlicher junger Nazis bedrängt wurden. Wieso sie einen „jüdischen Laden" fotografierten, wurden sie gefragt.

Mehr als zehn Jahre lang, ab Ende der 1950er-Jahre, hatte Gwynne einen Lebensgefährten, den Pianisten und Komponisten Geoffrey Rand, obwohl sie beide getrennte Schlafzimmer mit Einzelbetten hatten. Freunde, Familie und Kunden waren alle an der Wahrung des Gentlemen's Agreement beteiligt, das Gwynne ihnen auferlegte, so

Aufnahme des Wohnzimmers von The Homewood aus dem Jahr 1992

Photo from the living room of The Homewood from 1992

Patrick Gwynne's suppression of homosexual expression was more in his reticence and silence than in his actions. His first series of architectural commissions in the 1930s were all interiors for gay professional friends. Like a scene from Christopher Isherwood's novel *Goodbye to Berlin*, the twenty-one-year-old Gwynne was photographed with his travelling companion from Harrow, sunbathing on the shore of Lake Geneva as they motored carefree through Europe, marred only by a run in with a gang of Nazis. In Stuttgart they encountered the sleek modernism of the Schocken department store (1926-28, destroyed 1960) by the architect Eric Mendelsohn. Taking a photograph of the building, the two young men drew a crowd of "nasty" young Nazis, Gwynne said, asking why they were photographing "a Jewish store."

For more than ten years, from the end of the 1950s, Gwynne had a live-in companion, the pianist and composer Geoffrey Rand, although they both had separate bedrooms with single beds. Friends, family and clients were all complicit in maintaining the gentleman's agreement that Gwynne imposed upon them of never speaking to him about his homosexuality. Today, several decades after his death, many still find it irreverent and irrelevant, an invasion of Gwynne's privacy to bring his sexuality out into the open. However, approaches to sexuality in history have changed greatly and, beginning in 2017, even the staid old National Trust on the fiftieth anniversary of the partial decriminalisation of homosexuality in Britain, began to serve a public interested in the LBGTQ+ connections to their properties, such as Virginia Wolff's cottage Monk's House, and Lawrence of Arabia's home at Clouds Hill. The time of Oscar Wilde is past, and "the love that dare not speak its name" may now be spoken.

dass mit ihm niemals über seine Homosexualität gesprochen wurde. Heute, mehrere Jahrzehnte nach seinem Tod, empfinden viele es immer noch als respektlos und irrelevant, als eine Verletzung von Gwynnes Privatsphäre, seine Sexualität in die Öffentlichkeit zu bringen. Doch die Herangehensweise an Sexualität hat sich im Verlauf der Geschichte stark verändert. Zum fünfzigsten Jahrestag der teilweisen Entkriminalisierung von Homosexualität in Großbritannien wandte sich ab 2017 sogar der alte, behäbige National Trust an ein neues Publikum, das sich für LGBTQ+-Persönlichkeiten und ihre Wohnsitze interessiert, wie Virginia Wolffs Cottage Monk's House und Lawrence von Arabiens Haus in Clouds Hill. Die Zeit von Oscar Wilde ist vorbei, und „die Liebe, die ihren Namen nicht zu sagen wagt", darf nun ausgesprochen werden.

Uwe Bresan

Der Architekt und sein Engel: Chen Kuen Lee

Wie Eisschollen schieben sich die Deckenplatten ineinander. Wo sie sich übereinander legen, dringen schmale Lichtstreifen ins Innere. Der Raum fließt auf unterschiedlichen Niveaus darunter hinweg und durch die große Glasfront in den Garten hinaus. Der schwarze Steinboden folgt ihm nahtlos. Ein kleiner Teich zieht sich wiederum von außen hinein und bildet mitten im Wohnzimmer ein amorphes Tauchbecken. An seinem Rand entfaltet sich ein grüner, dichter Wald aus großblättrigen Gewächsen, aus Palmen und tropischen Kletterpflanzen, die sich um eine filigrane, frei in den Raum schwingende Stahltreppe in die Höhe entwickeln und damit den Aufstieg zur offenen Galerieebene, wo die privaten Räume des Hausherrn und seiner Frau liegen, in einen Dschungel einhüllen. Daneben liegt die offene Bar und durch eine freistehende Wand ist ein kleiner Kinosaal abgetrennt. Im Zentrum des Grundrisses steht wiederum ein großer offener Kamin aus schwerem dunklen Bruchsteinmauerwerk. Zwei Stufen führen in das halboffene holzvertäfelte Rund, das ihn umgibt, hinunter. Eine mit schwarzem Leder bezogene Sitzbank folgt der offenen Rundung und schließt den höhlenartigen Raum gegen die Umgebung ab. Folgt man ihrem Verlauf, gelangt man vom Wohnraum in den offenen Essbereich, dessen Wände mit edlen, markant gemaserten Hölzern verkleidet sind. Kinder- und Gästezimmer schließen sich in einem eigenen Gebäudeflügel an. Ein dritter Flügel markiert in Richtung Straße den Eingang und nimmt die Mädchenkammer sowie die Küche auf.

Wir kennen solche Häuser aus frühen James Bond-Filmen. 1971 etwa lässt sich Sean Connery in der Rolle des britischen Geheimagenten von zwei exotischen Akrobatinnen – ihre Namen sind Bambi und Klopfer – in einem ganz ähnlichen Interieur verprügeln, bevor er mit den beiden – im wahrsten Sinne atemberaubenden – Schönheiten im Pool des Hauses landet. Im Film, es ist übrigens die Episode *Diamonds are Forever*, sehen wir das berühmte Elrod House, das John Lautner 1968 in den Bergen über der mondänen Wüstenstadt Palm Springs realisierte.[1] Wir sind hingegen zu Gast in der südwestdeutschen Provinz, in einer Kleinstadt zwischen Rhein und Neckar im Städtedreieck von Stuttgart, Karlsruhe und Heilbronn. (Mehr soll auf Wunsch der aktuellen Bewohner nicht verraten werden. Sie fürchten um ihre behagliche Ruhe.) Und doch verbindet die beiden Häuser ein gemeinsamer Geist. Wie die Natur ins Haus hinein geholt wird, wie Steine, Pflanzen und Wasser einen tropischen Hintergrund bilden, wie sich der Raum über Treppen, Ebenen und Niveausprünge verteilt und sich der dunkle Steinboden zum Kamin hin zur Sitzlandschaft entwickelt, das sind

The Architect And His Angel: Chen Kuen Lee

The ceiling plates interlock like ice floes. Where they are overlapping, narrow shafts of light penetrate the interior. The room extends on different levels below them and out into the garden through the large glass front. The black stone floor follows it seamlessly. A small pond extends indoors from outside and forms an amorphous plunge basin in the middle of the living room. At its edge, a green, dense forest of large-leafed plants, of palm trees and tropical climbers unfolds which rise up around a filigree steel staircase freely swinging into the room. Like a jungle, the plants envelop the way up to the open gallery level where the private rooms of the owner and his wife are located. Next to the stairs is the open bar and a small cinema auditorium separated by a free-standing wall. In the centre of the layout is a large, open fireplace of heavy, dark quarry-stone masonry. Two steps lead down into the half-open, wood-panelled circle which surrounds it. A seating bench covered with black leather follows the open curvature and screens the cave-like space against the surrounding area. If one follows the curvature, one gets from the living room into the open dining area with walls panelled in extravagant, strikingly grained types of wood. The children's and the guest room are adjacent in their own wing. A third wing marks the entrance from the street and provides space for the maid's room as well as the kitchen.

We are familiar with such houses from early James Bond films. In 1971, for instance, Sean Connery in the role of the British secret agent has himself beaten up by two exotic female acrobats – their names are Bambi and Thumper – in quite a similar interior before he ends up in the pool of the house with the two – in the truest sense of the word – breath-taking beauties. In the film, by the way it is the Diamonds are Forever episode, we see the famous Elrod House which John Lautner had built in the mountains above the glamorous desert city of Palm Springs.[1] We, in contrast, are guests in a parochial south-western part of Germany, in a small town between the Rhine and the Neckar in the city triangle of Stuttgart, Karlsruhe and Heilbronn. (Upon the current residents' request, more information about the location is not to be disclosed. They fear for their cosy tranquillity) And yet the two houses are connected by a shared spirit. How nature is brought into the house, how stones, plants and water form a tropical background, how space is distributed across stairs, levels and differences in levels and how the dark stone floor becomes a seating landscape towards the fireplace – those are motifs of the especially future-oriented and utopia-loving American post-war architecture whose style we today like to call mid-century modernism.

Der Architekt Chen Kuen Lee bei Zen-Übungen in seinem Garten

Architect Chen Kuen Lee doing Zen exercises in his garden

Motive der besonders zukunftsfreudigen und utopieverliebten amerikanischen Nachkriegsarchitektur, deren Stil wir heute gern als Midcentury-Moderne bezeichnen. In Deutschland ist es die Zeit des sogenannten Wirtschaftswunders, und so spießig der Begriff heute klingt, so spießig stellt man sich gemeinhin auch die deutsche Architektur jener Jahre vor. Und deshalb überrascht dieses Haus in der deutschen Provinz auch so über alle Maßen. Es steht eben nicht im milden Klima Kaliforniens und ein James Bond hat sich nie hierhin verirrt, stattdessen stehen wir im Haus des Polstermöbelfabrikanten Carl Straub, errichtet in den Jahren 1955/56. Sein Architekt war Chen Kuen Lee (1914-2003).[2]

In einer Ausgabe der legendären Nachkriegsillustrierten *Film und Frau* aus dem Jahr 1963 sind das Haus und sein Architekt beschrieben.[3] Die Rede ist von einem „Traumbauwerk", das der „Hauskünstler" Lee hier gestaltet habe. Im Text wird auf die „Gefahr" angespielt, „daß manches an solchem Traumbauwerk sich zu phantasiegeladen in spielerische Tändeleien mit Formen, Farben und Baustoffen verlieren" könne. Mit dem Haus sei jedoch ein „Balanceakt" gelungen, „in dem ein Architekt mit atemberaubender Könnerschaft so tut, als ob bei allen seinen Tricks doch eigentlich gar nichts dabei wäre." Und so schließt sich der Vergleich mit dem „Ballzauberer Rastelli" an, „der im Spiel mit seinen Bällen, die ihn nach seinem Willen umschwebten, auch immer wie ein lächelnder Knabe" gewirkt habe. Der Architekt als gefeierter Jongleur und Ballakrobat, der mit dem Raum und seinen Elementen spielt, als hätten Mauern, Wände und Decken kein Gewicht; der hoch elaborierte Grundrisse mit komplexen Statiken und verschwenderischen Formen entwickelt und sich dabei die Leichtigkeit, Freude und Unverzagtheit eines spielenden Kindes bewahrt?

Chen Kuen Lee mit einem
Freund während seiner
Studienzeit in Berlin,
1930er-Jahre

*Chen Kuen Lee with a
friend during his student
days in Berlin, 1930s*

In Germany, it is the time of the so-called economic miracle and as stuffy as the concept sounds today, as one generally imagines the German architecture of those years to be. And that is why this house in an otherwise parochial German region is such an enormous surprise. It does not stand in the mild climate of California and a James Bond never got lost here. We are instead standing in the house of Carl Straub, the manufacturer of upholstered furniture, built in the years 1955/56. Its architect was Chen Kuen Lee.[2]

In an issue of the legendary post-war illustrated magazine *Film und Frau* from 1963, the house and its architect are described.[3] Mention is made of a true "dream building" which the "artisan of homes" Lee is said to have designed here. In the text, an allusion is made to the "danger" that "many features of such a dream building too full of fancy might be lost in

Chen Kuen Lee, Haus Straub, Süddeutschland, 1955/56, Gartenseite

Chen Kuen Lee, Straub House, southern Germany, 1955/56, garden side

– Wenn man die Porträts betrachtet, die von Chen Kuen Lee überliefert sind, so ist der Vergleich vielleicht gar nicht so weit hergeholt, wie man zunächst vermuten könnte. Denn selbst wenn einmal kein Lächeln seine Lippen umspielt, was selten ist, so sind es doch seine Augen, die Lees schier unverwüstliche, innere Vergnügtheit zu verraten scheinen.

Es mag sein, dass das Foto, das Lee bei Zen-Übungen im Garten zeigt, unsere Vorstellung des allzeit in sich ruhenden Architekten, der auch noch den widrigsten äußeren Umständen stets mit einem Lächeln begegnet, mehr prägt, als es der Wirklichkeit entsprach. Es sind Klischees und Projektionen, doch nach allem, was wir über Lee wissen, scheint sich das Bild, das wir uns von dem Architekten durch die Porträts machen können, zu bestätigen. Überprüfen können wir dieses Bild heute nicht mehr. Lee starb um die Jahrtausendwende. Vergessen war er schon zu Lebzeiten: Die große Zeit des Architekten endete in der Ölkrise der 1970er-Jahre, als seine in der Nachkriegszeit entstandenen Landhausentwürfe mit ihren vielfach gebrochenen Geometrien, ihren leichten Dächern und Wänden und ihren übergroßen Glasflächen nicht mehr in die Zeit endlicher fossiler Energieträger passen wollten. Knapp drei Dutzend Villen hatte Lee seit den 1950er-Jahren im südwestdeutschen Raum realisiert und dafür viel Aufmerksamkeit erhalten. Nun stand er plötzlich ohne Aufträge da. Den neuen Anforderungen an die Architektur konnte sich Lee in den 1980er-Jahren nicht mehr anpassen. Die kompakten Formen, welche die neuen Wärmeschutzverordnungen nötig machten, liefen seinen Ideen des offenen Raumes und der fließenden Verbindung von innen und außen entgegen. Und die Postmoderne lag ihm nicht. Auch der Versuch, sich in Taiwan, wohin Lee in den späten 1980er-Jahren als Professor berufen wurde, eine zweite Karriere aufzubauen, scheiterte. Es war das Ende von Lees einst so glänzender Laufbahn. Als er 2003 in einer winzigen Berliner Sozialwohnung verstarb, war er vollkommen mittellos.[4]

Chen Kuen Lee, Haus Straub, Süddeutschland, 1955/56, Wohnzimmer

Chen Kuen Lee, Straub House, South Germany, 1955/56, living room

playful dalliances with forms, colours and construction materials." With the house, however, a "balancing act" is reported to have succeeded "where an architect with breath-taking skill pretends that there is actually nothing to all his tricks." And thus, the article goes on by comparing the house to the "juggling magician Rastelli" who, "by juggling the balls as they orbited around him, still managed to look like a smiling boy." The architect as a celebrated juggler and acrobat who plays with space and its elements as if walls and ceilings had no weight; who develops highly elaborated layouts with complex static and lavish forms and, in the process, preserves the lightness, joy and dauntlessness of a child at play – If one looks at the portraits of Chen Kuen Lee the comparison may, after all, not be as far-fetched as one might at first assume. In pictures, the architect with his petite, almost boyish physique looks strangely ageless at an advanced age. And even if, for once, there is no smile on his face, which is rare, it is his eyes that appear to reveal Lee's almost indestructible inner cheerfulness.

It may well be that it is only the eye of a European which is so blind for the individual features and subtleties of far-eastern physiognomies and is convinced of always only seeing the ageless boy in the portraits of Lee the Chinese. And it may well be that the photograph showing Lee doing Zen exercises in the garden has contributed more to our notion of the perpetually calm architect who always faces even the most adverse external circumstances with a smile than was the actual reality. It is a matter of clichés and projections yet, after all we know about Lee, the image we can construct of the architect based on the portraits seems to be confirmed. Today, we are no longer able to verify this image. Lee died at the turn of the millennium. He was already forgotten during his lifetime: The heyday of the architect ended with the Oil Crisis of the 1970s when his country-home designs with their repeatedly fractured geometries, their lightweight roofs and walls and their oversized glass surfaces appeared to no longer fit into the time of limited fossil energy sources. Lee had

Die Umstände seines Todes bilden dabei den denkbar größten Kontrast zu seiner Herkunft und den Verhältnissen, in denen Lee in Schanghai aufwuchs. Der Großvater war ein bedeutender Seidenfabrikant und belieferte den chinesischen Hof. Der Vater wiederum leitete ein angesehenes Bankhaus und der 1914 geborene Lee wuchs so unter geradezu fürstlichen Bedingungen auf. Das Elternhaus war ein Palast mit Personal, einer eigenen Leibwache und privaten Hauslehrern und so groß, dass nach der Enteignung durch die neuen kommunistischen Herrscher in den späten 1940er-Jahren mehr als 50 Familien in dem Gebäude Platz fanden. 1931 schickte der Vater Lee nach Berlin, wo ein Onkel lebte. Hier lernte er die deutsche Sprache und begann ein Architekturstudium an der Technischen Hochschule. Der berühmte Hans Scharoun, der Begründer des organischen Bauens in Deutschland und bis heute als Architekt der Berliner Philharmonie weltweit verehrt, wurde sein Freund und Mentor. Bei ihm arbeitete Lee von 1937 bis 1953, bis er sich als Architekt in Stuttgart selbständig machte und sich – wie wir gesehen haben – schnell als gefragter Villenarchitekt im südwestdeutschen Raum etablierte.

Damals, auf dem Höhepunkt seiner Karriere, lernte er auch seinen Engel kennen – Werner Engel. Bilder zeigen Engel zum ersten Mal im Jahr 1962 bei einem gemeinsamen Ausflug nach Helgoland. Engel, damals gerade Anfang 20, steht an Deck eines kleinen Motorbootes. Er trägt ein weißes Hemd, unter dem sich deutlich seine muskulöse Statur abzeichnet. Ein schwarzer Wollschal ist eng um seinen Hals gebunden und unter einem modischen, schwarz-weiß gestreiften Hut mit schmaler Krempe schaut sein dunkles Haar hervor. Alles an ihm verrät den Handwerker, den Baugesellen, der unter freiem Himmel arbeitet und dabei allein der Kraft seines Körpers vertraut. Tatsächlich lernt Lee Engel auf einer seiner Baustellen kennen und verliebt sich augenblicklich in den kräftigen Burschen. Die Zuneigung beruht auf Gegenseitigkeit und entwickelt sich bald zu einer großen Liebe, die ein ganzes Leben lang halten wird. In Stuttgart wohnen sie gemeinsam in einer von Lee errichteten Häuserzeile am Rande der Großstadt.[5] Obwohl in den Dimensionen viel bescheidener als seine großbürgerlichen Villen und mehr in die Höhe ragend als in die Breite gehend, ist das kleine Haus, das sie bewohnen, ganz von Lees Architekturidealen durchdrungen. Alles ist offen und einsichtig, nur die Bäder und Toiletten besitzen Türen. Acht Ebenen, die durch kurze Treppen miteinander verbunden sind, hat Lee in dem nach außen gerade einmal dreigeschossigen Bau untergebracht. Zu ebener Erde liegen die Büroräume. Darüber entfalten sich die verschiedenen Lebensbereiche mit einem teilweise zweigeschossigen Wohnraum auf der Höhe des ersten Obergeschosses als Höhepunkt. Spiegel und farbige Wandflächen verleihen dem Raum Dynamik, während eine große Bar mit breitem Tresen den Grundriss dominiert. Sie ist Lees Lieblingsplatz und ein Markenzeichen seiner Architektur. In keiner seiner Villen fehlt sie. Der Architekt ist auch ein Lebemann! Er ist oft zu Gast auf den Festen und Partys seiner vermögenden Bauherren, er ist charmant und unterhaltsam und er tanzt gern. Bei ihm zu Hause stapeln

Chen Kuen Lee, Haus Straub, Süddeutschland, 1955/56, Kaminecke

Chen Kuen Lee, Straub House, South Germany, 1955/56, fireplace corner

completed almost three dozen mansions in the southwest region of Germany since the 1950s and received much attention for them. Now he suddenly found himself without any commissions. In the 1980s, Lee was no longer able to adapt to the new demands on architecture. The compact forms required by the new thermal-insulation regulations ran counter to his ideas of the open space and the flowing transition between the outside and the inside. And he did not like post-modernism. His attempt to build a second career for himself in Taiwan, where he was appointed as a professor in the late 1980s, failed. It was the end of Lee's formerly bright career. When he died in a tiny Berlin council flat in 2003, he was completely destitute.[4]

The facts of his death represent the strongest contrast imaginable to his origin and the conditions in which Lee grew up in Shanghai. His grandfather was a famous silk-manufacturer and supplied the Chinese court. His father directed a respected bank and thus Lee, born in 1915, grew up in princely circumstances. His parental home was a palace with servants, bodyguards and private tutors and it was so large that, after it was confiscated by the new communist rulers in the late 1940s, more than 50 families could be accommodated in the building. In 1931, his father sent Lee to Berlin where an uncle of his was living. This was where he learned German and began studying architecture at the technical university. The famous Hans Scharoun, the founder of organic architecture in Germany and, to this day, revered worldwide as the architect of the Berlin Philharmonie, became his friend and mentor. Lee worked in Scharoun's office from 1937 to 1953 when he became self-employed in Stuttgart and – as we have seen – quickly established himself as a sought-after architect of mansions in the south-west region of Germany.

At the time, at the peak of his career, he also met his "angel" – Werner Engel. The pictures in Lee's private photo albums which are today stored together with his estate of

Gemeinsamer Ausflug von Chen Kuen Lee und Werner Engel zur Insel Helgoland, 1962

Joint excursion by Chen Kuen Lee and Werner Engel to the island of Helgoland, 1962

sich die Jazzplatten in den Regalen. Und Engel ist immer an seiner Seite – auch dann noch, als die Bauherren wegbleiben und die Einladungen weniger werden; und auch noch, als der Architekt zuerst in Berlin dann in Taiwan nach einer zweiten Chance sucht; und zuletzt noch, als Lee gezwungen ist, sich auf eine Wohnung mit zwei kleinen Zimmern im Märkischen Viertel, einer Trabantenstadt am Rande Berlins, zu beschränken.[6] Lee hatte das Haus, ein bis zu 17 Geschosse hoch aufragendes Wohngebirge, zum Ende der 1960er-Jahre noch selbst gebaut.

Werner Engel lebt noch heute hier – in der Wohnung im 14. Stock, die er mit Lee nach ihrer Rückkehr aus Taiwan bezogen hat. Über seine Beziehung zu dem Architekten will er aber nicht sprechen. Er kommt aus einer anderen Generation: Als sich Lee und Engel kennen lernten, galt noch der berüchtigte Paragraph 175 des deutschen Strafgesetzbuches, ein Relikt aus dem Deutschen Kaiserreich, unter den Nationalsozialisten verschärft und nach 1945 unverändert in bundesdeutsches Recht umgewandelt, der bis 1969 jegliche sexuelle Handlung zwischen Personen männlichen Geschlechts unter schwere Strafe stellte und erst 1994 endgültig abgeschafft wurde. Dass der über 80-jährige Engel heute schweigt, ist also irgendwie verständlich. Unverständlich ist hingegen das Schweigen des Biografen: Als 2015 vor allem die frühen Villen und Landhäuser des Architekten in einer fulminanten Ausstellung in Stuttgart und Berlin neu zu entdecken waren, begleitet von einem ansonsten tadellosen Ausstellungskatalog, wird Engel auch hier verschwiegen. Viel mehr noch, Engel kommt in der Publikation nicht nur nicht vor, sondern er wird zugunsten einer eigenwilligen Ersatz-

drawings in the Baukunstarchiv of the Berlin Akademie der Künste, show Engel for the first time in 1962 during an excursion with Lee to Helgoland. Engel, in his early twenties at the time, is standing on the deck of a small motorboat. He wears a white shirt, and his muscular physique is clearly visible underneath it. A black woollen scarf is tightly wrapped around his neck and his dark hair shows under a fashionable hat with a narrow rim and black-and-white stripes. Everything about him indicates the craftsman, the builder who works under the open sky and trusts solely in the strength of his body. Lee in fact got to know Engel at one of his construction sites and immediately fell in love with the robust builder. The affection was mutual and soon developed into a great love which was to last for a whole life. In Stuttgart, they live together in a row house that Lee designed on the periphery of the major city.[5] Although far more modest in its dimensions than his bourgeois mansions and extending up rather than sideways, the small house they live in is completely permeated by Lee's architectural ideas. Everything is open and observable, only the bathrooms and the toilets have doors. Lee fitted eight levels, which are linked by short stairs, into the building that only has three storeys when seen from the outside. At ground level are the office premises. Above them are the various living areas with a two-level living room at the height of the first upper floor as a climax. Mirrors and coloured wall areas give the room dynamism and a large bar with a wide counter dominates the layout. It is Lee's favourite spot and a trademark of his architecture. It is missing in none of his mansions. The architect is also a *bon vivant*. He is frequently a guest at the celebrations and parties of his wealthy building clients, he is charming and entertaining, and he likes to dance. In his home, there are stacks of jazz records on the shelves. And Engel is always at his side – even when the building clients stay away and the number of invitations dwindles; and even when the architect looks for a second chance first in Berlin and then in Taiwan; and also in the end, when Lee is forced to limit himself to a flat with two small rooms in the Märkisches Viertel, a satellite city on the periphery of Berlin.[6] At the end of the 1960s, Lee himself had designed the building, a residential mountain rising by up to 17 storeys.

Werner Engel still lives here today – in the flat on the 14th floor he moved into together with Lee after their return from Taiwan. But he does not want to talk about his relationship with the architect. He is part of a different generation: When Lee and Engel met, the infamous "Paragraph 175" of the German criminal code was still valid, a relic from the German Reich which was tightened by the National Socialists and, after 1945, was unmodified turned into a federal law. Until 1969, it made any sexual act between persons of the male sex heavily punishable and was finally completely abolished in 1994. That the almost 80 years old Engel keeps silent today is thus somehow understandable. Not understandable, on the other hand, is the silence of the biographers: Since, in 2015, above all the early mansions and country homes planned by the architect could be newly discovered in brilliant exhibitions in Stuttgart and Berlin, architectural history once again

familie gleich ganz aus der Biografie gestrichen. Und so heißt es über Lee: „Die Bauherren waren seine Familie, die Häuser seine Kinder."[7] – Klar! Wer braucht da noch einen Engel an seiner Seite?

Lees Häuser, könnten sie sprechen, würden eine andere Geschichte erzählen! Sie dürfte gerade dem Biografen des Ausstellungskatalogs nicht verborgen geblieben sein, arbeitete er doch viele Jahre lang in Lees Stuttgarter Architekturbüro; in dem Haus also, das Lee zusammen mit Engel bewohnte! Dass in den Biografien von großen Künstlern und Architekten auch über ihr private Existenz gesprochen und geschrieben wird, ist heute unumstrittener Standard. Viele Werke der Kunst- und Architekturgeschichte lassen sich oft nur richtig interpretieren, wenn das Privatleben ihrer Schöpfer Eingang in den Prozess der Deutung findet. Nicht so bei schwulen Architekten: Sie werden gern – wie Lee – als allein in ihr Fach und ihre Profession vernarrte Helden der Baukunst verklärt, die für ein schnödes Privatleben einfach keine Zeit gehabt hatten.

focuses more intensely on Lee. Since then, numerous contributions have been published in newspapers, journals and magazines about the exhibitions, about Lee and his œuvre. In not a single one of them is Engel mentioned who lived at the architect's side for more than 40 years. And even the in other respects faultless exhibition catalogue of 2015 keeps silent regarding it. However, Engel not only does not get mentioned in the publication, but he is completely erased from the biography in favour of an arbitrary "pseudo" family. And thus, it is written about Lee: "The building clients were his family, the houses were his children." [7] – But of course: Who then still needs an angel at his side?

Lee's houses, if they could talk, would tell a different story. It should not have been hidden especially to the biographer who, after all, worked for many years in Lee's architectural office in Stuttgart; in exactly the house where Lee lived together with Engel. That the biographies of great artists and architects also tell and write about their private lives is today the undisputed standard. Many works of the history of art and of architecture can often only be correctly interpreted if the private lives of their creators become part of the process of the interpretation. Not so in the case of gay architects: They are readily – as happened with Lee – glorified as heroes of architecture who are exclusively in love with their discipline and their profession and who simply had no time for a mundane private life.

Uwe Bresan

Das Geheimnis des Architekten: Paul Rudolph

Vielen Zeitgenossen galt Paul Rudolph (1918-1997), der ohne Zweifel zu den führenden amerikanischen Architekten seiner Generation gezählt werden darf, als verschlossen und unnahbar. Schon sein militärisch wirkender Kurzhaarschnitt signalisierte – sicher nicht unbewusst – eine steife männliche Beherrschtheit und Strenge. Ihre Entsprechung findet diese nach außen getragene Seite von Rudolphs Persönlichkeit in zahlreichen seiner Bauwerke. Die Macher der Architekturzeitschrift *Progressive Architecture* gingen 1964 sogar soweit, für das Cover ihrer Februar-Ausgabe ein Porträtfoto Rudolphs direkt mit einer Nahaufnahme seines Art + Architecture Buildings in New Haven zu überblenden.[1] Es ist das bekannteste Gebäude des Architekten und gleichzeitig einer der berühmtesten Kunstschulbauten des 20. Jahrhunderts.[2] Der mitten auf dem traditionsreichen Campus der Yale University gelegene Fakultätsbau schließt sich nach außen nicht nur hermetisch gegen seine Umwelt ab, sondern wirkt vor allem in der Nahsicht geradezu bedrohlich. Rudolph hatte den gesamten Bau mit schmalen, spitz zulaufenden Betonlisenen überzogen, die nach dem Ausschalen mit einem Hammer gebrochen wurden und so eine fast martialisch scharfkantige Oberfläche erzeugten. Timothy Rohan, einer der profiliertesten Kenner von Rudolphs Werk, interpretiert diese später zu einem Markenzeichen von Rudolphs Bauten avancierte Betonbehandlung als „hyper-maskuline" Geste,[3] mit der der Architekt das ganz andere Wesen seiner Innenräume – und letztlich auch das „Geheimnis" um seine eigene Person – zu maskieren suchte.

Tatsächlich überraschen Rudolphs brutalistische Großbauten im Inneren durch die sensible Behandlung der Themen Raum, Material und Farbe.[4] Gerade für europäische Besucher, die Rudolphs Bauten oft nur aus zeitgenössischen Schwarzweiß-Aufnahmen kennen, vermitteln vor allem die weichen, rot oder orange leuchtenden Teppichböden, die der Architekt in vielen seiner öffentlichen Bauprojekte verwendete, einen vollkommen unerwarteten Eindruck, der zunächst nur schwer mit dem äußeren Bild der Bauten an sich beziehungsweise mit unserer Vorstellung des amerikanischen Beton-Brutalismus der Zeit in Einklang zu bringen ist. Gleichzeitig eröffnet sich im Inneren der Gebäude ein reiches, fast schon barockes Spiel mit Raum, der sich oft über mehrere Ebenen hinweg öffnet und dadurch vielfältigste Blick- und Wegebeziehungen generiert; sich mitunter aber auch in seiner labyrinthischen Struktur einer vollständigen Erfassbarkeit entzieht.

The Architect's Secret:
Paul Rudolph

Many contemporaries regarded Paul Rudolph, who can certainly be considered one of the leading American architects of his generation, as withdrawn and unapproachable. His short, military-looking haircut already signalled – certainly not unconsciously – a stiff, manly self-mastery and rigour. This outward side of Rudolph's personality is reflected in many of his buildings. In 1964, the people behind the architecture magazine *Progressive Architecture* even went so far as to cross-fade a portrait photo of Rudolph directly with a close-up of his Art + Architecture Building in New Haven for the cover of their February issue.[1] It is the architect's most famous building and at the same time one of the most famous art school buildings of the 20th century.[2] The faculty building, located in the middle of the traditional campus of Yale University, is not only hermetically sealed from the surroundings, but also appears almost menacing when viewed from up close. Rudolph had covered the entire building with narrow, tapering concrete pilaster strips, which were broken with a hammer after the formwork had been stripped, thus creating an almost martial sharp-edged surface. Timothy Rohan, one of the most distinguished experts on Rudolph's work, later interprets this treatment of concrete, which later became a trademark of Rudolph's buildings, as a *hyper-masculine* gesture[3] with which the architect sought to mask the completely different character of his interiors – and ultimately also the secret surrounding his own person.

In the interior, Rudolph's brutalist large-scale buildings actually surprise us with their sensitive approach to the themes of space, material and colour.[4] Especially to European visitors, who often only know Rudolph's buildings from contemporary black-and-white photographs, the soft red or orange carpets the architect used in many of his public building projects, convey a completely unexpected impression, which at first is hard to reconcile with the external appearance of the buildings respectively with our idea of American concrete brutalism of the time. At the same time, a rich, almost baroque play with space unfolds inside the buildings that often extends across several levels, generating a wide variety of visual links and connecting paths; but occasionally it also evades complete comprehensibility owing to its labyrinthine structure.

Paul Rudolph, fotografiert im Art + Architecture Building in New Haven

Paul Rudolph, photographed in the Art + Architecture Building in New Haven

Mit seinem eigenen New Yorker Penthouse-Apartment, das sich Rudolph ab Ende der 1970er-Jahre unter der Adresse Beekman Place 23 am Ufer des East Rivers und in unmittelbarer Nähe zum Sitz der Vereinten Nationen errichtete,[5] erreichte der Architekt zweifellos den Höhepunkt und – im Sinne eines für Außenstehende kaum mehr zu erfassenden räumlichen Zusammenhangs – die äußerste Grenze seiner Raumspielkunst. Zugleich scheint es, als fände die komplexe Persönlichkeit des Architekten gerade hier ihren stärksten Ausdruck.[6] Von der Straße aus gesehen, schließt sich der viergeschossige Dachaufbau mit massiven Betonscheiben vollkommen nach außen ab. Sie kragen, von einem Stahlträgergerüst gehalten, auf der Höhe des sechsten Obergeschosses weit über die historische Fassade des Bestandsgebäudes hinaus. Im Inneren des Apartments wiederum werden die Sinne des Besuchers durch gläserne Wände und Böden, verspiegelte Oberflächen und semitransparente Raumabschlüsse verwirrt. Selbst Stühle und Tische bestehen aus Plexiglas. Dazu kommt ein irritierendes räumliches Zusammenspiel von insgesamt 17 horizontalen Ebenen, über die sich das Apartment erstreckt und deren innerer Zusammenhang sich auch durch ein intensives Studium der von Rudolph publizierten Grundrisse nur schwer nachvollziehen lässt. Letztlich, so scheint es, hatte nur der Architekt selbst die Kontrolle über seine Schöpfung, was es Rudolph auch erlaubte, dem Apartment eine mehr oder weniger geheime zweite Wohnung einzuschreiben.

Offenbar wird das doppelte Gesicht von Rudolphs Penthouse-Apartment erst im Schnitt: Hier zeigt sich einerseits der „offizielle" und durch zahlreiche Veröffentlichungen wohl bekannte Wohnbereich Rudolphs, der sich über große Panoramascheiben zum East River hin öffnet und sich über insgesamt drei Geschosse erstreckt, die über ein zentrales Atrium miteinander verbunden sind. Andererseits offenbart sich ein weiterer, vollkommen

Mit der Planung seines eigenen New Yorker Apartments erreichte Paul Rudolph den Höhepunkt seiner Raumspielkunst.

With the planning of his own New York apartment, Paul Rudolph reached the pinnacle of his art of spatial play.

With his own penthouse apartment in New York, which Rudolph built at the end of the 1970s at 23 Beekman Place on the banks of the East River and in the immediate vicinity of the United Nations Headquarters,[5] the architect undoubtedly reached his climax and – in the sense of a spatial context that is almost impossible for outsiders to comprehend – the ultimate limit of his artistic play with space. At the same time, it seems as if the architect's complex personality is most strongly expressed in this apartment.[6] Viewed from the street, the four-storey roof structure with massive concrete slabs is completely closed off from the outside. Supported by a steel beam scaffold, they project far beyond the historical façade of the existing building at the height of the sixth floor. Inside the apartment, the visitor's senses are confused by glass walls and floors, mirrored surfaces and semi-transparent room enclosures. Even chairs and tables are made of Plexiglas. This is complemented with a confusing spatial interplay of 17 horizontal levels inside the apartment, the internal connections of which are difficult to comprehend even after intensive studies of the floor plans Rudolph had published. Ultimately, it seems, only the architect himself had control over his creation, which also allowed Rudolph to incorporate a more or less secret second flat into the apartment.

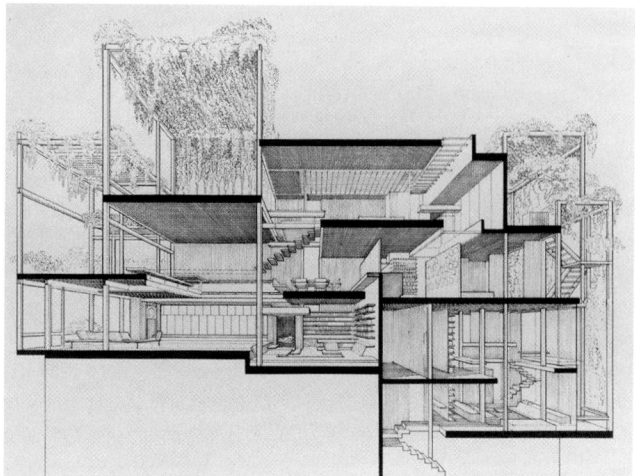

Im Schnitt lässt sich die räumliche Komplexität von Paul Rudolphs Apartment erahnen.

An inkling of the spatial complexity of Paul Rudolph's apartment can be seen in the section.

autarker und ebenfalls dreigeschossiger zur Stadtseite hin orientierter Wohntrakt, über dessen Existenz wohl die meisten Besucher von Rudolphs Penthouse im Unklaren gelassen wurden. Auch finden sich in den zeitgenössischen Publikationen des Penthouses kaum aussagekräftige Fotos des Bereichs. In ihm lebte bis zu Rudolphs Tod im Jahr 1997 dessen Lebensgefährte Ernst Wagner.

In den veröffentlichten Grundrissen werden die beiden unteren, ebenfalls über einen Luftraum verbundenen Wohnräume Ernst Wagners stets als „Bibliothek", das darüber liegende Schlafzimmer als „Gästetrakt" bezeichnet. Von der „offiziellen" Seite des Apartments unterscheiden sich die Räume aber nicht nur durch ihre intimere Größe, sondern auch durch ihren ganz eigenen Charakter. Während in den Haupträumen Weißtöne dominieren und damit die Offenheit und Größe des Apartments noch betont wird, überwiegen in den „geheimen" Räumen dunkle Oberflächen und „harte" Materialien. Schwarze Ledersofas und Einbauten aus poliertem Stahl lassen schnell Assoziationen an schwule Milieus entstehen, wie sie einem großen Publikum erstmals 1980 in dem Skandalfilm *Cruising* mit Al Pacino bekannt wurden. An zwei Stellen hat Rudolph auf geradezu spektakuläre Art und Weise die zwei ganz unterschiedlichen Welten seines Penthouses optisch miteinander verbunden: Zum einen installierte er in einem zu seinem „offiziellen" Wohnbereich gehörenden Badezimmer einen gläsernen Waschtisch, der in den Luftraum der vermeintlichen „Bibliothek", den Wohnraum seines Lebensgefährten, auskragte. Zum anderen gab er dem großen Whirlpool in seinem privaten Badezimmer einen gläsernen Boden, der sich unmittelbar über Ernst Wagners Schlafzimmer und dessen Bett öffnete.

Ein gläserner Waschtisch dient in Paul Rudolphs Apartment der optischen Verbindung zwischen verschiedenen Räumen.

A glass vanity serves as a visual link between different rooms in Paul Rudolph's apartment.

The two-faced character of Rudolph's penthouse apartment only becomes apparent in cross-section: On the one hand, Rudolph's official and due to numerous publications well-known living area appears; it opens up towards the East River with large panoramic windows and extends over three levels that are connected by a central atrium. On the other hand, another completely independent and also three-storey living area facing the city side is revealed, the existence of which remained unknown to most visitors to Rudolph's penthouse. Informative photographs of this area can hardly be found in contemporary publications featuring the penthouse. This is where his partner in life, Ernst Wagner, lived until Rudolph's death in 1997.

In published floor plans, the two living spaces on the lower level, which are also connected via a void, are referred to as library, while the bedroom located above is called *guest apartment*. Compared to the *official* side of the apartment, these rooms not only differ in their more intimate size but also owing to their very own character. While shades of white dominate the main rooms and thus further emphasize the openness and size of the apartment, dark surfaces and "hard" materials prevail in the "secret" rooms. Black

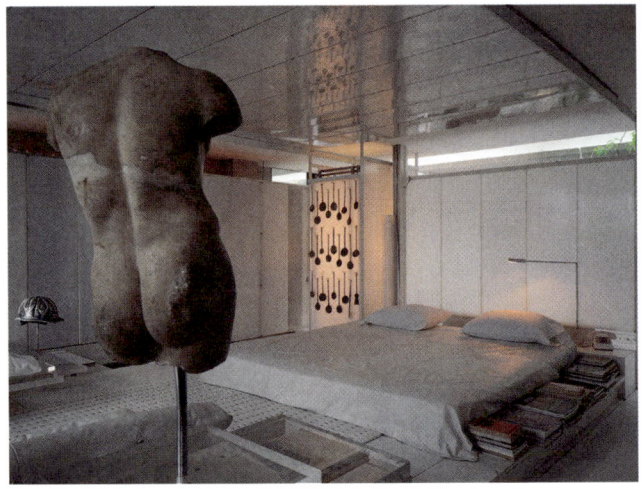

Aufnahme des Schlafzimmers in Paul Rudolphs Apartment

Shot of the bedroom in Paul Rudolph's apartment

Lässt man nun das private und in der breiten Öffentlichkeit kaum bekannte Zusammenleben Rudolphs mit seinem Partner in der Analyse unberücksichtigt, so lassen sich die komplexe Grundstruktur des Apartments und die aufwendige Überlagerung zweier getrennter Wohneinheiten nur schwer erklären. Natürlich begründete der Architekt selbst seinen gläsernen Whirlpool immer wieder mit der Notwendigkeit einer natürlichen Belichtung des darunter liegenden „Gästezimmers", das dadurch direkt an einem über dem Pool gelegenen Oberlicht partizipiert. Und natürlich lässt sich mit solch vermeintlich funktionalistischer Stringenz vieles begründen, weshalb die Architekturgeschichte gern auf so saubere Erklärungen zurückgreift. Ob damit jedoch der wahre Kern einer Sache getroffen wird und sich die Umsetzung einer bautechnisch so hoch-komplexen Konstruktion allein mit der Belichtung eines „Gästezimmers" hinreichend erklären lässt, bleibt fraglich. Eine andere Architekturgeschichte jenseits der engen Grenzen, in denen sich die Profession vor allem im deutschsprachigen Raum bewegt, könnte zweifellos auch zu ganz anderen Deutungen kommen. Nicht zuletzt könnte davon auch eine noch 2005 an der Universität Stuttgart entstandene Dissertation zu Rudolphs Lebenswerk profitieren,[7] der es tatsächlich gelingt, über den stattlichen Umfang von 544 Seiten hinweg nicht einmal den Namen von Rudolphs Lebensgefährten Ernst Wagner zu erwähnen.

leather sofas and built-in units made of polished steel immediately evoke associations with gay milieus, as the general public first saw them in 1980 in the scandalous film *Cruising* starring Al Pacino. Rudolph visually connected the two very different worlds of his penthouse in two places in a truly spectacular way: Firstly, he installed a glass washstand in a bathroom belonging to his *official* home, which protruded into the void of the alleged *library*, the living room of his partner. Secondly, he designed the large whirlpool with a glass bottom in his private bathroom, which was situated directly above the bed in Wagner's bedroom.

If one ignores Rudolph's private life with his partner, which was hardly known to the general public, the complex basic structure of the apartment and the elaborate overlapping of two separate residential units are difficult to explain. The architect repeatedly reasoned this arrangement, which is clearly recognisable in section, with the necessity of providing the guest room with natural light, which thus benefits from a skylight located directly above the whirlpool. Of course, such allegedly functionalist explanations can help to solve the puzzle, which is why architectural history prefers to fall back upon such clean explanations. However, whether this gets to the true heart of the matter, and the lighting of a guest room adequately explains the implementation of a structurally highly complex construction, remains debatable. A different architectural history beyond the strict boundaries of this profession, particularly in German-speaking countries, could undoubtedly provide completely different insights. A dissertation on Rudolph's lifework,[7] written at the University of Stuttgart as late as 2005, could also benefit from this, as it actually succeeds in not even mentioning the name of Rudolph's life companion, Ernst Wagner, over an impressive length of 544 pages.

Wolfgang Voigt

Ich danke für die entsprechende Anrede: Die Trans-Architektin Hildegard Schirmacher

Unter dem Namen Ernst Schirmacher hatte sie die längste Zeit ihres Lebens verbracht. Als engagierter Architekt, Denkmalpfleger und Fachautor war sie bekannt und genoss hohes Ansehen, so dass es für alle eine Überraschung war, als sie sich noch im Alter als Transgender bekannte. Den verblüfften Mitbürgern präsentierte sie sich als Dame und forderte sie auf, ihr als solcher mit Respekt zu begegnen.[1]

Die im männlichen Körper in Stuttgart aufgewachsene Hildegard Schirmacher (1924-2015) empfand schon als Kind den Wunsch, ein Mädchen zu sein. Während ihrer Jugend im Nationalsozialismus zog sie es vor, sich nichts anmerken zu lassen. Zwar gab es keine organisierte Verfolgung von Transgender-Personen, solange sie sich nicht dem Verdacht homosexueller Handlungen aussetzten.[2] Jedoch waren auch sie durch die aggressive Zementierung der Geschlechterrollen bedroht, so dass die meisten von ihnen zurückgezogen existierten. So gut es ging, vermied Schirmacher Männergesellschaften. Während des Krieges war das nicht mehr möglich; sie musste Soldat werden und empfand den Dienst in der Wehrmacht als Hölle. Davon war sie 1945 befreit, nicht jedoch vom quälenden Gefühl, im falschen Körper zu stecken. An Hilfe aus dem Dilemma war damals nicht zu denken. Hildegard Schirmacher ging eine Ehe ein, aus der ein Sohn hervorging.

Als Ernst Schirmacher absolvierte sie in der ersten Nachkriegszeit das Architekturstudium an der Technischen Hochschule Darmstadt. Eine für sie prägende Erfahrung, die ihren späteren Weg bestimmte, war dort der Unterricht des Städtebauers und Denkmalpflegers Karl Gruber,[3] der durch sein virtuos gezeichnetes Werk *Die Gestalt der deutschen Stadt* (1937) bekannt geworden war.[4] Wie kein anderer verstand dieser, die Morphologie der alten Städte zu erklären. Mit dem Diplom versehen, trat Schirmacher 1951 in die Hochbauverwaltung des neu gegründeten Bundeslandes Hessen ein, die nach den Zerstörungen des Krieges viel zu tun bekam. Unter der Leitung von Hans Köhler, eines Schülers von Hans Poelzig, versorgte die Hochbauverwaltung das Land mit zeitgemäßen Neubauten für Ministerien, Universitäten und andere öffentliche Gebäude.[5]

Zu den herausragenden Leistungen dieser Bauverwaltung zählte das Gebäude der Oberfinanzdirektion in Frankfurt am Main, für die deren Chefarchitekt Hans Köhler einen Entwurf geliefert hatte. Seine Formen erhielt es 1952 bis 1955 auf den Reißbrettern von

Thank You For The Appropriate Form of Address: Trans-Architect Hildegard Schirmacher

She had spent most of her life with the name Ernst Schirmacher. She was known and held in high esteem as a committed architect, monument conservator and specialist author, so it was a surprise to everyone when she confessed to being a transgender in her later years. She presented herself as a lady to her astounded fellow citizens and asked them to treat her as such with respect.[1]

Hildegard Schirmacher (1924-2015), who grew up in a male body in Stuttgart, already felt the desire to be a girl when she was a child. During her youth under National Socialism, she preferred not to let anything show. There was no organised persecution of transgender persons as long as they did not expose themselves to the suspicion of homosexual activities.[2] However, they too were threatened by the oppressive rigor of gender roles, so that most of them lived in seclusion. Schirmacher avoided male companionships as best as she could. During the war this was no longer possible; she had to become a soldier and felt service in the Wehrmacht as hell. She was freed from this in 1945, but not from the agonising feeling of being in the wrong body. Help to escape from the dilemma was out of the question at that time. Hildegard Schirmacher entered into marriage and had a son.

As Ernst Schirmacher, she studied architecture at the Technical University of Darmstadt in the immediate post-war period. A formative experience for her, which determined her later path in life, was the instruction from urban planner and monument conservator Karl Gruber,[3] who had become famous for his virtuosic work *Die Gestalt der deutschen Stadt* (1937).[4] Like no other, Gruber was able to explain the morphology of the old cities. After graduating, Schirmacher joined the Department for Building Construction of the newly founded Federal State of Hesse in 1951, which had plenty to do due to the destruction of the war. Under the direction of Hans Köhler, a student of Hans Poelzig, the Department of Building Construction provided the federal state with modern new ministry, university and other public buildings.[5]

One of the outstanding achievements of this building authority was the Oberfinanzdirektion building in Frankfurt on the Main, which was designed between 1952 and 1955 on the drawing boards of Schirmacher and her colleague Rolf Himmelreich: an eleven-storey, flat high-rise with a pavilion supported by slender columns in front of it, ac-

| Verschiedenes |

Namens-Änderung

Das Amtsgericht Frankfurt/M. hat gemäß TS-Gesetz meine Vornamen geändert:

Dr.-Ing. Hildegard Schirmacher (ehemals Ernst Sch.)

Es beginnt ein neuer Lebensabschnitt als Frau. Für Verstehen und entsprechende Anrede danke ich.

Ich bin jetzt eine Frau: Zeitungsannonce in der *Nassauischen Neuen Presse*, 14. Mai 1997

I am now a woman: newspaper advertisement in the Nassauische Neue Presse, *May 14, 1997*

Schirmacher und ihres Kollegen Rolf Himmelreich: eine elf Geschosse hohe Hochhausscheibe mit einem davor auf schlanken Stützen ruhenden Pavillon für Konferenzräume und den Präsidenten der Behörde. Das „Haus der 800 Fenster" fiel durch seine in Quadrate gerasterte Fassade auf, die mit erdfarbenen Keramikplatten in Gelb über Rot nach Dunkelbraun verkleidet war. Zwischen dem Mosaik der farbenfroh changierenden Flächen waren leicht vorstehende, quadratische Kastenfenster aus Stahlrahmen eingesetzt.[6] Eine gescheiterte Sanierung der Fassade mit einem Kleber, der sich als giftig erwies, erzwang 2009 erst die Räumung und dann den Abriss des Gebäudes. Einer der besten Bauten der Nachkriegsmoderne in der Region ging damit verloren.

Bald verließ Schirmacher die Bauverwaltung und verfasste als Doktorarbeit eine Stadtgeschichte von Limburg, einer mit viel historischer Substanz versehenen Stadt in der Nähe von Frankfurt am Main.[7] Während die Mehrzahl der Architektenkollegen noch die Flächensanierung mit dem Abrissbagger vertraten, propagierte sie mutig die erhaltende Erneuerung. In Limburg, der von einem romanischen Dom gekrönte Fachwerkstadt, bewirkte ein von ihr verfasstes Gutachten, dass sich die Stadt ab den 1970er-Jahren zum Modellfall der behutsamen Stadterneuerung entwickelte. Schirmacher zog nach Limburg um; die Altstadt wurde ihr Wohn- und Arbeitsort. Haus für Haus wurde denkmalgerecht saniert und dabei das historische Fachwerk von späteren Verkleidungen befreit. Die Haus-

Hildegard Schirmacher, 2010

commodating conference rooms and the offices of the president of the fiscal authority. The "House of 800 Windows" stood out because of its square-grid façade, which was clad with earth-coloured ceramic panels changing from yellow to red to dark brown. Between the mosaic of colourful, iridescent surfaces, slightly protruding, square box windows made of steel frames were inserted.[6] A failed renovation of the façade with an adhesive that turned out to be toxic forced the evacuation and then the demolition of the building in 2009. One of the finest buildings of post-war modernism in the region was thus lost.

Schirmacher soon left the Department of Building Construction and wrote her PhD thesis on the city history of Limburg, a city with a wealth of historical substance near Frankfurt on the Main.[7] While the majority of fellow architects were still advocating area rehabilitation with demolition machinery, she courageously propagated a conservational renewal. In Limburg, a city with half-timbered houses crowned by a Romanesque cathedral, an expert report prepared by her caused the city to become a model case of careful urban renewal from the 1970s onwards. Schirmacher moved to Limburg; the old town became her place of residence and work. House after house was renovated in accordance with monument preservation requirements, freeing the historic timber framing from subsequently installed cladding. The house owners developed pride in "their" house. The decisive idea for the change in consciousness was – in common with Karl Gruber –

Oberfinanzdirektion Frankfurt, erbaut 1955

Frankfurt Chief Finance Office, built in 1955

besitzer entwickelten Stolz auf „ihr" Haus. Der für den Bewusstseinswandel entscheidende Gedanke bestand darin, wie Karl Gruber die historische Stadt als Einheit zu sehen und nicht einzelne Bauten, sondern das Ganze in seinem Gefüge der Straßen und öffentlichen Räume als erhaltenswert zu begreifen.[8]

Ein anderes Werk, das Schirmacher übertragen wurde, waren die 1983 neu errichteten sechs Häuser der Ostzeile am Römerberg in Frankfurt am Main, mit denen eine seit dem Zweiten Weltkrieg bestehende Lücke in der Platzfront geschlossen wurde. Es handelte sich um Rekonstruktionen der 1944 an dieser Stelle zerstörten Bauten. Millionen von Touristen haben diese Häuser inzwischen gesehen und viele von ihnen dürften geglaubt haben, dass es sich um 300 bis 400 Jahre alte Bürgerhäuser handelt.

Nach dem Tod ihrer Ehefrau im Jahre 1987 war die zeitweise verdrängte Sehnsucht wieder da. Dass Transgender zur normalen Diversität der Geschlechter gehört und dass sie mit ihrem Wunsch nicht allein stand, war Schirmacher nicht bewusst. Für Transgender-Personen hatten sich die Rahmenbedingungen durch das in der BRD ab 1981 geltende Transsexuellengesetz verbessert, wovon sie aber nichts mitbekommen hatte.[9] Es dauerte lange, bis eine in die Öffentlichkeit wirkende Aufklärung stattfand. Von der Möglichkeit der Geschlechtsangleichung durch Hormone und Operation erfuhr die Architektin 1991 durch eine Fernsehsendung. Zur Behandlung, die inzwischen medizinischer Standard geworden war, die aber auch heute noch Mut und Geduld erfordert, entschloss sie sich im Alter von 70 Jahren. Einem Kollegen eröffnete sie, dass sie sich ihr Leben lang im falschen Körper gefühlt habe, um nun etwas zu unternehmen, um „ihr" Geschlecht anzunehmen.[10]

to see the historical city as a unity and not to understand individual buildings but the whole in its structure of streets and public spaces as worthy of preservation.[8]

Another work entrusted to Schirmacher was the six buildings of the eastern section of the Römerberg, a public square in Frankfurt on the Main, newly built in 1983, which closed a gap in the square's front that had existed since the Second World War. These were reconstructions of the buildings destroyed on this site in 1944. Millions of tourists have meanwhile seen these buildings and many of them may have believed that they are town houses that are 300 to 400 years old.

After the death of her wife in 1987, the temporarily suppressed longing returned. Schirmacher was unaware that transgender was part of the normal diversity of the sexes and that she was not the only one with her desire. For transgender persons, the general conditions had improved due to the Transsexuals Act, which had been in force in the Federal Republic of Germany since 1981, but which she had not noticed.[9] . It took a long time for public education to take place. In 1991, the architect learned about the possibility of sex reassignment through hormones and surgery in a TV programme. At the age of 70 she decided to undergo the treatment, which had become medical standard in the meantime but still requires courage and patience. She revealed to a colleague that she had felt she had been in the wrong body all her life and that she was now doing something to change this and switch to "her" sex.[10]

A close girlfriend was the first to whom she confided in a letter in 1994: "I have to start with this at some point, the change is too obvious. […] I know that I am entering an intermediate realm, an unlimited and unnamed one. But the world demands unambiguous signals: man or woman. Now that it has to be, I have decided to be a woman – in attitude and clothing. The id has always tended towards this form of being. […] It's annoying enough when, dressed as a woman, you present your credit card with your male first name. I don't know where this will all lead to. Perhaps it is a sign of necessity to go step by step, without imagining the consequences."[11] She had not yet arrived at herself, but the first steps had been taken: "It is wonderful, good and deeply satisfying."[12]

In the provincial city of Limburg, this was easier said than done; here, the protecting anonymity of the metropolis during the transition phase was missing. With unerring instinct, she decided to go off with a bang. From one day to the next, she changed her clothing and took on the role of the distinguished lady. In an advertisement in the local newspaper on May 14, 1997, she announced that from now on Dr. Ernst Schirmacher was Dr. Hildegard Schirmacher: "This is the beginning of a new chapter in my life as a woman. I thank you for your understanding and the appropriate form of address."[13] She

Eine enge Freundin war die erste, der sie sich 1994 in einem Brief anvertraute: „Ich muß einmal damit anfangen, zu offensichtlich ist die Wandlung. [...] Ich weiß, daß ich ein Zwischenreich betrete, ein unbegrenztes und unbenanntes. Doch die Welt fordert eindeutige Signale: Mann oder Frau! Nun, da es sein muß, habe ich mich für das Frau-Sein entschieden – in Haltung und Kleidung. Das Es neigte schon immer zu diesem Sein. [...] Es ist schon lästig, wenn man weiblich gekleidet die Kreditkarte mit dem männlichen Vornamen vorlegt. [...] Wohin das Ganze im Einzelnen führt, weiß ich nicht. Es ist vielleicht ein Zeichen von Notwendigkeit, daß man Schritt für Schritt geht, ohne sich die Folgen auszumalen."[11] Sie war bei sich noch nicht angekommen, aber erste Schritte waren getan: „Es ist herrlich, gut und tief befriedigend."[12]

Im provinziellen Limburg war das leichter gesagt als getan, hier fehlte die während der Phase des Übergangs schützende Anonymität der Metropole. Mit sicherem Instinkt entschied sie sich zum Paukenschlag. Von einem auf den anderen Tag wechselte sie die Garderobe und übernahm die Rolle der vornehmen Dame. In einer Anzeige in der Lokalzeitung machte sie am 14. Mai 1997 bekannt, Dr. Ernst Schirmacher sei von nun an Dr. Hildegard Schirmacher: „Es beginnt ein neuer Lebensabschnitt als Frau. Für Verstehen und entsprechende Anrede danke ich."[13] Sie tat es mit Stil und gewann. In Limburg war die Nachricht eine Sensation, obwohl sich, wie es heißt, viele zunächst damit schwer taten.[14] Mehr als die Männer waren es Frauen, die ihr den Schritt erleichterten: „Man beobachtete mich auf der Straße. Frauen kamen auf mich zu und versicherten mir, daß mein Weg richtig gewesen sei und bald redete man in Limburg darüber, daß ich zu den eleganten und gut angezogenen Frauen der Stadt gehöre (Was in Limburg nicht besonders schwierig ist)."[15]

Die Stadtgesellschaft erwies sich trotz katholisch-konservativer Grundstimmung als lernfähig und akzeptierte sie in ihrem neuen Leben. In einer Stadt von bescheidener Größe war das keine Selbstverständlichkeit. Schirmacher blieb als Frau, was sie gewesen war: die „Stimme der Altstadt", eine bekannte und geschätzte Figur in der lokalen Öffentlichkeit, in Ehrenämtern und weiterhin als Akteurin in allen Fragen des historischen Baubestandes. 2004 verlieh man ihr die Ehrenplakette der Stadt. Noch im hohen Alter wanderte die weißhaarige Dame am Stock durch die Altstadt und wurde respektvoll gegrüßt. Ihr frühes Werk, die Oberfinanzdirektion in Frankfurt am Main, wurde ein Jahr vor ihrem Tod 2015 abgerissen. Aber noch immer und auch in Zukunft erinnert Limburgs hervorragend erhaltene Altstadt an die Pionierarbeit dieser Transgender-Architektin.[16]

Ostzeile am Römerberg in Frankfurt, nach der Zerstörung im 2.Weltkrieg rekonstruiert

East row at the Römerberg in Frankfurt, reconstructed after the destruction in World War II.

did it with style and won. In Limburg, the news was a sensation, although, many people had a hard time with it at first. More than the men, it was women who made it easier for her to make the move: "They were watching me in the street. Women came up to me and assured me that my decision was the right one, and soon people in Limburg were talking about me being one of the most elegant and well-dressed women in town (which is not particularly difficult in Limburg)".[15]

Despite the Catholic-conservative basic attitude, the city society proved to be capable of learning and accepted her in her new life. In a city of modest size this was not a matter of course. As a woman, Schirmacher remained what she had been: the "voice of the old town," a well-known and esteemed figure in the local public, in honorary posts and still as a protagonist in all matters of historical building stock. In 2004 she was awarded the city's medal of honour. Even in her old age, the white-haired lady wandered through the old town with a walking stick and was greeted respectfully. Her early work, the Oberfinanzdirektion in Frankfurt on the Main, was demolished one year before her death in 2015. Yet Limburg's excellently preserved old town still reminds us and will continue to do so in the future of the pioneering work of this transgender architect.[16]

Uwe Bresan

To Be Openly Gay at That Time Would Not Have Been Good For Business: Arthur Erickson und Francisco Kripacz

Das Titelbild ist verführerisch! Im Vordergrund formen elegante weiße Polstermöbel, die sich um einen offenen Kamin gruppieren, ein intimes Arrangement, während große Glasfronten den Blick über die hölzerne Terrasse hinweg auf das Meer öffnen und der überhohe Innenraum von oben herab in intensives Sonnenlicht getaucht wird. Es ist das mondäne Interieur eines modernen Strandhauses in den Dünen, das zunächst unsere Aufmerksamkeit einfängt, bevor uns der Name des Architekten, der sich in großen schwarzen Lettern über das obere Drittel der Bildfläche legt, ins Auge fällt: Francisco Kripacz (1944-2000). Rein äußerlich unterscheidet sich der knapp 200 Seiten starke Bildband, der dem Werk des im Jahr 2000 verstorbenen kanadischen Interior Designers gewidmet ist,[1] damit kaum von anderen zeitgenössischen Architektenmonografien. Gleichwohl dürfte das Buch zu den bemerkenswertesten Architekturtiteln der vergangenen Jahre zählen. Denn hinter dem kleinen, feinen Band verbirgt sich die Geschichte einer großen und tragischen Liebe, deren Spuren in den Bildern und kurzen Texten des Buches aufgehoben sind. Sie führen unter anderem in ein idyllisches kleines Haus in einem ruhigen Vorort von Vancouver, dessen mit samtigen Wildleder-Fliesen verkleideter Wohnraum fast nahtlos in einen verwunschenen chinesischen Garten übergeht. Sie führen aber auch in den gediegenen Umbau einer alten Wagenremise auf einem herrschaftlichen Anwesen auf einer Anhöhe über Toronto. Die in edlem Grau gehaltenen Räume beherbergen Möbel von Le Corbusier und Mies van der Rohe, während sich Kunstwerke von Jasper Johns und Roy Lichtenstein über die Wände verteilen. Von hier aus geht es weiter in das elegante Haus am Strand von Fire Island bei New York, das auch auf dem Buchumschlag abgebildet ist und dessen verschiebbares Dach den Wohnraum zum Himmel öffnet, sowie in das luxuriöse Apartment im 37. Stockwerk des Olympic Towers im Herzen von Manhattan mit seinen verspiegelten Wänden und glänzenden Böden, in denen sich das Glitzern der Metropole vervielfacht. Und nicht zuletzt führen die Spuren auch in das vornehme Bürohaus am legendären Robertson Boulevard in Beverly Hills, dessen geschwungene Betonfassade von einer dünnen Schicht Glas bedeckt wird, was dem Gebäude eine geheimnisvolle Tiefe verleiht, während das graue Interieur durch kräftige farbige Akzente zu vibrieren scheint. Eine solche Auflistung von Orten und Gebäuden ist für eine Architektenmonografie zunächst nichts Ungewöhnliches. Was sie jedoch zu einer Geschichte verbindet, ist die Tatsache, dass es sich dabei nicht um eine Liste von Auftragsarbeiten handelt, sondern vielmehr um die wichtigsten Lebensstationen des Architek-

To Be Openly Gay at That Time Would Not Have Been Good For Business: Arthur Erickson and Francisco Kripacz

The cover photo is tempting! In the foreground, elegant, white upholstered furniture centred on the open fireplace forms an intimate arrangement while large glass fronts allow a view onto the sea across the wooden terrace and the extremely high interior is immersed in intense sunlight from above. It is the glamorous interior of a modern beach house in the dunes which initially attracts our attention before the name of the architect, which in large, black letters covers the top third of the image, catches the eye: Francisco Kripacz. At least on the outside, the close to 200 page-illustrated book dedicated to the Canadian interior designer who died in 2000 hardly differs from other contemporary monographs of architects.[1] Nevertheless, the book may well rank among the most remarkable publications on architecture of the past years. This is because behind the small, exquisite volume is the story of a great and tragic love whose traces are contained in the images and short texts of the book. Among other places, they lead us to an idyllic little house in a quiet suburb of Vancouver. Its living room covered with tiles of velvety suede almost seamlessly flows into an enchanted Chinese garden. But they also lead us into the tasteful conversion of an old coach house on a grand estate located on a hill above Toronto. The rooms designed in a noble shade of grey have furniture by Le Corbusier and Mies van der Rohe while works of art by Jasper Johns and Roy Lichtenstein decorate the walls. From here, we continue on into the elegant house on the beach of Fire Island near New York which is also pictured on the book cover. Its sliding roof opens the living room to the sky, as well as into the luxurious apartment on the 37th floor of the Olympic Tower in the heart of Manhattan with its mirrored walls and shiny floors where the glittering of the metropolis is multiplied. And not to be forgotten are the traces leading into the elegant office building on the legendary Robertson Boulevard in Beverly Hills whose curved concrete façade is covered by a thin layer of glass, which gives the building a mysterious depth while the grey interior appears to vibrate from the strong color contrasts. At first, such a list of places and buildings is nothing unusual. What combines them into a story, however, is the fact that this is not a list of commissioned works but rather of the most significant stations in the life of the architect himself. This is because Francisco Kripacz designed the interiors mentioned with their expensive fittings, the extravagant materials and furniture and the numerous works of art not for any clients but he created them for himself and his partner, probably the most famous Canadian architect of the 20th century: Arthur Erickson.[2]

Francisco Kripacz und Arthur Erickson waren ab den 1960er-Jahre Partner im Leben und im Beruf.

Francisco Kripacz and Arthur Erickson were partners in life and work beginning in the 1960s.

ten selbst. Denn Francisco Kripacz gestaltete die erwähnten Interieurs mit ihren teuren Innenausbauten, den extravaganten Materialien und Möbeln und den zahlreichen Kunstwerken nicht für irgendwelche Auftraggeber, sondern er gestaltete sie für sich und seinen Lebensgefährten, den wohl berühmtesten kanadischen Architekten des 20. Jahrhunderts: Arthur Erickson (1924-2009).[2]

Wie kein Zweiter prägte Erickson seit den frühen 1960er-Jahren mit seinen Gebäuden das Gesicht des modernen Kanada. Er realisierte riesige Universitätsbauten und Museen, große Konzert- und Theaterhäuser, Gerichtsgebäude, Banken und Krankenhäuser. Er war für die zentralen Bauten der Weltausstellung 1967 in Montreal verantwortlich und schuf den kanadischen Pavillon auf der Expo in Tokio 1970. Er gestaltete die offiziellen Büroräume des kanadischen Premierministers und die kanadische Botschaft in Washington. Später plante und baute er auch in Europa, in Asien und im Nahen Osten.[3] Nebenbei hinterließ er einige der spektakulärsten Wohnhäuser des 20. Jahrhunderts. Für seine Arbeiten erhielt er zahlreiche Auszeichnungen. Unter anderem wurde er 1986 als erster und bis heute einziger kanadischer Architekt mit der renommierten Goldmedaille des AIA, des US-amerikanischen Architektenverbandes, geehrt. Die Presse feierte Erickson damals als „Beton-Poeten" und Philip Johnson, der Doyen der amerikanischen Nachkriegsarchitektur, nannte ihn „den vielleicht größten Architekten des amerikanischen Kontinents."[4] Was allerdings nur wenige seiner Bewunderer damals wussten, war, dass Erickson all diese Erfolge auch seinem Lebensgefährten Francisco Kripacz zu verdanken hatte, der seit den frühen 1960er-Jahren an der Seite des berühmten Architekten lebte und arbeitete. Für Kripacz war es ein Leben im Geheimen. Nur wenige enge Freunde, darunter

Since the early 1960s, Erickson like no one else has made an impact on the face of modern Canada with his buildings. He designed huge university buildings and museums, large concert and theatre halls, courthouses, banks and hospitals. He was in charge of the central buildings of the world exhibition 1967 in Montreal and planned the Canadian pavilion at the Tokyo Expo of 1970. He designed the official office premises of the Canadian Prime Minister and the Canadian embassy in Washington. Subsequently, he planned and built in Europe, Asia and the Middle East as well.[3] Besides this, he left behind some of the most spectacular residential buildings of the 20th century. He received numerous rewards for his works. Among others, in 1986 he was honored with the gold medal of the AIA, the US-American association of architects, as the first and, until today, the only Canadian architect. At the time, the press celebrated Erickson as the "poet of concrete" and Philip Johnson, the doyen of American post-war architecture, called him the "probably greatest architect of the American continent".[4] Yet what only few of his admirers knew at the time was that Erickson owed all these successes also to his companion Francisco Kripacz who, since the early 1960s, had lived and worked at the side of the famous architect. For Kripacz, it was a life in secret. Just a few, close friends, among them also the Canadian Prime Minister for many years, Pierre Trudeau – he is the father of Justin Trudeau, the current Prime Minister of the country – were privy to it. Because Erickson knew very well that the revelation of his homosexuality would have barred the way to his success as an architect. "To be openly gay at that time would not have been good for business,"[5] Erickson later justified keeping his relationship with Kripacz a secret from the public and hiding the contribution his partner had made to many of his works. The Kripacz monograph which Erickson himself compiled after the death of his companion and which – seven years after Erickson's own death in 2009 – was published from his estate, can thus be read as a kind of belated recognition – as a last, strong declaration of love.

Erickson, born in 1924, and the almost 20 years younger Kripacz first met in 1961 at a party in Vancouver. The mysterious young man with his dark complexion and his coal-black hair immediately attracted Erickson's attention. When friends of Erickson then organized a party in 1962 to celebrate his brilliant success in the competition for the new building of Simon Fraser University in Burnaby/Canada, Kripacz was already a natural part of Erickson's entourage. It was the first successful competition for the architect and – apart from several smaller contracts – the actual start of his career. From now on, it seemed, Kripacz hardly left Erickson's side which unsettled many of the architect's friends. On the one hand, they were surprised by Erickson's sudden coming-out, on the other, they considered the temperamental young man to be immature and advised the rather calm and reserved Erickson against the relationship. He, however, would not be deterred and supported his youthful lover's ambitions. For a short period, Kripacz at the time enrolled for design studies at the art academy but very soon – encouraged by Erickson – shifted his focus onto

auch der langjährige kanadische Premierminister Pierre Trudeau – er ist der Vater von Justin Trudeau, dem heutigen Premier des Landes –, waren eingeweiht. Denn Erickson wusste genau, dass das Bekanntwerden seiner Homosexualität seinem geschäftlichen Erfolg als Architekt im Wege gestanden hätte. „To be openly gay at that time would not have been good for business",[5] rechtfertigte sich Erickson später dafür, dass er seine Beziehung zu Kripacz vor der Öffentlichkeit geheim hielt und den Anteil, den sein Lebensgefährte an vielen seiner Werke hatte, verschwieg. Die Kripacz-Monografie, die Erickson selbst nach dem Tod seines Lebensgefährten zusammenstellte und die sieben Jahre nach Ericksons eigenem Ableben im Jahr 2009 aus dem Nachlass heraus veröffentlicht wurde, kann deshalb als eine Art nachträgliche Wiedergutmachung gelesen werden – als eine letzte große Liebeserklärung.

Kennengelernt hatten sich der 1924 geborene Erickson und der fast 20 Jahre jüngere Kripacz 1961 auf einer Party in Vancouver. Augenblicklich erregte der geheimnisvolle junge Mann mit seinem dunklen Teint und seinen tiefschwarzen Haaren Ericksons Aufmerksamkeit. Als Freunde von Erickson dann 1962 eine Party organisierten, um dessen fulminanten Erfolg im Wettbewerb für den Neubau der Simon Fraser University im kanadischen Burnaby zu feiern, gehörte Kripacz bereits wie selbstverständlich zu Ericksons Entourage. Es war der erste große Wettbewerbsgewinn für den Architekten und – abgesehen von einigen kleineren Aufträgen – der eigentliche Beginn seiner Karriere. Von nun an, so scheint es, wich Kripacz kaum mehr von Ericksons Seite, was viele Freunde des Architekten verstörte. Einerseits waren sie von Ericksons plötzlichem *coming-out* überrascht, zum anderen hielten sie den temperamentvollen jungen Mann für unreif und rieten dem eher ruhigen und zurückhaltenden Erickson von der Verbindung ab. Der ließ sich jedoch nicht beirren und unterstützte seinen jugendlichen Liebhaber in dessen Ambitionen. Für kurze Zeit schrieb sich Kripacz damals für ein Designstudium an der Kunsthochschule ein, verlegte sich aber schon bald – unterstützt von Erickson – auf den Handel mit teuren europäischen Designermöbeln, die damals in Nordamerika noch kaum bekannt waren. Zusammen lebten sie in dem kleinen Haus in Vancouver, das Erickson nach seinem Studium erworben hatte und das ihm zeitlebens als Rückzugsort diente. Als Kripacz hier in den frühen 1960er-Jahren einzog, entstanden auch die edlen Wandvertäfelungen aus beigem Wildleder, die den Wohnraum in die moderne Version eines klassischen Salons verwandelten. Dazu kam der geheimnisvolle Garten, den Erickson nach chinesischen Vorbildern realisierte und der den großen Wohnraum nach draußen verlängerte. Der zunehmende Erfolg des Architekten und seine Aufträge für die Weltausstellung in Montreal veranlassten das Paar jedoch Mitte der 1960er-Jahre zum Umzug. Von Vancouver an der kanadischen Westküste ging es mehr als 4.000 Kilometer ostwärts nach Toronto. Die Ortswahl war dabei in mehrfacher Hinsicht strategisch. So suchte Erickson gezielt die Nähe zu einflussreichen Kreisen, um sich für neue Aufträge zu empfehlen. Montreal, der

In den 1970er-Jahren errichteten sich Kripacz und Erickson ein extravagantes Haus auf Fire Island.

In the 1970s, Kripacz and Erickson built themselves an extravagant home on Fire Island.

selling expensive European design furniture which, at the time, was still hardly known in North America. They lived together in the little house in Vancouver which Erickson had bought after his studies and which all his life served as his retreat. When Kripacz moved into it in the early 1960s, it was when the upscale wall panelling of beige suede leather was also installed which turned the living room into the modern version of a classic salon. Then there was also the mysterious garden, which Erickson designed based on Chinese models and which extended the large living room to the outside. The increasing success of the architect and his commissions for the Montreal world exhibition, however, caused the couple to move in the mid-1960s. From Vancouver on the Canadian west coast, they relocated more than 4,000 kilometres east to Toronto. The choice of place was strategic in several respects. Erickson specifically looked for proximity to influential circles to recommend himself for new contracts. Montreal, the site of the world exhibition in 1967, as well as Ottawa, the Canadian capital, was only a few hours by car from Toronto. More decisive than the proximity to the political and cultural centres of power in Canada, however, was the proximity to New York. In the 1960s, the city was considered to be the gay Mecca and Erickson and Kripacz from Toronto quickly established contacts to the American metro-

Schauplatz der Weltausstellung 1967, wie auch Ottawa, die kanadische Hauptstadt, lagen nur wenige Autostunden von Toronto entfernt. Entscheidender als die Nähe zu den politischen und kulturellen Machtzentren Kanadas war allerdings die Nähe zu New York. Die Stadt galt in den 1960er-Jahren als schwules Mekka und Erickson und Kripacz knüpften von Toronto aus schnell Kontakte in die amerikanische Ostküstenmetropole – und hier vor allen zu den Künstlerkreisen um Andy Warhol, Roy Lichtenstein und Jasper Johns. Ihr gemeinsames Zuhause in Toronto, eine umgebaute Wagenremise, legte davon Zeugnis ab. Das Wohnzimmer beherrschte ein monumentaler Lichtenstein-Fries, während das runde, mit roter Seide ausgeschlagene Badezimmer eine Bilderserie von Jasper Johns aufnahm. Die Möbel und Leuchten wiederum stammten von bekannten europäischen Marken wie Cassina, B&B Italia und Flos, deren kanadischen Vertrieb Kripacz betreute. Für das kleine Haus in Toronto ließ er zudem zahlreiche Stahlrohrklassiker der frühen Moderne von Le Corbusier, Mies van der Rohe, Marcel Breuer und Eileen Grey importieren – ein unerhörtes Novum für die damalige Zeit in Kanada! Das fertige Haus verwaiste jedoch schnell, denn immer öfter zog es Erickson und Kripacz von hier weg zu ausgedehnten Aufenthalten nach New York. Ein berühmtes Pressebild aus dem Getty-Archiv zeigt Kripacz auf der Tanzfläche des legendären New Yorker Nachtclubs Studio 54 – gemeinsam mit Margaret Trudeau, der damaligen kanadischen First Lady und der Mutter des heutigen Premiers Justin Trudeau.[6] Ihr Mann und Arthur Erickson hatten sich 1968 bei einem Empfang kennen gelernt. Die enge Freundschaft der beiden Männer übertrug sich schnell auch auf ihre jeweiligen Partner, wobei die Nähe zur mächtigen Premiersfamilie auch einen gewissen Schutz für Erickson und Kripacz darstellte.

Von New York aus eroberten Erickson und Kripacz auch die Insel Fire Island vor den Toren der Stadt. Die Inselgemeinden The Pines und Cherry Grove genossen schon damals unter Schwulen in ganz Nordamerika einen einzigartigen Ruf als Urlaubsparadies. Dem Charme des schwulen Insellebens erlagen auch Erickson und Kripacz, die jede Möglichkeit nutzten, um in den Sommermonaten von Toronto aus hierher zu kommen, bis sich schließlich Mitte der 1970er-Jahre die Möglichkeit bot, ein kleines Haus am Strand zu erwerben. Zunächst war nur ein einfacher Umbau geplant. Tatsächlich entstand hier jedoch eines der größten und aufwendigsten Häuser der Insel. Es ist das Haus auf dem Titelbild der Kripacz-Monografie! Das Dach über dem zweigeschossigen Wohnraum konnte automatisch zur Seite fahren und der Zaun, der die Terrasse und den Pool von der Umgebung abtrennte, ließ sich im Boden versenken, um einen direkten Zugang zum Strand und in die Dünen zu öffnen. Das Haus und seine beiden Bewohner wurden schnell zu lokalen Berühmtheiten, und noch heute berichten Weggefährten euphorisch von den glamourösen Festen, die Erickson und Kripacz auf der Insel veranstalteten. Vor allem eine Party im Sommer 1979, als die Gastgeber das Haus bis zur Decke mit goldenen und silbernen Luftballons füllten, hat sich tief in das kollektive Gedächtnis von Fire Island

Das Haus auf Fire Island gehörte zu den größten Anwesen auf der unter schwulen New Yorkern beliebten Ferieninsel.

The home on Fire Island was among the largest estates on the resort island popular among gay New Yorkers

polis on the East Coast – and here above all to the artistic circles around Andy Warhol, Roy Lichtenstein and Jasper Johns. Their shared home in Toronto, a converted coach house, bears witness to it. The living room was dominated by a monumental Lichtenstein freeze whereas the circular dressing room covered in red silk had a series of pictures by Jasper Johns. The furniture and the luminaires were well-known European brands such as Cassina, B&B Italia and Flos, whose Canadian marketing was organized by Kripacz. For the little house in Toronto, he also had numerous classic steel-tube items of early modernism by Le Corbusier, Mies van der Rohe, Marcel Breuer and Eileen Grey imported – an unheard-of novelty for that time in Canada. Yet the finished house was soon vacant since Erickson and Kripacz were more and more frequently lured away from here for long stays in New York. A famous press photograph from the Getty Archive shows Kripacz on the dance floor of the legendary New York nightclub Studio 54 – together with Margaret Trudeau, the then Canadian First Lady and the mother of the current Prime Minister Justin Trudeau.[6] Her husband and Arthur Erickson had met at a reception in 1968. The close friendship of the two men quickly also transferred to their respective partners with the proximity to the powerful family of the Prime Minister also representing a certain protection for Erickson and Kripacz.

From New York, Erickson and Kripacz also conquered Fire Island outside the city. Already at the time, the island communities The Pines and Cherry Grove enjoyed a unique reputation among gays as a holiday paradise. Erickson and Kripacz also succumbed to the charm of the gay island life and used every opportunity to come here from Toronto during the summer months until, in the mid-1970s, there was eventually a chance to purchase a

eingebrannt. Punkt Mitternacht öffnete sich das Dach und entließ die Ballons in den Himmel, während auf der Terrasse die Sängerin France Joli, umringt von hunderten halbnackter Männer, ihre Disco-Hymne *Come to Me* in die Nacht hinaus schmetterte. Der Abend gilt vielen als eine Art „letzter Walzer",[7] bevor Anfang der 1980er-Jahre die AIDS-Krise ihren dunklen Schatten nicht nur über Fire Island, sondern über das gesamte schwule Leben in Nordamerika warf. Seinen Möbelhandel hatte Kripacz zu dieser Zeit längst eingestellt. Er war nun finanziell vollkommen abhängig von Erickson. Der wiederum vertraute immer stärker auf die Fähigkeiten seines Lebensgefährten und begann damit, Kripacz auch offiziell in sein Büro einzuführen. Zur gleichen Zeit ließ das Paar Toronto hinter sich und siedelte endgültig nach New York über. Ihr neues Zuhause war ein Apartment im 37. Stockwerk des Mitte der 1970er-Jahre fertiggestellten Olympic Tower an der Fifth Avenue. Der gläserne Turm gehörte dem griechischen Reeder Aristoteles Onassis und war ein Werk des deutschen Architekten Cäsar Pinnau, dessen Karriere einst im Dritten Reich mit der Gestaltung von Hitlers Privaträumen in der Berliner Reichskanzlei begonnen hatte. Für das Apartment entwarf Kripacz ein fantastisches Interieur: Der Boden wurde leicht angehoben, wodurch die Rahmen der raumhohen Fenster verschwanden und der Eindruck entstand, das Apartment besitze gar keine Grenze nach außen. Zugleich sorgten verspiegelte Wände und der Wohnzimmerboden aus grauem Glas für ein futuristisches Ambiente, in dem sich vor allem nachts das Lichterspiel der Großstadt reflektierte.

Doch auch New York sollte nur eine kurze Zwischenstation bleiben, denn schon bald zog es Erickson und Kripacz weiter nach Los Angeles. Auch diesmal war der Umzug nur teilweise durch einige Aufträge, die Erickson an der Westküste hatte, gerechtfertigt. Viel entscheidender war, dass sich Kalifornien in den 1980er-Jahren zu einem neuen Zentrum der amerikanischen Schwulenbewegung entwickelte und in dieser Hinsicht New York den Rang ablief. Erickson und Kripacz folgten dieser Entwicklung. Es sollte jedoch der Anfang vom Ende sein: Hatten Erickson und Kripacz auch schon in New York einen nicht unaufwendigen Lebensstil gepflegt, so vervielfachten sich die privaten Ausgaben in Los Angeles und überstiegen bald schon jedes Maß. Das neue Haus lag im teuren Bel Air. Ein zweites musste gekauft werden, weil sich die Umbauarbeiten in die Länge zogen. Es lag im nicht weniger teuren Beverly Hills. Dazu kamen die Ausgaben für den Haushälter, den Gärtner und den Koch, für Ericksons Maserati und für Kripaczs Lamborghini und – nicht zuletzt – für das neue Bürohaus am Robertson Boulevard in der unmittelbaren Nachbarschaft des legendären Promi-Restaurants The Ivy. Die Büroräume waren in zarten Grautönen gestaltet, einer Spezialität von Kripacz, während leuchtend rote Möbel, Tischplatten und Stühle einen vibrierenden Kontrast erzeugten. Noch aufwendiger war die geschwungene Betonfassade, die mit einer feinen Schicht Glas bedeckt wurde und dadurch eine irritierende Tiefenwirkung entfaltete. Kripacz, der für den Bau verantwortlich war, trat nun auch ganz offiziell als wichtigster Mitarbeiter von Erickson in Erscheinung

small house on the beach. At first, just a simple conversion was planned. In actual fact, however, one of the largest and most lavish houses on the island was the result. It is the house on the cover of the Kripacz monograph. The roof above the two-level living room could be automatically moved to the side and the fence which separated the terrace and the pool from the surroundings could be lowered in the ground to allow direct access to the beach and the dunes. The house and its two residents quickly became local celebrities and, to this day, companions euphorically tell about the glamorous parties Erickson and Kripacz gave on the island. Above all a bash in the summer of 1979, when the hosts filled the house up to the ceiling with golden and silver balloons is deeply anchored in the collective memory of Fire Island. At the stroke of midnight, the roof opened up and let the balloons rise into the sky while, on the terrace, the singer France Joli surrounded by hundreds of half-naked men belted out her disco hymn "Come to Me" into the night. For many, the evening is seen as a kind of "last waltz" before,[7] at the beginning of the 1980s, the AIDS crisis cast its dark shadow not only over Fire Island but over the whole gay life in North America. At the time, Kripacz had long given up selling furniture. He was now financially completely dependent on Erickson. The latter, in turn, increasingly relied on the capabilities of his partner and started to also bring Kripacz officially into his office. At the same time, the couple left Toronto and moved permanently to New York. Their new home was an apartment on the 37th floor of the Olympic Tower completed in the middle of the 1970s on Fifth Avenue. The glass tower belonged to the Greek ship owner Aristoteles Onassis and was a work by the German architect Cäsar Pinnau, whose career had formerly begun during the Third Reich when he designed Hitler's private rooms in the Berlin Reich Chancellery. Kripacz produced a fantastic interior for the apartment: The floor was slightly elevated which made the frames of the room-high windows disappear and created the impression that the apartment had no boundaries towards the outside at all. At the same time, mirrored walls and the living-room floor of grey glass resulted in a futurist ambience where, especially at night, the play of the lights of the metropolis was reflected.

But New York was to only be another short stop since soon Erickson and Kripacz moved on to Los Angeles. This time as well, the move was only in part justified with some contracts Erickson had on the west coast. What was much more decisive was that California in the 1980s developed into a new centre of the American gay movement and dethroned New York in this respect. Erickson and Kripacz followed this trend. It was, however, to be the beginning of the end: If, in New York, Erickson and Kripacz had already maintained a far from modest lifestyle, their private expenses in Los Angeles multiplied and soon exceeded any limits. The new house was located in expensive Bel Air. A second one had to be bought since the conversion work dragged on. This house stood in the not less expensive Beverly Hills. Then there were the costs for the housekeeper, the gardener and the cook, for Erickson's Maserati and for Kripacz's Lamborghini and – last but not least – for the

Neben dem Haus auf Fire Island bewohnten Erickson und Kripacz auch ein Apartment im Herzen von Manhattan.

In addition to the house on Fire Island, Erickson and Kripacz also occupied an apartment in the heart of Manhattan.

und wurde zum Bürochef der neuen Dependance ernannt, was in Ericksons Büros in Vancouver und Toronto auf wenig Gegenliebe stieß. Kripacz galt den Kollegen als verschwenderisch und im Umgang mit Zahlen wenig verlässlich. Und tatsächlich trugen die hohen Kosten des Büros in Los Angeles wesentlich dazu bei, dass Ericksons Firma in den späten 1980er-Jahren zunehmend in Zahlungsschwierigkeiten geriet. Dazu kam, dass sich Kripacz mittlerweile einen jüngeren Liebhaber hielt, was Erickson in eine tiefe persönliche Krise stürzte. Die Trennung folgte auf Raten: Obwohl auch Erickson bald darauf in Allen Steele einen neuen Begleiter fand, ließ er Kripacz nicht fallen, sondern organisierte sogar gemeinsame Urlaubsreisen für alle vier. Sie waren ein seltsames Paar! Der nächste Tiefschlag ließ jedoch nicht lange auf sich warten: Sowohl bei Steele als auch bei Kripaczs Partner wurde AIDS diagnostiziert. Erickson kümmert sich nun kaum noch um seine Büros. Langjährige Mitarbeiter kündigten. Aufträge gingen verloren. Und so war der Architekt Anfang der 1990er-Jahre gezwungen, in Insolvenz zu gehen. Seine Schulden beliefen sich auf 10,5 Millionen Dollar.

Sein kleines Haus in Vancouver mit dem großen chinesischen Garten hatte Erickson vorsorglich in eine Stiftung, die Arthur Erickson Foundation, überführt, die sich noch heute um das Vermächtnis des Architekten kümmert.[8] So konnte es aus der Konkursmasse gerettet werden und diente dem Architekten bis zu seinem Lebensende als Zuhause. Alle anderen Immobilien, die Erickson gemeinsam mit Kripacz bewohnte, gingen hingegen verloren – das Haus in Toronto, die Wohnung in New York, das Strandhaus auf Fire Island und die Häuser und das Büro in Los Angeles. Auf Vermittlung eines ehemaligen Angestellten fand Erickson jedoch schnell eine neue Beschäftigung – als gefeierter Entwerfer bei einem jungen Architekturbüro in Vancouver, das sich gern mit dem berühmten Namen

Für das New Yorker Apartment im 37. Stock des Olympic Towers an der 5ᵗʰ Avenue entwarf Kripacz ein fantastisches Interieur.

Kripacz designed a fantastic interior for the New York apartment on the 37ᵗʰ floor of the Olympic Tower on 5ᵗʰ Avenue.

new office building on Robertson Boulevard in the immediate vicinity of the legendary VIP restaurant The Ivy. The office premises were designed in subtle shades of grey, a speciality of Kripacz, while bright red furniture, table tops and chairs produced a vibrant contrast. Even more extravagant was the curved concrete façade which was covered with a fine layer of glass and thus created a perplexing effect of depth. Kripacz, who was in charge of the building, was now also officially Erickson's most important employee and was appointed office manager of the new branch which met with little approval in Erickson's offices in Vancouver and Toronto. Among his colleagues, Kripacz was seen as too extravagant and as not very reliable when it came to figures. And indeed the high costs of the Los Angeles office contributed considerably to Erickson's company increasingly getting into payment difficulties in the late 1980s. What's more: Kripacz meanwhile had a younger love which threw Erickson into a deep personal crisis. The separation happened in stages: Although Erickson soon afterwards found a new companion in Allen Steele, he did not drop Kripacz but even organized joint trips. They were indeed a strange couple. The next low blow, however, was not long in coming: Steele as well as Kripacz's partner were diagnosed with AIDS. Erickson hardly dealt with his offices anymore. Long-time employees resigned. Contracts were lost. And thus, at the beginning of the 1990s, the architect was forced to declare bankruptcy. His debts amounted to 10.5 million dollars.

Erickson had providently made his little house in Vancouver with the large Chinese garden part of a foundation, the Arthur Erickson Foundation, which to this day handles the legacy of the architect.[8] Thus it could be saved from the bankruptcy estate and was the architect's home right up to the end of his life. In contrast, all the other properties where Erickson had resided together with Kripacz were lost – the house in Toronto, the

schmückte. Als sein letztes Werk, das er vor seinem Tod bearbeitete, gilt der Trump Tower in Vancouver, der sich fast 200 Meter hoch wie eine Spirale in den Himmel schraubt. Auch Kripacz kam nach dem AIDS-Tod seines neuen Lebensgefährten zurück nach Vancouver und lebte in der Nähe von Erickson, der sich rührend um seinen nun ebenfalls an AIDS erkrankten Ex-Partner kümmerte. Erickson organisierte gemeinsame Reisen, vermittelte kleinere Aufträge und bezahlte Krankenhausrechnungen, bis er Kripacz im Frühjahr des Jahres 2000 tot in seinem Haus auffand.

Er hatte sich an einem Dachbalken erhängt. Sein tragisches Ende war für Erickson der endgültige Auslöser, um ein Buch über Kripaczs Verdienste an der gemeinsamen Arbeit und am gemeinsamen Leben zu schreiben. Es wurde eine späte Würdigung für Francisco Kripacz – den unbekannten Mann hinter Arthur Erickson.

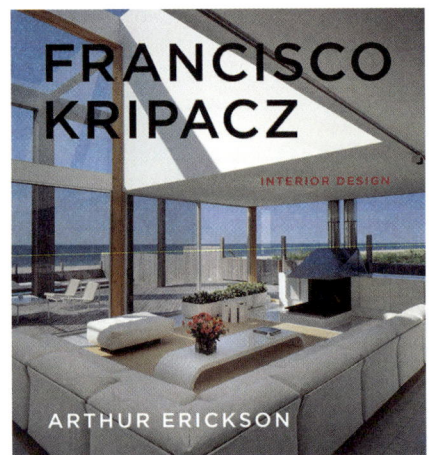

Die Monografie war eine späte Liebeserklärung von Erickson an Kripacz, die fast 30 Jahre zusammenlebten und arbeiteten.

The monograph was Erickson's late declaration of love to Kripacz; they lived and worked together for nearly 30 years.

apartment in New York, the beach house on Fire Island and the houses and the office in Los Angeles. Thanks to a former employee, however, Erickson quickly found a new job – as a celebrated designer in a young architectural office in Vancouver which liked to embellish itself with the famous name. The last work he was involved in prior to his death is the Trump Tower in Vancouver which spirals up into the sky for almost 200 metres. Kripacz as well came back to Vancouver after his new partner had died of AIDS and lived close to Erickson who touchingly took care of his ex-companion who also had AIDS. He went on trips with him, assigned him minor contracts and paid for the hospital bills until, in the spring of 2000, he found him dead in his house. Kripacz had hung himself from a roof beam. His tragic end was for Erickson the final trigger for writing a book about Kripacz's merits regarding their joint work and their shared life. It became a late appreciation of Francisco Kripacz – the unknown man behind Arthur Erickson.

Uwe Bresan

Der Architekt im Playboy: Charles Moore

Die Geschichte der modernen Architektur wird gern als eine Abfolge genialischer Architekten und Ingenieure beschrieben, die in den letzten 100 Jahren allein durch die Kraft ihrer visionären Ideen und den Mut, Neues zu wagen, das Antlitz unserer Welt und damit die Art unseres in der Welt Seins verändert haben. Wir lieben diese Art der Geschichtserzählung mit all ihren gottgleichen Heroengestalten und samt ihrer vielen Heldenbiografien. Tritt man jedoch einen Schritt zurück und schaut sich das Bild genauer an, so taucht hinter der Gestalt des visionären Entwerfers noch eine andere Figur auf, deren Einfluss auf die Architekturgeschichte nur allzu gern vergessen wird. Es ist die Figur des Bauherrn und Auftraggebers, ohne den kein Architekt seine Einfälle und Vorstellungen jemals realisieren könnte. So steht hinter jedem visionären Architekten mindestens ein Bauherr mit Visionen und hinter jedem wagemutigen Entwurf ein Auftraggeber, der auch den Mut hat, es zu wagen. Früher waren es Kaiser und Könige, Päpste und Patriarchen, die ihre Architekten und Ingenieure zu immer neuen Höchstleistungen antrieben. Aber welche Art von Bauherren kennt eigentlich das 20. Jahrhundert? Wer waren die Auftraggeber unserer Moderne? Wer also prägte unsere Vorstellung vom modernen Wohnen? Um es kurz zu machen: Es waren allesamt gesellschaftliche Außenseiter und Randfiguren, die sich mit ihren Lebensumständen und vor allem ihren Lebensvorstellungen an den normativen Grenzen ihrer jeweiligen Zeit bewegten.[1]

Es waren Frauen wie Truus Schröder, Witwe und Mutter von drei kleinen Kindern, die 1924 in der niederländischen Stadt Utrecht den Architekten Gerrit Rietveld mit dem Bau eines neuen Hauses in der Prins Hendriklaan Nr. 50 beauftragte. Ihr Mann war da gerade seit einem Jahr tot. Ob das Haus, das am Ende der pittoresken Siedlungszeile mit ihren traditionellen Backsteinbauten stand und scheinbar nur aus einer Ansammlung frei schwebender Kuben und losgelöster Betonscheiben bestand, der größere Skandal war oder aber die Tatsache, dass der Architekt nach der Fertigstellung gemeinsam mit seiner Bauherrin einzog, können wir heute nur noch erahnen. Das Haus jedenfalls hat die Zeit überdauert und gehört heute zum Weltkulturerbe. Le Corbusiers berühmte Villa in Garches bei Paris, entstanden zwischen 1926 und 1928, die zweifellos zu den am häufigsten publizierten Bauten der Klassischen Moderne gehört, verdankt sich wiederum einer dreiköpfigen Bauherrenschaft, deren unkonventionelles Miteinander damals für ein aufgeregtes Tuscheln in der Pariser Gesellschaft sorgte. In die fertige Villa, in deren strenges weißes Volumen der Architekt sich teilweise überlagernde Loggien, Terrassen und

The Architect in Playboy: Charles Moore

The history of modern architecture is often described as a succession of brilliant architects and engineers who, over the last 100 years, have changed the appearance of our world and thus the way of us being in it, solely through the power of their visionary ideas and the courage to try something new. We love this kind of storytelling with all its godlike heroes and their many hero biographies. If, however, one takes a step back and has a closer look at the bigger picture, another character emerges behind the figure of the visionary designer whose influence on the history of architecture is all too readily forgotten. It is the personality of the building owner and client, without whom no architect could ever implement his ideas and concepts. Behind every visionary architect there is at least one client with visions, and behind every daring design there is a client who has the courage to support it. In former times it was emperors and kings, popes and patriarchs who spurred their architects and engineers on to ever new outstanding achievements. So, what kind of developers and clients can actually be found in the 20th century? Who were the clients of our modern architecture? Who shaped our idea of modern living? To cut a long story short: They were all social outsiders and marginal figures who, with their circumstances and above all their ideas of life, acted on the accepted normative boundaries of their respective times.[1]

It was women like Truus Schröder, widow and mother of three small children, who in 1924 commissioned architect Gerrit Rietveld to build a new house at No. 50 Prins Hendriklaan in the small Dutch town of Utrecht. Her husband had died just a year ago. Today we can only guess what the bigger scandal was: the house at the end of a picturesque row of traditional brick buildings, which was seemingly made up of nothing but an arrangement of free-floating cubes and detached concrete slabs, or the fact that the architect moved in together with his client after completion of the building. In any case, the house has outlasted time and is today listed as a World Heritage Site. Le Corbusier's famous villa in Garches near Paris, built between 1926 and 1928 and undoubtedly one of the most frequently published buildings of classical modernism, in turn, owes its existence to a group of three clients whose unconventional relationship caused the Paris society to gossip. The completed villa, in whose austere, white volume the architect inserted partially overlapping loggias, terraces and balconies and thus created a highly complex interplay of rooms, was occupied by the wealthy American art collector Sarah Stein, her husband Michael and the couple's friend, Gabrielle de Monzie, the equally wealthy ex-wife of well-known French politician

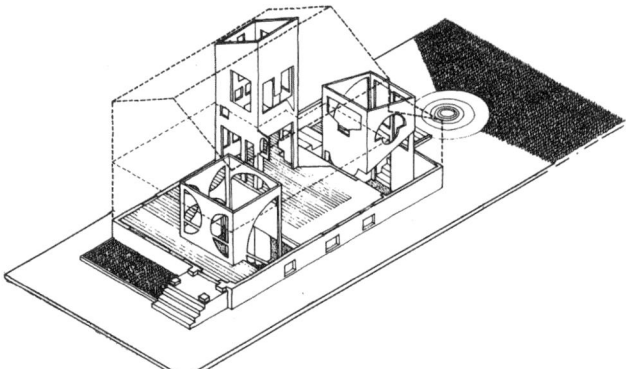

Charles Moore House in New Haven, Isometrie

Charles Moore House in New Haven, isometric view

Balkone einschnitt und damit ein hoch komplexes Zusammenspiel von Räumen realisierte, zogen ein: die vermögende amerikanische Kunstsammlerin Sarah Stein, ihr Mann Michael sowie die gemeinsame Freundin Gabrielle de Monzie, die nicht weniger wohlhabende Ex-Frau des bekannten französischen Politikers Anatole de Monzie. Auch die Chicagoer Ärztin Edith Farnsworth, die 1945 den aus Deutschland emigrierten Architekten Mies van der Rohe mit der Planung eines Wochenendhauses in der knapp eine Autostunde von Chicago entfernten Stadt Plano beauftragte, musste immer wieder um ihre gesellschaftliche Anerkennung kämpfen. Als alleinstehende Frau galt sie in der prüden amerikanischen Nachkriegsgesellschaft als Außenseiterin und Sonderling. Ihr von dünnen Stahlstützen getragenes und nach allen Seiten hin verglastes Weekend Retreat am Ufer des Fox Rivers hingegen gilt heute als eines der berühmtesten Wohnhäuser des 20. Jahrhunderts.

Schaut man sich nun die wenig konventionellen Lebensstile ihrer vornehmlich weiblichen Bauherrenschaft an, so scheint es fast absurd, dass die Häuser Schröder, Stein-de Monzie und Farnsworth zu Lifestyle-Ikonen werden konnten, deren Namen und Architekten heutzutage jeder Leser der einschlägigen Wohnzeitschriften von *Architectural Digest* bis *Schöner Wohnen* im Schlaf aufsagen kann. Was einst als Experiment gesellschaftlicher Außenseiter begann, taugt also längst auch noch der spießigsten Kleinfamilie, die am Stadtrand ihre so genannte "Bauhausvilla" bezieht, als vermeintliches Distinktionsmerkmal.

Dahinter steckt eine feine Ironie! Und die ist zweifellos auch am Werk, als 1969 in der Oktoberausgabe des *Playboys* ausgerechnet das private Wohnhaus des amerikanischen Architekten Charles Moore (1925-1993) auftaucht.[2] In Europa kennt man Moore hauptsächlich als Architekten der Piazza d'Italia in New Orleans. Die farben- und formenprächtige Plaza inmitten des Geschäftsviertels der Stadt gilt als Ikone der Postmo-

Anatole de Monzie. Similarly, physician Edith Farnsworth from Chicago had to repeatedly fight for social recognition. She commissioned architect Mies van der Rohe, who had emigrated from Germany in 1945, to design her weekend house in Plano, a town just under an hour's drive from Chicago. In America's prudish post-war society, the single woman was regarded as an outsider and eccentric. Today, Farnsworth House, her glazed weekend retreat with its slender steel supports located on the banks of Fox River, is considered one of the most famous 20th century residential buildings.

Looking at the rather unconventional lifestyles of these mainly female clients, it seems almost absurd that the residences of Schröder, Stein-de Monzie and Farnsworth could become lifestyle icons whose names and architects are familiar to all readers of the relevant home magazines from *Architectural Digest* to *Schöner Wohnen*. What once started as an experiment carried out by those regarded as social outsiders has long since proved its worth as a distinguishing feature even for the most conventional of small families, who move into their so-called Bauhaus mansion on the outskirts of the city

And it is doubtlessly a factor when in 1969 the October issue of *Playboy* featured, of all things, the private home of American architect Charles Moore.[2] In Europe, Moore is known mainly as the architect who designed Piazza d'Italia in New Orleans. The colorful plaza featuring a plethora of different shapes in the middle of the city's business district is considered an icon of postmodernism and is still capable of sparking controversy even today – almost 50 years after its creation. In America, on the other hand, Moore had been considered a celebrated innovator of American architecture since the mid-1960s. His small, inexpensive private homes, built mainly on the East Coast of the United States, represented a new and lively contrast to the International Style that had dominated the urban American landscape since the 1940s and whose increasingly rigorous canon of forms and materials had typically resulted in bland monotony. Unlike the houses built in the International Style, which hardly responded to the existing contexts at all in their rigid adherence to set rules, Moore's houses were adapted to their environments in question, incorporating typical regional materials and experimenting with various traditions and symbolism from older American residential architecture, without attempting to replicate rigid patterns and conventions.[3]

Moore's approach suited the zeitgeist of the 1960s: At the time, American society was undergoing a tremendous process of transformation that involved questioning the prevailing system and its strict forms of representation. Given this background, Moore's architectural designs, some of which were highly subversive, were popular among students and young architects in particular, who felt they represented alternative lifestyle choices. This led in 1965 to Moore's appointment as dean of the Yale School of Architecture, then as

derne und spaltet noch heute – fast 50 Jahre nach ihrer Entstehung – die Gemüter. In Amerika galt Moore hingegen schon seit Mitte der 1960er-Jahre als gefeierter Erneuerer der Architektur, der mit kleinen kostengünstigen Wohnhäusern vor allem an der Westküste der USA dem seit den 1940er-Jahren vorherrschenden International Style, dessen immer strenger gehandhabter Formen- und Materialkanon zunehmend in gesichtsloser Monotonie verkam, ein neues, lebendiges Bild der Architektur entgegensetzte. Anders als die Bauten des International Style, die in ihrem engen Schematismus kaum auf vorhandene Kontexte reagieren konnten, waren seine Wohnhäuser auf die jeweilige Landschaft abgestimmt, nahmen regional typische Materialien auf und spielten mit verschiedenen Traditionalismen und Symboliken der älteren amerikanischen Wohnhausarchitektur, ohne dabei starre Muster und Konventionen zu wiederholen.[3]

Damit traf Moore den Zeitgeist der 1960er-Jahre: Die gesamte amerikanische Gesellschaft befand sich damals in einem gewaltigen Transformationsprozess, in dem das herrschende System samt seiner strengen Repräsentionsformen in Frage gestellt wurde. In diesem Kontext gewannen Moores zum Teil äußerst subversive Architekturen als Modelle einer alternativen Lebenswirklichkeit vor allem bei Studenten und jungen Architekten viel Aufmerksamkeit, was 1965 letztlich zu Moores Berufung als Dekan der Yale School of Architecture, damals wie heute eine der führenden Architekturschulen des Landes, führte. In New Haven, der knapp eineinhalb Autostunden nördlich von New York gelegenen Universitätsstadt, bezog Moore kurz nach seiner Ankunft aus Kalifornien ein kleines Haus im Kolonialstil in der Nähe der Schule und begann neben dem Unterricht augenblicklich mit

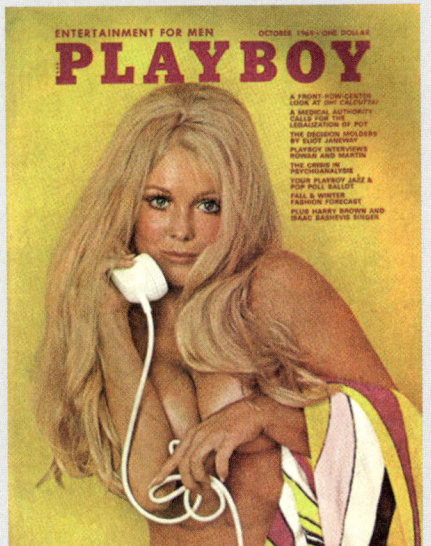

Charles Moore House in New Haven, Blick aus dem Garten und Blick aus dem Haus durch die Küche in den Garten

Playboy-Ausgabe, in der das Moore House als Bachelor Pad unter dem Titel *New Haven Haven* veröffentlicht wurde

Charles Moore House in New Haven, view from the garden and view from the house through the kitchen into the garden

Playboy *issue, in which the Moore House was published as a Bachelor Pad under the title* New Haven Haven

today one of the country's leading schools of architecture. Shortly after his arrival from California, Moore moved into a small colonial-style house near the school in New Haven, the university town just under an hour and a half's drive north of New York, and immediately commenced extensive renovation and extension work alongside his teaching activities. It was already the fourth house that Moore constructed for himself as client and architect. Three more should follow in the future. And like all of the architect's earlier and later houses, this one was tailored to his very special personality as a builder-owner.

From the outside, the extensive alterations Moore made to the interior of his home were barely noticeable. Indeed, his two-storey white clapboard house with its flat saddle roof and the small colonnaded porch over the front door exuded a quiet classicist charm. Yet Moore did not leave a single part of the interior architecture untouched. He demolished all of the interior walls, removed the panelling from the outer walls and finally opened the ceilings and floors to install three open towers in the house, some of which extended from the basement to the roof. Moore nicknamed these towers Howard, Berengaria, and Ethel. They provided voids and visually linked the house's individual levels, creating an amusing interplay of sight lines. This effect was further heightened by Moore's special treatment of the tower walls. These were made of thin plywood with geometric cut-outs arranged in several layers to form diverse overlaps and allow a range of views. The architect appropriated patterns, shapes and colours from the emerging Pop Art movement, to which he also owed his love of neon signage and ironically alienated quotes from American everyday culture. This resulted in an interior that was shaped by the wild zeitgeist of

umfangreichen Umbau- und Erweiterungsmaßnahmen. Es war bereits das vierte Haus, das Moore als Bauherr und Architekt für sich selbst realisierte. Drei weitere sollten in Zukunft noch folgen. Und es war wie alle früheren und alle späteren Häuser des Architekten auf seine ganz spezielle Bauherren-Persönlichkeit hin zugeschnitten.

Von außen sah man dem zweigeschossigen Haus, das mit seinem flachen Satteldach, den weiß gestrichenen Holzfassaden und dem kleinen Säulenportikus vor der Eingangstür einen moderaten klassizistischen Charme versprühte, die Umbauten im Inneren kaum an. Dabei ließ Moore keinen Teil der bestehenden Innenarchitektur unberührt. Was zwischen den Fassaden lag, riss er alles nieder, entfernte die Vertäfelungen der Außenwände und öffnete schließlich Decken und Böden, um drei offene Türme im Haus zu installieren, die teilweise vom Keller bis unter das Dach reichten. Moore nannte sie Howard, Berengaria und Ethel. Sie dienten als Lufträume und verbanden so optisch die einzelnen Ebenen des Hauses, was ein amüsantes Spiel von Blickbeziehungen in Gang setzte. Verstärkt wurde dieser Effekt noch durch Moores spezielle Behandlung der Turmwände. Sie bestanden aus dünnen, mit geometrischen Ausschnitten versehenen Wandschirmen, die in mehreren Schichten hintereinander angeordnet vielfältige Überschneidungen und Durchblicke bildeten. Muster, Formen und Farben entlieh der Architekt dafür aus der aufkommenden Pop Art, aus der Moore auch die Vorliebe für Neonlicht-Schriftzeichen und andere, ironisch verfremdete Zitate aus der amerikanischen Alltagskultur übernahm. So entstand ein vom wilden Zeitgeist der 1960er-Jahre geprägtes Interieur, dass schnell für Furore sorgte und sogar zur ersten Veröffentlichung über Moore in einer deutschsprachigen Architekturzeitschrift führte.[4]

Die bemerkenswerteste Publizität erfuhr das Haus jedoch in der Oktoberausgabe des *Playboy* 1969: Unter dem Titel *A Playboy Pad: New Haven Haven* widmete das für seine freizügigen ausklappbaren Bildstrecken bekannte Männermagazin dem Haus ganze sechs durchgehend mit Farbaufnahmen besetzte Seiten.[5] Inszeniert wurde die Fotostrecke des Magazins dabei als nächtliche Party. So zeigen die Aufnahmen größere und kleinere Gruppen von Gästen, die sich in den unterschiedlichen Ecken und Winkeln des Hauses amüsieren, und man meint fast, das Stimmengewirr, das Klirren der Cocktail-Gläser und die schummrige Paartanzmusik der späten Swinging Sixties zu hören. Der begleitende Text spricht von ein paar Freunden, die der das Haus bewohnende Junggeselle eingeladen habe.

Die Betonung liegt natürlich auf Junggeselle! Der ist, weil er von den Zwängen eines durchschnittlichen Familienlebens befreit ist und sich deshalb ständig auf der Jagd nach neuen weiblichen Bekanntschaften befinden kann, nicht nur das Idealbild des *Playboys*, sondern im urbanen Amerika der 1960er-Jahre das Idealbild des Mannes schlechthin.[6] Man denke etwa nur an den durchschlagenden Erfolg, den Ian Flemings Figur des James Bond gerade damals hatte. Die Wohnung des *Playboy*-Junggesellen, so die Idee der *Play-*

the 1960s and quickly caused a sensation, even leading to the first publication about Moore in a German-language architecture magazine.[4]

But it was the coverage in the October issue of *Playboy* that really made the house famous. In an article titled *A Playboy Pad: New Haven* the magazine otherwise notorious for its nude centrefolds devoted six pages of colour photographs to the building.[5] The photo series was produced to look as though it documented a late-night party at Moore's home, with the images showing smaller and larger groups of guests enjoying themselves in the house's various nooks and crannies. Looking at the series, you can almost hear the babble of voices, the chinking of cocktail glasses and the low dance music of the late 1960s. The accompanying text mentioned *a few friends the bachelor had invited to his home.*

The emphasis was, of course, on bachelor. As someone freed from the constraints of an average family life, who could constantly be on the lookout for new female acquaintances, the bachelor was not only the playboy ideal, but in 1960s America represented the ideal image of man per se.[6] The sweeping success enjoyed by Ian Fleming's James Bond figure at the time makes this abundantly clear. The apartment of the playboy bachelor, so the idea of the *Playboy* authors, played a special role as a place of his many conquests. Any woman entering the playboy's pad should feel overwhelmed. At the same time, she should never have the feeling of being alone. After all, as soon as the playboy would leave her, say to go next door and mix her a cocktail, she might change her mind and made a quick exit. The men behind *Playboy* therefore saw Moore's open interior, with its many views and perspectives, as the perfect bachelor pad. They orchestrated the party photos to have a special focus on those spatial situations where the individual levels of the house were visually connected, as in the three open towers.

The striking irony behind the *Playboy* story is that although the architect, client and occupant of the featured playboy pad was a bachelor, he could never have been considered a typical playboy in the sense of the eponymous magazine. Moore was quite simply gay. That is why there was no need for closed rooms in the design of his house – for example for children's rooms and the like – and it thus generated the spatial interplay the *Playboy* producers needed for their story.

We do not know if the people at *Playboy* knew Moore was homosexual when they featured his house as the prototype of a *Playboy* Pad. Moore himself was discreet in this regard at work in Yale, arguably above all, because in the early 1960s rumours about sexual orientation had already cost someone considered a sure candidate for a professorship in Berkeley his academic career. Moore's biographers also acted discreetly – strikingly discretely. Although David Littlejohn admits in his Moore biography that "[i]n a year of

boy-Autoren, spielt wiederum als Ort der Eroberung eine besondere Rolle. Die Frau, die hier eintritt, soll sich überwältigt fühlen! Zugleich soll sie aber nie das Gefühl haben, alleine zu sein. Denn sobald der Playboy die Frau allein lässt, etwa um im Nachbarzimmer einen Cocktail zuzubereiten, könnte sie es sich anders überlegen und das Haus hastig verlassen. Moores offenes Interieur mit seinen vielfältigen Ein- und Durchblicken ist deshalb für die Macher des *Playboys* ideal und so fokussieren die vermeintlichen Partyfotos immer wieder auf räumliche Situationen, in denen sich – wie etwa in den drei offenen Türmen – die verschiedenen Ebenen des Hauses optisch miteinander verbinden.

Allerdings verbirgt sich hinter der Playboy-Geschichte um Moores New Haven Haven eine feine ironische Wendung: Denn der Architekt, Bauherr und Bewohner der abgebildeten „Playboy-Bude" war zwar Junggeselle, aber keineswegs ein Playboy im Sinne des gleichnamigen Magazins. Moore war schlicht und einfach schwul! Deshalb konnte er bei der Gestaltung seines Hauses auf abgeschlossene Räume – etwa für Kinderzimmer und dergleichen – verzichten und eben jenes räumliche Zusammenspiel generieren, das die Macher des *Playboys* für ihre Geschichte brauchten.

Ob sie von Moores Homosexualität wussten, als sie das Haus als prototypisches „Playboy Pad" porträtierten, wissen wir nicht! Moore selbst jedenfalls behandelte das Thema in Yale diskret – wohl vor allem deshalb, weil ihn zu Beginn der 1960er-Jahre Gerüchte über seine sexuelle Orientierung schon einmal eine sicher geglaubte Professorenstelle in Berkeley gekostet hatten. Auch Moores Biografen verhielten sich in der Folge diskret – auffällig diskret! David Littlejohn gesteht in seiner Moore-Biografie zwar, „in einem Jahr voller Interviews und Gespräche Gerüchte in Hülle und Fülle gehört" zu haben, kommt danach allerdings zu dem überraschenden Schluss, dass der Architekt wahrscheinlich gar „kein Privatleben hatte".[7] Kevin P. Keim wiederum beschreibt Moore in seiner Biografie als „komplexe Persönlichkeit". Den Architekten habe zeitlebens „ein Schatten des Geheimnisses" umgeben, das keiner seiner zahllosen guten Freunde und Bekannten hätte „ganz entschleiern" können.[8]

Im beredten Schweigen der Biografen offenbart sich uns Moore als ein weiterer Bauherr des 20. Jahrhunderts, dessen Lebensumstände und Lebensvorstellungen mit den normativen Grenzen seiner Zeit in Konflikt gerieten. Und wie Truus Schröder, Edith Farnsworth, die Steins und Gabrielle de Monzie prägt auch Moore mit seinem vermeintlichen „Playboy Pad" unsere Idee vom modernen Wohnen entscheidend mit. Anders als die Häuser Schröder, Stein-de Monzie und Farnsworth hat Moores Haus in New Haven die Zeit allerdings nicht überdauert. Schon in den frühen 1970er-Jahren verkaufte der Architekt die Immobilie. Die neuen Eigentümer ließen Moores Einbauten entfernen und versetzten das Haus in seinen ursprünglichen Zustand zurück – ob trotz oder gerade wegen seiner kuriosen Veröffentlichung im *Playboy*, wissen wir nicht.

Charles Moore House in New Haven: der Architekt in seinem Studio im Erdgeschoss des eingestellten Turmes „Howard"

Charles Moore House in New Haven: the architect in his studio on the first floor of the tower "Howard" inserted here

interviews and conversations, I had heard rumors galore," he finally arrives at the surprising conclusion that the architect probably "had no private life whatsoever." Kevin P. Keim in turn describes Moore in his biography as a "complex man." Throughout his life, the architect was surrounded by "a shade of mystery," another layer that none of his countless good friends and acquaintances had been able to "reveal".[8]

The eloquent silence of the biographers reveals Moore to us as another client of the 20th century whose circumstances and ideas of life came into conflict with the normative boundaries of his time. Like Truus Schröder, Edith Farnsworth, the Stein Couple and Gabrielle de Monzie, Moore's alleged playboy pad also played a decisive role in shaping our idea of modern living. Unlike the houses of Schröder, Stein-de Monzie and Farnsworth, Moore's residence in New Haven has not survived time. The architect already sold the property in the early 1970s. The new owners had Moore's fixtures removed and returned the house to its original condition – we don't know if they did so despite or because of its curious publication in *Playboy*.

Uwe Bresan

Der Architekt von Fire Island: Horace Gifford

Fire Island, keine zwei Autostunden vom Stadtzentrum entfernt, ist ein beliebtes Ausflugsziel der New Yorker. Die knapp 50 Kilometer lange und an vielen Stellen nur wenige hundert Meter breite Insel liegt vor der Südküste von Long Island im Osten der Metropole und teilt die sogenannte Great South Bay vom Atlantik ab. Zum offenen Meer hin zieht sich ein breiter Sandstrand die gesamte Insel entlang. Er verbindet die etwa 20 Gemeinden, die sich wie an einer Perlenkette aufgereiht über Fire Island verteilen. Eine Inselstraße gibt es nicht. Überhaupt ist nur ein kleiner Teil im Westen des fast vollständig unter Naturschutz stehenden Eilands über eine Brücke mit dem Festland verbunden. Daneben bilden Fährschiffe, die durch die Great South Bay kreuzen, das Haupttransportmittel von Fire Island. Seit dem Ende des 19. Jahrhunderts dient die Insel als Sommerdomizil. Anders als die zur gleichen Zeit erschlossenen Hamptons am östlichen Ende von Long Island, wohin sich noch heute der mondäne New Yorker Geldadel in den Sommermonaten auf seine stattlichen Anwesen und schlossartigen Herrenhäuser zurückzieht,[1] entwickelte sich Fire Island zu Beginn des 20. Jahrhunderts zum Naherholungsgebiet der städtischen Mittelschicht sowie der Kreativen und Intellektuellen. Die relative Abgeschiedenheit der Insel und ihr fast endlos erscheinender weißer Sandstrand, in dessen bewaldete Dünen man sich jederzeit ungestört zurückziehen konnte, machten Fire Island in den dreißiger Jahren des vergangenen Jahrhunderts zudem zu einem Mekka der New Yorker Schwulen, die hier ihre Sexualität mehr oder weniger frei von den alltäglichen gesellschaftlichen Nachstellungen ausleben konnten, denen sie in der Stadt ausgeliefert waren.

Noch heute bilden die zwei benachbarten Siedlungen The Pines und Cherry Grove in den Sommermonaten einen zentralen Lebensmittelpunkt vieler New Yorker Schwuler. Kaum ein Gebäude hier ist älter als 60 Jahre. Nachdem 1938 zunächst ein schwerer Sturm die Insel verwüstet hatte, dauerte es bis zum Ende des Zweiten Weltkriegs, bevor die ehemaligen Feriengäste in großer Zahl zurückkehrten und die Hotels sich erneuerten. Den größten Bauboom ihrer Geschichte erlebten die beiden Orte jedoch in den 1950er- und 1960er-Jahren. Die amerikanische Wirtschaft florierte und ermöglichte breiten Bevölkerungsschichten einen nie gekannten Wohlstand. Immer mehr New Yorker konnten es sich nun leisten, dem schwülen und drückenden Klima der Stadt zu entfliehen, um die heißen Sommermonate oder zumindest die Wochenenden in eigenen Strandhäusern auf Fire Island zu verbringen. Wie schon vor dem Krieg nahmen The Pines und Cherry Grove aufgrund ihres überwiegend schwulen Publikums dabei eine Sonderstellung ein. Vor allem

The Architect of Fire Island: Horace Gifford

Fire Island, located less than two hours by car from the downtown Manhattan, is a popular destination for New Yorkers. The almost 50-kilometre long and in many places only a few hundred metres wide barrier island is situated off the Long Island south coast, east of the metropolis, and separates the so-called Great South Bay from the Atlantic Ocean. Towards the open sea, a wide sandy beach stretches along the entire island, which connects the more or less 20 municipalities, which are distributed across Fire Island like pearls on a string. There is no island road, and only a small western part of the island, the majority of which is under nature conservation, is connected with the mainland via a bridge. Ferries cruising through the Great South Bay are the main means of transport of Fire Island. Since the end of the 19th century, the island has served as a summer domicile for New York's residents. Unlike the Hamptons at the eastern end of Long Island, which were developed at the same time and where the members of the glamorous New York money aristocracy still retreat to in the summer months to their imposing estates and palatial mansions,[1] Fire Island developed at the beginning of the 20th century into a local recreation area for the urban middle class as well as creative people and intellectuals. The relatively remote island and its seemingly endless white sandy beach, where the wooded dunes provided an undisturbed retreat at any time, made Fire Island in the 1930s a Mecca for New York's homosexuals, who were able to live out their sexuality more or less free from everyday social harassment they had to endure in the city.

To this day, the two neighbouring communities of The Pines and Cherry Grove are a focal point for many gays from New York during the summer months. Hardly any of the buildings here is older than 60 years. After a severe storm devastated the island in 1938, it took until the end of the Second World War before the former holiday guests returned in large numbers and hotels were renovated. However, the two municipalities experienced the biggest building boom in their history in the 1950s and 1960s. The American economy flourished and brought broad sections of the population unprecedented prosperity. More and more New Yorkers were able to afford to escape from the city's sticky and stifling climate and spend the hot summer months or at least the weekends in their own beach houses on Fire Island. As before the war, The Pines and Cherry Grove took a special position due to their predominantly gay clientele. Particularly in the climate of the McCarthy era, which was characterized by denunciations, the dunes which still separate the two places from each other, provided some kind of area of social freedom, where an open gay

in der von Denunziationen geprägten McCarthy-Ära bildete das Dünenfeld, das die beiden Orte noch heute voneinander trennt, eine Art gesellschaftlichen Freiraum, in dem ein offen schwules Leben zumindest vorübergehend möglich war. Der freiheitliche Ruf von The Pines und Cherry Grove verbreitete sich damals über ganz Nordamerika. 1971 drehte der Broadway-Choreograph Wakefield Poole hier den legendären Schwulenporno *Boys in the Sand*,[2] der zu den Klassikern des Genres zählt. Mit seinen gefühlvollen Aufnahmen zeichnete der Filmenthusiast und Autodidakt ein realistisches Bild des schwulen Lebens auf Fire Island jenseits aller gesellschaftlichen Klischees homoerotischer Sexualität. Weil den Film auch seriöse Zeitungen ausgiebig in ihren Feuilletons besprachen, löste *Boys in the Sand* eine nationale Debatte über Homosexualität aus, die wesentlich zu einer Liberalisierung der gesamten Gesellschaft beitrug.

Neben Wakefield Poole darf auch Tom Bianchi als Chronist des schwulen Insellebens gelten. Der bekannte New Yorker Fotograf verbrachte in den 1970er-Jahren viele Sommer auf Fire Island und hielt das Leben am Strand und in den Dünen mit seiner Polaroid SX-70 fest.[3] Die typischen, etwas blassen Aufnahmen der legendären Klapp-Kamera zeigen aber nicht nur muskulöse sonnengebräunte Männerkörper in knappen Badehosen, sondern sie erlauben auch – ganz nebenbei – einen Einblick in die spezifische Architektur von The Pines und Cherry Grove. Kleine Bungalows, die sich über riesige Glasflächen nach außen öffnen und deren Terrassen den Innenraum in die Natur erweitern; Häuser auf massiven Stützen, die sich turmartig über die Landschaft erheben, um ein Maximum an Ausblick zu generieren; und große Villen, deren sanft gerundete Anbauten den Außenraum einfangen und ins Haus zu holen scheinen – mit Zedernholz verkleidet und spektakulär in die wilde Dünenlandschaft hinein komponiert, sind sie Zeugen für das außergewöhnliche Talent von Horace Gifford (1932-1992), der wie kein anderer die Architektur von The Pines und Cherry Grove prägte. In nicht einmal 20 Jahren – zwischen 1960 und 1980 – realisierte der Architekt mehr als 60 Sommerhäuser in den beiden Gemeinden und schuf damit ein einmaliges und bis heute weitgehend erhaltenes Ensemble des späten Mid-Century-Modernism.[4]

Zugleich dürfte Gifford zu den schillerndsten Architektenpersönlichkeiten der damaligen Zeit gehören. Überliefert ist, dass er seine Bauherren gerne nur mit einer Badehose bekleidet am Strand empfing. Dass er sich diese Auftritte augenscheinlich leisten konnte, zeigt schon ein Blick in das Jahrbuch seiner Highschool, wo Gifford als Best Looking Boy seines Jahrgangs gefeiert wird. Zudem arbeitete er nach dem Studium zeitweilig als Model. Man darf also annehmen, dass die Strandauftritte gerade im Hinblick auf die spezielle Klientel von The Pines und Cherry Grove einen nicht unerheblichen Anteil am Erfolg Giffords hatten. Und der Architekt zeigte sich gegenüber den Avancen seiner Bauherrn durchaus aufgeschlossen. So verband Gifford mit seinen ersten New Yorker Auftraggebern, dem Set Designer Edwin Wittstein und dessen Lebensgefährten, dem Art

Porträt des Architekten
Horace Gifford, 1963

*Portrait of the architect
Horace Gifford, 1963*

life was possible, at least temporarily. At the time, the liberal spirit of The Pines and Cherry Grove spread throughout North America. In 1971, Broadway choreographer Wakefield Poole chose this area as location for his legendary gay porn *Boys in the Sand*,[2] which ranks among the classics of this genre. With his sensitive shots, the film enthusiast and autodidact drew a realistic picture of gay life on Fire Island beyond all social clichés of homoerotic sexuality. Since the film was also thoroughly reviewed in the features section of serious newspapers, *Boys in the Sand* triggered a national debate about homosexuality, which decisively contributed to a liberalization of the entire society.

Besides Wakefield Poole, Tom Bianchi can also be regarded as chronicler of gay life on the island. In the 1970s, the renowned photographer from New York spent many summers on Fire Island and captured life on the beach and in the dunes on his Polaroid SX-70.[3] The typical, somewhat faint photographs of the legendary folding camera not only show muscular, sun-tanned male bodies in tight swimming trunks, but also – incidentally – allow an insight into the specific architecture of The Pines and Cherry Grove: small bungalows that open out towards the exterior with huge glazed areas and with terraces that extend the interiors into nature; houses supported by massive columns that tower above the landscape to afford as much view as possible; and large mansions whose gently rounded extensions embrace the exterior space and seem to bring it into the house. Clad in cedar wood and spectacularly set into the wild dune landscape, they bear witness to the extraordinary talent of Horace Gifford, who shaped the architecture of The Pines and Cherry Grove like no one else. In less than 20 years – between 1960 and 1980 – the architect built more than 60 summer houses in the two communities, creating a unique ensemble of late mid-century modernism that is largely preserved to this day.[4]

Der Fotograf Tom Bianchi dokumentierte in den 1970er-Jahren das Leben auf Fire Island mit seiner Polaroid SX-70.

Photographer Tom Bianchi documented life on Fire Island in the 1970s with his Polaroid SX-70.

Director Robert Miller, eine mehrjährige ménage-à-trois. Das Paar hatte für den Bau seines gemeinsamen Wochenendhauses zunächst Andrew Geller beauftragt, der damals mit einer Reihe experimenteller Strandhäuser auf Long Island für viel Aufsehen sorgte.[5] Nachdem sich Wittstein jedoch auf eine Affäre mit Gifford eingelassen hatte, wurde der Vertrag mit Geller gekündigt und stattdessen Gifford mit dem Bau beauftragt. So begann – mit nicht einmal 30 Jahren – die steile Karriere des 1932 in Florida geborenen Architekten.

Dieser hatte seine Ausbildung zunächst an der University of Florida begonnen, wo er unter anderem bei Paul Rudolph studierte, dessen legendäre Florida Houses an den Stränden von Sarasota einen nachhaltigen Eindruck auf Gifford machten.[6] Als seinen eigentlichen Mentor betrachtete Gifford jedoch Louis Kahn, dem er 1958 zu einem Master-Kurs an die University of Pennsylvania folgte. Nach seinem Studium zog es den jungen Architekten wiederum nach New York, wo er im Büro von J. Gordon Carr, einem damals gefragten Innenarchitekten, Arbeit fand. Aufgewachsen an den sonnigen Stränden von Florida und sexuellen Abenteuern nicht abgeneigt, entdeckte Gifford schon bald nach seiner Ankunft in New York die Dünen von The Pines und Cherry Grove für sich und verbrachte einen Großteil der Sommermonate auf Fire Island. Tatsächlich fühlte er sich nur am Strand lebendig. In der Stadt und vor allem in den Wintermonaten überfiel ihn oft eine tiefe Schwermut. „I'm gay, and I'm manic-depressive", charakterisierte sich Gifford – wohl nur halb im Scherz – einmal selbst.[7] Aber auch das erotisch-eskapistische Strandleben wurde Gifford zum Verhängnis, als er 1965 in den Dünen von The Pines und Cherry Grove bei einer Razzia der Polizei festgenommen und wegen eines „Verstoßes gegen die guten Sitten" verurteilt wurde. Gifford beantragte in der Folge niemals eine offizielle

Horace Gifford, Gifford
House II, Fire Island,
1965

Simultaneously, Gifford probably was one of the most colourful personalities in architecture at the time. It is said that he liked to greet his clients on the beach – only dressed in swimming trunks. A look at the yearbook of his high school, where Gifford was celebrated as best-looking boy of his year, proves that he was obviously able to run such a risk. In addition, he occasionally worked as a model after completing his studies. Particularly with regard to the special clientele of The Pines and Cherry Grove, one can assume that his beach appearances made a significant contribution to Gifford's success. And the architect was indeed receptive to the advances of his clients. Gifford was involved with his first client from New York, set designer Edwin Wittstein, and his life partner, art director Robert Miller, in a ménage à trois lasting several years. The couple had initially commissioned Andrew Geller with the construction of their common weekend home. Geller had caused great sensation with a series of experimental beach houses on Long Island.[5] However, after Wittstein had started an affair with Gifford, the contract with Geller was cancelled and Gifford was instead commissioned with the project. That's how the stellar career of the architect, who had not yet reached 30, started.

Horace Gifford, Travis-Wall House, Fire Island, 1972-75

Zulassung als Architekt, etwa um ein eigenes Büro zu eröffnen. Er hätte jederzeit die Ablehnung seines Antrags unter Verweis auf seinen fehlenden „good moral character" fürchten müssen;[8] der betreffende Paragraph ist noch heute vor allem im US-amerikanischen Einwanderungsrecht gebräuchlich und ermöglicht es, schon bei kleinsten Vergehen Aufenthaltsgenehmigungen zu verweigern. So war Gifford im Umgang mit Baubehörden zeitlebens auf die Unterstützung befreundeter Architekten angewiesen; eine Beteiligung an öffentlichen Ausschreibungen war nahezu aussichtslos.

Umso mehr, so scheint es, konzentrierte sich Gifford in der Folge auf seine privaten Aufträge, die von Jahr zu Jahr an Umfang zunahmen und es dem Architekten erlaubten, mit einem reichen gestalterischen Repertoire zu experimentieren. In den Boden eingelassene Sitzgruppen, die sich bei Bedarf in große Liegelandschaften vor dem offenen Kamin verwandeln ließen, waren dabei nur eine von Giffords Spezialitäten. Ein anderes Thema waren verspiegelte Wand- und Deckenflächen, die nicht nur dazu dienten, Räume optisch zu erweitern, sondern durchaus auch ein voyeuristisches Spiel in Gang setzen konnten, wenn sie gebrochene, kaleidoskopische Einblicke in vermeintlich abgeschlossene Bäder und Schlafzimmer ermöglichten. Irgendwann begann Gifford sogar damit, die Wandspiegel in den Bädern seiner Bauherren gegen Fenster mit getönten Scheiben einzutauschen, um die Erotik des Sehens und Gesehenwerdens nach draußen zu erweitern. Auch die obligatorischen Außenduschen auf den weiten Terrassen, unter denen man sich nach dem Strandaufenthalt

Horace Gifford, Lipkins House, Fire Island, 1970

Gifford was born in 1932 in Florida and had initially started his education at the University of Florida, where he studied with, amongst others, Paul Rudolph, whose legendary Florida Houses on the beaches of Sarasota made a lasting impression on Gifford.[6] However, Gifford regarded Louis Kahn as his actual mentor, whom he followed to attend a master course at the University of Pennsylvania in 1958. After completing his studies, the young architect moved back to New York, where he found a job in the office of J. Gordon Carr, a then much sought-after interior designer. Growing up on the sunny beaches of Florida and not averse to sexual adventures, Gifford soon discovered the dunes of The Pines and Cherry Grove after having moved to New York and spent most of the summer months on Fire Island. In fact, he only felt alive on the beach. In the city and especially in the winter months he was often struck by deep melancholy. "I'm gay, and I'm manic-depressive," Gifford once characterized himself – probably only half in jest.[7] However, Gifford's erotic and escapist beach life was also his undoing when he was arrested in 1965 in the dunes of The Pines and Cherry Grove during a police raid and convicted of an "offence against good manners." As a consequence, Gifford never applied for official approval as an architect, for example in order to open his own office. He would have had to fear the rejection of his application at any time with reference to his lack of "good moral character";[8] a paragraph, by the way, which is still commonly used in US immigration law today to refuse residence permits even for the smallest of offences. Thus, Gifford was throughout his life dependent on the support of architect friends when dealing with building authorities; participation in public tenders was almost pointless.

All the more, so it seems, Gifford now focused on private commissions, which increased in number and scope year after year and allowed the architect to experiment

sauber machte, gestaltete der Architekt immer ein wenig offener und einsehbarer als notwendig. Der New Yorker Architekt Christopher Rawlins, der in den frühen 2010er-Jahren eine wunderbare Monografie über Gifford verfasst hat,[9] beschreibt dessen Arbeiten deshalb vielleicht nicht zu unrecht als eine „Architektur der Verführung".

Auch auf die Frage, weshalb Gifford trotz seines beachtlichen und vielfach publizierten Œuvres nach seinem frühen Tod, 1992, fast vollkommen in Vergessenheit geraten konnte, hat Rawlins eine einfache Antwort: AIDS. Der Immunschwächekrankheit fiel in den späten 1980er- und frühen 1990er-Jahren eine ganze Generation homosexueller Männer zum Opfer, weshalb die Krankheit zunächst panisch als Schwulenseuche gebrandmarkt wurde. Auch Gifford war betroffen – genauso wie ein Großteil seines Bekanntenkreises: Auftraggeber, Bauherrn und Freunde. Es blieb kaum jemand übrig, der sich an Gifford hätte erinnern und für dessen Nachruhm sorgen können. Dass wenigstens sein Nachlass gerettet wurde, verdanken wir Robert Greenfield, Giffords langjährigem Lebensgefährten, der den Architekten zwar nur um wenige Monate überlebte, seine Erben jedoch im Testament verpflichtete, Giffords Archiv zu erhalten. Mit dem Ausbruch von AIDS ging auch auf Fire Island eine Epoche zu Ende. Das sorgenfreie und unbeschwerte Leben in den Dünen von The Pines und Cherry Grove, wie es Gifford verkörperte, war nachher nicht mehr dasselbe.

with a rich design repertoire. Sitting areas sunken into the floor, which can be turned into large lounge landscapes in front of the open fireplace if required, were just one of Gifford's specialities. Another theme was mirrored wall and ceiling areas, which not only served to visually extend the rooms but could also stimulate voyeuristic games as they afforded broken up, kaleidoscopic insights into allegedly separated bathrooms and bedrooms. At some point, Gifford even started to replace the wall mirrors in the bathrooms of his clients with tinted windows to extend the eroticism of seeing and been seen to the outside. The architects also designed the obligatory outdoor showers on the generous terraces, which were used to clean and refresh oneself after spending time on the beach, slightly more open and visible than necessary. Architect Christopher Rawlins from New York, who wrote a wonderful monograph on Gifford in the early 2010s[9] describes his projects, maybe quite rightly, as *Architecture of Seduction*. Rawlins also has a simple answer to the question as to why Gifford, despite his considerable and frequently published œuvre, was almost completely forgotten after his early death in 1992: AIDS. In the late 1980s and early 1990s, a whole generation of homosexual men fell victim to the immunodeficiency disease, which is why the disease was at first branded as a gay disease. Gifford was also affected, as was a large part of his circle of acquaintances: clients, builder-owners and friends. There was hardly anyone left who could remember Gifford and provide for his fame after his death. We owe it to Robert Greenfield, Gifford's long-time partner, who survived the architect by only a few months, but in his will obliged his heirs to preserve Gifford's archive, that at least his estate was secured. With the outbreak of AIDS, an era also came to an end on Fire Island. The carefree and easy-going life in the dunes of The Pines and Cherry Grove, as Gifford embodied it, was never the same afterwards.

Wolfgang Voigt & Uwe Bresan
Last, But Not Least: Von Ashbee bis Gropius

Einige Architektenbiografien seien hier kurz skizziert, die sich in unserer Kollektion genauso gut machen würden wie die anderen Porträts in diesem Band. Wir haben sie schweren Herzens ausgelassen, um die schon lange herausgeschobene Publikation unseres Buches nicht weiter zu verzögern.

In der Arts-and-Crafts-Bewegung in England war der homosexuelle Architekt, Kunsthandwerker und Dichter **Charles Robert Ashbee** (1863-1942) um 1900 einer der führenden Köpfe. Die industrielle Herstellung von Gegenständen des Alltags hatte diese zwar billiger gemacht, jedoch um den Preis minderer Qualität und minderwertiger Gestaltung. Ashbee und seine sozialreformerisch inspirierten Zeitgenossen antworteten darauf mit Aktivitäten zur Neubelebung des Kunsthandwerks und zur Schulung des Geschmacks. In Ashbees erster Guild and School of Handicraft in London wurden junge Männer in der Gold- und Kupferschmiedekunst sowie in Design und Herstellung von Möbeln ausgebildet. Der 1902 vollzogene Umzug aus der Metropole ins ländliche Gloucestershire war mit der Hoffnung verbunden, die kooperative Gilde als ideale Arbeits- und Lebensgemeinschaft zu gestalten. Wie nahe sich Ashbee und die von ihm „men friends" genannten Mitglieder dabei auch körperlich gekommen waren, blieb ihr Geheimnis, nachdem die handgeschriebene *confessio amantis* (Bekenntnisse eines Liebenden) nach seinem Tod von Ashbees Witwe vorsichtshalber vernichtet wurde.[1] Über seine Homosexualität und die Absicht, die „treue Zuneigung zu seinen Männerfreunden" („loyal reference of affection that I have given to my men friends") nicht aufzugeben, hatten sich Charles und Janet Ashbee vor der Heirat kameradschaftlich verständigt.[2] Ab 1918 erlaubte ihm ein Aufenthalt in Palästina das Eintauchen in die Welt des Orients. Die britische Militärregierung hatte ihn mit Familie nach Jerusalem berufen, wo er sich als Berater für Denkmalpflege und Bauwesen um die Erhaltung der Altstadt kümmerte. Seine jüngste Tochter, die Jerusalem als Kind erlebte, war sich sicher: „... he fell in a big way for the beautiful Arab young men – but I don't mean physically".[3] (WV)

Stanford White (1853-1906) gehörte zur gleichen Generation wie Ashbee. Er war nur zehn Jahre älter als der Engländer, stammte allerdings aus New York, wo er gemeinsam mit seinen Partnern Charles McKim und William Rutherford Mead auch seine größten Erfolge feierte. Berühmt wurde ihr gemeinsames Büro, McKim Mead & White, mit mondänen Sommerhäusern an den Küsten von Rhode Island und großen Stadtpalästen für die New Yorker High Society des Gilded Age, des goldenen amerikanischen Zeitalters der

Last, But Not Least:
From Ashbee to Gropius

A few architect's biographies are briefly outlined here, which would be as suitable for our compilation as the other portraits in this volume. We have reluctantly decided to leave them out so as not to delay the publication of our book any longer.

The homosexual architect, craftsman and poet **Charles Robert Ashbee** (1863-1942) was one of the leading figures in the Arts and Crafts movement in England around 1900. The industrial production of everyday objects had made them cheaper, but at the price of inferior quality and inferior design. Ashbee and his contemporaries, who were inspired by social reform, responded to this with activities aimed at revitalising handicrafts and cultivating taste. At Ashbee's first Guild and School of Handicraft in London, young men were trained in goldsmithing, coppersmithing and furniture design and manufacture. Moving from the metropolis to rural Gloucestershire in 1902 was motivated by the hope of creating the cooperative guild as an ideal working and living community. How close Ashbee and the members he called "men friends" had become physically, remained their secret after the handwritten *confessio amantis* (confessions of a lover) was destroyed by Ashbee's widow after his death.[1] Before their wedding, Charles and Janet Ashbee had reached an amicable agreement about his homosexuality and the intention not to give up the "loyal reference of affection that I have given to my men friends."[2] From 1918, a stay in Palestine allowed him to immerse himself in the world of the Orient. The British military government had called him and his family to Jerusalem, where he worked as an advisor for the preservation of historical monuments and buildings and was responsible for the preservation of the Old City. His youngest daughter, who experienced Jerusalem as a child, was certain: "[...] he fell in a big way for the beautiful Arab young men – but I don't mean physically."[3] (WV)

Stanford White (1853-1906) was of the same generation as Ashbee. He was only ten years older than the Englishman, but came from New York, where he also celebrated his greatest successes together with his partners, Charles McKim and William Rutherford Mead. Their joint office, McKim Mead & White, became famous with chic summer homes on the coasts of Rode Island and large city palaces for New York's high society of the Gilded Age, the golden American age of steel barons, oil magnates and railway kings. Their clients included the Carnegies, Rockefellers and Vanderbilts. White designed for them sinfully expensive interiors in the style of Beaux-Arts and imported furniture, fabrics

Das Porträt zeigt C.R. Ashbee im Jahr 1903, nach der Übersiedelung der Guild of Handicraft von London in die alte Seidenmühle nach Chipping Campden in Gloucestershire.

The portrait shows C.R. Ashbee in 1903, shortly after the Guild of Handicraft moved from London to the old silk mill at Chipping Campden in Gloucestershire.

Stahlbarone, Ölmagnaten und Eisenbahnkönige. Zu ihren Auftraggebern gehörten die Carnegies, Rockefellers und Vanderbilts. Für sie entwarf White sündhaft teure Inneneinrichtungen im Beaux-Arts-Stil und importierte aus Europa Möbel, Stoffe und Tapeten, aber auch hölzerne Wand- und Deckenverkleidungen, marmorne Kamine und anderen historischen Zierrat, den er bei Kunst- und Antiquitätenhändlern auf dem ganzen Kontinent erstand. Sie sollten dem neuen amerikanischen Geldadel den Anschein von Historizität verleihen. Zugleich entwarfen McKim Mead & White zahllose öffentliche Bauten für New York – darunter die berühmte Pennsylvania Station, das Rathaus sowie den Campus der Columbia University –, für die sie Vorbilder aus der europäischen Renaissance-Architektur zitierten. Auch der legendäre zweite Bau des Madison Square Gardens, eines riesigen Vergnügungspalastes im Zentrum von New York mit Veranstaltungs-, Theater-, Konzert- und Kabarett-Sälen für mehr als 10.000 Besuchern, war ein Werk der Architekten. White, der für den Entwurf des Gebäudes maßgeblich verantwortlich war, später auch ein Apartment innerhalb des Komplexes bewohnte und schließlich unter tragischen Umständen auf der Dachterrasse des Madison Square Gardens ums Leben kam – er wurde von einem psychopathischen Millionärssohn erschossen, der anschließende Prozess wurde von der sensationshungrigen New Yorker Presse zum „Trial of the Century" ausgerufen –,[4] arbeitete für die Ausgestaltung eng mit dem Künstler Augustus Saint-Gaudens zusammen. Mit dem Bildhauer, der unter anderem die den Turm des Gebäudes bekrönende Diana-Figur schuf, verband White, wie wir heute wissen, eine lebenslange Liaison. Den wahren Charakter ihrer Beziehung, die in der Vergangenheit immer wieder als Künstlerfreundschaft und enger Männerbund gedeutet wurde, konnte erst Mosettte Broderick entschlüsseln, die für ihre 2011 erschienene fulminante Studie über McKim Mead & White auf Briefe Whites und Saint-Gaudens zurückgreifen konnte, die zuvor von den Nachfahren unter Verschluss gehalten wurden.[5] Besonders bemerkenswert ist, dass diese Briefe nicht nur die homoerotische Beziehung der beiden Künstlerpersönlichkeiten offenbaren, sondern auch auf einen größeren Kreis von Männern

Der Bau des zweiten Madison Square Gardens in New York, eröffnet 1890, ist eng mit dem Schicksal des Architekten Stanford White verbunden.

The building of the second Madison Square Garden in New York, opened in 1890, is closely linked to the fate of architect Stanford White.

and wallpaper from Europe, as well as wooden wall and ceiling panelling, marble fireplaces and other historical decoration, which he purchased from art and antique dealers throughout the continent. They were to give the new American moneyed aristocracy the appearance of historicity. At the same time, McKim Mead & White designed countless public buildings for New York – including the famous Pennsylvania Station, the City Hall and the Columbia University campus – for which they used models from European Renaissance architecture. The legendary second building of the Madison Square Garden, a huge amusement palace in downtown New York with event, theatre, concert and cabaret halls for more than 10,000 visitors, was also created by the architects. White, who was mainly responsible for the design of the building, later also lived in an apartment within the complex and finally died under tragic circumstances on the roof terrace of Madison Square Gardens – he was shot dead by a psychopathic millionaire's son; the subsequent trial was proclaimed "Trial of the Century" by the sensation-hungry New York press.[4] He worked closely with the artist Augustus Saint-Gaudens on the interior design. As we now know, White had a lifelong liaison with the sculptor who created, among other things, the Diana figure crowning the tower of the building. The true nature of their relationship, which in the past was repeatedly interpreted as a friendship between artists and a close male bond, could only be revealed by Mosettte Broderick, who for her brilliant study on McKim Mead & White, published in 2011, was able to draw on letters from White and Saint-Gauden that had previously been kept under lock and key by their descendants.[5] It is particularly noteworthy that these letters not only reveal the homoerotic relationship between the two artistic personalities, but also point to a larger circle of men from White's and Saint-Gauden's acquaintances who met for regular sexual debauchery. This so-called Sewer Club included mutual artist friends of White and Saint-Gauden, employees of the McKim Mead & White office, and quite a few prominent clients of the office. (UB)

1893 verfasste Ralph Adams Cram den Roman *The Decadent*. Bertram Grosvenor Goodhue steuerte das Frontispiz bei. Es lässt sich als sinnlich-erotisches Doppelporträt der beiden Architekten deuten.

In 1893 Ralph Adams Cram wrote the novel The Decadent. *Bertram Grosvenor Goodhue contributed the frontispiece. It can be understood as a sensual and erotic double portrait of the two architects.*

aus dem Umfeld Whites und Saint-Gaudens hindeuten, der sich zu regelmäßigen sexuellen Ausschweifungen traf. Dieser sogenannten Sewer Club umfasste sowohl gemeinsame Künstlerfreunde Whites und Saint-Gaudens als auch Mitarbeiter des Büros McKim Mead & White sowie nicht wenige prominente Auftraggeber des Büros. (UB)

Auch **Ralph Adams Cram** (1863-1942) und **Bertram Grosvenor Goodhue** (1869-1924) schrieben um die Wende vom 19. zum 20. Jahrhundert amerikanische Architekturgeschichte. Beide gelten als bedeutende Vertreter des amerikanischen Gothic Revival beziehungsweise der Collegiate Gothic, die ihren Namen den großen, neogotischen College-Neubauten der Jahrhundertwende an der amerikanischen Ostküste verdankt. Auch Cram und Goodhue waren für Universitätsbauten unter anderem in Princeton, Exeter, Yale und Chicago verantwortlich. Der eigentliche Schwerpunkt ihrer Arbeit lag jedoch bei Kirchen- und Kathedralbauten. Allein Cram lassen sich heute mehr als 50 überwiegend neogotische Kirchenbauwerke zwischen New Hampshire im Norden und Florida im Süden der amerikanischen Ostküste zuordnen. Ihr wahrscheinlich bekanntestes und zugleich letztes gemeinsames Werk stellt die Saint Thomas Church an der New Yorker Fifth Avenue dar. Die zwischen 1911 und 1913 im Stil der französischen Hochgotik errichtete und von mächtigen Wolkenkratzern eng umstandene Kirche an der Ecke zur 53. Straße ist heute ein beliebtes Film- und Fotomotiv. Cram und Goodhue arbeiteten seit 1892 zusammen und hatten ihr gemeinsames Büro in Boston. Nach der Fertigstellung von Saint Thomas verließ Goodhue die Arbeitsgemeinschaft jedoch und siedelte nach Kalifornien über, wo er sich zunehmend der Architektur des Spanish Colonial Revival zuneigte und bald auch in diesem

In den 1890er-Jahren waren die Architekten Ralph Adams Cram (l.) und Bertram Grosvenor Goodhue (r.) Büro- und wohl auch Lebenspartner.

In the 1890s, the architects Ralph Adams Cram (l.) and Bertram Grosvenor Goodhue (r.) were office partners and probably also a couple.

Ralph Adams Cram (1863-1942) and **Bertram Grosvenor Goodhue** (1869-1924) also made American architectural history at the turn of the 19th to the 20th century. Both are considered important representatives of the American Gothic Revival and the Collegiate Gothic, which owes its name to the large neo-Gothic college buildings on the American East Coast at the turn of the century. Cram and Goodhue were also responsible for university buildings in Princeton, Exeter, Yale and Chicago, amongst others. The actual focus of their work, however, was on church and cathedral buildings. Cram alone realized more than 50 predominantly neo-Gothic church buildings between New Hampshire in the north and Florida in the south of the American east coast. Their probably most famous and also last joint work is the Saint Thomas Church on New York's 5th Avenue. Built between 1911 and 1913 in the style of French High Gothic and closely surrounded by mighty skyscrapers, the church on the corner of 53rd Street is today a popular film and photo motif. Cram and Goodhue had worked together since 1892 and had their joint office in Boston. After the completion of Saint Thomas, however, Goodhue left the joint venture and moved to California, where he increasingly turned to the architecture of the Spanish Colonial Revival and soon enjoyed great success with this style.[6] Architectural historian Douglass Shand-Tucci, who dedicated a two-volume biography to Cram,[7] assumes that Cram and Goodhue were lovers, at least in the 1890s.[8] In the first volume of his biography, *Boston Bohemia*, he recapitulates, among other things, the architects' illustrious circle of friends and acquaintances, which mainly comprised homosexuals.[9] He also quotes Cram, who describes the relationship with Goodhue not as a collaboration between two individuals, but rather as the interaction of two brain halves.[10] Yet Shand-Tucci also points to Cram's and Goodhue's acquaintance with the aforementioned homosexual English Arts and Crafts architect Charles Robert Ashbee[11] and, not least, to Cram's and Goodhue's joint work on *The Decadent*. The novel, written by Cram in 1893,[12] deliberately follows in the tradition of the sultry decadence poems of Joris-Karl Huysmans (*À rebours*, 1884)

Stil große Erfolge feierte.[6] Der Architekturhistoriker Douglass Shand-Tucci, der Cram eine zweibändige Biografie widmete,[7] geht davon aus, das Cram und Goodhue zumindest in den 1890er-Jahren ein Liebespaar waren.[8] Im ersten Band seiner Biografie, *Boston Bohemia*, rekapituliert er unter anderem den illustren Freundes- und Bekanntenkreis der Architekten, der sich zu großen Teilen aus Homosexuellen zusammensetzte.[9] Außerdem zitiert er Cram, der die Beziehung zu Goodhue nicht als Zusammenarbeit zweier Individuen schildert, sondern vielmehr als das Zusammenspiel der zwei Hälften eines Gehirns.[10] Shand-Tucci verweist aber auch auf die Bekanntschaft von Cram und Goodhue mit dem bereits erwähnten, homosexuellen, englischen Arts-and-Crafts-Architekten Charles Robert Ashbee[11] und nicht zuletzt auf die gemeinsame Arbeit von Cram und Goodhue an *The Decadent*. Der Roman, 1893 von Cram verfasst,[12] steht bewusst in der Tradition der schwülen Dekadenzdichtungen von Joris-Karl Huysmans (*À rebours*, 1884) und Oscar Wilde (*The Picture of Dorian Gray*, 1890/1891).[13] Cram widmete den Text ausdrücklich seinem Partner Goodhue, der seinerseits wiederum die Frontispiz-Zeichnung für den Druck beisteuerte. Sie lässt sich unschwer als sinnlich-erotisches Doppelporträt der beiden Architekten deuten.[14] (UB)

Ein wohl unerwarteter Name an dieser Stelle ist der vor allem als Soziologe (*Das Ornament der Masse*, 1927) und Filmhistoriker berühmt gewordene **Siegfried Kracauer** (1889-1966). In seinem Brotberuf, den er bis zum Ende des Ersten Weltkriegs ausübte, war er Architekt in Frankfurt am Main. Als 34-Jähriger lernte er 1921 den 14 Jahre jüngeren Theodor Adorno kennen, der zu dieser Zeit noch zur Schule ging. Mit dem später berühmt gewordenen Philosophen verband ihn damals eine komplizierte Beziehung, die erst kürzlich durch die Publikation ihrer Briefe ans Licht gekommen ist.[15] „Ich fühlte in diesen beiden Tagen wieder eine solch quälende Liebe zu Dir, daß es mir jetzt so vorkommt, als könne ich allein gar nicht bestehen", schrieb er 1923 an seinen „Teddie" genannten Freund.[16] In Kracauers autobiografischem Roman *Ginster* (1928) über einen jungen Architekten in Frankfurt, der sich zwischen 1914 und 1918 mit Erfolg dem Kriegsdienst entziehen kann, wird um dessen homosexuelle Neigungen kein Geheimnis gemacht.[17] (WV)

Der jüdische Architekt **Otto Eisler** (1893-1968) gehört neben Bohuslav Fuchs und Ernst Wiesner zu den bekanntesten Protagonisten des Brünner Funktionalismus der 1920er- und 1930er-Jahre.[18] Internationale Bekanntheit erlangte er 1932 durch die von **Philip Johnson** (1906-2005) und **Henry-Russell Hitchcock** (1903-1987) – beide waren homosexuell – verfasste Publikation *The International Style: Architecture since 1922*[19] sowie durch die ebenfalls von Johnson und Hitchcock kuratierte Ausstellung *Modern Architecture: International Exhibition* am New Yorker Museum of Modern Art. In der Ausstellung war Eisler mit einem „Haus für zwei Brüder" in Brünn aus dem Jahr 1931 vertreten.[20] Es ist auch als „Haus für zwei Junggesellen"[21] sowie als „Haus für zwei junge Männer"[22] bekannt. Otto Eisler bewohnte das Haus selbst mit seinem ebenfalls unverhei-

Siegfried Kracauer,
um 1930

*Siegfried Kracauer,
around 1930*

and Oscar Wilde (*The Picture of Dorian Gray*, 1890/1891).[13] Cram expressly dedicated the text to his partner Goodhue, who in turn contributed the frontispiece drawing for the print. It can easily be understood as a sensual-erotic double portrait of the two architects.[14] (UB)

A probably unexpected name at this point is **Siegfried Kracauer** (1889-1966), who became famous above all as a sociologist (*Das Ornament der Masse*, 1927) and film historian. In his bread-and-butter profession, which he pursued until the end of World War I, he was an architect in Frankfurt am Main. In 1921, at the age of 34, he met Theodor Adorno, 14 years his junior, who still attended school at that time. He had a complicated relationship with the philosopher, who later became famous, which only recently came to light through the publication of their letters.[15] "I felt such an agonizing love for you again during these two days that it now seems to me as if I could not exist on my own," he wrote to his friend he called "Teddie" in 1923.[16] In Kracauer's autobiographical novel *Ginster* (1928) about a young architect in Frankfurt who successfully escaped military service between 1914 and 1918, no secret is made of his homosexual inclinations.[17] (WV)

The Jewish architect **Otto Eisler** (1893-1968) is one of the best-known protagonists of functionalism in Brno in the 1920s and 1930s, besides Bohuslav Fuchs and Ernst Wiesner.[18] He achieved international fame in 1932 through the publication *The International Style: Architecture since 1922*[19] written by **Philip Johnson** (1906-2005) and **Henry-Russell Hitchcock** (1903-1987) – who were both homosexual –, and through the exhibition *Modern Architecture: International Exhibition* at the New York Museum of Modern Art, also curated by Johnson and Hitchcock. Eisler was represented in the exhibition with a "House for Two Brothers" in Brno from 1931.[20] It is also known as the "House for Two Bachelors"[21] and the "House for Two Young Men"[22]. Otto Eisler lived in

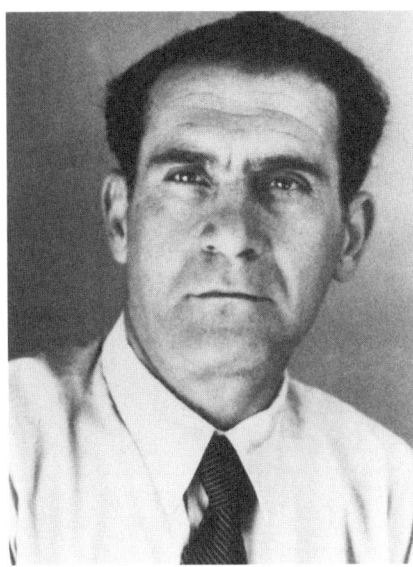

Der jüdische Architekt Otto Eisler gehört zu den bekanntesten Protagonisten des Brünner Funktionalismus der 1920er- und 1930er-Jahre.

The Jewish architect Otto Eisler is one of the best-known protagonists of functionalism in Brno in the 1920s and 1930s.

rateten, fünf Jahre älteren Bruder Moritz Eisler, der zwar auch eine Ausbildung als Architekt besaß, jedoch im Bauunternehmen der Familie tätig war. (Die Baufirma der Eislers gehörte zu den größten in der Region und war unter anderem an der Realisierung der Villa Tugendhat (1929-30) von Ludwig Mies van der Rohe in Brünn beteiligt.) Der gemeinsame Hausbau verweist auf das ungewöhnlich enge Verhältnis der beiden Junggesellen-Brüder, die damals bereits ein mittleres Alter erreicht hatten. Sie pflegten einen ähnlichen Lebensstil und teilten zahlreiche Interessen und Vorlieben. Beide waren sportlich sehr aktiv und nahmen rege am gesellschaftlichen Leben der Stadt teil. Sie sammelten Gemälde und andere Kunstgegenstände und machten ihr gemeinsames Haus zu einem Treffpunkt von Künstlern und Intellektuellen. Später überlebten sie gemeinsam das Konzentrationslager Auschwitz und fanden nach ihrem Tod in einem gemeinsamen Grab ihre letzte Ruhe.[23] Dass sich hinter dem vermeintlichen Junggesellen-Dasein der beiden Brüder jeweils eine mehr oder weniger offen ausgelebte Homosexualität verbarg, ist zumindest für Otto Eisler verbürgt. Niemand Geringeres als Philip Johnson darf dafür als Zeuge gelten.[24] Er hatte Eisler 1930 in Brünn im Rahmen einer Europareise kennen gelernt, die der Vorbereitung auf die Ausstellung und das Buch zum International Style diente.[25] Johnson nannte Otto Eisler „the best architect in Czechoslovakia."[26] (UB)

Zu den herausragenden Figuren in der Architektur des 20. Jahrhunderts zählt zweifellos auch der Mexikaner **Luis Barragán** (1902-1988). Für seine Fähigkeit, mittelamerikanische Tradition mit der Moderne verschmelzen zu lassen und auratische Räume

Otto Eisler, Haus für zwei Junggesellen, Brünn, 1931

Otto Eisler, House for Two Bachelors, Brno, 1931

this house himself with his brother Moritz Eisler, who was also unmarried and five years his senior. Although he was also trained as an architect, he worked in the family's construction company. (The Eislers' construction company was one of the largest in the region and was involved, among other things, in the realization of the Villa Tugendhat (1929-30) by Ludwig Mies van der Rohe in Brno). The joint construction of the house indicates the unusually close relationship between the two bachelor brothers, who were already middle-aged at the time. They cultivated a similar lifestyle and shared numerous interests and preferences. Both were very active in sports and took an active part in the city's social life. They collected paintings and other works of art and turned their common home into a meeting place for artists and intellectuals. Later they survived the Auschwitz concentration camp together and found their final resting place in a common grave.[23] At least for Otto Eisler, the fact that the supposed bachelor existence of the two brothers concealed a more or less open homosexuality is proven. No one less than Philip Johnson can be considered a witness to this.[24] He had got to know Eisler in 1930 in Brno during a trip to Europe, which served as preparation for the exhibition and the book on the International Style.[25] Johnson referred to Otto Eisler as "the best architect in Czechoslovakia."[26] (UB)

The Mexican **Luis Barragán** (1902-1988) is undoubtedly one of the outstanding figures in 20th-century architecture. He received the Pritzker Prize in 1980, which had only been established the year before, for his ability to fuse Central American tradition with modernism and to create auratic spaces of simplicity and calm, always with a rare sense of colour.[27] His homosexuality was a well-kept secret for a long time. Barragán's

von Einfachheit und Stille zu schaffen, stets mit einem seltenen Sinn für Farbe, erhielt er 1980 den Pritzker-Preis, der erst im Jahr zuvor gestiftet worden war.[27] Seine Homosexualität war lange ein gut gehütetes Geheimnis. Barragáns 1948 errichtetes eigenes Wohnhaus in Mexico City ist heute ein Museum. Im Inneren trifft der Besucher auf einen beinahe labyrinthischen Grundriss und an vielen Stellen eingebaute mannshohe Trennwände und Paravents, die die einzelnen Funktionen der Räume voneinander trennen und Blickbeziehungen unterbrechen. Die wegen ihres perfekten Spiels von Flächen und Farben oft abgebildete Dachterrasse ist an allen Seiten von schützenden Mauern umgeben. Man hat das mit der extremen Persönlichkeit des Architekten erklärt, der sich vor der Öffentlichkeit als mönchisch lebender Eremit inszenierte. Neuerdings ist ein queeres Narrativ hinzugekommen.[28] Das Haus kann als penibel gestaltete Zuflucht eines streng katholischen und zugleich homosexuellen Architekten entziffert werden, der panisch bemüht war, Einblicke in seine Privatsphäre zu unterbinden. Einige spiegelnde Kugeln in diesem Ambiente waren nicht nur Dekoration: Sie erlaubten Barragán die visuelle Kontrolle über Eingänge, die sich in seinem Rücken befanden. (WV)

So wie Barragán Elemente der Moderne mit den traditionellen Bauformen seiner mexikanischen Heimat zu einem neuen Ganzen zu verschmelzen verstand, so entwickelte auch der sri-lankische Architekt **Geoffrey Bawa** (1919-2003) eine ganz eigene, auf die klimatischen Bedingungen seines Heimatlandes abgestimmte Spielart der Moderne. Er gilt damit als Begründer des sogenannten tropical modernism.[29] Obwohl sein Werk nahezu alle gängigen Bauaufgaben umfasst, wird Bawa heute vor allem mit seinen Wohnhäusern sowie seinen zahlreichen Hotelbauten in Verbindung gebracht.[30] Mit 20 Jahren verließ Bawa, der aus einer vermögenden Familie stammte, Sri Lanka, um in Großbritannien zunächst englische Literatur und später Jura zu studieren. In Cambridge und London lebte Bawa seine Homosexualität erstmals offen aus, wie sein Biograf David Robson berichtet.[31] Wir müssen

Von schützenden Mauern umgeben: Luis Barragáns eigenes Wohnhaus in Mexico City, errichtetet 1948

Enclosed by protecting walls: Luis Barragán's own residence in Mexico City, built in 1948

Porträt des Architekten Luis Barragán

Portrait of architect Luis Barragán

own residence in Mexico City, built in 1948, is now a museum. Inside, the visitor finds an almost labyrinthine layout and man-high partitions and screens installed in many places, which separate the individual functions of the rooms from each other and interrupt visual relationships. The rooftop terrace, often depicted because of its perfect play of areas and colours, is enclosed by protecting walls on all sides. This has been explained by the extreme personality of the architect, who presented himself to the public as a hermit with a monastic lifestyle. Recently, a queer narrative has been added.[28] The house can be read as the meticulously designed refuge of a strictly Catholic and at the same time homosexual architect, who was panic-stricken and tried to prevent insights into his private life. Some reflective spheres in this ambience were not just decoration: they allowed Barragán visual control over entrances located behind him. (WV)

Just as Barragán was able to fuse elements of modernism with the traditional building styles of his Mexican homeland to form a new whole, the Sri Lankan architect **Geoffrey Bawa** (1919-2003) also developed his very own version of modernism, adapted to the climatic conditions of his home country. He is thus considered the founder of the so-called tropical modernism.[29] Although his work encompasses almost all the usual construction tasks, Bawa is today mainly associated with his residential houses and numerous hotel buildings.[30] At the age of 20, Bawa, who came from a wealthy family, left Sri Lanka to study English literature and later law in Britain. In Cambridge and London, Bawa lived out his homosexuality openly for the first time, as his biographer David Robson reports.[31] We must imagine Bawa at that time as a youthful dandy; always elegantly dressed and with a penchant for fast and expensive cars. Only reluctantly did he turn his back on this existence in the mid-1940s to work as a lawyer in Colombo, the capital of Sri Lanka. This was soon followed by an extensive trip to Europe lasting several years and studies of architecture at the Architectural Association (AA) in London, which

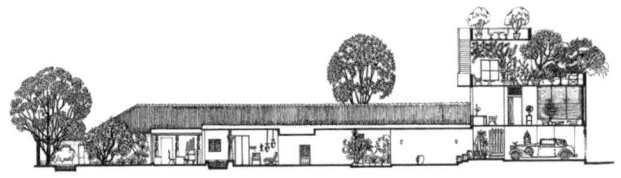

Geoffrey Bawa, Stadthaus, 33rd Lane, Colombo, Schnitt und Grundriss

Geoffrey Bawa, Townhouse, 33rd Lane, Colombo, section and floor plan

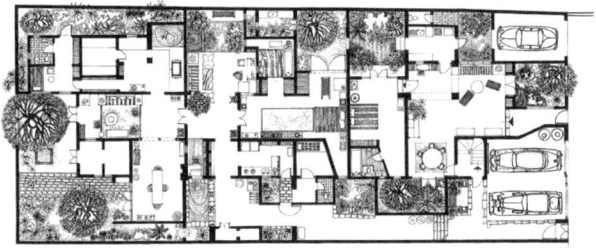

Herbert Tayler, Club Room of a Small Sports Club, Architectural Association, 1930er-Jahre

Herbert Tayler, Club Room of a Small Sports Club, Architectural Association, 1930s

uns Bawa zu jener Zeit als jugendlichen Dandy vorstellen; immer elegant gekleidet und mit einer Vorliebe für schnelle und teure Autos. Nur unwillig kehrte er Mitte der 1940er-Jahre diesem Dasein den Rücken, um in Colombo, der Hauptstadt von Sri Lanka, als Anwalt tätig zu werden. Es folgten schon bald eine ausgedehnte, mehrjährige Europareise und ein Architekturstudium an der Architectural Association (AA) in London, das den Grundstein für Bawas eigentliche Karriere bilden sollte. Diese nimmt nach seiner Rückkehr, Ende der 1950er-Jahre, schnell Fahrt auf und Bawa wird innerhalb der nächsten Jahrzehnte der führende Architekt seines Landes. Gleichwohl muss Bawa in Sri Lanka seine Homosexualität mit Diskretion behandeln. Davon zeugen nicht zuletzt die beiden eigenen Anwesen des Architekten: sein Stadthaus in der 33rd Lane in Colombo[32] sowie das etwa 70 Kilometer südlich der Hauptstadt gelegene Landgut Lunuganga.[33] Ersteres besticht durch ein komplexes Gefüge von Räumen, die über schmale verwinkelte Gänge und kleine Höfe auf unterschiedlichste Arten miteinander verbunden sind. In diesem räumlichen Geflecht verhüllte Bawa geschickt die wahre Natur der Beziehungen, die er über die Jahre hinweg zu vermeintlichen „Hausangestellten" unterhielt. In Lunuganga wiederum schützte schon allein die Größe des ländlichen Anwesens vor allzu neugierigen Einblicken. Trotzdem verzichtete Bawa auch hier bei der Gestaltung von Garten und Haus auf allzu eindeutige Symbole und Anspielungen, die ihn als Homosexuellen hätten verraten können. Er verhielt sich damit ganz anders als sein knapp zehn Jahre älterer Bruder **Bevis Bawa** (1909-1992). Auch er war homosexuell und machte sich vor allem als Landschaftsarchitekt einen Namen. Parallel zu Lunuganga und nur wenige Kilometer entfernt, realisierte Bevis Bawa seinen Brief Garden, eine exaltierte Gartenanlage mit zahlreichen und oft eindeutig posierenden männlichen Aktfiguren. Beide Anwesen gelten heute als herausragende Beispiele sri-lankischer Gartenkunst des 20. Jahrhunderts[34] und können besichtigt werden. (UB)

was to form the foundation for Bawa's actual career. After his return in the late 1950s, his career quickly gathered momentum, and within the next few decades Bawa became the leading architect in his country. Nevertheless, in Sri Lanka, Bawa had to handle his homosexuality with discretion. The architect's two own estates bear witness to this: his townhouse on 33rd Lane in Colombo[32] and the Lunuganga estate, located about 70 kilometres south of the capital.[33] The former impresses with a complex structure of rooms, which are connected in many different ways by narrow, winding corridors and small courtyards. In this spatial network, Bawa skilfully concealed the true nature of the relationships he maintained over the years with supposed "domestics". In Lunuganga, on the other hand, the size of the rural estate alone protected him from overly curious glimpses. Nevertheless, here, too, Bawa avoided all too obvious symbols and allusions in the design of the garden and house that could have betrayed him as a homosexual. He thus behaved quite differently from his brother **Bevis Bawa** (1909-1992), who was almost ten years older. He, too, was homosexual and made a name for himself as a landscape architect. Parallel to Lunuganga and only a few miles from it, Bevis Bawa created his Brief Garden, an exalted garden with numerous and often unambiguously posing male nude figures. Both estates are today regarded as outstanding examples of 20th-century Sri Lankan garden art[34] and are open to visitors. (UB)

Der deutsche Architekt Hans Broos wanderte in den 1950er-Jahren nach Brasilien aus.

German architect Hans Broos emigrated to Brazil in the 1950s.

Herbert Tayler (1912-2000) und **David Green** (1912-1998), die sich Anfang der 1930er-Jahre während des Studiums an der Architectural Association (AA) in London kennen lernten, lebten nicht nur mehr als sechs Jahrzehnte als Paar zusammen. Sie betrieben auch von 1938 bis 1973 ihr gemeinsames Architekturbüro in der Grafschaft Norfolk, das wegen seiner vorbildlichen ländlichen Wohnbauten einen guten Ruf besaß.[35] Im Nachlass gibt es von der Hand Taylers, der ein künstlerisch hochbegabter Zeichner war, ein bemerkenswertes Blatt mit erotischem Subtext.[36] Das im Rahmen des Studiums an der AA angefertigte Aquarell „Club Room of a Small Sports Club" zeigt am Fenster zwei Männer im Flirt und an der Rückwand ein extravagantes Bild im Bild: auf einer Bank aufgereihte Männer, oben mit Zylinderhüten und drolligen Vollbärten und unten mit wenig mehr als Strümpfen bekleidet. Nichts deutet darauf hin, dass die Studienarbeit unterdrückt oder abgelehnt wurde – was auf ein ausgesprochen liberales Klima an der AA zu jener Zeit schließen lässt, fast vierzig Jahre vor den Stonewall Riots im Jahr 1969. (WV)

Hans Broos (1921-2011) erwarb sein Architekturdiplom 1948 an der Technischen Hochschule in Braunschweig, wo Friedrich Wilhelm Kraemer[37] sein wichtigster Lehrer war. Danach zog es ihn nach Karlsruhe, wo er Mitarbeiter von Egon Eiermann, der potentesten Figur der westdeutschen Nachkriegsmoderne, wurde. Mit 32 Jahren suchte er jedoch das Weite und wanderte nach Brasilien aus, weil er, wie es heißt, die Dominanz „dieses geistigen Giganten" nicht mehr ertrug.[38] Vermutlich störte ihn auch das westdeutsche Strafgesetz gegen Homosexualität, das in den 1950er-Jahren rigoros zur Anwendung kam. In Brasilien gab es seit dem 19. Jahrhundert kein solches Gesetz mehr. Zunächst in der Provinz, ab 1968 mit Büro in São Paulo, schuf Broos einige der prägnantesten Werke des brasilianischen Brutalismus – unter anderem die als schwebende Box geformte Kirche San Bonifacio aus dem Jahr 1966. Nur wenige Jahre später, 1971, baute er sich dann auf einem Hanggrundstück in São Paulo seine eigene Villa mit Atelier. Beide Gebäude sind durch einen subtropischen

Herbert Tayler (1912-2000) and **David Green** (1912-1998), who met in the early 1930s while studying at the Architectural Association (AA) in London, not only lived together as a couple for more than six decades. From 1938 to 1973, they also ran their joint architecture firm in the county of Norfolk, which enjoyed a good reputation for its exemplary rural housing projects.[35] The estate includes a remarkable drawing by Tayler, who was a highly talented illustrator, with an erotic subtext.[36] The watercolour "Club Room of a Small Sports Club", which he painted while studying at the AA, shows two men flirting at the window and an extravagant picture on the back wall: men lined up on a bench, with top hats and droll full beards, wearing little more than stockings. There is nothing that suggests that the student work was suppressed or rejected; this indicates a decidedly liberal attitude at the AA at the time, almost forty years before the Stonewall Riots in 1969. (WV)

Hans Broos (1921-2011) earned his diploma in architecture in 1948 at the Technische Hochschule in Brunswick, where Friedrich Wilhelm Kraemer[37] was his most important teacher. He then moved to Karlsruhe, where he worked with Egon Eiermann, the most potent figure in West German post-war modernism. At the age of 32, however, he left the country and emigrated to Brazil because, as the saying goes, he could no longer bear the dominance of "this intellectual giant".[38] He was probably also bothered by the West German penal law against homosexuality, which was rigorously applied in the 1950s. In Brazil there had been no such law since the 19th century. Initially in the province, and from 1968 with an office in São Paulo, Broos created some of the most striking works of Brazilian Brutalism – including the church of San Bonifacio in 1966, designed as a floating box; and only a few years later, in 1971, he built his own maison and studio on a hillside property in São Paulo. Both buildings are connected by a subtropical garden designed by homosexual landscape architect **Roberto Burle Marx** (1909-1994). Completely separated from the studio at the lower end of the complex, the living area extends under a mighty concrete table, which also seems to symbolically shield the gay architect's private zone. (WV)

Walter Gropius (1883-1969), founder of the Bauhaus and probably the most famous name in classical modern architecture alongside Le Corbusier and Ludwig Mies van der Rohe, must, however, be left out of this presentation of homosexual architects' biographies. Even though a biography was published about him in the Bauhaus anniversary year 2019, in which interesting episodes are reported, we must assume that far too many of these accounts are freely invented by the author Bernd Polster.[39] It is known that the young Walter Gropius was a highly attractive gentleman who was for a time the lover and husband of the artist Alma Mahler-Werfel, a famous femme fatale of the time. It is also not new that the banker Karl-Ernst Osthaus also played a role in Gropius' life. At a time when Gropius had little contact with the early modern movement, he had already been active for years as a reformer and patron of the arts. The two men met in 1907 during a

Garten verbunden, den ihm der ebenfalls homosexuelle Landschaftsarchitekt **Roberto Burle Marx** (1909-1994) entworfen hatte. Vom Atelier am unteren Ende der Anlage vollständig getrennt, erstreckt sich die Wohnebene unter einem mächtigen Tisch aus Beton, der die private Zone des schwulen Architekten auch symbolisch zu beschützen scheint. (WV)

Walter Gropius (1883-1969), Gründer des Bauhauses und neben Le Corbusier und Ludwig Mies van der Rohe der wohl berühmteste Name der klassischen Architekturmoderne, muss aus dieser Darstellung homosexueller Architektenbiografien allerdings draußen bleiben. Auch wenn über ihn im Bauhaus-Jubiläumsjahr 2019 eine Biographie erschien, in der interessante Episoden berichtet werden, so müssen wir doch davon ausgehen, dass allzu viele dieser Geschichten vom Autor Bernd Polster frei erfunden sind.[39] Bekannt ist, dass der junge Walter Gropius ein höchst attraktiver Herr gewesen ist, der eine zeitlang der Geliebte und Ehemann der Künstlerin Alma Mahler-Werfel war, einer berühmten femme fatale der Epoche. Nicht neu ist auch die Rolle, die der Bankier Karl-Ernst Osthaus für Gropius spielte. Als Gropius noch kaum Berührung mit der frühen modernen Bewegung hatte, war dieser bereits jahrelang als Reformer und Mäzen aktiv. Die beiden lernten sich 1907 auf einer Reise in Spanien kennen; von da an war Osthaus für Gropius ein Freund, Mentor und Förderer. Aber warum nur, fragt sich Polster, bemühte sich der zehn Jahre ältere Bankier und „Schöngeist"[40] um den damals 24-jährigen, den noch niemand kannte und der in seinem Architekturstudium alles andere als erfolgreich war? Polster ist sich sicher, die Antwort gefunden zu haben: „Dass der Grandseigneur sich Hals über Kopf in den jungen Kerl verliebte, wäre eine Erklärung. [...] Es drängt sich der Gedanke auf, dass zwischen den beiden gertenschlanken Dandys, die mit so feurigen Herzen ihre Ziele verfolgten, die viel auf ihr elegantes Äußeres gaben und gern in schönen Formulierungen schwelgten, mehr war als nur die Liebe zur Architektur. [...] Dass einer von beiden oder beide schwul waren, davon ist nichts bekannt. Aber ist das ausgeschlossen?"[41] Eine reine Spekulation also! Abgesehen von den Klischees, die hier bemüht werden und zeigen, wie der Autor sich schwule Männer als blasierte Ästheten vorstellt, hinterlässt die These einen schlechten Nachgeschmack. Heutzutage unbestritten ist, dass das Bild von Gropius als einer Heldenfigur der Moderne zu großen Teilen ein zu hinterfragender Mythos ist. Polster geht es aber um weit mehr als eine Revision; er zeichnet Gropius als einen zu eigenen Leistungen unfähigen Hochstapler, dessen Karriere in allen Phasen vor allem auf Zufällen beruhte und auf der Begabung, auf geniale Art andere Menschen für sich auszubeuten. Obwohl Polster in manchen Aspekten Recht hat, ist das Narrativ so einseitig vernichtend, dass am Ende buchstäblich nichts übrig bleibt. In diesem Rahmen ist die angebliche Affäre mit Osthaus nicht mehr als eine homophobe Arabeske mit dem Zweck, den gestürzten Helden vollends zu demontieren. (WV)

Ein mächtiger Betontisch als symbolischer Schutz: Hans Broos, Haus und Studio, São Paulo, 1971

A mighty concrete table as symbolic shield: Hans Broos, villa and studio, São Paulo, 1971

trip to Spain; from then on Osthaus was a friend, mentor and patron of Gropius. But why, Polster asks himself, did the banker and "aesthete",[40] who was ten years older than Gropius, make such an effort to support the then 24-year-old, whom no one knew yet and who was anything but successful in his architectural studies? Polster is certain to have found the answer: "That the grand seigneur fell head over heels in love with the young guy would be one explanation. […] The thought suggests itself that there was more than just a love of architecture between the two willowy dandies, who pursued their goals with such fervent ambition, who paid great attention to their elegant appearance and liked to indulge in beautiful formulations. […] That one or both of them were gay is not known. But is it impossible?" This is pure speculation. Apart from the clichés that are used here and show how the author imagines gay men as smug aesthetes, the thesis has a bad aftertaste. Today it is undisputed that the image of Gropius as a heroic figure of modernism is largely a questionable myth. For Polster, however, it is much more than just a revision; he portrays Gropius as an impostor incapable of achieving anything on his own, whose career in all phases was based above all on coincidence and on the talent of exploiting other people for his own benefit in an ingenious way. Although Polster is right in some respects, the narrative is so one-sidedly devastating that in the end literally nothing remains. Seen in this light, the alleged affair with Osthaus is nothing more than a homophobic arabesque with the purpose of thoroughly damaging the reputation of the fallen hero. (WV)

Anmerkungen

You Can't Be What You Can't See – ein Vorwort

– **1** – Dietrich, Verena: Architektinnen. Ideen – Projekte – Bauten, Stuttgart/Berlin/Köln/Mainz (Kohlhammer), 1986 – **2** – Rodenstein, Marianne: Wege zur nicht-sexistischen Stadt. Architektinnen und Planerinnen in den USA, Freiburg (Kore), 1994 – **3** – Baldessarini, Sonja Ricon: Wie Frauen bauen: Architektinnen von Julia Morgan bis Zaha Hadid, Berlin (AvivA), 2001 – **4** – Kullack, Tanja: Architektur: eine weibliche Profession, Berlin (Jovis), 2011 – **5** – Schwartz, Frederic (Hg.): Alan Buchsbaum, Architect & Designer: The Mechanics of Taste, New York (Monacelli), 1996 – **6** – ebd., S. 152f. – **7** – ebd., S. 164-171 – **8** – ebd., S. 178-182 – **9** – ebd., S. 76-83 – **10** – Southern Alleghenies Museum of Art (Hg.): Roger Ferri: Architectural Visionary, Loretto (Southern Alleghenies Museum of Art), 1999 – **11** – Hines, Thomas S. (Hg.): Franklin D. Israel: Buildings and Projects, New York (Rizzoli), 1993; Betsky, Aaron: Drager House: Franklin D. Israel (Architecture in Detail), London (Phaidon), 1996 – **12** – vgl. Schwartz (Anm. 5), S. 5. – **13** – Twombly, Robert: Louis Sullivan: His Life and Work, New York (Viking), 1986, S. 399 – **14** – ebd., S. 399-406 – **15** – Bloomer, Jennifer: „D'OR" (For Donnie), in: Colomina, Beatriz (Hg.): Sexuality & Space, New York (Princeton Architectural Presse), 1992, S. 163-184 – **16** – Snyder, Daniel: Louis H. Sullivan: That Object He Became, in: Heuvel, Dirk van den; Gorny, Robert Alexander (Hg.): Trans-Bodies / Queering Spaces, Footprint – Delft Architectural Theory Journal 21, Jg. 11 (2017), Ausgabe 2 (Herbst/Winter), S. 67-85 – **17** – N.N.: The Master Builder. Architect Philip Johnson Designs the World's Largest Gay Church, in: Out. Americas Best-Selling Gay and Lesbian Magazine, Jg. 5 (1996), Ausgabe 5 (Mai) – **18** – Schulze, Franz: Philip Johnson. Life and Work, Chicago (The University of Chicago Press), 1994 – **19** – zitiert nach der deutschen Ausgabe: Schulze, Franz: Philip Johnson. Leben und Werk (1994), Wiesbaden (Springer), 1996, S. 43 – **20** – ebd., S. 79 – **21** – ebd., S. 104 – **22** – Pehnt, Wolfgang: Philip Johnson Superstar. Der nahezu unaufhaltsame Aufstieg eines Architekten, in: F.A.Z. Frankfurter Allgemeine Zeitung, Jg. 49, Ausgabe 36 (12.02.1997), S. 32 – **23** – Sunselson, Avner (Hg.): Antoine Laroche. Innenräume, Köln (Verlag der Buchhandlung Walther König), 1991, S. 9 – **24** – Ramchurn, Rakesh: Findings of the AJ Lesbian, Gay and Bisexual Survey, in: AJ Architects' Journal, 11.07.2013 (Online: www.architectsjournal.co.uk/home/exclusive-findings-of-the-aj-lesbian-gay-and-bisexual-survey/8650559.article / letzter Zugriff: 02.04.2018) – **25** – Stonewall (Hg.): Stonewall Top 100 Employers 2013. The Workplace Equality Index, London (Stonewall), 2013 – **26** – Ramchurn, Rakesh: Is Architecture Really LGBT Friendly?, in: AJ Architects' Journal, 27.08.2015 (Online: www.architectsjournal.co.uk/news/daily-news/is-architecture-really-lgbt-friendly/8688184.article / letzter Zugriff: 29.04.2018); Waite, Richard: The AJ's LGBT+ Survey 'Reflects a Less Tolerant Society', in: AJ Architects' Journal, 26.01.2018 (Online: www.architectsjournal.co.uk/news/the-ajs-lgbt-survey-reflects-a-less-tolerant-society/10027332.article / letzter Zugriff: 29.04.2018) – **27** – vgl. www.nowwhat-architexx.org/articles/2018/5/25/the-organization-of-lesbian-and-gay-architects-designers, letzter Zugriff: 03.12.2019 – **28** – Arcidi, Philip: Defining Gay Design. Homosexual Designers, Gathering in New York Ask Whether their Work Differs from that of Straight Colleagues, in: PA Progressive Architecture, Jg. 75 (1994), Ausgabe 8 (August), S. 36 – **29** – OLGAD Organization of Lesbian and Gay Architects and Designers; DIFFA Design Industries Foundation Fighting AIDS; Elsie de Wolfe Foundation (Hg.): Design Legacies: A Tribute to Architects and Designers who Have Died of AIDS, New York (Design Pride '94 International Lesbian and Gay Design Conference), 1994 – **30** – OLGAD Organization of Lesbian and Gay Architects and Designers: A Guide to Lesbian and Gay New York Historical Landmarks, New York (Organization of Lesbian and Gay Architects and Designers), 1994 – **31** – Shockley, Jay: Preservation of LGBTQ Historic & Cultural Sites – A New York City Perspective, in: Springate, Megan E. (Hg.): LGBTQ America: A Theme Study of Lesbian, Gay, Bisexual, Transgender, and Queer History, Washington (National Park Foundation), 2016, S. 26/1-26/33 – **32** – Sontag, Susan: Notes on Camp, in: Partisan Review, Ausgabe 31, 1964, S. 515-530 (deutsche Übersetzung: Sontag, Susan: Anmerkungen zu Camp (1964), in: Sontag, Susan: Kunst und Antikunst. 24 literarische Analysen, Frankfurt am Main (Fischer), 1982, S. 322-341) – **33** – Betsky, Aaron: Queer Space. Architecture and Same-Sex Desire, New York (William Morrow & Company), 1997 – **34** – vgl. die entsprechenden Beiträge in diesem Band – **35** – Pepchinksi, Mary; Budde, Christina; Voigt, Wolfgang; Schmal, Peter Cachola (Hg.): Frau Architekt. Seit mehr als 100 Jahren: Frauen im Architekturberuf, Tübingen (Wasmuth), 2017 – **36** – Friedrich, Jan: Definitionen eines verdrängten Raumes. Learning from Queer Spaces, in: Bauwelt 2009, Ausgabe 47, S. 2; Kasiske, Michael: Cruising als Architekturmodell, in: TAZ Die Tageszeitung, 18.11.2009

Hamburg im 18. Jahrhundert: Der Baumeister Ernst Georg Sonnin und sein Liebling

– **1** – Heckmann, Herbert: Ernst Georg Sonnin – Baumeister des Rationalismus, in: Heckmann, Herbert: Barock und Rokoko in Hamburg. Baukunst des Bürgertums, Berlin (Verlag für Bauwesen), 1990, S. 294-327 – **2** – Reinke, Johann Theodor: Lebensbeschreibung des ehrenwerthen Ernst Georg Sonnin, Baumeisters und Gelehrten in Hamburg, Hamburg (Auf Kosten d. Verf. u. in Comm. i. d. Heroldschen Buchhdlg.), 1824, S. 13 – **3** – ebd. – **4** – Artikel Johann Theodor Reinke, in: Historische Commission bei der königl. Akademie der Wissenschaften (Hg.): Allgemeine Deutsche Biographie, Leipzig (Duncker & Humblot), 1889, Bd. 28 (Reinbeck-Rodbertus), S. 88f. (Online: http://de.wikisource.org/wiki/ADB:Reinke,_Johann_Theodor / letzter Zugriff: 05.01.2020) – **5** – Reinke (Anm. 2), S. 34f. – **6** – Artikel Reinke (Anm. 4) – **7** – Reinke (Anm. 2), S. 104 – **8** – ebd., S. 13 – **9** – ebd., S. 102 – **10** – Grimm, Jacob und Wilhelm: Deutsches Wörterbuch, Leipzig, 1885, Bd. 6 – **11** – Voigt, Wolfgang: Geschichte der Schwulen in Hamburg, in: Voigt, Wolfgang; Weinrich, Klaus (Hg.): Hamburg ahoi! Der schwule Lotse durch die Hansestadt, Berlin (Verlag Rosa Winkel), 1982, S. 7-49 – **12** – Heckmann (Anm. 1), S. 320, 327

Annotations

You Can't Be What You Can't See – a Preface

– 1 – Dietrich, Verena: Architektinnen. Ideen – Projekte – Bauten, Stuttgart (Kohlhammer), 1986 – 2 – Rodenstein, Marianne: Wege zur nicht-sexistischen Stadt. Architektinnen und Planerinnen in den USA, Freiburg (Kore), 1994 – 3 – Baldessarini, Sonja Ricon: Wie Frauen bauen: Architektinnen von Julia Morgan bis Zaha Hadid, Berlin (AvivA), 2001 – 4 – Kullack, Tanja: Architektur: eine weibliche Profession, Berlin (Jovis), 2011 – 5 – Schwartz, Frederic (ed.): Alan Buchsbaum, Architect & Designer: The Mechanics of Taste, New York (Monacelli), 1996 – 6 – ibid., pp. 152f. – 7 – ibid., pp. 164-171 – 8 – ibid., pp. 178-182 – 9 – ibid., pp. 76-83 – 10 – Southern Alleghenies Museum of Art (ed.): Roger Ferri: Architectural Visionary, Loretto (Southern Alleghenies Museum of Art), 1999 – 11 – Hines, Thomas S. (ed.): Franklin D. Israel: Buildings and Projects, New York (Rizzoli), 1993; Betsky, Aaron: Drager House: Franklin D. Israel (Architecture in Detail), London (Phaidon), 1996 – 12 – cf. Schwartz 1996 (note 5), p. 5. – 13 – Twombly, Robert: Louis Sullivan: His Life and Work, New York (Viking), 1986, p. 399 – 14 – ibid., pp. 399-406 – 15 – Bloomer, Jennifer: "D'OR" (For Donnie), in: Colomina, Beatriz (ed.): Sexuality & Space, New York (Princeton Architectural Presse), 1992, pp. 163-184 – 16 – Snyder, Daniel: Louis H. Sullivan: That Object He Became, in: Heuvel, Dirk van den; Gorny, Robert Alexander (eds.): Trans-Bodies / Queering Spaces, Footprint – Delft Architectural Theory Journal 21, vol. 11 (2017), issue 2 (autumn/winter), pp. 67-85 – 17 – N.N.: The Master Builder. Architect Philip Johnson designs the World's largest gay Church, in: Out. Americas bestselling gay and lesbian Magazine, vol. 5 (1996), issue 5 (May) – 18 – Schulze, Franz: Philip Johnson. Life and Work, Chicago (The University of Chicago Press), 1994 – 19 – quoted from the German edition: Schulze, Franz: Philip Johnson. Leben und Werk, Wiesbaden (Springer), 1996 (1994), p. 43 – 20 – ibid., p. 79 – 21 – ibid., p. 104 – 22 – Pehnt, Wolfgang: Philip Johnson Superstar. Der nahezu unaufhaltsame Aufstieg eines Architekten, in: F.A.Z. Frankfurter Allgemeine Zeitung, vol. 49, issue 36 (12/02/1997), p. 32 – 23 – Sunselson, Avner (ed.): Antoine Laroche. Innenräume, Köln (Verlag der Buchhandlung Walther König), 1991, p. 9 – 24 – Ramchurn, Rakesh: Findings of the AJ lesbian, gay and bisexual Survey, in: AJ Architects' Journal, 11/07/2013 (online: www.architectsjournal.co.uk/home/exclusive-findings-ofthe-aj-lesbian-gay-and-bisexual-survey/8650559.article / last accessed on 02/04/2018) – 25 – Stonewall (ed.): Stonewall Top 100 Employers 2013. The Workplace Equality Index, London (Stonewall), 2013 – 26 – Ramchun, Rakesch: Is Architecture really LGBT friendly?, in: AJ Architects' Journal, 27/08/2015 (online: www.architectsjournal.co.uk/news/daily-news/is-architecture-really-lgbtfriendly/8688184.article / last accessed on 29/04/2018); Waite, Richard: The AJ's LGBT+ Survey "reflects a less tolerant Society," in: AJ Architects' Journal, 26/01/2018 (online: www.architectsjournal.co.uk/news/the-ajs-lgbt-survey-reflects-a-less-tolerantsociety/10027332.article / last accessed on 29/04/2018) – 27 – cf. www.nowwhat-architexx.org/articles/2018/5/25/the-organization-oflesbian-and-gay-architects-designers, last accessed on 03/12/2019 – 28 – Arcidi, Philip: Defining Gay Design. Homosexual designers, gathering in New York ask whether their work differs from that of straight colleagues, in: PA Progressive Architecture, vol. 75 (1994), issue 8 (August), p. 36 – 29 – OLGAD Organization of Lesbian and Gay Architects and Designers; DIFFA Design Industries Foundation Fighting AIDS; Elsie de Wolfe Foundation (eds.): Design Legacies: A Tribute to Architects and Designers who have died of AIDS, New York (Design Pride '94 International Lesbian and Gay Design Conference), 1994 – 30 – OLGAD Organization of Lesbian and Gay Architects and Designers: A Guide to Lesbian and Gay New York Historical Landmarks, New York (Organization of Lesbian and Gay Architects and Designers), 1994 – 31 – Shockley, Jay: Preservation of LGBTQ Historic & Cultural Sites – A New York City Perspective, in: Springate, Megan E. (ed.): LGBTQ America: A Theme Study of Lesbian, Gay, Bisexual, Transgender, and Queer History, Washington (National Park Foundation), 2016, pp. 26/1-26/33 – 32 – Sontag, Susan: Notes on Camp, in: Partisan Review, issue 31, 1964, pp. 515-530 (German translation: Sontag, Susan: Anmerkungen zu Camp [1964], in: Sontag, Susan: Kunst und Antikunst. 24 literarische Analysen, Frankfurt am Main [Fischer], 1982, pp. 322-341) – 33 – Betsky, Aaron: Queer Space. Architecture and Same-Sex Desire, New York (William Morrow & Company), 1997 – 34 – cf. corresponding contributions in this book – 35 – Pepchinksi, Mary; Budde, Christina; Voigt, Wolfgang; Schmal, Peter Cachola (eds.): Frau Architekt. Seit mehr als 100 Jahren: Frauen im Architekturberuf, Tübingen (Wasmuth), 2017 – 36 – Friedrich, Jan: Definitionen eines verdrängten Raumes. Learning from Queer Spaces, in: Bauwelt, vol. 100 (2009), issue 47, p. 2; Kasiske, Michael: Cruising als Architekturmodell, in: TAZ Die Tageszeitung, 18/11/2009

Hamburg in the 18th Century: The Architect Ernst Georg Sonnin and his "Liebling"

– 1 – Heckmann, Herbert: Ernst Georg Sonnin – Baumeister des Rationalismus, in: Heckmann, Herbert: Barock und Rokoko in Hamburg. Baukunst des Bürgertums, Berlin (Verlag für Bauwesen), 1990, pp. 294-327 – 2 – Reinke, Johann Theodor: Lebensbeschreibung des ehrenwerthen Ernst Georg Sonnin, Baumeisters und Gelehrten in Hamburg, Hamburg (at the expense of the author in commission in the Heroldsche Buchhdlg.), 1824, p. 13 – 3 – ibid. – 4 – Article Johann Theodor Reinke, in: Historische Commission bei der königl. Akademie der Wissenschaften (ed.): Allgemeine Deutsche Biographie, Leipzig (Duncker & Humblot), 1889, vol. 28 (Reinbeck – Rodbertus), pp. 88f. (online: http://de.wikisource.org/wiki/ADB:Reinke,_Johann_Theodor / last accessed on 01/05/2020) – 5 – Reinke (note 2), p. 34f. – 6 – Article Reinke (note 4) – 7 – Reinke (note 2), p. 104 – 8 – ibid., p. 13 – 9 – ibid., p. 102 – 10 – Grimm, Jacob und Wilhelm: Deutsches Wörterbuch, Leipzig, 1885, vol. 6 – 11 – Voigt, Wolfgang: Geschichte der Schwulen in Hamburg, in: Voigt, Wolfgang; Weinrich, Klaus (eds.): Hamburg ahoi. Der schwule Lotse durch die Hansestadt, Berlin (Verlag Rosa Winkel), 1982, pp. 7-49 – 12 – Heckmann (note 1), pp. 320, 327

Die Erfindung der Queer Gothic: Horace Walpole

– **1** – Miller, Norbert: Strawberry Hill. Horace Walpole und die Ästhetik der schönen Unregelmässigkeit, München/Wien (Hanser), 1986 – **2** – Walpole, Horace: Das Schloss von Otranto (1764), München (C.H. Beck), 2014 – **3** – Walpole, Horace: A Description of the Villa of Mr. Horace Walpole, Youngest Son of Sir Robert Walpole Earl of Orford, at Strawberry-Hill near Twickenham, Middlesex, with an Inventory of the Furniture, Pictures, Curiosities, etc., Strawberry-Hill, 1784 – **4** – Sedgwick, Eve Kosofsky: Between Men. English Literature and Male Homosocial Desire, New York (Columbia University Press), 1985 – **5** – Haggerty, George E.: Queer Gothic, Champaign (University of Illinois Press), 2006 – **6** – Reeve, Matthew M.: Gothic Architecture, Sexuality, and License at Horace Walpole's Strawberry Hill, in: The Art Bulletin, Ausgabe 3, 2013, S. 411-439 – **7** – vgl. den entsprechenden Beitrag in diesem Band – **8** – ebd. – **9** – Bohl, David: Beauport. The Sleeper-McCann House, Boston (David R. Godine Publisher), 1990; Murphy, Kevin D.: 'Secure from All Intrusion' Heterotopia, Queer Space, and the Turn-of-the-Twentieth-Century American Resort, in: Winterthur Portfolio, Ausgabe 2/3, 2009, S. 185-228 – **10** – Welter, Volker M.: Schloss Murnau, Hollywoodland, CA 90068, in: Cabinet. A Quarterly of Art and Architecture, Ausgabe 63, 2017, S. 41-48

Exzentrisches Eremitentum: William Beckford

– **1** – Beckford, William: An Arabian Tale, From an Unpublished Manuscript [Vathek], London (J. Johnson), 1787 (deutsche Übersetzung: Beckford, William: Vathek (1787), Frankfurt am Main (Suhrkamp), 1999 – **2** – Zur Biografie William Beckfords und zur Geschichte seines Landsitzes in Fonthill Gifford siehe: Miller, Norbert: Fonthill Abbey. Die dunkle Welt des William Beckford, München (Hanser), 2012 – **3** – vgl. Britton, John: Graphical and Literary Illustrations of Fonthill Abbey, Wiltshire. With Heraldical and Genealogical Notices of the Beckford Family, London (Longman), 1823; Rutter, John: Delineations of Fonthill and its Abbey, Shaftesbury, 1823 – **4** – Zum Werk und zur Biografie von James Wyatt siehe: Robinson, John Martin: James Wyatt, 1746-1813, Architect to George III, New Haven (Yale University Press), 2012 – **5** – vgl. Alexander, Boyd: England's Wealthiest Son. A Study of William Beckford, London (Centaur Press), 1962 – **6** – Norton, Rictor: William Beckford. The Fool of Fonthill, in: Gay History and Literature, 16.11.1999 (Online: www.rictornorton.co.uk/beckfor1.htm / letzter Zugriff: 01.11.2019) – **7** – Holzschuh, Robert: Das verlorene Paradies Ludwig II. – Die persönliche Tragödie des Märchenkönigs, Frankfurt (Eichborn Verlag), 2001; Spangenberg, Marcus: Ludwig II. – Der andere König, Regensburg (Verlag Friedrich Pustet), 2011 – **8** – Norton (Anm. 6)

Wie Castor und Pollux für immer verbunden: Percier und Fontaine, die Architekten Napoleons

– **1** – Halévy, (Jacques Fromental): Institut impérial de France. Académie des beaux-arts. Notice historique sur la vie et sur les travaux de M. Fontaine par M. F. Halévy, scrétaire perpétuel, lue à la séance publique du samedi 7 octobre 1854, Paris (Firmin-Didot), 1854 (zitiert nach: Garric, Jean-Philippe: Percier et Fontaine. Les architectes de Napoléon, Paris (Belin) 2012, S. 200) – **2** – Foucart, Bruno: P. F. L. Fontaine. Du journal au mémorial, in: Fontaine, Pierre François Léonard: Journal 1799-1853 (2 Bände), Paris (École nationale supérieure des Beaux-Arts, Institut français d'architecture, Société de l'histoire de l'art français), 1987, Bd. 1, S. XIX-XXXVI, Zitat XXXVI – **3** – Rapp, Linda: Percier & Fontaine, in: Summers, Claude J. (Hg.): The Queer Encyclopedia of the Visual Arts, New York (Cleis Press), 2004, S. 244-246 – **4** – Fouché, Maurice: Percier et Fontaine. Biographie critique (Les grands artistes. Leur vie – leur oeuvre), Paris (H. Laurens), 1904, S. 72 – **5** – Garric (Anm. 1), S. 38 – **6** – Friedhof: Cimetière du Père Lachaise, Boulevard de Ménilmontant, Paris (20. Arrondissement); Grab: 28. Abteilung, Linie 8/29, Nummer 1/37 – **7** – Fontaine (Anm.2) – **8** – ebd., S. 525 – **9** – Rapp (Anm. 3), S. 246 – **10** – Foucart (Anm. 2), Bd. 1, S. XIX-XXXVI

Die Architekten der Wiener Hofoper: Eduard van der Nüll und August Sicard von Sicardsburg

– **1** – Uhl, Friedrich: Feuilleton, Wiener Chronik, in: Neue Freie Presse, 25.11.1866, S. 1f. – **2** – Springer, Elisabeth: Geschichte und Kulturleben der Wiener Ringstraße (=Wagner-Rieger, Renate (Hg.): Die Wiener Ringstraße. Bild einer Epoche, Band 2), Wiesbaden (Franz Steiner Verlag), 1979, S. 364f. – **3** – N.N.: Selbstmord des Oberbaurathes Professor van der Nüll, in: Gemeinde-Zeitung, 05.04.1868, S. 6 – **4** – Die nach wie vor umfassendste Studie zu den beiden Architekten: Hoffmann, Hans-Christoph: Die Architekten Eduard van der Nüll und August von Sicardsburg, in: Hoffmann, Hans-Christoph; Krause, Walter; Kitlitschka, Werner: Das Wiener Opernhaus (=Wagner-Rieger, Renate (Hg.): Die Wiener Ringstraße. Bild einer Epoche, Band 8/1), Wiesbaden (Franz Steiner Verlag), 1972, S. 1-206 – **5** – Eder, Franz X.: Homosexualitäten. Diskurse und Lebenswelten 1870-1970, Weitra (Verlag Bibliothek der Provinz), o.J. (2010), S. 26-28 – **6** – Brunner, Andreas; Sulzenbacher, Hannes (Hg.): Schwules Wien. Reiseführer durch die Donaumetropole, Wien (Promedia), 1998, S. 33 – **7** – Dabei ging es auch um die Nachfolgeregelung der Professuren der beiden Architekten an der Aka-

The Invention of Queer Gothic: Horace Walpole

– 1 – Miller, Norbert: Strawberry Hill. Horace Walpole und die Ästhetik der schönen Unregelmässigkeit, Munich/Vienna (Hanser), 1986 – 2 – Walpole, Horace: The Castle of Otranto (1764), London (Penguin Classics), 2001 – 3 – Walpole, Horace: A Description of the Villa of Mr. Horace Walpole, Youngest Son of Sir Robert Walpole Earl of Orford, at Strawberry-Hill near Twickenham, Middlesex, with an Inventory of the Furniture, Pictures, Curiosities, etc., Strawberry-Hill, 1784 – 4 – Sedgwick, Eve Kosofsky: Between Men. English Literature and Male Homosocial Desire, New York (Columbia University Press), 1985 – 5 – Haggerty, George E.: Queer Gothic, Champaign (University of Illinois Press), 2006 – 6 – Reeve, Matthew M.: Gothic Architecture, Sexuality, and License at Horace Walpole's Strawberry Hill, in: The Art Bulletin, vol. 95 (2013) issue 3, pp. 411-439 – 7 – cf. the corresponding contribution in this book – 8 – ibid. – 9 – Bohl, David: Beauport. The Sleeper-McCann House, Boston (David R. Godine Publisher), 1990; Murphy, Kevin D.: "Secure from All Intrusion'Heterotopia," Queer Space, and the Turn-of-the-Twentieth-Century American Resort, in: Winterthur Portfolio, vol. 43 (2009), issue 2/3, pp. 185-228 – 10 – Welter, Volker M.: Schloss Murnau, Hollywoodland, CA 90068, in: Cabinet. A Quarterly of Art and Architecture, issue 63, 2017, pp. 41-48

Eccentric Hermitism: William Beckford

– 1 – Beckford, William: An Arabian Tale. From an Unpublished Manuscript [Vathek], London (J. Johnson), 1787 – 2 – On the Biography of William Beckford and the History of his Country Estate at Fonthill Gifford cf. Miller, Norbert: Fonthill Abbey. Die dunkle Welt des William Beckford, Munich (Hanser), 2012 – 3 – cf. Britton, John: Graphical and Literary Illustrations of Fonthill Abbey, Wiltshire. With Heraldical and Genealogical Notices of the Beckford Family, London (Longman), 1823; Rutter, John: Delineations of Fonthill and its Abbey, Shaftesbury, 1823 – 4 – For the Work and Biography of James Wyatt cf. Robinson, John Martin: James Wyatt, 1746-1813, Architect to George III, New Haven (Yale University Press), 2012 – 5 – cf. Alexander, Boyd: England's Wealthiest Son. A Study of William Beckford, London (Centaur Press), 1962 – 6 – Norton, Rictor: William Beckford. The Fool of Fonthill, in: Gay History and Literature, 11/16/1999 (online: www.rictornorton.co.uk/beckfor1.htm / last accessed on 11/01/2019) – 7 – Holzschuh, Robert: Das verlorene Paradies Ludwigs II. Die persönliche Tragödie des Märchenkönigs, Frankfurt (Eichborn Verlag), 2001; Spangenberg, Marcus: Ludwig II. – Der andere König, Regensburg (Verlag Friedrich Pustet), 2011 – 8 – Norton (note 6)

Like Castor and Pollux Forever United:
Percier and Fontaine, Napoleon's Architects

– 1 – Halévy, (Jacques Fromental): Institut imperial de France. Académie des beaux-arts. Notice his-torique sur la vie et sur les travaux de M. Fontaine par M. F. Halévy, secrétaire perpétuel, lue à la sé-ance publique du samedi 7 octobre 1854, Paris (Firmin-Didot), 1854 (quoted from: Garric, Jean-Philippe: Percier et Fontaine. Les architectes de Napoléon, Paris (Belin) 2012, p. 200 – 2 – Foucart, Bruno: P. F. L. Fontaine. Du journal au mémorial, in: Fontaine, Pierre François Léonard: Journal 1799-1853 (2 vol.), Paris (École nationale supérieure des Beaux-Arts, Institut français d'architecture, Société de l'histoire de l'art français), 1987, vol. 1, pp. XIX-XXXVI, quotation XXXVI – 3 – Rapp, Linda: Percier & Fontaine, in: Summers, Claude J. (ed.): The Queer Encyclopedia of the Visual Arts, New York (Cleis Press), 2004, pp. 244-246 – 4 – Fouché, Maurice: Percier et Fontaine. Biographie critique (Les grands artistes. Leur vie – leur œuvre), Paris (H. Laurens), 1904, p. 72 – 5 – Garric (note 1), p. 38 – 6 – Cemetery: Cimetière du Père Lachaise, Boulevard de Ménilmontant, Paris (20. Arrondissement); grave: 28. section, line 8/29, number 1/37 – 7 – Fontaine (note 2) – 8 – ibid., p. 525 – 9 – Rapp (note 3), p. 246 – 10 – Foucart (note 2), vol. 1, pp. XIX-XXXVI

The Architects of the Vienna Court Opera: Eduard van der Nüll and August Sicard von Sicardsburg

– 1 – Uhl, Friedrich: Feuilleton, Wiener Chronik, in: Neue Freie Presse, 11/25/1866, pp. 1f. – 2 – Springer, Elisabeth: Geschichte und Kulturleben der Wiener Ringstraße (=Wagner-Rieger, Renate [ed.]: Die Wiener Ringstraße. Bild einer Epoche, vol. 2), Wiesbaden (Franz Steiner Verlag), 1979, pp. 364f. – 3 – N.N.: Selbstmord des Oberbaurathes Professor van der Nüll, in: Gemeinde-Zeitung, 04/05/1868, p. 6 – 4 – Still the most comprehensive study on the two architects: Hoffmann, Hans-Christoph: Die Archi-tekten Eduard van der Nüll und August von Sicardsburg, in: Hoffmann, Hans-Christoph; Krause, Walter; Kitlitschka, Werner: Das Wiener Opernhaus (=Wagner-Rieger, Renate [ed.]: Die Wiener Ringstraße. Bild einer Epoche, vol. 8/1), Wiesbaden (Franz Steiner Verlag), 1972, pp. 1-206 – 5 – Eder, Franz X.: Homosexualitäten. Diskurse und Lebenswelten 1870-1970, Weitra (Verlag Bibliothek der Provinz), n.d. (2010), pp. 26-28 – 6 – Brunner, Andreas; Sulzenbacher, Hannes (eds.): Schwules Wien. Reiseführer durch die Donaumetropole, Vienna (Promedia), 1998, p. 33 – 7 – This also involved the succession of the professorships of the two architects at the Academy of

demie der bildenden Künste, der zentralen Kunstausbildungsstätte der habsburgischen Monarchie. (vgl. Hoffmann, Karl: Akademische Intrigen, in: Neues Wiener Tagblatt, 20.04.1868, S. 1) – **8** – Bresan, Uwe; Voigt, Wolfgang: The Queer Architect in Germany: Invisible in Practice, Missing from History, in: Brown, James B.; Harriss, Harriet; Morrow, Ruth; Soane, James (Hg.): A Gendered Profession: The Question of Representation in Space Making, London (RIBA Publishing) 2016, S. 88-94, besonders 91f. – **9** – N.N.: Eduard van der Nüll, in: Neues Fremden-Blatt (Abendblatt), 04.04.1868, S. 3 – **10** – So in der Rubrik: Theater und Kunst, in: Beilage des Fremden-Blattes, 02.09.1868, o. S. sowie in der Rubrik: Theater- und Kunstnachrichten, in: Neue Freie Presse (Morgenblatt), 02.09.1868, S. 7 – **11** – N.N.: Die Todten-Liste von 1868, in: Extra-Beilage der Gemeinde-Zeitung, 03.01.1869, S. 11 – **12** – Nach dem Mord an Agamemnon wurde dessen Sohn Orestes zu König Strophios in Sicherheit gebracht, wo er zusammen mit dessen Sohn Pylades aufwuchs. Sie verbrachten ihr gesamtes Leben gemeinsam: Pylades begleitete Orestes nach Athen zum Prozess wegen des Muttermordes an Klytämnestra und beide wollten, als einer der beiden in Aulis der Göttin Artemis geopfert werden sollte, nicht ohne den anderen weiterleben. – **13** – Jonathan, der Sohn König Sauls, „liebte David wie sein eigenes Leben", bewahrte ihn mehrmals vor den Mordabsichten seines Vaters und verhalf ihm zur Flucht (1 Samuel 18: 1–9, 1 Samuel 19: 1–7, 1 Samuel 20: 1–42). – **14** – N.N.: August v. Sicardsburg, in: Neues Fremden-Blatt, 14.06.1868, S. 6 – **15** – N.N.: Eduard van der Nüll, in: Neues Wiener Tagblatt, 04.04.1868, S. 2 – **16** – W., K. (Weiß, Karl): August v. Sicardsburg, in: Wiener Abendpost, 22.06.1868, S. 583 – **17** – Voigt, Wolfgang: Mit Sorgfalt verschwiegen. Verborgene Biographien homosexueller Architekten. Drei Fälle aus dem 18. und 20. Jahrhundert in Hamburg, in: Küppers, Carolin; Schneider, Martin (Hg.): Orte der Begegnung. Orte des Widerstands. Zur Geschichte homosexueller, trans*geschlechtlicher und queerer Räume (Geschichte der Homosexuellen in Deutschland nach 1945, Band 7), Hamburg (Männerschwarm Verlag), 2018, S. 104-116 – **18** – N.N.: Eduard van der Nüll, in: Fremden-Blatt (Morgenblatt), 04.04.1868, S. 4f. – **19** – ebd. – **20** – wie Anm. 15 – **21** – Telesko, Werner (Hg.): Die Wiener Hofburg 1835-1918. Der Ausbau der Residenz vom Vormärz bis zum Ende des Kaiserforums, Wien (Verlag der Österreichischen Akademie der Wissenschaften) 2012, S. 58, 130, 132 – **22** – N.N.: Selbstmord des Oberbauraths Professor van der Nüll, in: Morgen-Post, 04.04.1868, S. 1 (Die heutige Adresse lautet Schadekgasse 4. Eine 1957 durch das Bezirksvertretung Mariahilf und das lokale Bezirksmuseum angebrachte Gedenktafel nennt zwar auch Sicardsburg als Bewohner dieses Hauses, jedoch stimmen weder die offiziellen Wohnadressen von van der Nüll noch von Sicardsburg mit dieser Anschrift überein. Sicardsburg wohnte seit spätestens 1859 in der Inneren Stadt in der Wipplingerstraße 4 (Konskriptionsnummer 382); van der Nülls Adresse lautete offiziell Coburgbastei 12 (Konskriptionsnummer 1191) und lag ebenfalls in der Inneren Stadt. Tatsächlich war das Mariahilfer Haus die offizielle Wohnadresse von August La Vigne (Lehmann, Adolph: Allgemeiner Wohnungs-Anzeiger nebst Handels- und Gewerbe-Adreßbuch der k. k. Reichshaupt- und Residenzstadt Wien und Umgebung etc., Wien (Verlag Carl Gerold's Sohn), Ausgaben der Jahre 1859, 1860, 1861, 1864, 1865, 1867 und 1868). Für die frühen 1840er-Jahre dagegen können wir eine gemeinsame Adresse von Sicadsburg und van der Nüll offiziell feststellen: Jägerzeile (Konskriptionsnummer 401) – heute Praterstraße 63 – in der Leopoldstadt (Högn, J.: Bau-Schematismus oder: Adressbuch aller mit Bauten und Bauarbeiten sich beschäftigenden Künstler und Professionisten etc., Wien (Verlag der Jasper'schen Buchhandlung) 1844, S.3).) – **23** – ebd. – **24** – Gugitz, Gustav: Das Wiener Kaffeehaus. Ein Stück Kultur- und Lokalgeschichte, Wien (Verlag Jugend und Volk), 1940, S. 201 – **25** – wie Anm. 22 (zur Wohnadresse Koburgbastei 12 (ehemals Konskriptionsnummer 1191) vgl. auch: Lehmann (Anm. 22), S. 426) – **26** – wie Anm. 15 – **27** – wie Anm. 22 – **28** – N.N.: Eduard van der Nüll, in: Fremden-Blatt (Morgenblatt), 04.04.1868, S. 1 – **29** – Karlmann: Siccardsburg, in: Neues Wiener Tagblatt, 13.06.1868, S. 1 – **31** – N.N.: Siccardsburg, in: Morgen-Post, 15.06.1868, S. 2 – **32** – wie Anm. 30 – **33** – Payer, Peter: 'Wien bei Nacht, wie es tanzt und lacht'. Stadtimage und Erotik, 1840-1930, in: Brunner, Andreas; Kreutler, Frauke; Lindinger, Michaela; Milchram, Gerhard; Nußbaumer, Martina; Sulzenbacher, Hannes (Hg.): Sex in Wien. Lust. Kontrolle. Ungehorsam (Ausstellungskatalog Wien Museum), Wien (Metroverlag), 2016, S. 248–253, besonders 249 – **34** – Brunner, Andreas; Sulzenbacher, Hannes: Die verborgene schwule Topografie der Stadt, in: Brunner (Anm. 33), S. 260-266, besonders 261 – **35** – Albertina Wien, CHA 356 – **36** – Museo Archeologico Nazionale di Napoli, Inv.-Nr. 27.874 – **37** – Saint Non, Jean Claude Richard de: Voyage Pittoresque ou Descripition des Royaumes de Naples et de Sicile. Second Partie du Premier Volume. Tome Second, Paris, 1782, Tafel 13

Der Architekt und der Kürassier: Franz Heinrich Schwechten

– **1** – Baumgardt, Manfred; Dose, Ralf; Herzer, Manfred; Klein, Hans-Günter; Kokula, Ilse; Lindemann, Gesa: Magnus Hirschfeld – Leben und Werk (Ausstellungskatalog), Berlin (Rosa Winkel), 1985; Wolff, Charlotte: Magnus Hirschfeld. A Portrait of a Pioneer in Sexology, London/New York (Quartet Books), 1986 – **2** – Hirschfeld, Magnus: Berlins Drittes Geschlecht (1904), Berlin (Rosa Winkel), 1991, S. 13 – **3** – Ostwald, Hans: Männliche Prostitution im kaiserlichen Berlin (1906), Berlin (Janssen), 1991, S. 21 – **4** – Dobler, Jens: Hans von Tresckow (1866-1934), in: Archiv für Polizeigeschichte, Jg. 10 (1999), Ausgabe 2 (Nr. 28), S. 47-52 – **5** – Tresckow, Hans von: Von Fürsten und anderen Sterblichen. Erinnerungen eines Kriminalkommissars, Berlin (Fontane & Co.), 1922 – **6** – ebd., S. 114 – **7** – Hirschfeld (Anm. 2), S. 87 – **8** – Tresckow (Anm. 5), S. 114 – **9** – ebd. – **10** – Zietz, Peer: Franz Heinrich Schwechten. Ein Architekt zwischen Historismus und Moderne, Stuttgart/London (Menges), 1999; Streich, Wolf Jürgen: Franz Heinrich Schwechten. 1841-1924. Bauten für Berlin, Petersberg (Imhof), 2005 – **11** – ebd., S. 36 – **12** – ebd., S. 10

Zwei Stadtbauräte, zwei Junggesellen: Fritz Schumacher und Gustav Oelsner

– **1** – Frank, Hartmut (Hg.): Fritz Schumacher. Reformkultur und Moderne, Stuttgart (Hatje Cantz), 1994 – **2** – Timm, Christoph: Gustav Oelsner und das Neue Altona. Kommunale Architektur und Stadtplanung in der Weimarer Republik, Hamburg (Ernst Kabel), 1984; Dogramaci, Burcu (Hg.): Gustav Oelsner Stadtplaner und Architekt der Moderne, Hamburg (Junius), 2008 – **3** – Schaefer-Lübeck, Karl (Hg.): Hamburger Staatsbauten von Fritz Schumacher (2 Bände), Berlin (Der Zirkel), 1919/21; siehe auch: Fischer, Manfred (Bearb.): Fritz Schumacher. Hamburger Staatsbauten 1909-1919/21. Eine Bestandsaufnahme (Arbeitshefte zur Denkmalpflege in

Fine Arts, the central art training institution of the Habsburg Monarchy (cf. Hoffmann, Karl: Akademische Intrigen, in: Neues Wiener Tagblatt, 20/04/1868, p. 1). – **8** – Bresan, Uwe; Voigt, Wolfgang: The Queer Architect in Germany: Invisible in Practice, Missing from History, in: Brown, James B.; Harriss, Harriet; Morrow, Ruth; Soane, James (eds.): A Gendered Profession: The Question of Representation in Space Making, London (RIBA Pub-lishing), 2016, pp. 88-94, in particular pp. 91f. – **9** – N.N.: Eduard van der Nüll, in: Neues Fremden-Blatt (Abendblatt), 04/04/1868, p. 3 – **10** – As under the heading: Theater und Kunst, in: Beilage des Frem-den-Blattes, 09/02/1868, n.p. as well as under the heading: Theater- und Kunstnachrichten, in: Neue Freie Presse (Morgenblatt), 09/02/1868, p. 7 – **11** – N.N.: Die Todten-Liste von 1868, in: Extra-Beilage der Gemeinde-Zeitung, 01/03/1869, p. 11 – **12** – After the murder of Agamemnon his son Orestes was taken to safety to King Strophios, where he grew up together with his son Pylades. They spent their entire lives together: Pylades accompanied Orestes to Athens for the trial for his matricide of Clytem-nestra, and when one of them was to be sacrificed to the goddess Artemis in Aulis, they both did not want to live without the other. – **13** – Jonathan, the son of king Saul, "loved David as much as he loved himself," saved him several times from his father's murderous intentions and helped him escape. (1 Samuel 18: 1–9, 1 Samuel 19: 1–7, 1 Samuel 20: 1–42). – **14** – N.N.: August v. Sicardsburg, in: Neues Fremden-Blatt, 06/14/1868, p. 6 – **15** – N.N.: Eduard van der Nüll, in: Neues Wiener Tagblatt, 04/04/1868, p. 2 – **16** – W., K. (Weiß, Karl): August v. Sicardsburg, in: Wiener Abendpost, 06/22/1868, p. 583 – **17** – Voigt, Wolfgang: Mit Sorgfalt verschwiegen. Verborgene Biographien homosexueller Architekten. Drei Fälle aus dem 18. und 20. Jahrhundert in Hamburg, in: Küppers, Carolin; Schneider, Martin (eds.): Orte der Begegnung. Orte des Widerstands. Zur Geschichte homosexueller, trans*geschlechtlicher und queerer Räume (Geschichte der Homosexuellen in Deutschland nach 1945, vol. 7), Hamburg (Männerschwarm Verlag), 2018, pp. 104-116 – **18** – N.N.: Eduard van der Nüll, in: Fremden-Blatt (Morgenblatt), 04/04/1868, pp. 4f. – **19** – ibid. – **20** – as note 15 – **21** – Telesko, Werner (ed.): Die Wiener Hofburg 1835-1918. Der Ausbau der Residenz vom Vormärz bis zum Ende des Kai-serforums, Wien (Verlag der Österreichi-schen Akademie der Wissenschaften), 2012, pp. 58, 130, 132 – **22** – N.N.: Selbstmord des Oberbauraths Professor van der Nüll, in: Morgen-Post, 04/04/1868, p. 1 (The current address is Schadekgasse 4. A commemorative plaque attached in 1957 by the Mariahilf dis-trict council and the local district museum also mentions Sicardsburg as the resident of this house, but neither the official residential addresses of van der Nüll nor of Sicardsburg coincided with this address. Sicardsburg had lived in the inner city at Wipplingerstrasse 4 (conscription number 382) since 1859 at the latest; van der Nüll's official address was Coburgbastei 12 (conscription number 1191) and was also situated in the inner city. Actually, the Mariahilf house was the official residential address of August La Vigne (Lehmann, Adolph: Allgemeiner Wohnungs-Anzeiger nebst Handels- und Gewerbe-Adreßbuch der k. k. Reichshaupt- und Residenzstadt Wien und Umgebung etc., Vienna [Verlag Carl Gerold's Sohn], editions of 1859, 1860, 1861, 1864, 1865, 1867 and 1868). For the early 1840s, on the contrary, we can officially state a common address of Sicardsburg and van der Nüll: Jägerzeile (con-scription number 401) – today Praterstrasse 63 – in the Leopoldstadt published by J.: Bau-Schematismus oder: Adressbuch aller mit Bauten und Bauarbeiten sich beschäftigenden Künstler und Professionisten etc., Vienna (Verlag der Jasper'schen Buchhandlung) 1844, p. 3 – **23** – ibid. – **24** – Gugitz, Gustav: Das Wiener Kaffeehaus. Ein Stück Kultur- und Lokalgeschichte, Vienna (Verlag Jugend und Volk), 1940, p. 201 – **25** – as note 22 (for the home address Koburgbastei 12, formerly conscription no. 1191), see also: Lehmann 1864 (note 22), p. 426 – **26** – as note 15 – **27** – as note 22 – **28** – N.N.: Eduard van der Nüll, in: Fremden-Blatt (Morgenblatt), 04/04/1868, p. 1 – **29** – as note 22 – **30** – Karlmann: Siccardsburg, in: Neues Wiener Tagblatt, 06/13/1868, p. 1 – **31** – N.N.: Siccardsburg, in: Morgen-Post, 06/15/1868, p. 2 – **32** – as note 30 – **33** – Payer, Peter: "Wien bei Nacht, wie es tanzt und lacht." Stadtimage und Erotik, 1840-1930, in: Brunner, Andreas; Kreutler, Frauke; Lindinger, Michaela; Milchram, Gerhard; Nußbaumer, Martina; Sulzenbacher, Hannes (eds.): Sex in Wien. Lust. Kontrolle. Ungehorsam (Exhibition catalogue Vienna Museum), Vienna (Metroverlag), 2016, pp. 248-253, in particular p. 249 – **34** – Brunner, Andreas; Sulzenbacher, Hannes: Die verborgene schwule Topografie der Stadt, in: Brunner (note 33), pp. 260-266, in particular p. 261 – **35** – Albertina Vienna, CHA 356 – **36** – Museo Archeologico Nazionale di Napoli, inventory no. 27,874 – **37** – Saint Non, Jean Claude Richard de: Voyage Pittoresque ou Description des Royaumes de Naples et de Sicile. Second Partie du Premier Volume, Tome Second, Paris, 1782, plate 13

The Architect and the Cuirassier: Franz Heinrich Schwechten

– **1** – Baumgardt, Manfred; Dose, Ralf; Herzer, Manfred; Klein, Hans-Günter; Kokula, Ilse; Lindemann, Gesa: Magnus Hirschfeld – Leben und Werk (Exhibition catalogue), Berlin (Rosa Winkel), 1985; Wolff, Charlotte: Magnus Hirschfeld. A Portrait of a Pioneer in Sexology, London/New York (Quartet Books), 1986 – **2** – Hirschfeld, Magnus: Berlins Drittes Geschlecht (1904), Berlin (Rosa Winkel), 1991, p. 13 – **3** – Ostwald, Hans: Männliche Prostitution im kaiserlichen Berlin (1906), Berlin (Janssen), 1991, p. 21 – **4** – Dobler, Jens: Hans von Tresckow (1866-1934), in: Archiv für Polizeigeschichte, vol. 10 (1999), issue 2 (no. 28), pp. 47-52 – **5** – Tresckow, Hans von: Von Fürsten und anderen Sterblichen. Erinnerungen eines Kriminalkommissars, Berlin (Fontane & Co.), 1922 – **6** – ibid., p. 114 – **7** – Hirschfeld (note 2), p. 87 – **8** – Tresckow (note 5), p. 114 – **9** – ibid. – **10** – Zietz, Peer: Franz Heinrich Schwechten. Ein Architekt zwischen Historismus und Moderne, Stuttgart/London (Menges), 1999; Streich, Wolf Jürgen: Franz Heinrich Schwechten. 1841-1924. Bauten für Berlin, Petersberg (Imhof), 2005 – **11** – Zietz (note 10) p. 36 – **12** – ibid., p. 40

Two City Planning Officials, Two Bachelors: Fritz Schumacher and Gustav Oelsner

– **1** – Frank, Hartmut (ed.): Fritz Schumacher. Reformkultur und Moderne, Stuttgart (Hatje Cantz), 1994 – **2** – Timm, Christoph: Gustav Oelsner und das Neue Altona. Kommunale Architektur und Stadtplanung in der Weimarer Republik, Hamburg (Ernst Kabel), 1984; Dogramaci, Burcu (ed.): Gustav Oelsner Stadtplaner und Architekt der Moderne, Hamburg (Junius), 2008 – **3** – Schaefer-Lübeck, Karl (ed.): Hamburger Staatsbauten von Fritz Schumacher (2 vols.), Berlin (Der Zirkel), 1919/21; see also: Fischer, Manfred (revision): Fritz Schumacher. Hamburger Staatsbauten 1909-1919/21. Eine Bestandsaufnahme (Arbeitshefte zur Denkmalpflege in

Hamburg, Nr. 15/1), Hamburg (Christians), 1995. Zur integrierenden Wirkung des Backsteins siehe auch: Voigt, Wolfgang: Backstein als Erzieher. Gedanken über Gemeinsamkeiten in der klassischen Hamburger Architekturmoderne, in: Schädel, Dieter (Hg.): Fritz Schumacher in der Moderne. Beiträge und Ergebnisse des Fritz-Schumacher-Kolloquiums 2002 (Arbeitshefte zur Denkmalpflege in Hamburg, Nr. 22), Hamburg (Christians), 2003, S. 53-56 – **4** – So offenbarte es in hohem Alter Erich Lüth, ein enger Freund Oelsners, dem Historiker Axel Schildt im Gespräch am 23.01.1984. Für diesen Hinweis bedanke ich mich bei Axel Schildt. Zur Quellenangabe siehe: Schildt, Axel: Die Grindelhochhäuser. Eine Sozialgeschichte der ersten deutschen Wohnhochhausanlage Hamburg Grindelberg 1945-1956 (Schriftenreihe des Hamburgischen Architekturarchivs), Hamburg (Dölling und Galitz), 2007, S. 232 – **5** – zu Krupp vgl.: Hergemöller, Bernd-Ulrich: Mann für Mann. Biographisches Lexikon zur Geschichte von Freundesliebe und mannmännlicher Sexualität im deutschen Sprachraum, Hamburg (LIT), 1994, S. 448-449 – **6** – Jungblut, Peter: Famose Kerle. Eulenburg – eine wilhelminische Affäre, Hamburg (Männerschwarm), 2003 – **7** – Kayser, Werner: Fritz Schumacher. Architekt und Städtebauer. Eine Bibliographie (Arbeitshefte zur Denkmalpflege in Hamburg, Nr. 5), Hamburg (Christians), 1984 – **8** – Bartels, Olaf (Hg.): Die Architekten Langmaack. Planen und Bauen in 75 Jahren (Schriftenreihe des Hamburgischen Architekturarchivs), Hamburg (Dölling und Galitz), 1998 – **9** – Stockhausen, Tilmann von: Die Kulturwissenschaftliche Bibliothek Warburg. Architektur, Einrichtung und Organisation, Hamburg (Dölling und Galitz), 1992 – **10** – Für diesen Hinweis aus ihren Gesprächen mit türkischen Schülern Oelsners bedanke ich mich bei Burcu Dogramaci. – **11** – Lüth, Erich (Hg.): Gustav Oelsner. Porträt eines Baumeisters, Hamburg (Verlag der Werkberichte Justus Buekschmitt), 1960 – **12** – Kallmorgen, Werner: Öl, weiche Kreide und verschwommene Diktion = Architektur, in: ebd., S. 67-71, Zitat S. 70 – **13** – Lodders, Rudolf: Gustav Oelsners Werk, in: ebd., S. 83-89, Zitat S. 84 – **14** – Den Hinweis auf den Zirkel Lüth/Lodders/Oelsner gab Axel Schildt, dem Erich Lüth davon berichtete (siehe Anm. 4). – **15** – ebd. – **16** – Schildt, Axel: Max Brauer, Hamburg (Ellert & Richter), 2002 – **17** – Brauer, Max: Gustav Oelsners Altonaer Jahre, in: Lüth (Anm. 11), S. 61-66 – **18** – Briefwechsel in der Staats- und Universitätsbibliothek Hamburg, Nachlass Fritz Schumacher, XI B 14 Korrespondenz Fritz Schumacher - Gustav Oelsner – **19** – Gustav Oelsner an Conny Schumacher, 02.12.1947, Briefwechsel (Anm. 18)

Die erste deutsche Architektin und die bauende Lesbe als Zerrbild im homophoben Roman: Emilie Winkelmann und Blanka Wild

– **1** – Pepchinksi, Mary; Budde, Christina; Voigt, Wolfgang; Schmal, Peter Cachola (Hg.): Frau Architekt. Seit mehr als 100 Jahren: Frauen im Architekturberuf, Tübingen (Wasmuth), 2017 – **2** – Lippert, Hans-Georg: Emilie Winkelmann. Deutschlands erste Architektin, in: ebd., S. 79-86; Witzel, Beate: Emilie Winkelmann (1875-1951). „Ich weiß, wie man es machen könnte", in: Stiftung Stadtmuseum Berlin; Spies, Paul; Weiland, Martina (Hg.): Berlin – Stadt der Frauen. Couragiert und feminin. 20 außergewöhnliche Biografien, Berlin (Verlag M), 2016, S. 77-88 – **3** – vgl. Stratigakos, Despina: „I myself want to build": Women, Architectural Education and the Integration of Germany's Technical Colleges, in: Paedagogica Historica, Jg. 43 (2007), Ausgabe 6, S. 727-756 – **4** – vgl. www.frauenorte-brandenburg.de/index.php?article_id=99 / letzter Zugriff: 02.12.2019 – **5** – heute Ottilie-von-Hansemann-Haus, vgl. https://de.wikipedia.org/wiki/Ottilie-von-Hansemann-Haus, letzter Zugriff: 02.12.2019; Lippert (Anm. 2), S. 83 – **6** – Pepchinski, Mary: Vom Woman's Building zum Haus der Frau: Kulturexport, Typologie und das Problem der Repräsentation, 1893-1914, in: Köth, Anke; Krauskopf, Kai; Schwarting, Andreas (Hg.): Building America. Eine große Erzählung, Dresden (Thelem), 2008, S. 183-205; Lippert (Anm. 2), S. 85 – **7** – Lippert (Anm. 2), S. 85 – **8** – Scheffler, Karl: Die Frau und die Kunst, Berlin (Julius Bard), 1908, zitiert nach: Stratigakos, Despina: The Uncanny Architect: Fears of Lesbian Builders and Deviant Homes in Modern Germany, in: Heynen, Hilde; Baydar, Gulsum (Hg.): Negotiating Domesticity: Spatial Productions of Gender in Modern Architecture, Abingdon (Routledge), 2005, S. 145-161, Zitate S. 146 – **9** – Scheffler, Karl: Vom Beruf und von den Aufgaben des modernen Architekten, in: Süddeutsche Bauzeitung, Jg. 19 (1909), Ausgabe 14, S. 110 – **10** – Bartning, Otto: Sollen Damen bauen?, in: Die Welt der Frau (Gartenlaube), 1911, Ausgabe 40, S. 625 – **11** – Jessen, Peter: Die Deutsche Werkbund-Ausstellung 1914, in: Jahrbuch des Deutschen Werkbundes. Deutsche Form im Kriegsjahr. Die Ausstellung 1914, Jg. 4 (1915), S. 1-42, hier: S. 30 – **12** – Scheffler, Karl: Der neue Mensch, Leipzig (Insel-Verlag) 1932, S. 33 – **13** – ebd., S. 162 – **14** – Stratigakos (Anm. 8), S. 152-155 – **15** – Boutelle, Sara Holmes: Julia Morgan Architect, New York (Abbeville Press), 1988 – **16** – Tattelman, Ira: Architecture, in: Summers, Claude J. (Hg.): The Queer Encyclopedia of the Visual Arts, New York (Cleis Press), 2004 (Online: www.glbtqarchive.com/arts/architecture_A.pdf / letzter Zugriff: 02.12.2019)

Mein Zuhause soll nicht sein: Austen St. Barbe Harrison

– **1** – Durrell, Lawrence: Bitter Lemons, London (Faber & Faber), 1957, S. 99 – **2** – Veröffentlichtes Material zu Harrison siehe: Fuchs, Ron; Herbert, Gilbert: Representing Mandatory Palestine, Austen St. Barbe Harrison and the Representational Buildings of the British Mandate in Palestine 1922-37, in: Architectural History, Journal of the Society of Architectural Historians of Great Britain, Band 43 (2000), S. 281-333; Fuchs, Ron: Public Works in the Holy Land: Government Buildings under the British Mandate in Palestine, 1917-48, in: Campbell, Louise (Hg.): Twentieth Century Architecture And Its Histories. Millennial Volume, London (Society of Architectural Historians of Great Britain), 2000, S. 275-306; Fuchs, Ron; Herbert, Gilbert: A Colonial Portrait of Jerusalem, British Architecture in Jerusalem of the Mandate 1917-48, in: Alsayyad, Nezar (Hg.): Hybrid Urbanism: On the Identity Discourse and the Built Environment, Westpoint (Praeger Publishers), 2001, S. 81-108. Archivmaterial zu Harrison siehe: Harrisons persönliche Dokumente, die sich ursprünglich im Besitz seines Erben Dimitri Papadimos in Athen befanden. Dazu gehörte ein maschinengeschriebener Band mit persönlicher Korrespondenz, die Harrison neu abtippte [im Folgenden: Briefe]. Mappen, Fotos und einige Dokumente, die ebenfalls zu dieser Sammlung gehörten, wurden der Israel Antiquities Authority (IAA) geschenkt. Anderes Material wird in entsprechenden Akten im Public Record Office, London, und im Israelischen Staatsarchiv aufbewahrt. Siehe weitere Hinweise in: Fuchs, Herbert: Representing (s.o.) – **3** – Für einen Überblick über diese

Hamburg, Nr. 15/1), Hamburg (Christians), 1995. On the integrating effect of brick see also: Voigt, Wolfgang: Backstein als Erzieher. Gedanken über Gemeinsamkeiten in der klassischen Hamburger Architekturmoderne, in: Schädel, Dieter (ed.): Fritz Schumacher in der Moderne. Beiträge und Ergebnisse des Fritz-Schumacher-Kolloquiums 2002 (Arbeitshefte zur Denkmalpflege in Hamburg, Nr. 22), Hamburg (Christians), 2003, pp. 53-56 – 4 – This is how Erich Lüth, a close friend of Oelsner, revealed it in a conversation with historian Axel Schildt on 01/23/1984. I would like to thank Axel Schildt for this information. For reference cf. Schildt, Axel: Die Grindelhochhäuser. Eine Sozialgeschichte der ersten deutschen Wohnhochhausanlage Hamburg Grindelberg 1945-1956 (Schriftenreihe des Hamburgischen Architekturarchivs), Hamburg (Doelling und Galitz), 2007, p. 232 – 5 – On Krupp cf.: Hergemüller, Bernd-Ulrich: Mann für Mann. Biographisches Lexikon zur Geschichte von Freundesliebe und mannmännlicher Sexualität im deutschen Sprachraum, Hamburg (LIT), 1994, pp. 448-449 – 6 – Jungblut, Peter: Famose Kerle. Eulenburg – eine wilhelminische Affäre, Hamburg (Männerschwarm), 2003 – 7 – Kayser, Werner: Fritz Schumacher. Architekt und Städtebauer. Eine Bibliografie (Arbeitshefte zur Denkmalpflege in Hamburg, Nr. 5), Hamburg (Christians), 1984 – 8 – Bartels, Olaf (ed.): Die Architekten Langmaack. Planen und Bauen in 75 Jahren (Schriftenreihe des Hamburgischen Architekturarchivs), Hamburg (Doelling und Galitz), 1998 – 9 – Stockhausen, Tilmann von: Die Kulturwissenschaftliche Bibliothek Warburg. Architektur, Einrichtung und Organisation, Hamburg (Dölling und Galitz), 1992 – 10 – I would like to thank Burcu Dogramaci for this reference from her conversations with Oelsner's Turkish pupils. – 11 – Lüth, Erich (ed.): Gustav Oelsner. Porträt eines Baumeisters, Hamburg (Verlag der Werkberichte Justus Buekschmitt), 1960 – 12 – Kallmorgen, Werner: Öl, weiche Kreide und verschwommene Diktion, Architektur, in: ibid., pp. 67-71, quotation p. 70 – 13 – Lodders, Rudolf: Gustav Oelsner|s Werk, in: ibid., pp. 83-89, quotation p. 84 – 14 – The reference to the Lüth/Lodders/Oelsner compass was made by Axel Schildt, who learned about it from Erich Lüth (note 4). – 15 – ibid. – 16 – Schildt, Axel: Max Brauer, Hamburg (Ellert & Richter), 2002 – 17 – Brauer, Max: Gustav Oelsners Altonaer Jahre, in: Lüth (note 11), pp. 61-66 – 18 – Correspondence in the Hamburg State and University Library, Fritz Schumacher Estate, XI B 14 Correspondence Fritz Schumacher – Gustav Oelsner – 19 – Gustav Oelsner to Conny Schumacher, 12/02/1947, correspondence (note 18)

The First German Female Architect and the Lesbian Builder as a Caricature in a Homophobic Novel: Emilie Winkelmann and Blanka Wild

– 1 – Pepchinksi, Mary; Budde, Christina; Voigt, Wolfgang; Schmal, Peter Cachola (eds.): Frau Architekt. Seit mehr als 100 Jahren: Frauen im Architekturberuf, Tübingen (Wasmuth), 2017 – 2 – Lippert, Hans-Georg: Emilie Winkelmann. Deutschlands erste Architektin, in: ibid., pp. 79-86; Witzel, Beate: Emilie Winkelmann (1875-1951). "Ich weiß, wie man es machen könnte," in: Stiftung Stadtmuseum Berlin; Spies, Paul; Weiland, Martina (eds.): Berlin – Stadt der Frauen. Couragiert und feminin. 20 außergewöhnliche Biografien, Berlin (Verlag M), 2016, pp. 77-88 – 3 – cf. Stratigakos, Despina: "I myself want to build." Women, Architectural Education and the Integration of Germany's Technical Colleges, in: Paedagogica Historica, vol. 43 (2007), issue 6, pp. 727-756 – 4 – cf. www.frauenortebrandenburg.de/index.php?article_id=99, last accessed on 12/02/2019 – 5 – today Ottilie-von-Hansemann-Haus, cf. https://de.wikipedia.org/wiki/Ottilie-von-Hansemann-Haus / last accessed on 12/02/2019; Lippert (note 2), p. 83 – 6 – Pepchinski, Mary: Vom Woman's Building zum Haus der Frau. Kulturexport, Typologie und das Problem der Repräsentation, 1893-1914, in: Köth, Anke; Krauskopf, Kai; Schwarting, Andreas (eds.): Building America. Eine große Erzählung, Dresden (Thelem), 2008, pp. 183-205; Lippert (note. 2), p. 85 – 7 – Lippert (note 2), p. 85 – 8 – Scheffler, Karl: Die Frau und die Kunst, Berlin (Julius Bard), 1908, quoted from: Stratigakos, Despina: The Uncanny Architect: Fears of Lesbian Builders and Deviant Homes in Modern Germany, in: Heynen, Hilde; Baydar, Gulsum (eds.): Negotiating Domesticity: Spatial Productions of Gender in Modern Architecture, Abingdon (Routledge), 2005, pp. 145-161, quotations p. 146 – 9 – Scheffler, Karl: Vom Beruf und von den Aufgaben des modernen Architekten, in: Süddeutsche Bauzeitung, vpl. 19 (1909), issue 14, p. 110 – 10 – Bartning, Otto: Sollen Damen bauen? in: Die Welt der Frau (Gartenlaube), issue 40, 1911, p. 625 – 11 – Jessen, Peter: Die Deutsche Werkbund-Ausstellung 1914, in: Jahrbuch des Deutschen Werkbundes. Deutsche Form im Kriegsjahr. Die Ausstellung 1914, vol. 4 (1915), pp. 1-42, here: p. 30 – 12 – Scheffler, Karl: Der neue Mensch, Leipzig (Insel-Verlag) 1932, p. 33 – 13 – ibid., p. 162 – 14 – Stratigakos (note 8), pp. 152-155 – 15 – Boutelle, Sara Holmes: Julia Morgan Architect, New York (Abbeville Press), 1988 – 16 – Tattelman, Ira: Architecture, in: Summers, Claude J. (ed.): The Queer Encyclopedia of the Visual Arts, New York (Cleis Press), 2004 (online: www.glbtqarchive.com/arts/architecture_pdf / last accessed on 12/02/2019)

My Home Is Not To Be: Austen St. Barbe Harrison

– 1 – Durrell, Lawrence: Bitter Lemons, London (Faber & Faber), 1957, p. 99 – 2 – For published material on Harrison cf. Fuchs, Ron; Herbert, Gilbert: Representing Mandatory Palestine: Austen St. Barbe Harrison and the Representational Buildings of the British Mandate in Palestine 1922-37, in: Architectural History, Journal of the Society of Architectural Historians of Great Britain, vol. 43 (2000), pp. 281-333; Fuchs, Ron: Public Works in the Holy Land: Government Buildings under the British Mandate in Palestine, 1917-48, in: Campbell, Louise (ed.): Twentieth Century Architecture and Its Histories, Millennial Volume, London (Society of Architectural Historians of Great Britain), 2000, pp. 275-306; Fuchs, Ron; Herbert, Gilbert: A Colonial Portrait of Jerusalem. British Architecture in Jerusalem of the Mandate 1917-48, in: Alsayyad, Nezar (ed.): Hybrid Urbanism, Westpoint (Praeger Publishers), 2001, pp. 81-108. For archival sources cf. Harrison's personal documents originally in possession of his heir, Dimitri Papadimos, Athens. This included a typescript volume of personal correspondence that Harrison retyped [hereafter: Letters]. Portfolios, photographs, and some documents belonging to this collection were donated to the Israel Antiquities Authority (IAA). Other material is kept in relevant files in the Public Record Office, London, and Israel State Archives. See further references in: Fuchs/Herbert (note 2). – 3 – Survey of these projects in: Fuchs, Ron: Austen St. Barbe Harrison. A British Architect in the Holy Land, D. Sc. Dissertation (Technion – Israel Institute of Technology, Faculty of Architecture & Town Planning), 1992 – 4 – Most of these projects were designed in partnership

Projekte siehe: Fuchs, Ron: Austen St. Barbe Harrison, a British Architect in the Holy Land, Dissertation (Technion – Israel Institute of Technology, Faculty of Architecture & Town Planning), 1992 – **4** – Die meisten dieser Projekte wurden in Partnerschaft mit Pearce Hubbard und Thomas S. Barnes entworfen, wobei Harrison die dominierende Figur des Trios bildete. Hubbard studierte Architektur an der Universität Liverpool (unter Charles Reilly) und arbeitete in den 1930er-Jahren in Palästina mit dem Architekten Clifford Holliday zusammen. Harrison kannte Hubbard seit ihrer gemeinsamen Zeit in Jerusalem. Zu Hubbard siehe: Nachruf, in: The Times, 13.09.1965; Reilly, Charles: Scaffolding in the Sky, a Semi-Architectural Autobiography, London (Routledge), 1938, S. 209-211; Durrell (Anm. 1). Zu Barnes siehe: Nachruf, in: The Times (?), 02.04.1968 (Zeitungsausschnitt im IAA). Offenbar war er für die finanziellen Belange der Partnerschaft verantwortlich. – **5** – Man könnte von einem „Kolonialen Regionalismus" sprechen. Zu Harrisons Arbeiten in Palästina siehe: Anm. 2; vgl. auch: Metcalf, Thomas R.: An Imperial Vision, Indian Architecture and Britain's Raj, Berkeley (University of California Press), 1989 – **6** – vgl. den entsprechenden Beitrag zu Charles Robert Ashbee in diesem Band – **7** – Seine abgetippten Briefe sind jedoch eine wichtige Quelle. Siehe dazu: Anm. 2 – **8** – Durrell (Anm. 1), S. 98 – **9** – Brief von Harrison an Bomberg, 15.01.1932, Tate Gallery – **10** – Brief an Reiner, 12.08.1947, Briefe (Anm. 2) (Reiner war Wissenschaftler und wanderte 1922 nach Palästina ein, wo er als Bauingenieur beim Public Works Department arbeitete.) – **11** – Der Vorfall wird berichtet in: Hoffman, Adina: Till We Have Built Jerusalem, New York (Farrar, Straus and Giroux), 2017, S. 128, mit folgender Quellenangabe: Erich und Luise Mendelsohn Papers, Getty Research Institute, Los Angeles, EM/LM 33/3, 294-295 – **12** – Brief an seine Mutter, 22.01.1941, Briefe (Anm. 2) Zu John Gayer-Anderson siehe: Foxcroft, Louise: Gayer-Anderson, the Life and Afterlife of the Irish Pasha, Kairo (American University in Cairo Press), 2016 – **13** – Durch den Kriegsbeginn wurde das Studium unterbrochen. – **14** – Einige seiner Fotografien dokumentieren Harrisons gesellschaftlichen Kreis. Das Papadimos-Archiv befindet sich im Besitz der National Bank of Greece Cultural Foundation (MIET) in Athen. – **15** – In Palästina wurde Homosexualität 1936, kurz vor Harrisons Abreise, kriminalisiert. Siehe dazu: Han, Enze; O'Mahoney, Joseph: British Colonialism and the Criminalization of Homosexuality, London (Routledge), 2018. Die Autoren zeigen in ihrem Buch, wie sich die Kriminalisierung von Homosexualität in den postkolonialen Ländern als „dunkles Erbe" der britischen Kolonialherrschaft erweisen sollte. – **16** – Brief an seine Mutter, 12.01.1942, Briefe (Anm. 2) – **17** – Brief an Reiner, 02.12.1946, Briefe (Anm. 2) – **18** – Briefe (Anm. 2)

Die Jagd auf schwule Architekturlehrer – drei amerikanische Fälle: Bruce Goff, Charles Moore, Lionel Pries

– **1** – De Long, David Gilson: Bruce Goff. Toward Absolute Architecture. Cambridge (The MIT Press), 1988 – **2** – ebd., S. 135f. – **3** – Scanian, Joe: No Place Like Home. The Architecture of Bruce Goff, in: Frieze, Ausgabe 26, (Januar/Februar) 1996 (Online: www.frieze.com/article/no-place-home-0 / letzter Zugriff: 03.11.2019) – **4** – Otero-Pailos, Jorge: Architecture's Historical Turn. Phenomenology and the Rise of the Postmodern, Minneapolis (University of Minnesota Press), 2010, S. 100 – **5** – Über Moores Lehre in Princeton siehe das Kapitel: LSDesign, in: ebd., S. 101ff. – **6** – zitiert nach: ebd., S. 108 („Single at 35, Moore did not seem stable or mature in respect to his relationships with students, and while brilliant, was an uncertain quantity personally for the long pull.") – **7** – zitiert nach: ebd., S. 109 („... to avoid a climate too often associated with art centers.") – **8** – Ochsner, Jeffrey Karl: Lionel H. Pries, Architect, Artist, Educator: From Arts and Crafts to Modern Architecture, Seattle (University of Washington Press), 2007 – **9** – ebd., S. 288f. – **10** – ebd., S. 291 – **11** – vgl. den entsprechenden Beitrag in diesem Band

Nur die Sonne war Zeuge: Barry Dierks und Eric Sawyer

– **1** – Fray, François: La Clientèle de l'Architecte Barry Dierks sur la Côte d'Azur, in: In Situ. Revue des Patrimoines, Ausgabe 4, 2004 (Online: www.journals.openedition.org/insitu/2131 / letzter Zugriff: 26.10.2019) – **2** – Das gemeinsame Leben von Barry Dierks und Eric Sawyer an der Côte d'Azur hat die Schriftstellerin Maureen Emerson hinlänglich erforscht. Ihr Buch *Riviera Dreaming* bildet in weiten Teilen die Grundlage für die folgende Darstellung der Biographien. (Emerson, Maureen: Riviera Dreaming. Love and War on the Côte d'Azur, London (Bloomsburry), 2018) – **3** – Zwischen 2012 und 2014 war das Stuttgarter Architekturbüro 4a Architekten mit der Sanierung des Hauses beauftragt. Das Gästebuch diente den Architekten als Arbeitsgrundlage. Für die Zurverfügungstellung einer digitalen Kopie danke ich den Architekten Matthias Burkart und Ernst Ulrich Tillmanns. – **4** – Gloeden, Wilhelm von: Taormina. Mit einem Text von Ulrich Pohlmann, München (Schirmer/Mosel), 1998 – **5** – Briolle, Cécile; Fuzibet, Agnès; Monnier, Gérard: Rob Mallet-Stevens La Villa Noailles (Monographies d'Architecture), Paris (Éditions Parenthèses), 1990 – **6** – Wang, Wilfried; Adam, Peter (Hg.): Eileen Gray, E.1027, 1926-1929 (O'Neil Ford Monograph Series, Vol. 7), Tübingen (Wasmuth), 2018 – **7** – Bachmann, Wolfgang (Hg.): 4a Architekten. Orte setzen, Räume bilden, Licht geben, Farbe bekennen, Zürich (Parkbooks), 2015

Sissie Architects: John Seely und Paul Paget

– **1** – Eine kurze Darstellung der Lebensgeschichte von John Seely und Paul Paget ist auf der Internetseite der Organisation English Heritage, die sich um die Verwaltung aller in Staatsbesitz befindlichen Denkmäler und archäologischen Stätten Englands kümmert, abrufbar. (www.english-heritage.org.uk/learn/histories/lgbtq-history/seely-and-paget-at-eltham-palace / letzter Zugriff: 08.11.2019) – **2** – Zur Geschichte von Eltham Palace siehe: www.english-heritage.org.uk/visit/places/eltham-palace-and-gardens/history / letzter Zugriff: 08.11.2019 – **3** – www.stevenagechurch.org / letzter Zugriff: 10.11.2019 – **4** – Rule, Fiona: The Oldest House in London,

with Pearce Hubbard and Thomas S. Barnes, with Harrison as the dominant figure. Hubbard studied at the architectural school at Liverpool University (under Charles Reilly). He worked in Palestine with architect Clifford Holliday in the 1930s. Harrison knew Hubbard since their Jerusalem days. On Hubbard see: Obituary, in: The Times, 09/13/1965; Reilly, Charles: Scaffolding in the Sky. A Semi-Architectural Autobiography, London (Routledge), 1938, pp. 209-211; Durrell 1957 (note 1). For Barnes cf. Obituary, in: The Times (?), 04/02/1968, newspaper cutting IAA. Apparently he was responsible for the partnership's financial dealings. – 5 – "Colonial Regionalism" this may be dubbed. For Harrison's work in Palestine see note 2; cf. Metcalf, Thomas R.: An Imperial Vision. Indian Architecture and Britain's Raj, Berkeley (University of California Press), 1989 – 6 – cf. the corresponding essay on Charles Robert Ashbee in this book – 7 – However, his retyped letters are an important source. See note 2 – 8 – Durrell 1957 (note 1), p. 98 – 9 – Letter, Harrison to Bomberg, 01/15/1932, Tate Gallery – 10 – Letter to Reiner, 08/12/1947, Letters (note 2) (Reiner was a scientist who immigrated to Palestine in 1922, and worked as civil engineer in the Public Works Department.) – 11 – The incident is reported in Hoffman, Adina: Till We Have Built Jerusalem, New York (Farrar, Straus and Giroux), 2017, p. 128, with source given as Erich and Luise Mendelsohn Papers, Getty Research Institute, Los Angeles, EM/LM 33/3, 294-295 – 12 – Letter to his mother, 01/22/1941, Letters (note 2). On John Gayer-Anderson cf. Foxcroft, Louise: Gayer-Anderson. The Life and Afterlife of the Irish Pasha, Cairo (American University in Cairo Press), 2016 – 13 – Though eventually his studies were interrupted by the War. – 14 – Some on his photographs document Harrison's social circle. Papadimos archive at National Bank of Greece Cultural Foundation (MIET), Athens – 15 – In Palestine criminalization of homosexuality was introduced in 1936 just before his departure. See: Han, Enze; O'Mahoney, Joseph: British Colonialism and the Criminalization of Homosexuality, London (Routledge), 2018. The authors demonstrate how criminalization of homosexuality proved "a dark legacy" of British colonial rule in post-colonial countries. – 16 – Letter to his mother, 01/12/1942, Letters (note 2) – 17 – Letter to Reiner, 12/02/1946, Letters (note 2) – 18 – Letters (note 2)

The Hunt for Gay Architecture Professors - Three American Cases: Bruce Goff, Charles Moore, Lionel Pries

– 1 – De Long, David Gilson: Bruce Goff. Toward Absolute Architecture. Cambridge (The MIT Press), 1988 – 2 – ibid., pp. 135ff. – 3 – Scanian, Joe: No Place Like Home. The Architecture of Bruce Goff, in: Frieze, issue 26, 1996 (January/February) (Online: www.frieze.com/article/no-place-home-0 / last accessed on 11/03/2019) – 4 – Otero-Pailos, Jorge: Architecture's Historical Turn. Phenomenology and the Rise of the Postmodern, Minneapolis (University of Minnesota Press), 2010, p. 100 – 5 – Regarding Moore's teaching in Princeton cf. the chapter LSDesign, in: ibid., pp. 101ff. – 6 – quoted from: ibid., p. 108 – 7 – quoted from: ibid., p. 109 – 8 – Ochsner, Jeffrey Karl: Lionel H. Pries. Architect, Artist, Educator: From Arts and Crafts to Modern Architecture, Seattle (University of Washington Press), 2007 – 9 – ibid., pp. 288f. – 10 – ibid., p. 291 – 11 – cf. the corresponding contribution in this book

The Sun Was the Only Witness: Barry Dierks and Eric Sawyer

– 1 – Fray, François: La Clientèle de l'Architecte Barry Dierks sur la Côte d'Azur, in: In Situ. Revue des Pat-rimoines, issue 4, 2004 (online: www.journals.openedition.org/insitu/2131 / last accessed on 10/26/2019) – 2 – The Life of Barry Dierks and Eric Sawyer on the Côte d'Azur has been sufficiently explored by the writer Maureen Emerson. Her book Riviera Dreaming is to a large extent the basis for the following biographies (Emerson, Maureen: Riviera Dreaming. Love and War on the Côte d'Azur, London (Bloomsbury), 2018) – 3 – Between 2012 and 2014, the Stuttgart-based architectural firm 4a Architekten was commissioned with the renovation of the building. The architects used the guest book as a basis for their work. I would like to thank the architects Matthias Burkart and Ernst Ulrich Tillmanns for providing a digital copy. – 4 – Gloeden, Wilhelm von: Taormina. Mit einem Text von Ulrich Pohlmann, Munich (Schirmer/Mosel), 1998 – 5 – Briolle, Cécile; Fuzibet, Agnès; Monnier, Gérard: La Villa Noailles: Rob Mallet-Stevens (Monographies d'Architecture), Paris (éditions Parenthèses), 1990 – 6 – Wang, Wilfried; Adam, Peter (eds.): Eileen Gray, E.1027, 1926-1929 (O'Neil Ford Monograph Series, vol. 7), Tübingen (Wasmuth), 2018 – 7 – Bachmann, Wolfgang (ed.): 4a Architekten. Orte setzen, Räume bilden, Licht geben, Farbe bekennen, Zurich (Parkbooks), 2015

Sissy Architects: John Seely and Paul Paget

– 1 – A brief account of the lives of John Seely and Paul Paget is available on the website of English Heritage, the organization which is responsible for managing all state-owned monuments and archaeological sites in England (www.englishheritage.org.uk/learn/histories/lgbtq-history/seely-and-paget-at-eltham-palace / last accessed on 11/08/2019) – 2 – For the history of Eltham Palace cf. www.english-heritage.org.uk/visit/places/eltham-palace-and-gardens/history / last accessed on 11/08/2019 – 3 – www.stevenagechurch.org / last accessed on 11/10/2019 – 4 – Rule, Fiona: The Oldest House in London, Cheltenham (The History Press), 2017 – 5 – www.london-walking-tours.co.uk/secret-london/sailors-home-coming-

Cheltenham (The History Press), 2017 – **5** – www.london-walking-tours.co.uk/secret-london/sailors-home-coming-window.htm / letzter Zugriff: 09.11.2019 – **6** – Aslet, Clive: An Interview with the late Paul Paget 1901-1985, in: The Thirties Society Journal, Ausgabe 6 (1987), S. 16-25 – **7** – ebd., S. 22 („The houses were so close that the neighbours across the alleyway could see us carving the Sunday joint – it was so close that you almost felt as though you should hand a plate across.") – **8** – ebd., S. 16 („It was just the marriage of two minds, I mean we became virtually one person.") – **9** – The Shack steht auf dem Anwesen von Mottistone Manor und befindet sich im Besitz des National Trust (for Places of Historic Interest or Natural Beauty). Das Anwesen und The Shack sind öffentlich zugänglich. (www.nationaltrust.org.uk/mottistone-gardens/features/the-shack-a-country-retreat / letzter Zugriff: 09.11.2019) – **10** – vgl. Brady, Sean: Masculinity and Male Homosexuality in Britain 1861-1913, London (Palgrave Macmillan), 2005 – **11** – Brittain-Catlin, Timothy J.: Bleak Houses. Disappointment and Failure in Architecture, Cambridge (The MIT Press), 2014, S. 100 („A strong partnership between two teenagers who wanted to grow up together and do things together.") – **12** – ebd., S. 97-102 – **13** – ebd., S. 100 – **14** – ebd., S. 101 – **15** – ebd., S. 101 („Most were bullied and lonely people, and their response to their condition may have been to try to design themselves into a more beautiful world: that is, a sentimental one.") – **16** – Das Haus steht heute unter Denkmalschutz. (www.historicengland.org.uk/listing/the-list/list-entry/1373510 / letzter Zugriff: 10.11.2019) – **17** – Brittain-Catlin (Anm. 11), S. 100

Eine Villa für zwei Junggesellen: St. Ann's Court von Raymond McGrath

– **1** – O'Donovan, Donal: God's Architect: A Life of Raymond McGrath, Wicklow (Kilbride Books), 1995; Biografische Kurzdarstellungen liefern auch: Buckman, David: Artists in Britain since 1945, Band 2 (M-Z), Bristol (Art Dictionaries Ltd.), 1998; Drew, Philip: Flashback. Raymond McGrath in Britain, in: Architecture Australia, Ausgabe 5, 2000 (Online: www.architectureau.com/articles/flashback-raymond-mcgrath-in-britain / letzter Zugriff: 29.10.2019) – **2** – Seinen ersten Auftrag erhielt Raymond McGrath von dem Historiker und Universitätsprofessor Mansfield Forbes. Für dessen Wohnhaus in Cambridge entwarf der Architekt eine spektakuläre Inneneinrichtung im Art-Deco-Stil, die noch heute als frühes Meisterwerk der Moderne in Großbritannien gefeiert wird. Das Haus ist unter dem Namen „Finella" bekannt. Aufgrund der Homosexualität des Bauherrn und der außergewöhnlichen Gestaltung des Hauses, hätte „Finella" durchaus auch einen eigenen Beitrag in diesem Sammelband verdient. Es sei an dieser Stelle aber auf die entsprechende Studie von Elisabth Darling verwiesen. (Darling, Elisabeth: Finella, Mansfield Forbes, Raymond McGrath, and Modernist Architecture in Britain, in: Journal of British Studies, Ausgabe 50, 2011, S. 125-155) – **3** – Hines, Mark: The Story of Broadcasting House. Home of the BBC, London (Merrell Publishers), 2008 – **4** – Die Liebesgeschichte von Gerald L. Schlesinger und Christopher Tunnard, die hinter dem Bau des Hauses steckt, wurde erstmals durch das von der staatlichen Denkmalpflegebehörde, Historic England, und der Leeds Beckett University initiierte Programm Pride of Place dokumentiert und 2016 öffentlich bekannt gemacht. (www.historicengland.org.uk/whats-new/news/england-queer-history-recognised-recorded-celebrated / letzter Zugriff: 29.10.2019) – **5** – Powers, Alan: Oliver Hill. Architect and Lover of Life, 1887-1968, London (Mouton Publications), 1989 – **6** – Eine ausführliche Beschreibung von Haus und Anwesen findet sich in der Denkmalbeschreibung von Historic England. (www.historicengland.org.uk/listing/the-list/list-entry/1260122 / letzter Zugriff: 29.10.2019) – **7** – vgl. Brady, Sean: Masculinity and Male Homosexuality in Britain 1861-1913, London (Palgrave Macmillan), 2005 – **8** – vgl. Cook, Matt: Queer Domesticities. Homosexuality and Home Life in Twentieth-Century London, London (Palgrave Macmillan), 2014; Potvin, John: Bachelors of a Different Sort. Queer Aesthetics, Material Culture and the Modern Interior in Britain, Manchester (Manchester University Press), 2015 – **9** – Tunnard, Christopher: Gardens in the Modern Landscape, London (The Architectural Press), 1938 – **10** – Jacques, David; Woudstra, Jan: Landscape Modernism Renounced. The Career of Christopher Tunnard (1910-1979), London (Routledge), 2009 – **11** – Aktuell steht das Haus abermals zum Verkauf. Die architektur-affine Immobilienplattform The Modern House hat dazu ein umfassendes Portfolio von St. Ann's Court zusammengestellt. (www.themodernhouse.com/sales-list/st-anns-hill / letzter Zugriff: 29.10.2019) – **12** – Historic England (Hg.): Pride of Place. A Guide to Understanding and Protecting Lesbian, Gay, Bisexual, Transgender and Queer (LGBTQ) Heritage, London (Historic England), 2016

Amüsante und weniger amüsante Erlebnisse: Alfred Roth

– **1** – Deutscher Werkbund (Hg.): Bau und Wohnung, Stuttgart (Fritz Wedekind & Co.), 1927; Kirsch, Karin: Die Weißenhofsiedlung, Stuttgart (DVA), 1987 – **2** – Roth, Alfred: Zwei Wohnhäuser von Le Corbusier und P. Jeanneret, Stuttgart (Fritz Wedekind & Co.), 1927 – **3** – Le Corbusier an Richard Döcker, 25. April 1927, zitiert in: Roth, Alfred: Amüsante Erlebnisse eines Architekten, Zürich (Ammann), 1988, S. 23 – **4** – Roth, Alfred: Architect of Continuity / Architekt der Kontinuität. Introduction by Stanislaus von Moos / Einführung von Stanislaus von Moos, Zürich (Waser), 1985 – **5** – Landeshauptstadt Stuttgart und Wüstenrot Stiftung (Hg.): Weißenhofmuseum im Haus Le Corbusier. Katalog zur Ausstellung, Stuttgart (Karl Krämer), 2008 – **6** – Rüegg, Arthur: Ein Hauptwerk des neuen Bauens in Zürich: Die Doldertalhäuser 1932-1936, Zürich (gta), 1996 – **7** – Roth (Anm. 3), S. 102f. – **8** – Moos, Stanislaus von: Alfred Roth zum Gedenken, in: Neue Zürcher Zeitung, 24./25. Oktober 1998

Dreischeibenhaus und Schloss: Helmut Hentrich

– **1** – Hitchcock, Henry-Russell: HPP Hentrich-Petschnigg & Partner, Düsseldorf (Econ-Verlag), 1973, S. IX – **2** – Burchard, John: The Voice of the Phoenix. Postwar Architecture in Germany, Cambridge (MIT Press), 1966, S. 144 – **3** – Hentrich, Helmut; Dressel, Hans J.: Kasteel Groot Buggenum. Biografie eines Hauses – Biography of a House, Köln (DuMont), 1992 – **4** – Tünkers, Sabine: Hentrich, Heuser, Petschnigg 1927-1955, Weimar (VDG), 2000 – **5** – Pehnt, Wolfgang; Schirren, Matthias (Hg.): Hans Poelzig. Architekt

window.htm / last accessed on 11/09/2019 – **6** – Aslet, Clive: An Interview with the late Paul Paget 1901-1985, in: The Thirties Society Journal, vol. 6 (1987), pp. 16-25 – **7** – ibid., p. 22 ("The houses were so close that the neighbor's across the alleyway could see us carving the Sunday joint – it was so close that you almost felt as though you should hand a plate across.") – **8** – ibid., p. 16 ("It was just the marriage of two minds, I mean we became virtually one person.") – **9** – The Shack is located on the Mottistone Manor estate and is owned by the National Trust (for Places of Historic Interest or Natural Beauty). The estate and The Shack are open to the public (www.nationaltrust.org.uk/mottistone-gardens/features/the-shack-a-country-retreat / last accessed on 11/09/2019) – **10** – cf. Brady, Sean: Masculinity and Male Homosexuality in Britain 1861-1913, London (Palgrave Macmillan), 2005 – **11** – Brittain-Catlin, Timothy J.: Bleak Houses. Disappointment and Failure in Architecture, Cambridge (The MIT Press), 2014, p. 100 – **12** – ibid., pp. 97-102 – **13** – ibid., p. 100 – **14** – ibid., p. 101 – **15** – ibid., p. 101 ("Most were bullied and lonely people, and their response to their condition may have been to try to design themselves into a more beautiful world: that is, a sentimental one.") – **16** – Today the house is under a preservation order (www.historicengland.org.uk/listing/the-list/list-entry/1373510 / last accessed on 11/10/2019) – **17** – Brittain-Catlin (note 11), p. 100

A Mansion For Two Bachelors: St Ann's Court by Raymond McGrath

– **1** – O'Donovan, Donal: God's Architect: A Life of Raymond McGrath, Wicklow (Kilbride Books), 1995; Brief biographic accounts are supplied as well by: Buckman, David: Artists in Britain since 1945, vol. 2 (M-Z), Bristol (Art Dictionaries Ltd.), 1998; Drew, Philip: Flashback. Raymond McGrath in Britain, in: Architecture Australia, issue 5, 2000 (online: www.architectureau.com/articles/flashback-raymond-mcgrath-in-britain / last accessed on 10/29/2019) – **2** – Raymond McGrath received his first commission from the historian and university professor Mansfield Forbes. For the latter's home in Cambridge, the architect designed a spectacular interior furnishing in Art Deco style which is today still celebrated as an early masterwork of modernism in Great Britain. The house is known by the name Finella. Due to the homosexuality of the client and the extraordinary design of the house, Finella would definitely have merited a contribution in this collection. Attention should, however, be drawn to a respective study by Elisabeth Darling (Darling, Elisabeth: Finella, Mansfield Forbes, Raymond McGrath, and Modernist Architecture in Britain, in: Journal of British Studies, vol. 50 (2011), pp. 125-155) – **3** – Hines, Mark: The Story of Broadcasting House. Home of the BBC, London (Merrell Publishers), 2008 – **4** – The love story of Gerald L. Schlesinger and Christopher Tunnard which is behind the construction of the house was first documented and made public in 2016 by the Pride of Place programme initiated by the government monument preservation department, Historic England, and Leeds Beckett University (www.historicengland.org.uk/whats-new/news/england-queer-history-recognisedre-corded-celebrated / last accessed on 10/29/2019) – **5** – Powers, Alan: Oliver Hill. Architect and Lover of Life, 1887-1968, London (Mouton Publications), 1989 – **6** – An extensive account of the house and the estate is found in the description of monuments of Historic England (www.historicengland.org.uk/listing/the-list/list-entry/1260122 / last accessed on 10/29/2019) – **7** – cf. Brady, Sean: Masculinity and Male Homosexuality in Britain 1861-1913, London (Palgrave Macmillan), 2005 – **8** – cf. Cook, Matt: Queer Domesticities. Homosexuality and Home Life in Twentieth-Century London, London (Palgrave Macmillan), 2014; Potvin, John: Bachelors of a Different Sort. Queer Aesthetics, Material Culture and the Modern Interior in Britain, Manchester (Manchester University Press), 2015 – **9** – Tunnard, Christopher: Gardens in the Modern Landscape, London (The Architectural Press), 1938 – **10** – Jacques, David; Woudstra, Jan: Landscape Modernism Renounced. The Career of Christopher Tunnard (1910-1979), London (Routledge), 2009 – **11** – The house is currently for sale once more. The real-estate platform The Modern House with an affinity to architecture has compiled a comprehensive portfolio on St Ann's Court (www.themodernhouse.com/sales-list/st-anns-hill / last accessed on 10/29/2019) – **12** – Historic England (ed.): Pride of Place. A Guide to Understanding and Protecting Lesbian, Gay, Bisexual, Transgender and Queer (LGBTQ) Heritage, London (Historic England), 2016

Amusing and Less Amusing Experiences: Alfred Roth

– **1** – Deutscher Werkbund (ed.): Bau und Wohnung, Stuttgart (Fritz Wedekind & Co.), 1927; Kirsch, Karin: Die Weißenhofsiedlung, Stuttgart (DVA), 1987 – **2** – Roth, Alfred: Zwei Wohnhäuser von Le Corbusier und P. Jeanneret, Stuttgart (Fritz Wedekind & Co.), 1927 – **3** – Le Corbusier to Richard Döcker, 25th April 1927, quoted in: Roth, Alfred: Amüsante Erlebnisse eines Architekten, Zurich (Ammann), 1988, p. 23 – **4** – Roth, Alfred: Architect of Continuity / Architekt der Kontinuität. Introduction by Stanislaus von Moos / Einführung von Stanislaus von Moos, Zurich (Waser), 1985 – **5** – Landeshauptstadt Stuttgart und Wüstenrot Stiftung (eds.): Weißenhofmuseum im Haus Le Corbusier. Catalogue for the exhibition, Stuttgart (Karl Kraemer), 2008 – **6** – Rüegg, Arthur: Ein Hauptwerk des neuen Bauens in Zürich: Die Doldertalhäuser 1932-1936, Zürich (gta), 1996 – **7** – Roth (note 3), pp. 102f. – **8** – Moos, Stanislaus von: Alfred Roth zum Gedenken, in: Neue Zürcher Zeitung, 24th/25th October 1998

Dreischeibenhaus and Castle: Helmut Hentrich

– **1** – Hitchcock, Henry-Russell: HPP Hentrich-Petschnigg & Partner, Düsseldorf (Econ Verlag), 1973, p. IX – **2** – Burchard, John: The Voice of the Phoenix. Postwar Architecture in Germany, Cambridge (MIT Press), 1966, p. 144 – **3** – Hentrich, Helmut; Dressel, Hans J.: Kasteel Groot Buggenum. Biografie eines Hauses / Biography of a House, Cologne (DuMont), 1992 – **4** – Tünkers, Sabine: Hentrich, Heuser, Petschnigg 1927-1955, Weimar (VDG), 2000 – **5** – Pehnt, Wolfgang; Schirren, Matthias (eds.): Hans Poelzig. Architekt Lehrer

Lehrer Künstler, Stuttgart (DVA), 2007 – **6** – Hentrich, Helmut: Bauzeit. Aufzeichnungen aus dem Leben eines Architekten, Düsseldorf (Droste-Verlag), 1995 – **7** – ebd., S. 19 – **8** – ebd., S. 24 – **9** – ebd., S. 233 – **10** – ebd., S. 237 – **11** – ebd., S. 245 – **12** – ebd., S. 274 – **13** – ebd., S. 148 – **14** – ebd., S. 178 – **15** – ebd., S. 93 – **16** – Brief Friedrich Tamms an Helmut Hentrich, 12.04.1933, in: Nachlass Hentrich, Akademie der Künste, Berlin – **17** – Durth, Werner: Düsseldorf: Demonstration der Modernität, in: Beyme, Klaus von; Durth, Werner; Gutschow, Niels; Nerdinger, Winfried; Topfstedt, Thomas (Hg.): Neue Städte aus Ruinen. Deutscher Städtebau der Nachkriegszeit, München (Prestel-Verlag), 1992, S. 231-250 – **18** – vgl. die entsprechenden Beiträge in diesem Band

Durch die Kollegen gerettet: Friedrich Wilhelm Kraemer

– **1** – Wilhelm, Karin; Gisbertz, Olaf; Jessen-Klingenberg, Detelf; Schmedding, Anne (Hg.): Gesetz und Freiheit. Der Architekt Friedrich Wilhelm Kraemer (1907-1990), Berlin (Jovis), 2007 – **2** – Gerkan, Meinhard von: Erinnerungen, in: ebd., S. 111-113 – **3** – Wilhelm (Anm. 1), S. 13 – **4** – Gespräch des Autors mit dem Zeitzeugen Helge Bofinger (1940-2018), Architekt und Kraemer-Schüler, geführt am 20.12.2009 – **5** – ebd. – **6** – ebd. – **7** – In Kraemers Personalakte (Universitätsarchiv, Signatur UniA BS B 7 : 338 [2 Bde.]), die später möglicherweise gereinigt worden ist, ist dieser Brief nicht enthalten. Es gibt darin jedoch Hinweise auf das 1950 stattgefundene Ermittlungsverfahren ebenso den Brief der Studentenschaft. Für diese Information bedanke ich mich bei Lars Strominski vom Universitätsarchiv der TU Braunschweig. – **8** – Gespräch Bofinger (Anm. 4) – **9** – Schmedding, Anne: Lehre in Braunschweig, in: Wilhelm (Anm. 1), S. 102-110 – **10** – Wilhelm (Anm. 1), S. 17

Der Abenteurer, sein Ghostwriter und ihr Architekt: William Alexander Levy

– **1** – Zur Biografie des Abenteurers und Reiseschriftstellers Richard Halliburton siehe: Alt, John H.: Don't Die in Bed. The Brief, Intense Life of Richard Halliburton, Atlanta (Quincunx Press) 2013 – **2** – Halliburton, Richard: The Royal Road to Romance, Indianapolis (Bobbs-Merrill), 1925 – **3** – Halliburton, Richard: Die Jagd nach dem Wunder. Eine abenteuerliche Weltreise (1925), Leipzig (Paul List), 1926 – **4** – Halliburton, Richard: The Glorious Adventure, Indianapolis (Bobbs-Merrill), 1927 – **5** – Halliburton, Richard: Auf den Spuren des Odysseus. Ein klassisches Abenteuer (1927), Leipzig (Paul List), 1933 – **6** – vgl. Max, Gerry: Horizon Chasers. The Lives and Adventures of Richard Halliburton and Paul Mooney, Jefferson/London (Mc Farland), 2007 – **7** – Zur Baugeschichte des Hauses und zur Biografie des Architekten siehe: Denzer, Anthony: The Halliburton House and its Architect, William Alexander, in: Southern California Quarterly, Berkeley (University of California Press), Ausgabe 3, 2009, S. 319-341 – **8** – In der Richard Halliburton Collection des Rhodes College Archives in Memphis sind zahlreiche Fotos aus der Bauzeit des Hauses vorhanden. – **9** – Fotos des fertigen Baus finden sich im Nachlass von William Alexander in der Architecture and Design Collection der University of California in Santa Barbara. – **10** – Rand, Ayn: The Fountainhead, Indianapolis (Bobbs-Merrill), 1943 (deutsche Übersetzung: Rand, Ayn: Der Ursprung, Hamburg (Gewis), 2000) – **11** – vgl. Sontag, Susan: Notes on Camp, in: Partisan Review, Ausgabe 31, 1964, S. 515-530 (deutsche Übersetzung: Sontag, Susan: Anmerkungen zu Camp (1964), in: Sontag, Susan: Kunst und Antikunst. 24 literarische Analysen, Frankfurt am Main (Fischer), 1982, S. 322-341) – **12** – zitiert nach: Max (Anm. 6), S. 216 – **13** – Hart, Kelli: Home for Sale of Adventurer Lost at Sea, in: Orange County Register, 14.03.2011 (Online: www.ocregister.com/2011/03/14/home-for-sale-of-adventurer-lost-at-sea / letzter Zugriff: 30.10.2019) – **14** – Für das Lookbook der Frühjahrskollektion 2012 der Streetwear-Modemarke LRG diente das Hangover House als grandiose Kulisse. (Online: www.direktconcept.com/2012/01/26/lrg-spring-2012-lookbook / letzter Zugriff: 30.10.2019) – **15** – Koerner, Claudia: Work Resumes on Historic Hangover House, in: Orange County Register, 26.04.2012 (Online: www.ocregister.com/2012/04/26/work-resumes-on-historic-hangover-house / letzter Zugriff: 30.10.2019)

Ein Gentlemen's Agreement: Patrick Gwynne

– **1** – The Homewood ist vermietet und nach vorheriger Anmeldung von April bis Oktober für die Öffentlichkeit zugänglich. Es gibt eine kleine Broschüre zum Haus: Bingham, Neil: The Homewood, Surrey, London (The National Trust), 2004 – **2** – Bingham, Neil: The Houses of Patrick Gwynne, in: Journal of the Twentieth Century Society: Post-War Houses (Ausgabe 4), 2000, S. 30-44 – **3** – Le Corbusier: Ausblick auf eine Architektur, Berlin (Ullstein), 1963. Zum Thema homosexueller Häuslichkeit siehe: Reed, Christopher (ed.): Not At Home: The Suppression of Domesticity in Modern Art and Architecture, London (Thames and Hudson), 1996

Der Architekt und sein Engel: Chen Kuen Lee

– **1** – Campbell-Lange, Barbara-Ann: John Lautner (1911-1994). Disappearing Space, Köln (Taschen), 2005 (deutsche Übersetzung: Campbell-Lange, Barbara-Ann: John Lautner (1911-1994). Der aufgelöste Raum, Köln (Taschen), 2005); Cygelman, Adele: Arthur Elrod. Desert Modern Design, Layton (Gibbs Smith Publisher), 2019 – **2** – Institut für Auslandsbeziehungen (Hg.): Chen Kuen Lee. Hauslandschaften. Organisches Bauen in Stuttgart, Berlin und Taiwan, Stuttgart (Karl Krämer), 2015 – **3** – N.N.: Die Natur zog in das Haus, in: Film und Frau, Ausgabe 7 (Architektur und kultiviertes Wohnen), 1963 , S. 44-47 – **4** – Grunert, Brigitte: Geboren 1915. Chen-Kuen Lee, in: Der Tagesspiegel, 24.10.2003 (Online: www.tagesspiegel.de/wirtschaft/geb-1915/459380.html / letzter Zugriff: 27.10.2019) – **5** – Es handelt sich um die Reihenhaus-Bebauung „Stetten", Jahnstraße 81, in Leinfelden-Echterdingen. – **6** – Strauss,

Künstler, Stuttgart (DVA), 2007 – **6** – Hentrich, Helmut: Bauzeit. Aufzeichnungen aus dem Leben eines Architekten, Düsseldorf (Droste Verlag), 1995 – **7** – ibid., p. 19 – **8** – ibid., p. 24 – **9** – ibid., p. 233 – **10** – ibid., p. 237 – **11** – ibid., p. 245 – **12** – ibid., p. 274 – **13** – ibid., p. 148 – **14** – ibid., p. 178 – **15** – ibid., p. 93 – **16** – Letter from Friedrich Tamms to Helmut Hentrich, 04/12/1933, in: Nachlass Hentrich, Akademie der Künste, Berlin – **17** – Durth, Werner: Düsseldorf: Demonstration der Modernität, in: Beyme, Klaus von; Durth, Werner; Gutschow, Niels; Nerdinger, Winfried; Topfstedt, Thomas (eds): Neue Städte aus Ruinen. Deutscher Städtebau der Nachkriegszeit, München (Prestel Verlag), 1992, pp. 231-250 – **18** – cf. the respective contribution in this book

Saved by Colleagues: Friedrich Wilhelm Kraemer

– **1** – Wilhelm, Karin; Gisbertz, Olaf; Jessen-Klingenberg, Detelf; Schmedding, Anne (eds.): Gesetz und Freiheit. Der Architekt Friedrich Wilhelm Kraemer (1907-1990), Berlin (Jovis), 2007 – **2** – Gerkan, Meinhard von: Erinnerungen, in: Wilhelm (note 1), pp. 111-113 – **3** – Wilhelm (note 1), p. 13 – **4** – Conversation with the contemporary Helge Bofinger (1940-2018), architect and student of Kraemer, on 12/20/2009. – **5** – ibid. – **6** – ibid. – **7** – In Kraemer's personnel file (Universitätsarchiv, Signatur UniA BS B 7:338 [2 vols.]), which may have been cleansed later on, this letter is not included. There are, however, references to the preliminary proceedings having taken place in 1950 as well as the letter from the student body. I thank Lars Strominski from the Universitätsarchiv of TU Braunschweig for this information. – **8** – Conversation with Bofinger (note 4) – **9** – Schmedding, Anne: Lehre in Braunschweig, in: Wilhelm (note 1), pp. 102-110 – **10** – Wilhelm (note 1), p. 17

The Adventurer, His Ghost-writer and Their Architect: William Alexander Levy

– **1** – On the biography of the adventurer and travel writer Richard Halliburton see: Alt, John H.: Don't Die in Bed. The Brief, Intense Life of Richard Halliburton, Atlanta (Quincunx Press) 2013. – **2** – Halliburton, Richard: The Royal Road to Romance, Indianapolis (Bobbs-Merrill), 1925 – **3** – Halliburton, Richard: Die Jagd nach dem Wunder. Eine abenteuerliche Weltreise (1925), Leipzig (Paul List), 1926 – **4** – Halliburton, Richard: The Glorious Adventure, Indianapolis (Bobbs-Merrill), 1927 – **5** – Halliburton, Richard: Auf den Spuren des Odysseus. Ein klassisches Abenteuer (1927), Leipzig (Paul List), 1933 – **6** – cf. Max, Gerry: Horizon Chasers. The Lives and Adventures of Richard Halliburton and Paul Mooney, Jefferson/London (Mc Farland), 2007 – **7** – On the building history of the house and the biography of its architect cf. Denzer, Anthony: The Halliburton House and its Architect, William Alexander, in: Southern California Quarterly, Berkeley (University of California Press), vol. 91 (2009), issue 3, pp. 319-341 – **8** – The Richard Haliburton Collection of the Rhodes College Archives in Memphis contains numerous photos taken during the construction of the house. – **9** – Photos of the completed building can be found in the estate of William Alexander in the Architecture and Design Collection of the University of California in Santa Barbara. – **10** – Rand, Ayn: The Fountainhead, Indianapolis (Bobbs-Merrill), 1943 – **11** – cf. Sontag, Susan: Notes on Camp, in: Partisan Review, issue 31, 1964, pp. 515-530 – **12** – quoted after: Max (note 6), p. 216 – **13** – Hart, Kelli: Home for Sale of Adventurer Lost at Sea, in: Orange County Register, 03/14/2011 (online: www.ocregister.com/2011/03/14/home-for-sale-of-adventurer-lost-at-sea / last accessed on 10/30/2019) – **14** – The Hangover House served as a grandiose backdrop for the lookbook of the spring 2012 collection of the streetwear fashion brand LRG (online: www.direktconcept.com/2012/01/26/lrg-spring-2012-lookbook / last access on 10/30/2019) – **15** – Koerner, Claudia: Work Resumes on Historic Hangover House, in: Orange County Register, 04/26/2012 (online: www.ocregister.com/2012/04/26/work-resumes-on-historichangover-house / last accessed on 10/30/2019)

A Gentleman's Agreement: Patrick Gwynne

– **1** – The Homewood is tenanted, open to the public from April to October. See guidebook: Bingham, Neil: The Homewood, Surrey, London (The National Trust), 2004 – **2** – Bingham, Neil: The Houses of Patrick Gwynne, in: Journal of the Twentieth Century Society: Post-War Houses, issue 4, 2000, pp. 30-44 – **3** – Le Corbusier: Towards a New Architecture (1st English Translation of Vers une Architecture by Frederick Etchells), London (J. Rodker), 1927. For a discussion of homosexual domesticity, see Reed, Christopher (ed.): Not At Home: The Suppression of Domesticity in Modern Art and Architecture, London (Thames and Hudson), 1996

The Architect And His Angel: Chen Kuen Lee

– **1** – Campbell-Lange, Barbara-Ann: John Lautner (1911-1994). Disappearing Space, Cologne (Taschen), 2005 (German translation: Campbell-Lange, Barbara-Ann: John Lautner [1911-1994]. Der aufgelöste Raum, Cologne [Taschen], 2005); Cygelman, Adele: Arthur Elrod. Desert Modern Design, Layton (Gibbs Smith Publisher), 2019 – **2** – Institut für Auslandsbeziehungen (ed.): Chen Kuen Lee. Hauslandschaften. Organisches Bauen in Stuttgart, Berlin und Taiwan, Stuttgart (Karl Kraemer), 2015 – **3** – N.N.: Die Natur zog in das Haus, in: Film und Frau, issue 7 (Architektur und kultiviertes Wohnen), 1963, pp. 44-47 – **4** – Grunert, Brigitte: Geboren 1915. Chen-Kuen Lee, in: Der Tagesspiegel, 10/24/2003 (online: www.tagesspiegel.de/wirtschaft/geb-1915/459380.html / last accessed on 10/27/2019) – **5** – It is the "Stetten" development of terraced houses, Jahnstrasse 81, in Leinfelden-Echterdingen. – **6** – Strauss, Stefan: "Zwei Zimmer im 14. Stock. Chen Kuen Lee entwarf einst das Märkische Viertel, jetzt lebt er selbst dort", in: Berliner Zeitung

Stefan: Zwei Zimmer im 14. Stock. Chen Kuen Lee entwarf einst das Märkische Viertel, jetzt lebt er selbst dort, in: Berliner Zeitung 22.01.2003 (Online: www.berliner-zeitung.de/chen-kuen-lee-entwarf-einst-das-maerkische-viertel--jetzt-lebt-er-selbst-dort-zwei-zimmer-im-14--stock-15955802 / letzter Zugriff: 27.10.2019) – **7** – Institut für Auslandsbeziehungen (Anm. 2), S. 122

Das Geheimnis des Architekten: Paul Rudolph

– **1** – Progressive Architecture, Ausgabe 2, 1964, S. 1 – **2** – Nobel, Philip: The Yale Art + Architecture Building, New York (Princeton Architectural Press), 1999 – **3** – Rohan, Timothy M.: Rendering the Surface. Paul Rudolph´s Art and Architecture Building at Yale, in: Grey Room, Ausgabe 1, 2000, S. 84-107 – **4** – Dem Werk von Paul Rudolph beziehungsweise einzelnen Werkphasen sind zahlreiche Monographien gewidmet – u.a. Moholy-Nagy, Sibyl: The Architecture of Paul Rudolph, New York (Praeger), 1970 (deutsche Übersetzung: Schwab, Gerhard (Hg.): Paul Rudolph. Bauten und Projekte, Stuttgart (Hatje Cantz), 1970); Yoshida, Yoshio (Hg.): 100 by Paul Rudolph, 1946-74, in: A+U Architecture and Urbanism, Ausgabe 80, 1977; Monk, Tony: The Art and Architecture of Paul Rudolph, Hoboken (Wiley), 1999; De Alba, Roberto: Paul Rudolph. The Late Work, New York (Princeton Architectural Press), 2003; Domin, Christopher; King, Joseph: Paul Rudolph. The Florida Houses, New York (Princeton Architectural Press), 2005; Rohan, Timothy M.: The Architecture of Paul Rudolph, New Haven (Yale University Press), 2014 – **5** – Der Architekt bewohnte das oberste Stockwerk des Hauses bereits länger. Einen ersten, kleineren Umbau dokumentierte 1976 die Zeitschrift *House & Garden* (N.N.: Mirror, Light, Carpeted Platforms, Storage in a Spectacular Apartment by Paul Rudolph, in: House & Garden, Ausgabe 10, 1976, S. 116-123). Auch dem folgenden Ausbau ab den späten 1970er-Jahren über insgesamt vier Geschosse widmete die Zeitschrift 1988 eine größere Text- und Bildstrecke (Sorkin, Michael: The Light House, in: House & Garden, Ausgabe 1, 1988, S. 88-95). – **6** – Rohan, Timothy M.: Paul Rudolph, Casa Rudolph, New York 1977-1997, Spettacoli pubblici e privati / Public and Private Spectacles, in: Casabella, Ausgabe 673/674, 1999, S. 138-149, 171-173 – **7** – Kühnle, Rüdiger Paul: Paul Rudolph und die zweite Generation der amerikanischen Moderne, Dissertation, Universität Stuttgart, 2005

Ich danke für die entsprechende Anrede:
Die Trans-Architektin Hildegard Schirmacher

– **1** – Für wertvolle Hinweise zur Person Hildegard Schirmacher bedanke ich mich bei Franz Josef Hamm, Bauingenieur und Partner von Hildegard Schirmacher bei den Altstadt-Projekten in Limburg, sowie bei Dr. Christoph Waldecker, Leiter des Stadtarchivs Limburg. – **2** – vgl. Weiß, Volker: „Eine weibliche Seele im männlichen Körper" – Archäologie einer Metapher als Kritik der medizinischen Konstruktion der Transsexualität, Dissertation, FU Berlin, 2007; Herrn, Rainer: Transvestitismus in der NS-Zeit – Ein Forschungsdesiderat, in: Zeitschrift für Sexualforschung, Ausgabe 4, 2013, S. 330-371 – **3** – Romero, Andreas: Baugeschichte als Auftrag. Karl Gruber, Architekt, Lehrer, Zeichner. Eine Biographie, Braunschweig (Vieweg), 1990 – **4** – Gruber, Karl: Die Gestalt der deutschen Stadt, Leipzig (Bibl. Institut), 1937 – **5** – Persicke, Erhard: Staatlicher Hochbau in Hessen, Wiesbaden (Staatsbauverwaltung), 1962 – **6** – Rimpl, Herbert: Verwaltungsbauten. Organisation, Entwurf, Konstruktion, Ausgeführte Bauen und Projekte, Berlin (Ullstein), 1959, S. 84-88; Sturm, Philipp; Schmal, Peter Cachola (Hg.): Hochhausstadt Frankfurt: Bauten und Visionen seit 1945 / High-Rise City Frankfurt: Buildings and Visions since 1945, München/London/New York (Prestel), 2014, S. 199; Opatz, Wilhelm E.; Deutscher Werkbund Hessen (Hg.): Architekturführer Frankfurt 1950-1959, Sulgen (Niggli), 2014, S. 66-73 – **7** – Schirmacher, Ernst: Limburg an der Lahn. Entstehung und Entwicklung der mittelalterlichen Stadt. Veröffentlichungen der Historischen Kommission für Nassau, Band 16, Wiesbaden (Historische Kommission für Nassau), 1963 – **8** – Stadtverwaltung Limburg (Hg.): Altstadtsanierung in Limburg an der Lahn 1972-2014, Limburg, 2017 (Broschüre) – **9** – Adamietz, Laura: Rechtliche Anerkennung von Transgeschlechtlichkeit und Anti-Diskriminierung auf nationaler Ebene – Zur Situation in Deutschland, in: Schreiber, Gerhard (Hg.): Transsexualität in Theologie und Neurowissenschaften. Ergebnisse, Kontroversen, Perspektiven, Berlin (De Gruyter), 2016, S. 357-372 – **10** – Gespräch mit Franz-Josef Hamm, geführt am 24. Juni 2015 – **11** – Brief an Ingeborg Möller in Bad Herrenalb, 07.08.1996, zitiert nach: Schirmacher, Hildegard: Verflogene Tage. Gespräche mit mir selbst und den Vielen, die vor mir und mit mir waren, Manuskript, o.J., S. 548 (Stadtarchiv Limburg) – **12** – ebd. – **13** – vgl. Nachruf von Laubach, Johannes: Hildegard Schirmacher gestorben. Die Stimme der Altstadt ist verstummt, in: Nassauische Neue Presse, 11.03.2015 – **14** – Anm. 10 – **15** – Anm. 11, S. 552 – **16** – In ihren *Stadtvorstellungen* hat sie die Erfahrungen in der Erhaltung der alten Städte mit konkreten Handlungsanweisungen weitergegeben. (Schirmacher, Ernst: Stadtvorstellungen. Die Gestalt der mittelalterlichen Städte. Erhaltung und planendes Handeln, Zürich (Artemis Verlag), 1988)

To Be Openly Gay At That Time Would Not Have Been Good For Business:
Arthur Erickson und Francisco Kripacz

– **1** – Erickson, Arthur: Francisco Kripacz. Interior Design, Vancouver (Figure 1 Publishing), 2015 – **2** – Die jüngste und umfassendste Biographie zu Arthur Erickson stammt von David Stouck aus dem Jahr 2013. Er beschäftigt sich ausführlich mit Ericksons Homosexualität und seiner Beziehung zu Francisco Kripacz. Die folgenden Ausführungen verdanken sich in weiten Teilen der Arbeit von Stouck. (Stouck, David: Arthur Erickson. An Architect's Life, Vancouver (Douglas & McIntyre), 2013) – **3** – Zum Werk Arthur Ericksons existieren eine Reihe von Monographien: Erickson, Arthur: The Architecture of Arthur Erickson, Montreal (Tundra Books), 1975; Iglauer, Edith: Seven

01/22/2003 (online: www.berliner-zeitung.de/chen-kuen-lee-entwarf-einst-das-maerkische-viertel-jetzt-lebt-er-selbst-dort-zwei-zimmer-im-14-stock-15955802 / last accessed on 10/27/2019) – **7** – Institut für Auslandsbeziehungen (note 2), p. 122

The Architect's Secret: Paul Rudolph

– **1** – Progressive Architecture, vol. 45 (1964), issue 2, p. 1 – **2** – Nobel, Philip: The Yale Art + Architecture Building, New York (Princeton Architectural Press), 1999 – **3** – Rohan, Timothy M.: Rendering the Surface. Paul Rudolph's Art and Architecture Building at Yale, in: Grey Room, issue 1, 2000, pp. 84-107 – **4** – Numerous monographs are dedicated to the work of Paul Rudolph or individual phases of his work – including Moholy-Nagy, Sibyl: The Architecture of Paul Rudolph, New York (Praeger), 1970; Yoshida, Yoshio (ed.): 100 by Paul Rudolph, 1946-74, in: A+U Architecture and Urbanism, issue 80, 1977; Monk, Tony: The Art and Architecture of Paul Rudolph, Hoboken (Wiley), 1999; De Alba, Roberto: Paul Rudolph. The Late Work, New York (Princeton Architectural Press), 2003; Domin, Christopher; King, Joseph: Paul Rudolph. The Florida Houses, New York (Princeton Architectural Press), 2005; Rohan, Timothy M.: The Architecture of Paul Rudolph, New Haven (Yale University Press), 2014 – **5** – The architect had been living on the top floor of the house for some time. A first, smaller reconstruction was documented in 1976 by the magazine House & Garden (N.N.: Mirror, Light, Carpeted Platforms, Storage in a Spectacular Apartment by Paul Rudolph, in: House & Garden, issue 10, 1976, pp. 116-123). In 1988, the magazine also devoted a large section of text and images to the subsequent conversion of a total of four storeys starting in the late 1970s (Sorkin, Michael: The Light House, in: House & Garden, issue 1, 1988, pp. 88-95). – **6** – Rohan, Timothy M.: Paul Rudolph, Casa Rudolph, New York 1977-1997, Spettacoli pubblici e private / Public and Private Spectacles, in: Casabella, issue 673/674, 1999, pp. 138-149, 171-173 – **7** – Kühnle, Rüdiger Paul: Paul Rudolph und die zweite Generation der amerikanischen Moderne, Dissertation, University of Stuttgart, 2005

Thank You For The Appropriate Form of Address:
Trans-Architect Hildegard Schirmacher

– **1** – I would like to thank Franz Josef Hamm, civil engineer and Hildegard Schirmacher's partner in projects in the old town of Limburg, as well as Dr. Christoph Waldecker, head of the Limburg City Archive, for valuable information about Hildegard Schirmacher. – **2** – Weiß, Volker: "Eine weibliche Seele im männlichen Körper" – Archäologie einer Metapher als Kritik der medizinischen Konstruktion der Transsexualität, Dissertation, FU Berlin, 2007; Herrn, Rainer: Transvestitismus in der NS-Zeit – Ein Forschungsdesiderat, in: Zeitschrift für Sexualforschung, Ausgabe 4, 2013, S. 330-371 – **3** – Romero, Andreas: Baugeschichte als Auftrag. Karl Gruber, Architekt, Lehrer, Zeichner. Eine Biographie, Brunswick (Vieweg), 1990 – **4** – Gruber, Karl: Die Gestalt der deutschen Stadt, Leipzig (Bibl. Institut), 1937 – **5** – Persicke, Erhard: Staatlicher Hochbau in Hessen, Wiesbaden (Staatsbauverwaltung), 1962 – **6** – Rimpl, Herbert: Verwaltungsbauten. Organisation, Entwurf, Konstruktion, Ausgeführte Bauen und Projekte, Berlin (Ullstein), 1959, pp. 84-88; Sturm, Philipp; Schmal, Peter Cachola (eds.): Hochhausstadt Frankfurt: Bauten und Visionen seit 1945 / High-Rise City Frankfurt: Buildings and Visions since 1945, Munich/London/New York (Prestel), 2014, p. 199; Opatz, Wilhelm E.; Deutscher Werkbund Hessen (eds.): Architekturführer Frankfurt 1950-1959, Sulgen (Niggli), 2014, pp. 66-73 – **7** – Schirmacher, Ernst: Limburg an der Lahn. Entstehung und Entwicklung der mittelalterlichen Stadt. Veröffentlichungen der Historischen Kommission für Nassau, vol. 16, Wiesbaden 1963 (Historische Kommission für Nassau) – **8** – Stadtverwaltung Limburg (ed.): Altstadtsanierung in Limburg an der Lahn 1972-2014, Limburg, 2017 (brochure) – **9** – Adamietz, Laura: Rechtliche Anerkennung von Transgeschlechtlichkeit und Anti-Diskriminierung auf nationaler Ebene. Zur Situation in Deutschland, in: Schreiber, Gerhard (ed.): Transsexualität in Theologie und Neurowissenschaften. Ergebnisse, Kontroversen, Perspektiven, Berlin (De Gruyter), 2016, pp. 357-372 – **10** – Conversation with Franz-Josef Hamm on 06/24/2015 – **11** – Letter to Ingeborg Müller in Bad Herrenalb, 08/07/1996, quoted after: Schirmacher, Hildegard: Verflogene Tage. Gespräche mit mir selbst und den Vielen, die vor mir und mit mir waren, manuscript, n.d., p. 548 (Limburg City Archive) – **12** – ibid. – **13** – cf. obituary from Laubach, Johannes: Hildegard Schirmacher gestorben. Die Stimme der Altstadt ist verstummt, in: Nassauische Neue Presse, 03/11/2015 – **14** – note 10 – **15** – note 11,p. 552 – **16** – In her Stadtvorstellungen she has passed on her experience in the preservation of the old cities with concrete instructions (Schirmacher, Ernst: Stadtvorstellungen. Die Gestalt der mittelalterlichen Städte. Erhaltung und planendes Handeln, Zurich (Artemis Verlag), 1988)

To Be Openly Gay At That Time Would Not Have Been Good For Business:
Arthur Erickson and Francisco Kripacz

– **1** – Erickson, Arthur: Francisco Kripacz. Interior Design, Vancouver (Figure 1 Publishing), 2015 – **2** – The latest and most comprehensive biography of Arthur Erickson is by David Stouck from 2013. He intensely focused on Erickson's homosexuality and his relationship with Francisco Kripacz. Large parts of the following statements are owed to Stouck's work (Stouck, David: Arthur Erickson. An Architect's Life, Vancouver (Douglas & McIntyre), 2013) – **3** – A series of monographs exists on the work by Arthur Erickson: Erickson, Arthur: The Architecture of Arthur Erickson, Montreal (Tundra Books), 1975; Iglauer, Edith: Seven Stones. A Portrait of

Stones. A Portrait of Arthur Erickson, Seattle (University of Washington Press), 1981; Steele, Allen (Hg.): The Architecture of Arthur Erickson, London (Thames & Hudson) 1988; Oldsberg, Nicholas R. (Hg.): Arthur Erickson. Critical Works, Vancouver (Douglas & McIntyre), 2006 – **4** – zitiert nach: Iglauer (Anm. 3), S. 11f. („Arthur Erickson is by far the greatest architect in Canada, and may be the greatest on this continent.") – **5** – zitiert nach: Stouck (Anm. 2), S. 208 – **6** – Getty Images, Bildnummer 585797947 (Online: www.gettyimages.de/detail/nachrichtenfoto/margaret-trudeau-and-francisco-kripacz-at-studio-54-nachrichtenfoto/585797947 /letzter Zugriff: 26.10.2019) – **7** – Brewster, Hugh: Remembering Arthur Erickson, in: Xtra, 03.06.2009 (Online: www.dailyxtra.com/re-membering-arthur-erickson-13078 / letzter Zugriff: 26.10.2019) – **8** – www.aefoundation.ca / letzter Zugriff: 26.10.2019

Der Architekt im Playboy: Charles Moore

– **1** – Friedman, Alice T.: Women and the Making of the Modern House, New Haven/London (Yale University Press), 2006 – **2** – N.N.: A Playboy Pad. New Haven Haven, in: Playboy, Ausgabe 10, 1969, S. 126-129, 186 – **3** – Dem Werk von Charles Moore sind diverse Monographien gewidmet – unter anderem: Allen, Gerald: Charles Moore, New York (Whitney Library of Design), 1980 (deutsche Übersetzung: Allen, Gerald: Charles Moore. Ein Architekt baut für den „einprägsamen Ort", Stuttgart (DVA), 1981); Johnson, Eugene J.: Charles Moore. Buildings and Projects, 1949-1986, New York (Rizzoli), 1986 (deutsche Übersetzung: Johnson, Eugene J.: Charles Moore. Bauten und Projekte, 1949-1986, Stuttgart (Klett-Cotta), 1987) – **4** – N.N.: Die Kunst und das Heim, in: db Deutsche Bauzeitung, Ausgabe 7, 1968, S. 536-538 – **5** – Anm. 2 – **6** – Preciado, Beatriz: Pornotopia. Architektur, Sexualität und Multimedia im „Playboy", Berlin (Klaus Wagenbach), 2012 (englische Übersetzung: Pornotopia. An essay on Playboy's Architecture and Biopolitics, New York (Zone Books), 2014) – **7** – Littlejohn, David: The Life & Work of Charles W. Moore, New York (Holt, Rinehart and Winston), 1984, S. 143 („In a year of interviews and conversations, I had heard rumors galore; but having assayed them all, I was nearly ready to conclude that Charles Moore had no private life whatsoever.") – **8** – Keim, Kevin P. (Hg.): An Architectural Life. Memoirs & Memories on Charles W. Moore, Boston/New York/Toronto/London (Little, Brown and Company), 1996, S. 12 („He was a complex man, and those who knew him throughout his life [...] knew him in their own special way, but many felt that they didn't know him entirely. There was always a shade of mystery, another layer to be revealed.")

Der Architekt von Fire Island: Horace Gifford

– **1** – Gordon, Alastair: Weekend Utopia. Modern Living in the Hamptons, New York (Princeton Architectural Press), 2001 – **2** – Poole, Wakefield: The Wakefield Poole Collection 1971-1986, Philadelphia (TLA Entertainment Group), 2002 – **3** – Bianchi, Tom: Fire Island Pines. Polaroids 1975-1983, Bologna (Damiani), 2013 – **4** – 2013 legte der New Yorker Architekt Christopher Rawlins mit *Fire Island Modernist* eine erste, viel beachtete Biographie zu Horace Gifford vor. Rawlins gelang es damit, Leben und Werk Giffords dem Vergessen zu entreißen. Der vorliegende Beitrag verdankt sich nicht zuletzt dieser Vorarbeit. (Rawlins, Christopher: Fire Island Modernist. Horace Gifford and the Architecture of Seduction, New York (Metropolis Books), 2013) – **5** – Gordon, Alastair: Andrew Geller. Beach Houses, New York (Princeton Architectural Press), 2003 – **6** – Domin, Christopher; King, Joseph: Paul Rudolph. The Florida Houses, New York (Princeton Architectural Press), 2005 – **7** – zitiert nach Rawlins (Anm. 4), S. 15 – **8** – ebd., S. 86 – **9** – ebd.

Last, But Not Least: Von Ashbee bis Gropius

– **1** – MacCarthy, Fiona: The Simple Life. C. R. Ashbee in the Cotswolds, London (Lund Humphries), 1981, S. 184 – **2** – ebd., S. 29 – **3** – Stummer, Robin: Felicity Ashbee, Memoirist of the Arts and Crafts Era, in: Independent, 09.08.2008 (Online: www.independent.co.uk/news/obituaries/felicity-ashbee-memoirist-of-the-arts-and-crafts-era-889306.html / letzter Zugriff: 03.11.2019) – **4** – 1955 rekapitulierte der Kinofilm *The Girl in the Red Velvet Swing* die Ereignisse, die zum Tod des Architekten führten. Stanford White wurde von Ray Milland verkörpert. 1975 wiederum verarbeitete der Schriftsteller E. L. Doctorow die Umstände von Whites Ableben in seinem gefeierten Roman *Ragtime*. In der Romanverfilmung von 1981 wird White von Norman Mailer gespielt. – **5** – Broderick, Mosette: Triumvirate. McKim Mead & White. Art, Architecture, Scandal, and Class in America's Gilded Age, New York (Alfred A. Knopf), 2011 – **6** – Oliver, Richard: Bertram Grosvenor Goodhue, Cambridge (The MIT Press), 1983 – **7** – Shand-Tucci, Douglass: Boston Bohemia, 1881-1900: Ralph Adams Cram – Life and Architecture, Amherst (University of Massachusetts Press), 1995; Shand-Tucci, Douglass: Ralph Adams Cram: An Architect's Four Quests – Medieval, Modernist, American, Ecumenical, Amherst (University of Massachusetts Press), 2005 – **8** – Shand-Tucci 1995 (Anm. 7), S. 140 – **9** – ebd., S. 3-56 (Kapitel: Pickney Street) – **10** – ebd., S. 255 („It sometimes seemed to me, [...] that [Bertram and I] were less two individuals than two lobes of the same brain.") – **11** – ebd., S. 300f. – **12** – Cram, Ralph Adams: The Decadent: Being the Gospel of Inaction, Boston (Copeland and Day), 1893 – **13** – Shand-Tucci 1995 (Anm. 7), S. 362 – **14** – ebd., S. 141 – **15** – Schopf, Wolfgang (Hg.): Theodor W. Adorno – Briefe und Briefwechsel, Bd. 7, Frankfurt am Main (Suhrkamp) 2008 – **16** – zitiert nach: Müller-Dohm, Stefan: Briefwechsel Adorno-Kracauer. Immer war einer von beiden zutiefst gekränkt, in: F.A.Z. Frankfurter Allgemeine Zeitung, 24.11.2008 (Online: www.faz.net/aktuell/feuilleton/buecher/rezensionen/sachbuch/briefwechsel-adorno-kracauer-immer-war-einer-von-beiden-zutiefst-gekraenkt-1731142.html / letzter Zugriff: 03.11. 2019) – **17** – Kracauer, Siegfried: Ginster, Frankfurt am Main (Suhrkamp), 2013 – **18** – Slapeta, Vladimir (Hg.): Die Brünner Funktionalisten. Moderne Architektur in Brünn (Brno), Innsbruck (Institut für Raumgestaltung der Technischen Fakultät der Universität Innsbruck), 1985 – **19** – Hitchcock, Henry-Russell; Johnson, Philip: The International Style: Architecture since 1922, New York (W.W. Norton & Co.), 1932, S. 132-135 – **20** – vgl. Hitchcock, Henry-Russell; Johnson, Philip: Modern Architecture: International Exhibition (Catalog), New York (Plandome

Arthur Erickson, Seattle (University of Washington Press), 1981; Steele, Allen (ed.): The Architecture of Arthur Erickson, London (Thames & Hudson) 1988; Oldsberg, Nicholas R. (ed.): Arthur Erickson. Critical Works, Vancouver (Douglas & McIntyre), 2006 – **4** – quoted from: Iglauer (note 3), pp. 11f. ("Arthur Erickson is by far the greatest architect in Canada, and may be the greatest on this continent.") – **5** – quoted from: Stouck (note 2), p. 208 – **6** – Getty Images, photo number 585797947 (online: www.gettyimages.de/detail/nachrichtenfoto/margaret-trudeau-and-francisco-kripacz-at-studio-54-nachrichtenfoto/585797947 / last accessed on 10/26/2019) – **7** – Brewster, Hugh: Remembering Arthur Erickson, in: Xtra, 06/03/2009 (online: www.dailyxtra.com/remembering-arthur-erickson-13078, last accessed on 10/26/2019) – **8** – www.aefoundation.ca / last accessed: 10/26/2019

The Architect in Playboy: Charles Moore

– **1** – Friedman, Alice T.: Women and the Making of the Modern House, New Haven/London (Yale University Press), 2006 – **2** – N.N.: A Playboy Pad. New Haven Haven, in: Playboy, issue 10, 1969, pp. 126-129, 186 – **3** – Various monographs are dedicated to the work of Charles Moore – among others: Allen, Gerald: Charles Moore, New York (Whitney Library of Design), 1980; Johnson, Eugene J.: Charles Moore. Buildings and Projects, 1949-1986, New York (Rizzoli), 1986 – **4** – N.N.: Die Kunst und das Heim, in: db Deutsche Bauzeitung, vol. 102 (1968), issue 7, pp. 536-538 – **5** – note 2 – **6** – Preciado, Beatriz: Pornotopia. An essay on Playboy's Architecture and Biopolitics, New York (Zone Books), 2014) – **7** – Littlejohn, David: The Life & Work of Charles W. Moore, New York (Holt, Rinehart and Winston), 1984, p. 143 ("In a year of interviews and conversations, I had heard rumors galore; but having assayed them all, I was nearly ready to conclude that Charles Moore had no private life whatsoever.") – **8** – Keim, Kevin P. (ed.): An Architectural Life. Memoirs & Memories on Charles W. Moore, Boston/New York/Toronto/London (Little, Brown and Company), 1996, p. 12 ("He was a complex man, and those who knew him throughout his life [...] knew him in their own special way, but many felt that they didn't know him entirely? There was always a shade of mystery, another layer to be revealed.")

The Architect of Fire Island: Horace Gifford

– **1** – Gordon, Alastair: Weekend Utopia. Modern Living in the Hamptons, New York (Princeton Architectural Press), 2001 – **2** – Poole, Wakefield: The Wakefield Poole Collection 1971-1986, Philadelphia (TLA Entertainment Group), 2002 – **3** – Bianchi, Tom: Fire Island Pines. Polaroids 1975-1983, Bologna (Damiani), 2013 – **4** – In 2013 the New York-based architect Christopher Rawlins published Fire Island Modernist, a first, highly acclaimed biography of Horace Gifford. Rawlins thus succeeded in rescuing Gifford's life and work from oblivion. This essay is not least due to this preparatory work (Rawlins, Christopher: Fire Island Modernist. Horace Gifford and the Architecture of Seduction, New York (Metropolis Books), 2013 – **5** – Gordon, Alastair: Andrew Geller. Beach Houses, New York (Princeton Architectural Press), 2003 – **6** – Domin, Christopher; King, Joseph: Paul Rudolph. The Florida Houses, New York (Princeton Architectural Press), 2005 – **7** – quoted after Rawlins (note 4), p. 15 – **8** – ibid., p. 86 – **9** – ibid.

Last, But Not Least: From Ashbee to Gropius

– **1** – MacCarthy, Fiona: The Simple Life. C. R. Ashbee in the Cotswolds, London (Lund Humphries), 1981, p. 184 – **2** – ibid., p. 29 – **3** – Stummer, Robin: Felicity Ashbee, Memoirist of the Arts and Crafts Era, in: Independent, 08/09/2008 (online: www.independent.co.uk/news/obituaries/felicity-ashbee-memoirist-of-the-arts-and-crafts-era-889306.html / last accessed on 11/03/2019) – **4** – In 1955, the film The Girl in the Red Velvet Swing recapitulated the events that led to the death of the architect. Stanford White was played by Ray Milland. In 1975, the writer E. L. Doctorow dealt with the circumstances of White's death in his acclaimed novel Ragtime. In the 1981 novel adaptation, White is depicted by Norman Mailer. – **5** – Broderick, Mosette: Triumvirate. McKim Mead & White. Art, Architecture, Scandal, and Class in America's Gilded Age, New York (Alfred A. Knopf), 2011 – **6** – Oliver, Richard: Bertram Grosvenor Goodhue, Cambridge (The MIT Press), 1983 – **7** – Shand-Tucci, Douglass: Boston Bohemia, 1881-1900: Ralph Adams Cram – Life and Architecture, Amherst (University of Massachusetts Press), 1995; Shand-Tucci, Douglass: Ralph Adams Cram. An Architect's Four Quests – Medieval, Modernist, American, Ecumenical, Amherst (University of Massachusetts Press), 2005 – **8** – Shand-Tucci 1995 (note 7), p. 140 – **9** – ibid., pp. 3-56 (chapter: Pickney Street) – **10** – ibid., p. 255 ("It sometimes seemed to me, [...] that [Bertram and I] were less two individuals than two lobes of the same brain"). – **11** – ibid., pp. 300f. – **12** – Cram, Ralph Adams: The Decadent: Being the Gospel of Inaction, Boston (Copeland and Day), 1893 – **13** – Shand-Tucci 1995 (note 7), p. 362 – **14** – ibid., p. 141 – **15** – Adorno, Theodor W.; Kracauer, Siegfried: Briefwechsel 1923-1966. Der Riß der Welt geht auch durch mich (= Schopf, Wolfgang [ed.]: Theodor W. Adorno. Briefe und Briefwechsel, vol. 7), Frankfurt am Main (Suhrkamp), 2008 – **16** – quoted after: Müller-Dohm, Stefan: Briefwechsel Adorno-Kracauer. Immer war einer von beiden zutiefst gekränkt, in: F.A.Z. Frankfurter Allgemeine Zeitung, 11/24/2008 (online: www.faz.net/aktuell/feuilleton/buecher/rezensionen/sachbuch/briefwechsel-adorno-kracauer-immer-war-einer-von-beiden-zutiefst-gekraenkt-1731142.html, last accessed on 11/03/2019) – **17** – Kracauer, Siegfried: Ginster, Frankfurt am Main (Suhrkamp), 2013 – **18** – Slapeta, Vladimir (ed.): Die Brünner Funktionalisten. Moderne Architektur in Brünn (Brno), Innsbruck (Institut für Raumgestaltung der Technischen Fakultät der Universität Innsbruck), 1985 – **19** – Hitchcock, Henry-Russell; Johnson, Philip: The International Style: Architecture since 1922, New York (W.W. Norton & Co.), 1932, pp. 132-135 – **20** – cf. Hitchcock, Henry-Russell; Johnson, Philip: Modern Architecture: International Exhibition (Catalog), New York (Plandome Press), 1932, p. 25 – **21** – www.bam.brno.cz/de/objekt/c058-haus-fur-zwei-junggesellen / last accessed on 03/07/2020 – **22** – www.bam.brno.cz/en/object/c058-house-for-two-young-men / last accessed on 03/07/2020 – **23** – www.yumpu.com/de/document/ read/4365034/fuhrer-durch-denjudischen-friedhof-in-brunn-bedeutende- / last accessed on 03/08/2020 – **24** – Schulze,

Press), 1932, S. 25 – **21** – www.bam.brno.cz/de/objekt/c058-haus-fur-zwei-junggesellen / letzter Zugriff: 07.03.2020 – **22** – www.bam.brno.cz/en/object/c058-house-for-two-young-men / letzter Zugriff: 07.03.2020 – **23** – www.yumpu.com/de/document/read/4365034/fuhrer-durch-den-judischen-friedhof-in-brunn-bedeutende- / letzter Zugriff: 08.03.2020 – **24** – Schulze, Franz: Philip Johnson. Leben und Werk, Wien (Springer), 1996, S. 151 – **25** – Lamster, Mark: The Man in the Glass House: Philip Johnson, Architect of the Modern Century, New York (Little, Brown and Company), 2018, S. 75 – **26** – ebd., S. 177 – **27** – Pauly, Daniele: Barragán. Raum und Schatten, Mauer und Farbe, Basel/Boston/Berlin (Birkhäuser), 2002 – **28** – Suess, Stephen: Luis Barragán was that Way, in: The Bilerico Project / LGBTQ Nation, 12.04.2008 (Online: www.bilerico.lgbtqnation.com/2008/04/luis_barragan_was_that_way.php / letzter Zugriff: 03.11.2019) – **29** – Flagge, Ingeborg: Bawa – Genius of the Place. An Architect of Sri Lanka, Frankfurt am Main (Deutsches Architekturmuseum), 2004, S. 20f. – **30** – Robson, David: Geoffrey Bawa. The Complete Works, London (Thames & Hudson), 2002 – **31** – Robson, David: In Search of Bawa. Master Architect of Sri Lanka, London (Laurence King Publishing), 2016, S. 9 – **32** – Robson 2002 (Anm. 30), S. 232-237; Robson 2016 (Anm. 31), S. 36-39 – **33** – Robson 2002 (Anm. 30), S. 238-261; Robson 2016 (Anm. 31), S. 116-121 – **34** – Robson, David: Bawa – Sri Lanka Gardens, London (Thames & Hudson), 2017 – **35** – Harwood, Elain; Powers, Alan (Hg.): Tayler and Green. Architects 1938-1973. The Spirit of Place in Modern Housing, London (Prince of Wales's Institute of Architecture), 1998 – **36** – ebd., S. 76 – **37** – vgl. den entsprechenden Beitrag zu Friedrich Wilhelm Kraemer in diesem Band – **38** – Weinstock-Montag, Judith: Hans Broos, ein deutsch-brasilianischer Architekt in São Paulo, in: Bauwelt, 2007, Ausgabe 19, S. 24-45 – **39** – Polster, Bernd: Walter Gropius. Der Architekt seines Ruhms. München (Hanser), 2019 – **40** – ebd., S. 109, 199 – **41** – ebd., S. 112

Franz: Philip Johnson. Leben und Werk, Wien (Springer), 1996, p. 151 – **25** – Lamster, Mark: The Man in the Glass House: Philip Johnson. Architect of the Modern Century, New York (Little, Brown and Company), 2018, p. 75 – **26** – ibid., p. 177 – **27** – Pauly, Daniele: Barragán. Raum und Schatten, Mauer und Farbe, Basel/Boston/Berlin (Birkhäuser), 2002 – **28** – Suess, Stephen: Luis Barragán was that Way, in: The Bilerico Project / LGBTQ Nation, 04/12/2008 (online: www.bilerico.lgbtqnation.com/2008/04/luis_barragan_was_that_way.php / last accessed on 11/03/2019) – **29** – Flagge, Ingeborg: Bawa – Genius of the Place. An Architect of Sri Lanka, Frankfurt am Main (Deutsches Architekturmuseum), 2004, pp. 20f. – **30** – Robson, David: Geoffrey Bawa. The Complete Works, London (Thames & Hudson), 2002 – **31** – Robson, David: In Search of Bawa. Master Architect of Sri Lanka, London (Laurence King Publishing), 2016, p. 9 – **32** – Robson 2002 (note 30), pp. 232-237; Robson 2016 (note 31), pp. 36-39 – **33** – Robson 2002 (note 30), pp. 238-261; Robson 2016 (note 31), pp. 116-121 – **34** – Robson, David: Bawa – Sri Lanka Gardens, London (Thames & Hudson), 2017 – **35** – Harwood, Elain; Powers, Alan (eds.): Tayler and Green. Architects 1938-1973. The Spirit of Place in Modern Housing, London (Prince of Wales's Institute of Architecture), 1998 – **36** – ibid., p. 76 – **37** – cf. the respective essay on Friedrich Wilhelm Kraemer in this book – **38** – Weinstock-Montag, Judith: Hans Broos, ein deutsch-brasilianischer Architekt in Sao Paulo, in: Bauwelt, vol. 47 (2007), issue 19, pp. 24-45 – **39** – Polster, Bernd: Walter Gropius. Der Architekt seines Ruhms. München (Hanser), 2019 – **40** – ibid., pp. 109, 199 – **41** – ibid., p. 112

Register

A
Adler, Dankmar 16, 17
Adorno, Theodor 268, 269
Adshead, Stanley Davenport 110, 111
Arabia, Lawrence of 197, 198
Ashbee, Charles Robert 112, 113, 262, 263
Ashbee, Janet 262, 263, 267, 268

B
Barragán, Luis 29, 30, 170, 171, 270-273
Barting, Otto 104, 105
Bavinger 121
Bavinger, Gene 118, 119
Bavinger, Nancy 118, 119
Bawa, Bevis 274, 275
Bawa, Geoffrey 170, 171, 272-275
Beauharnais, Joséphine 66, 67, 69
Beckford, William 50-63
Behrens, Peter 156, 157
Bergdoll, Barry 31, 32
Bernier, Claude-Louis 66, 67
Bernstein, Leonard 176, 177
Betsky, Aaron 26, 27
Bianchi, Tom 254-257
Bingham, Neil 32, 33
Bismarck, Otto von 84, 85
Blomberg, David 114, 115
Bofinger, Helge 31, 32
Bollmann, Ulf 31, 32
Bond, James 200-203
Borges, Jorge Luis 52, 53
Bonaparte, Napoleon 60, 61, 64-67, 69-71
Bosma, Koos 32, 33
Breuer, Marcel 158, 159, 234, 235
Brinkley, Christie 12, 13
Brittain-Catlin, Timothy 140, 143-145
Britten, Benjamin 154, 155
Broderick, Mosette 264, 265
Broos, Hans 276, 277, 279
Buchsbaum, Alan 12-15
Buonarotti, Michelangelo 14, 15
Burkart, Matthias 136, 137
Burle Marx, Roberto 276, 278
Byron, Lord George Gordon 48, 51-53

C
Carnegie 263, 264
Carr, J. Gordon 256, 259
Chermayeff, Serge 146, 147
Constable, John 56, 57
Coates, Welles 146, 147
Cooper, Gary 188, 190
Courtault, Stephen 138, 139
Courtault, Virginia 138.139
Courtenay, William 57, 58
Cram, Ralph Adams 265-269

D
Dierks, Barry 126-135
Dietrich, Verena 10, 11
Drexler, Alfred 166-168
Dupuis, Sophie 68, 69
Durrell, Lawrence 110-113

E
Edelman, Marian Wright 23, 24
Edward III., König 54, 55
Eiermann, Egon 172, 173, 276, 277
Eilers, Fritz 167, 168
Eisenhower, Dwight D., 118, 119
Eisler, Otto 268-271
Engel, Werner 206-209
Eschenbach, Christoph 176, 177
Enzo 159, 160
Erickson, Arthur 228-241
Eulenburg 92, 93
Evans, Lydia 153, 154

F
Farnsworth, Edith 244, 245
Farquhar, John 62, 63
Fathy, Hasan 112, 113
Ferri, Roger 12, 14, 15
Fischer, Jochen 32, 33
Follett, Ken 52, 53
Fontaine, Pierre François Léonard 64-71

Foucault, Michel 38, 39
Fouché, Maurice 66, 67
Foxwell, Peter 138, 139
Franco 159, 169
Frantz, Justus 176, 177
Franz Josef I., Kaiser 72, 73
Fuchs, Mathhias 176, 177
Fuchs, Ron 32, 33

G
Gaudí, Antoni 29, 30
Gayer-Anderson, John 114, 115
Gehry, Frank 14, 15
Geller, Andrew 256, 257
Gifford, Horace 252-261
Gill, Eric 112, 113, 116, 117
Gisbertz, Olaf 31, 32
Gloeden, Wilhelm von 130, 131
Goodhue, Bertram Grosvenor 266-268
Goethe, Johann Wolfgang 38, 39, 75, 76
Goff, Bruce 118-120, 122, 123
Green, David 276, 277
Greenfield, Robert 260, 261
Grey, Eileen 132, 133, 234, 235
Grimm, Brüder 38, 39
Gropius, Walter 156, 157, 278, 279
Gruber, Karl 220, 221, 223, 224
Gwynne, Patrick 170, 171, 194-199

H
Haggerty, George 48, 50, 51
Halliburton, Richard 180-187, 190-193

Hamm, Franz-Josef 31, 32
Haring, Keith 18, 19, 25, 26
Harrison, Austen St. Barbe 110-117
Henn, Walter 172, 173
Hentrich, Helmut 162-170
Herrenberger, Justus 174, 175
Heuser, Hans 164, 165
Heuvel, Dirk van den 32, 33
Hill, Oliver 148, 149
Himmelreich, Rolf 220, 221
Hirschfeld, Magnus 82-85
Hitchcock, Henry-Russell 162, 163, 268, 269
Hitler, Adolf 236, 237
Hockney, David 8, 9
Höfer, Candida 18, 19
Hoffmann, Ludwig 86, 87
Holden, Charles 110, 111
Holle 77, 78
Hood, Raymond 184, 185
Hudson, Rock 18, 19
Huysmans, Joris-Karl 59, 60, 268, 269

I
Ihne, Ernst von 86, 87
Isherwood, Christopher 196, 197
Israel, Frank 12, 14, 15

J
Janschky, Luise 80, 81
Joel, Billy 12, 13
Johns, Jasper 228, 229, 234, 235
Johnson, Philip 16-19, 176, 177, 268, 269
Joli, France 236, 237

K
Kaeßmann 77, 78
Kahn, Eli Jacques 184, 185
Kahn, Louis 256, 259
Kallmorgen, Werner 94, 95
Karl V., Kaiser 38-41
Keaton, Diane 12, 13
Keim, Kevin P. 250, 251
Kertbeny, Karl Maria 72, 73
Killer, Maria 78, 79
Koehler, Hans 220, 221
Kracauer, Siegfried 268, 269
Kraemer, Friedrich Wilhelm 124, 125, 172-179
Kripacz, Francisco 228-241
Krupp, Friedreich Alfred 92, 93
Kurdiovsky, Richard 32, 33

L
Langmaack, Gerhard 92, 93
Laroche, Anton 18, 19
Lautner, John 200, 201
La Vigne, August 77, 78
Le Corbusier 156, 157, 159, 195, 196, 228, 229, 234, 235, 242, 243
Lee, Chen Kuen 200-209
Levy, William Alexander 180, 181, 184-189, 191-193
Lichtenstein, Roy 228, 229, 234, 235
Lippert, Hans-Georg 31, 32, 102, 103
Littlejohn, David 249, 250
Lodders, Rudolf 94, 97
Lorenz, Gottfried 31, 32
Louis-Philippe, König 70, 71

Ludwig II., König 50, 51, 60, 61
Lüth, Erich 94, 95
Lutyens, Edwin 110, 111, 112, 113
Lyndon, Donlin 122, 123

M
Magne, Claude 134, 137
Mahler-Werfel, Alma 277, 278
Mallet-Stevens, Robert 132, 133
Mann, Thomas 8, 9
Manzanera, Phil 153, 154
Marco 159, 160
McCown, William Eugene 192, 193
McGrath, Raymond 146-155
McKim, Charles 262, 263
McKim Mead & White 264, 265
Mead, William Rutherford 262, 263
Meeteren, Olga van 165-168
Mendelsohn, Erich 112-115, 196, 197
Mendelsohn, Luise 114, 115
Mercury, Freddy 18, 19
Messel, Alfred 86, 87
Michele 159, 160
Midler, Bette 12, 13
Mies van der Rohe, Ludwig 156, 157, 176, 177, 228, 229, 234, 235, 270, 271
Möller, Cord Michael 34-37
Mondrian, Piet 160, 161
Monzie, Anatole de 243, 244
Monzie, Gabriel de 243, 244

Mooney, Paul 182-193
Moore, Charles 118-123, 242-251
Morgan, Julia 108, 109
Moser, Karl 156, 157
Murnau, Friedrich Wilhelm 50, 51

N
Nüll, Eduard van der 72-81

O
Obama, Barack 24, 25
O'Brien, James W. 125
Oelsner, Gustav 90-99
Oesterlen, Dieter 172, 173
Osthaus, Karl-Ernst 278, 279

P
Pacino, Al 216, 217
Paget, Paul 138-145
Palladio, Andrea 42, 43
Palucca, Gret 176, 177
Paolo 159, 160
Papadimos, Dimitri 113-117
Pepchinski, Mary 31, 33
Percier, Charles 64, 65
Petschnigg, Hubert 164, 165
Plecnik, Jože 29-31
Pierino 158-160
Pinnau, Cäsar 236, 237
Plummer, Lord 112, 113
Poelzig, Hans 162, 163, 167, 168, 220, 221
Polster, Bernd 277-279
Poole, Wakefield 254, 255
Prey, Johann Bernhard 34, 35
Pries, Lionel 118, 119, 122, 123, 124, 125

Poe, Edgar Allen 52, 53
Ponti, Gio 162, 163
Powers, Alan 31, 32

R
Rand, Ayn 187, 188
Rand, Geoffrey 196, 197
Raschdorff, Julius Carl 86-89
Rathenau, Walter 84, 85
Rawlins, Christopher 260, 261
Reiner, Markus 114, 117
Reinke, Johann Theodor 34-37, 40, 41
Renaut, Marc-Pierre 134, 137
Richard, Jean-Claude 80, 81
Rietvelt, Gerrit 242, 243
Roark, Howard 188, 190
Rockefeller 263, 264
Roth, Alfred 156-160
Roth, Emil 158, 159
Rudolph, Paul 212-219, 256, 259
Ruf, Sep 172, 173

S
Saint-Gaudens, Augustus 264, 265
Sawyer, Eric 126, 127, 129-135
Scharoun, Hans 206, 207
Scheffler, Karl 102, 103
Schildt, Axel 31, 32
Schiller, Friedrich 75, 76
Schirmacher, Ernst 220, 221, 225, 226
Schirmacher, Hildegard 220-227
Schlesinger, Gerald 146-154

Schröder, Truus 242, 243, 250, 251
Schulze, Franz 16, 17
Schumacher, Fritz 29, 30, 90-99
Schwechten, Franz 84-89
Scott, Wallace Thompson 192, 193
Shand-Tucci, Douglas 267, 268
Scitt, Zolite Elizabeth 192, 193
Sedgwick, Eve Kosofsky 46-49, 51
Seely, John 138-145
Sicard von Sicardsburg, August 72-81
Sleeper, Henry Davis 50, 51
Sontag, Susan 25, 26, 190, 192
Sonnin, Ernst Georg 34-41
Speer, Albert 168, 169
Steele, Allen 238, 239
Stein, Michael 243, 244
Stein, Sarah 243, 244
Storrs, Ronald 112, 113
Stratigakos, Despina 32, 33, 106, 107
Straub, Carl 202-205
Strominski, Lars 32, 33
Sullivan, Louis 14, 15

T
Tamms, Friedrich 168, 169
Tayler, Herbert 276, 277
Thomas, Brian 144, 145
Tillmanns, Ernst Ulrich 136, 137
Tresckow, Hans von 82-85, 88, 89
Trudeau, Justin 230, 231, 234, 235
Trudeau, Margaret 234, 235
Trudeau, Pierre 230, 231
Tschaikovsky, Peter 8, 9
Tunnard, Christopfer 146-154
Turnbull, William 122, 123
Turner, William 56, 57
Twombly, Robert 14-17

U
Ulrichs, Karl Heinrich 72, 73

V
Vanderbilt 263, 264
Visconti, Luchino 8, 9

W
Wagner, Ernst 216, 217
Wall, Jeff 18, 19
Wallot, Paul 86, 89
Walpole, Horace 42-51
Walpole, Sir Robert 46, 47
Warburg, Aby 92, 93
Warhol, Andy 25, 26, 234, 235
Waldecker, Christoph 32, 33
Weber, Roland 168, 169
Weston, Scott 14, 15
Whitaker, Richard 122, 123
White, Stanford 262-265
Whitney, David 16, 17
Wild, Blanka 100, 101, 106, 107
Wilde, Oscar 59, 60. 150, 151, 154, 155, 194, 195, 197, 198
Wilhelm II., Kaiser 84-87
Winkelmann, Emilie 100-109
Wittstein, Edwin 254, 257
Woolf, Virgina 197, 198
Wren, Christopher 138, 139

Wright, Frank Lloyd 184, 187
Wyatt, James 54, 55

Y
Yamasaki, Minoru 122, 123

Z
Zietz, Peer 88, 89

Abbildungen

– **S. 13** – Schwartz, Frederic (Hg.): Alan Buchsbaum, Architect & Designer: The Mechanics of Taste, New York (Monacelli), 1996 – **S. 17** – Fotograf unbekannt/Art Institute of Chicago; Fotograf unbekannt/Library of Congress – **S. 18** – Out, 5/1996 – **S. 24** – Privatbesitz – **S. 31** – Fotograf unbekannt/Creative Commons; 0000ff/Creative Commons – **S. 36/37** – Reinke, Johann Theodor: Lebensbeschreibung des ehrenwerthen Ernst Georg Sonnin, Baumeisters und Gelehrten in Hamburg, Hamburg (Auf Kosten d. Verf. u. in Comm. i. d. Heroldschen Buchhdlg.), 1824 – **S. 40** – Heckmann, Herbert: Barock und Rokoko in Hamburg. Baukunst des Bürgertums, Berlin (Verlag für Bauwesen), 1990 – **S. 44** – Chiswick Chap/Creative Commons – **S. 45** – Johannes Aegidius Eckardt, Horace Walpole, 1754/National Portrait Gallery – **S. 47/48/50** – Walpole, Horace: A Description of the Villa of Mr. Horace Walpole, Youngest Son of Sir Robert Walpole Earl of Orford, at Strawberry-Hill near Twickenham, Middlesex, with an Inventory of the Furniture, Pictures, Curiosities, etc., Strawberry-Hill, 1784 – **S. 49** – John Carter, The Cabinet at Strawberry Hill, 1789/Yale University – **S. 54** – Sir Joshua Reynolds, William (Thomas) Beckford, 1782/National Portrait Gallery – **S. 55/56/58/59** – Rutter, John: Delineations of Fonthill and its Abbey, Shaftesbury, 1823 – **S. 57** – Britton, John: Graphical and Literary Illustrations of Fonthill Abbey, Wiltshire. With Heraldical and Genealogical Notices of the Beckford Family, London (Longman), 1823 – **S. 61** – Fotograf unbekannt/Library of Congress – **S. 62** – Rictor Norton & David Allen/Creative Commons – **S. 66** – Robert Lefèvre, Charles Percier, 1807/Château de Versailles; Joseph Désiré Court, Pierre François Léonard Fontaine/Château de Versailles – **S. 67** – Pierre-Yves Beaudouin/Creative Commons – **S. 68** – Percier, Charles; Fontaine, Pierre François Léonard: Recueil de décorations intérieures, Paris, 1812 – **S. 69** – Gilles Messian/Creative Commons – **S. 70** – Thesupermat/Creative Commons – **S. 71** – Guilhem Vellut/Creative Commons – **S. 74** – Ludwig Angerer/Bildarchiv der Österreichischen Nationalbibliothek; Alois von Anreiter/Bildarchiv der Österreichischen Nationalbibliothek – **S. 76** – Josef Löwy/Creative Commons – **S. 77** – Eduard Bitterlich (nach Carl Rahl)/Albertina Wien, Inv.-Nr. 33.021 – **S. 79** – Albertina Wien, CHA 356; Fer.filol/Creative Commons – **S. 81** – GuentherZ/Creative Commons – **S. 84** – Ribbe, Wolfgang; Schäche, Wolfgang (Hg.): Baumeister, Architekten, Stadtplaner, Berlin (Stapp Verlag), 1987 – **S. 85** – Maler unbekannt/Privatarchiv Kuno Rogalla von Bieberstein, Hamburg/Creative Commons – **S. 86** – Deutsche Bauzeitung, 13/1879 – **S. 87/88** – Postkarte/Privatbesitz – **S. 89** – Wolfgang Voigt – **S. 92** – Hugo Meier-Thur/Privatbesitz – **S. 93** – Anny Breer/Staatsarchiv Hamburg – **S. 94/95/96/97** – Adolf und Carl Dransfeld/Staats- und Universitätsbibliothek Hamburg – **S. 98** – Wolfgang Voigt – **S. 102** – Fotograf unbekannt/Privatbesitz – **S. 103** – Fotograf unbekannt/TU Dresden, Institut für Baugeschichte, Architektur und Denkmalpflege – **S. 105** – Bodo Kubrak/Creative Commons – **S. 106** – Buchumschlag/Schweizerische Nationalbibliothek – **S. 107** – Fotograf unbekannt/Stadt Zürich, Creative Commons – **S. 113** – Dimitri Papadimos/Dimitri Papadimos Archive, MIET, Athen – **S. 113** – Fotograf unbekannt/Israel Antiquities Authority – **S. 116** – Archiv Ron Fuchs – **S. 117** – Wolfgang Voigt – **S. 120** – Courtesy of the Bruce Goff Collection, Ryerson and Burnham Archives, Art Institute of ChicagoJones – **S. 121** – 2jy/Creative Commons – **S. 122** – Charles Moore/Deutsches Architekturmuseum, Frankfurt am Main – **S. 122** – Heinrich Klotz/Heinrich-Klotz-Archiv, HfG Karlsruhe, Courtesy of DAM Deutsches Architekturmuseum – **S. 124** – Fotograf unbekannt/archinform.net – **S. 125** – Department of Architecture Archives/University of Washington Library – **S. 128/129/131/133/134/135** – Fotograf unbekannt/Gästebuch Le Trident, Courtesy of 4a Architekten, Stuttgart – **S. 136/137** – Uwe Ditz, Stuttgart/Courtesy of 4a Architekten, Stuttgart – **S. 141** – Fotograf unbekannt/Templewood Estate – **S. 142** – Judithcomm/Creative Commons; Tom Parnell/Creative Commons – **S. 143** – AnemoneProjectors/Creative Commons; Zoothorno/Creative Commons – **S. 144/145** – Steve Daniels/Creative Commons – **S. 148** – Fotograf unbekannt/Creative Commons – **S. 150/151/152/153** – Courtesy of The Modern House – **S. 158** – Roth, Alfred: Amüsante Erlebnisse eines Architekten, Zürich (Ammann), 1988 – **S. 159/160/161** – Wolfgang Voigt – **S. 164/166** – Hentrich, Helmut: Bauzeit. Aufzeichnungen aus dem Leben eines Architekten, Düsseldorf (Droste-Verlag), 1995 – **S. 167** – Werner Kortokraks/Stadtarchiv Ludwigshafen – **S. 169** – Wolfgang Voigt – **S. 171** – Hentrich, Helmut; Dressel, Hans J.: Kasteel Groot Buggenum. Biografie eines Hauses – Biography of a House, Köln (DuMont), 1992 – **S. 174/175/176/178** – Heinrich Heidersberger/ARTUR – **S. 177** – Fotograf unbekannt/Hochschularchiv TU Braunschweig, Diasammlung Kraemer – **S. 182** – Fotograf unbekannt/Rhodes College Archives, The Richard Haliburton Collection – **S. 183/185/187/188/189/190/191** – Fotograf unbekannt/University of California, Santa Barbara, Architecture and Design Collection – **S. 196** – Fotograf unbekannt/The National Trust – **S. 197** – Mark Fiennes/Country Life – **S. 202/204/205/207** – Fotograf unbekannt/Archiv Michael Koch, Stuttgart – **S. 203/208** – Fotograf unbekannt/Privatbesitz – **S. 214/216** – Fotograf unbekannt/Library of Congress, Prints and Photographs Division – **S. 215/217/218** – Paul Aaron/ESTO – **S. 222** – Stadtarchiv Limburg – **S. 223** – Dieter Fluck, Limburg – **S. 224** – Postkarte/Archiv Wolfgang Voigt – **S. 227** – Pedelecs/Creative Commons – **S. 230/233/235/238/239/240** – Erickson, Arthur: Francisco Kripacz. Interior Design, Vancouver (Figure 1 Publishing), 2015 – **S. 246** – Courtesy of Charles Moore Foundation – **S. 247** – Playboy, 10.1969 – **S. 251** – John Hill – **S. 255** – Edwin Wittstein, Courtesy of Christopher Rawlins – **S. 256** – Tom Bianchi, Courtesy of Christopher Rawlins – **S. 257** – Tom Sibley, Courtesy of Christopher Rawlins – **S. 258** – Tom Yee, Courtesy of Christopher Rawlins – **S. 259** – Michael Weber, Courtesy of Christopher Rawlins – **S. 264** – William Strang, C.R. Ashbee, 1903; MacCarthy, Fiona: The Simple Life. C. R. Ashbee in the Cotswolds, London (Lund Humphries), 1981 – **S. 265** – Fotograf unbekannt/Library of Congress; Fotograf unbekannt/National Park Service – **S. 266** – Cram, Ralph Adams: The Decadent: Being the Gospel of Inaction, Boston (Copeland and Day), 1893 – **S. 267** – Fotograf unbekannt/Library of Congress; Fotograf unbekannt/Creative Commons – **S. 269** – Fotograf unbekannt/Schiller-Nationalmuseum, Marbach – **S. 270/271** – Fotograf unbekannt/via bam.brno.cz – **S. 272** – Thomas Ledl/Creative Commons; Ymblanter/Creative Commons – **S. 273** – Fotograf unbekannt/Creative Commons – **S. 274** – Robson, David: Geoffrey Bawa. The Complete Works, London (Thames & Hudson), 2002 – **S. 275** – Harwood, Elain; Powers, Alan (Hg.): Tayler and Green. Architects 1938-1973. The Spirit of Place in Modern Housing, London (Prince of Wales's Institute of Architecture), 1998 – **S. 276** – Fotograf unbekannt/via archdaily.br – **S. 279** – Wolfgang Voigt